HOOVER'S GUIDE

THE TEXAS 500

EDITED BY THE REFERENCE PRESS

Hoover's Guides are intended to provide their readers with accurate and authoritative information about the enterprises profiled in them. The Reference Press asked all profiled companies and organizations to provide information for its books. Many did so; a number did not. The information contained herein is as accurate as we could reasonably make it. In many cases we have relied on third-party material that we believe to be trustworthy but were unable to independently verify. We do not warrant that the book is absolutely accurate or without any errors. Readers should not rely on any information contained herein in instances where such reliance might cause loss or damage. The editors, publisher, and their data suppliers specifically disclaim all warranties, including the implied warranties of merchantability and fitness for a specific purpose. This book is sold with the understanding that neither the editors nor the publisher is engaged in providing investment, financial, accounting, legal, or other professional advice.

The financial data (How Much section and Where and What tables) in this book are from a variety of sources. For publicly traded companies, Standard & Poor's Compustat, Inc., provided most of the data for the How Much section. For private companies and for historical information on public companies prior to their becoming public, we obtained information directly from the companies or from trade sources deemed to be reliable. We specifically wish to acknowledge TEXAS MONTHLY, Inc. for permitting us to reprint their list of the 100 richest Texans and selected profiles of individuals contained on that list. The copyright for all such reprinted materials resides with TEXAS MONTHLY, Inc. The Reference Press, Inc., is solely responsible for the presentation of all data.

Many of the names of products and services mentioned in this book are the trademarks or service marks of the companies manufacturing or selling them and are subject to protection under US law. Space has not permitted us to indicate which names are subject to such protection, and readers are advised to consult with the owners of such marks regarding their use. *Hoover's Handbook* ® is a registered trademark of The Reference Press, Inc.

™
The Reference Press, Inc.

Copyright © 1994 by The Reference Press, Inc. All rights reserved. No part of this book may be reproduced or transmitted in any form or by any means, electronic or mechanical, including by photocopying, facsimile transmission, recording, or using any information storage and retrieval system, without permission in writing from The Reference Press, Inc., except that brief passages may be quoted by a reviewer in a magazine, newspaper, on-line, or broadcast review.

10 9 8 7 6 5 4 3 2 1

Publisher Cataloging-In-Publication Data

The Texas 500: Hoover's Guide to the Top Texas Companies
Edited by The Reference Press

 Includes indexes.
 1. Business enterprises — Directories. 2. Corporations — Directories.
HF3010   338.7

The profiles in this book are also available on-line from America Online.

ISBN 1-878753-39-8 trade paper
ISBN 1-878753-46-0 clothbound

This book was produced by The Reference Press on Apple Macintosh computers using Aldus Corporation's PageMaker 4.2 software, Quark Inc.'s Quark XPress software and Adobe Systems, Inc.'s fonts from the Clearface and Futura families. Cover design is by Jane Yansky of Austin, Texas. Interior layout design is by Kristin M. Jackson. Electronic prepress was done by RJL Graphics at Austin, Texas, and the book was printed by Best Printing Company, Inc., at Austin, Texas. Text paper is 60# White Husky Smooth. Trade paper cover stock is 10 point, White Carolina coated one side, film laminated. Clothbound cover stock is 100#, coated two sides, Vintage Gloss Book.

Hoover's Guides are available in bookstores in the US, Canada, and many European countries through all major US book distributors and library jobbers, and directly from The Reference Press. The following companies are authorized distributors of *Hoover's Handbooks*:

US AND CANADA (except booksellers)
The Reference Press
6448 Highway 290 E., Suite E-104
Austin, Texas 78723
Phone: 512-454-7778
Fax: 512-454-9401

EUROPE
William Snyder Publishing Associates
5, Five Mile Drive,
Oxford, OX2 8HT,
England
Phone & fax: +44 865-513186

US BOOKSELLERS
Publishers Group West
4065 Hollis
Emeryville, California 94608
Phone: 510-658-3453
Fax: 510-658-1834

CANADIAN BOOKSELLERS
Publishers Group West
31A Westminster Ave. North
Montreal West, Quebec H4X 1Y8
Canada
Phone: 514-369-5753
Fax: 514-369-5755

TEXAS BOOKSELLERS
Publishers Group West
c/o Martin Beeman
309 Church St.
Georgetown, Texas 78626
Phone: 512-863-0521
Fax: 512-869-2770

CONTENTS

Acknowledgments 5
Letter from Cathy Bonner, Texas Department of Commerce 6
Letter from Ann Richards, Governor of Texas 7
About *The Texas 500: Hoover's Guide to the Top Texas Companies* 8
Overview of the Texas Economy and Business Environment 10

A List-Lover's Compendium 21
    The Texas 500 Companies Ranked by Sales 22
    The Texas 500 Companies Ranked by Number of Employees 27
    The Largest Employers in Texas 32
    Largest Companies in Austin, Dallas–Ft. Worth, Houston, and San Antonio 34
    Inc. 500 Fastest-Growing Private Companies in Texas 36

The 100 Richest Texans 37
    Selected Profiles from *TexasMonthly*'s 100 Richest Texans List 42

State of Texas Profile 47
    Texas Statistics 50

The Top 25 53
    American General Corporation 54
    AMR Corporation 56
    Burlington Northern Inc. 58
    The Coastal Corporation 60
    Compaq Computer Corporation 62
    Continental Airlines Holdings, Inc. 64
    Cooper Industries, Inc. 66
    Electronic Data Systems Corporation 68
    Enron Corp. 70
    Exxon Corporation 72
    Halliburton Company 74
    Houston Industries Incorporated 76
    Kimberly-Clark Corporation 78
    Lyondell Petrochemical Company 80
    Marathon Group 82
    J. C. Penney Company, Inc. 84
    Shell Oil Company 86
    The Southland Corporation 88
    Southwestern Bell Corporation 90
    SYSCO Corporation 92
    Tandy Corporation 94
    Tenneco Inc. 96
    Texas Instruments Incorporated 98
    Texas Utilities Company 100
    USAA 102

The Bubba 10 105
    Baker Hughes Incorporated 106
    Browning-Ferris Industries, Inc. 108
    Dell Computer Corporation 110
    Dr Pepper/Seven-Up Companies, Inc. 112
    Dresser Industries, Inc. 114
    King Ranch, Inc. 116
    Mary Kay Cosmetics Inc. 118

Pennzoil Company 120
Southwest Airlines Co. 122
Trammell Crow Company 124

The Hot 20 127
    50-Off Stores, Inc. 128
    Babbage's, Inc. 129
    BMC Software, Inc. 130
    The Bombay Company, Inc. 131
    Brinker International, Inc. 132
    Cash America International, Inc. 133
    CompuCom Systems, Inc. 134
    CompUSA Inc. 135
    Cyrix Corporation 136
    Destec Energy, Inc. 137
    EZCORP, Inc. 138
    Heritage Media Corporation 139
    Kaneb Services, Inc. 140
    The Men's Wearhouse, Inc. 141
    Serv-Tech, Inc. 142
    Snyder Oil Corporation 143
    Sterling Software, Inc. 144
    Tuesday Morning Corporation 145
    U.S. Long Distance Corp. 146
    Whole Foods Market, Inc. 147

The Texas 500 149

More Texas Information 251
    Texas Comers 252
    80 of the Largest Texas Employers Headquartered Out of State 254
    Big 6 Accounting Firms 262
    Major Banks 264
    Top 10 Advertising Agencies 268
    Top 10 Law Firms 272
    Major Texas Publications 276
    Major Media 276
    Largest Not-for-Profit Hospitals 279
    Professional Sports Teams in Texas 282
    Texas Zip Code Map 283

The Indexes 285
    Index of Companies by Industry 286
    Index of Companies by Headquarters Location 292

THE STAFF

Chairman: Gary Hoover
CEO, President, and Senior Editor: Patrick J. Spain
Senior Vice-President and Editor-in-Chief: Alta Campbell
Vice-President and Senior Editor: Alan Chai
Managing Editor: James Talbot
Art Director: Kristin M. Jackson
Proofreading/Fact Checking Manager: Jeanne Minnich
Director of Sales and Marketing: Dana L. Smith
Controller: Deborah L. Dunlap
Office Manager: Tammy Fisher
Customer Service Manager: Rhonda T. Mitchell

ACKNOWLEDGMENTS

Editor, *The Texas 500*
Deborah Stratton

Editors
Alta Campbell, Patrick J. Spain, Teri C. Sperry, James Talbot

Writers
Tim Barger, Christopher Barton, Dean Graber, Stuart Hampton, Jon Hockenyos, Edward Kozek, G. Keith McGowan, Paul Mitchell, Barbara M. Spain

Desktop Publishers
JoAnn Estrada, Kristin M. Jackson, Thomas Trotter

Fact Checkers/Proofreaders
Megan A. Brown, Melinda Freeman, Diane Lee, Jeanne Minnich, Elizabeth A. Morgan, Elizabeth Gagne Morgan, Rebecca P. Sankey, Tracy Sergo, Alice Wightman

Researchers
Patricia DeNike, Jill Holsinger, Valeria Verri

Other Contributors
Roy Bernstein, Stephen A. Childs, Marsha Cook, Kevin Taylor, Lisa Treviño, Wendy Weigant, Steve Wolk, Jane Yansky

Special Thanks
Governor Ann Richards, Comptroller John Sharp, Commerce Director Cathy Bonner

The Reference Press Mission Statement

1. To produce business information products and services of the highest quality, accuracy, and readability.
2. To make that information available whenever, wherever, and however our customers want it through mass distribution at affordable prices.
3. To continually expand our range of products and services and our markets for those products and services.
4. To reward our employees, suppliers, and shareholders based on their contributions to the success of our enterprise.
5. To hold to the highest ethical business standards, erring on the side of generosity when in doubt.

STATE OF TEXAS
DEPARTMENT OF COMMERCE

October 14, 1993

Dear Business Owners:

Texas created more jobs than any other state last year, and so far this year, we're number one again. This achievement is in part due to you, the business owners of Texas. At the Texas Department of Commerce, we know that the majority of new job growth is coming from the expansion of small- and medium-sized businesses. And with 97 percent of the state's businesses in that category, your continued prosperity is our number one goal!

Building a business requires a good foundation and the right tools. The Department of Commerce works hard to help businesses connect with the best resources for today's growing businesses. One of those tools is in your hands right now, *Texas 500: Hoover's Guide to the Top Texas Companies*. Within its pages you can find the information that can give your company a competitive edge.

I am hopeful you will use this resource, and the programs and services of the Department of Commerce, to turn potential into profits.

Sincerely,

Cathy Bonner
Executive Director

STATE OF TEXAS
OFFICE OF THE GOVERNOR
AUSTIN, TEXAS 78711

ANN W. RICHARDS
GOVERNOR

September 28, 1993

Greetings:

Texas is a big state--the home of big thinkers and big dreams. When you come to Texas you learn that one season quietly rolls into the next, and that the people really are as friendly as you've read about. It's a place residents love to call home and travelers love to visit.

It's also a state that's big on business--a business like those listed in this guide. But, whether yours is an international corporate headquarters with a multi-million dollar payroll, or a small business that helps make up the 99 percent of Texas companies with less than 500 employees, Texas is the place to go and grow.

Considering our strategic geographic location, our envied quality of life, our favorable tax climate and our world-renowned skilled and available work force, I think you'll agree that Texas is where the world, and the world of business, is headed.

Sincerely,

Ann Richards

ANN W. RICHARDS
Governor

About *The Texas 500: Hoover's Guide to the Top Texas Companies*

This first edition of *The Texas 500: Hoover's Guide to the Top Texas Companies* is the initial publication in a series of regional guides to U.S. companies. During the next 12 months, The Reference Press will publish company guides to Los Angeles, San Francisco, and New York City. Guides to other cities, states, and regions will follow. *Hoover's Guides*, which will be updated every two years, extend the acclaimed *Hoover's Handbook* series of company handbooks to a regional level.

The format of this book combines the company profile formats of *Hoover's Handbook of American Business* and *Hoover's Handbook of Emerging Companies* with information contained in *Hoover's MasterList of Major U.S. Companies*. More information on these publications is available in the back of this book.

To create *The Texas 500* we delved into our existing extensive database of information on Texas companies and conducted thousands of hours of research to identify and obtain additional information about the largest companies, public and private, in Texas. We used many sources to identify potential candidates for the book, including the Texas Department of Commerce, various publications by Dun & Bradstreet, the *Ward's* directories, the *Inc.* 500 list of private companies, the *Forbes* 400 list of private companies, and the Standard & Poor's database of public companies. Special credit is due to Demand Research of Chicago, Illinois, which supplied us with basic information about all Texas public companies.

Our research identified over 1,000 candidates for inclusion in the book. We then surveyed each of these companies to obtain and confirm information. Most companies were helpful and cooperative; some were not. For those that did not cooperate, we obtained the most reliable information we could find and in some cases made estimates about revenues and employment. Finally, we ranked the companies by revenues to determine the Texas 500. Where two companies had the same revenues, we next looked to total employees to determine rankings.

We wrote in-depth profiles of the largest 25 companies in Texas, from #1 Exxon to #25 Compaq. We then profiled 10 other large Texas companies that were not large enough to make the top 25 but that we felt were quintessentially Texan. These include the King Ranch, Mary Kay, Dr Pepper, and others. We then went looking for the future giants — 20 smaller companies growing at a rapid rate. These include Men's Wearhouse, Babbage's, and U.S. Long Distance. We even added a profile of the State of Texas. Many of these company profiles appear in other *Hoover's Handbook*s, but a number were written just for this book. (For a detailed explanation of how the various financial ratios in the profiles were calculated, see *Hoover's Handbook of American Business*.) Finally, we created capsule profiles for the remaining 445 companies. We also created and collected lists of Texas companies — the largest employers, fastest-growing private companies, etc.

Our Texas 500 list includes only companies headquartered in Texas, but in other sections of the book we have identified companies headquartered elsewhere with significant operations in Texas. In Austin, for example, the largest private-sector employers count IBM, Motorola, AMD, and 3M among their number. While other books on Texas companies might ignore these enterprises because they are not headquartered in Texas, we do not. We have gone to considerable effort to identify and provide information about these companies and their Texas employment levels.

In addition to public and private for-profit companies, we included consortia (e.g., Sematech) and cooperatives (e.g., Associated Milk Producers) in our book. We have included these enterprises because we believe they are as important to driving the Texas economy and creating jobs as the for-profit sector. Not-for-profit hospitals are among the largest employers in Texas. The top five of these hospitals in Houston alone employ over 41,900 people and generate revenues in excess of $2.9 billion. We have included information about 25 of Texas's largest not-for-profit hospital operators. We also tried to identify large public-sector employers but discovered that this task was too complicated to allow inclusion of the information at this time. We hope to add it to future editions.

In reviewing the companies that we identified as the top 500, we found a few things that we expected and some that we did not. Our largest company is Exxon at $103.2 billion in revenues; our smallest, H and H Meat Products at $67 million. As you might expect, oil and agriculture featured prominently in our list, but high-tech companies, retailers, wholesalers, and restaurants were hot on their heels. Most banks and S&Ls in Texas were destroyed during the financial debacle of the 1980s. We were able to identify only a handful of these institutions that remain headquartered in Texas. Somewhat to our surprise, several Texas law firms appear on our list as among the state's largest businesses, but none of the professional sports teams (the largest is the Texas Rangers at $66 million) made it.

Of the 500 companies in the Texas 500, some 262 of them (52%) are private. Many of these are well known (e.g., grocery store operator HEB), but some companies among the 1,000 largest private companies in the U.S. are not well known (e.g., Philp of Dallas, with $2.9 billion in revenues, which sells everything from gas to boats to toys).

Through the profiles, lists, company capsules, and the essay on the Texas economy, we have tried to anticipate the needs of our readers. If we have missed anything, let us know. If there are companies that should be in this book that are not, send us a note and we will add them to the next edition. We look forward to hearing from you.

The Editors
Austin, Texas
October 27, 1993

Overview of the Texas Economy and Business Environment

Jon Hockenyos and the Texas Comptroller's Office

Traditionally divergent from the United States economy, the Texas economy continues to perform counter-cyclically to the rest of the country. A total of 132,000 net new jobs were created during 1992, marking the third year in a row that Texas has ranked first among all states in job growth. Texas accounted for one out of five new jobs created in the United States last year.

The basis of this deviation from the national norm is rooted in structural and cyclical trends, as well as geographic location. For most of its history, the Texas economy has functioned much like those in the developing world, exporting commodities (first agricultural products and then oil and petrochemicals) and importing finished goods. At the same time, favorable demographics also have played a role in the economic development of the state, as both high birth rates and strong in-migration have expanded the available labor force. The net result of this diverging structure has meant that Texas has tended to fare well during times of national distress; rising oil prices, for example, boosted the Texas economy through most of the 1970s into the early 1980s, when annual growth rates exceeded 4 percent. However, the oil bust, followed closely by the real estate and financial crisis, meant that Texas was once again out of step with the rest of the country.

Out of this recession were born the seeds of the current level of relative prosperity. The impetus toward economic diversification was greatly enhanced, as economic necessity compelled both entrepreneurship and heightened focus on industrial recruitment. Meanwhile, the fact that Texas was first to suffer the slings and arrows of the S&L and banking downturn meant that our institutions were first to resolve the crisis, which in turn implied that the state was relatively well positioned to take advantage of opportunities presented by sluggishness in other regions of the country. When the growing integration with the expanding Mexican economy is factored into the equation, it is evident that macro-economic forces currently tend to run in Texas's favor.

The consensus of recent credible economic forecasts indicates that growth over the next eighteen months should be slightly better than the historical average. Real gross state product (the inflation-adjusted dollar value of goods and services produced in Texas) in 1993 and 1994 should grow about 3 percent a year, while total personal income is expected to increase at an annual rate of about 7 percent over the period. With most estimates suggesting that at least 100,000 more people will move to Texas in both 1993 and 1994, population growth will be somewhat higher than in recent years. Texas's employment should continue to grow by more than 2.5 percent a year in 1993 and 1994, gaining about 400,000 jobs over the two-year period.

The Texas Comptroller's Office provides extensive information concerning the performance and outlook for both the different regions and industries of the state. What follows is their recent assessment of the principal component sectors of the Texas economy, as well as the status and outlook for Austin, Dallas, Houston, and San Antonio.

OIL AND GAS

In response to federal tax credits, drilling in Texas and the U.S. increased through most of 1992. Because credits expired at the end of 1992, a speed-up in exploration at the end of the year led to a drop in activity for early 1993. The number of drilling rigs is beginning to rise again, but the outlook for the oil and gas industry over the next few years is for more of the same—lackluster activity with exploration continuing to shift overseas and little employment change in Texas.

The latest Comptroller's forecast calls for a loss of 3,900 mining jobs in 1993 and another 1,100 in 1994 before employment stabilizes at about 166,000 jobs statewide in 1995.

CONSTRUCTION

The number of new housing permits so far in 1993, at an annualized rate of over 70,500 houses, is up 19 percent from a year ago. Mortgage rates are at their lowest levels in over twenty years, creating a favorable environment for new construction projects. Even commercial and business construction, long suppressed by high vacancy rates, are beginning to respond to lower vacancy and interest rates. Nonresidential building is expected to rise 7 percent in 1993 and 11 percent in 1994.

Despite the gains, the number of construction employees is up by only 1.4 percent over a year ago. One possible explanation for this apparent mismatch is that undocumented workers are filling many of the new construction jobs, so the official numbers do not reflect actual economic increases.

Assuming that consumer confidence does not erode further, the outlook for Texas construction over the next two years is excellent. Double-digit growth rates are expected in the number of housing starts, with over 100,000 starts for 1994. There should be 26,000 construction jobs added in 1993 and 1994, rising about 3 to 4 percent per year.

MANUFACTURING

Texas manufacturing bottomed out in early 1992 and has gathered some steam in early 1993. A lack of confidence about the strength of the national economic recovery, a desire to keep productivity high, and the high cost to employers of worker benefits and insurance has suppressed new hiring in the manufacturing sector. But over the first four months of 1993, 10,300 new manufacturing jobs have been added in Texas, mostly in apparel, building materials, printing materials, and plastics.

Texas manufacturing is expected to add 14,000 jobs in 1993 and another 15,000 in 1994. The outlook for 1993 is that nondurable manufacturing will account for most of the new jobs, with the fastest rates of growth in apparel, textiles and plastics. In 1994, as the national economic recovery intensifies and Mexican trade continues to increase, the emphasis will shift to durable goods, particularly computers, electronics and building materials. The bleakest outlook is for defense transportation equipment, oil field machinery, petroleum refining, and for the long term, textiles and apparel.

If the North American Free Trade Agreement is not implemented, the level of trade with Mexico would be hampered. The consequent outlook for Texas manufacturing would be weaker, with the biggest loss of opportunity being felt by electronics, computers and transportation equipment.

SERVICES AND TRADE

Most of the employment growth in 1993 and 1994 in the service-producing industries will be concentrated in retail trade (71,000 jobs), business and miscellaneous services (113,000 jobs) and local government (64,000 jobs). Overall, the service-producing sectors will account for about 87 percent of all new jobs in Texas in 1993 and 1994.

Texas retail sales are expected to increase 7.6 percent in 1993 and 6.9 percent in 1994. In comparison, the average annual growth rate was 6.4 percent during the 1987–1992 period.

Health services will add an additional 36,000 jobs in 1993 and 1994, for growth rates of about 3.3 percent a year. Although a healthy rate of growth, this is substantially slower than the 6.3 percent average annual increases seen over the past five years, as high costs are beginning to cap the growth potential of the industry. A national health plan, if implemented, might slow the growth of health services even more.

Although most service-producing industries will benefit from a stronger national economy in 1993 and 1994, there is one exception. Federal government employment will actually decline in response to budget reductions, particularly for defense.

AUSTIN

Despite the closing of Bergstrom Air Force Base, metropolitan Austin's high-tech, silicon-chip economy continues to soar. After posting a very strong 4.1 percent employment increase in 1992, total non-farm employment should continue its rapid rise, increasing 3.7 percent in 1993 and 3.2 percent in 1994, reaching 436,000 jobs in that year. The slight post-1992 slowdown in one of Texas's fastest-growing metro areas stems largely from the dampening effect of decreasing federal governmental expenditures on the area's wholesale and retail trade and services sectors.

Expanding its already significant role as a high-tech Mecca, Austin added Applied Materials, Inc., in late 1992 to its growing constellation of firms involved with the microprocessor industry. In addition to the direct growth of firms like Applied Materials, these companies are attracting suppliers and support industries to the area, such as CDS Leopold, a precision machining company from California.

These new-to-area firms join an already impressive array of high-tech giants located in the metro, including Apple, Dell Computer, Motorola, CompuAdd, Advanced Micro Devices, Sematech and

MCC among others. These firms enjoy about the same access to a highly skilled workforce in Austin as is found in other high tech centers, but face lower wage, housing and other living costs in the Austin area. Even IBM, which suffered significant cutbacks at many of its sites throughout the world, continues with a strong local presence thanks to the company's fast-growing (and Austin-based) Advanced Workstation Systems division.

Together, these high-tech firms helped generate a remarkable 3.4 percent employment growth in manufacturing in 1992. As the nation's economy continues to recover, this growth should climb to 3.9 percent in 1993, and to 4.5 percent in 1994.

The fast-growing manufacturing sector has had a number of ripple effects on other parts of the metro's economy, but nowhere have the impacts been more apparent than in the new housing and construction market. Into early 1993, the Austin metro has the shortest supply of housing on the market of any Texas metropolitan area and among the highest rental occupancy rates. With the aid of low interest rates, new home construction is surging. During the 12 month period ending in April 1993, single-family housing permits were up 32.9 percent over the comparable preceding 12-month period. As a result, construction employment was up 10.3 percent in 1992. While this growth in construction employment is expected to slow somewhat during the next two years, the rate of increase will remain substantial, at 6.5 percent in both 1993 and 1994.

The closing of Bergstrom Air Force Base is, however, expected to slow growth in some sectors of the metro economy. Employment growth in wholesale and retail trade, after surging 5.4 percent in 1992, is expected to taper off to 3.6 percent in 1993 and to 2.5 percent in 1994. In part, this slowing of growth reflects the loss of purchasing power which the base brought to the local economy. Similarly, employment growth in services is expected to slow from the 6.6 percent posted in 1992, to 5.2 percent in 1993 and 4.4 percent in 1994. But, while the rate of growth may slow, the number of jobs will increase by 5,200 in wholesale and retail trade from 1992 to 1994, and by 10,500 in services during the same period.

The relatively strong local economy will have two other important impacts. First, because employment prospects are good, particularly relative to the chances of finding a job in many other parts of the nation, migration into the metro will continue at a relatively rapid pace. As a result, almost 24,000 net new residents should migrate into the metro between 1992 and 1994. Total metro population is expected to rise substantially, up 2.7 percent in 1993 and 2.4 percent in 1994, reaching 877,400 in the latter year, and nearly one million in the year 2000. Second, as a consequence of rapid population growth, local government employment will rise to meet expanding demands. This growth, coupled with more modest gains in state and federal employment, should generate an additional 3,000 jobs in 1993 and 2,200 in 1994.

In line with solid employment growth led by high-tech manufacturing, total personal income should rise by a strong 7.8 percent in 1993, following a 10.4 percent jump in 1992. Total income growth should remain strong in 1994, rising by 6.8 percent to $18.5 billion. Similarly, the growth in retail sales in the metro should remain relatively rapid, rising by 9.8 percent in 1993 and 7.9 percent in 1994.

The area's unemployment rate, already among the lowest in the state, should drop to 4.9 percent in 1993 and decline further to 4.6 percent by 1994.

DALLAS

Following very weak nonagricultural employment growth of 0.5 percent in 1992, Metropolitan Dallas can expect 2.2 percent employment growth in 1993. This rate translates into an increase of over 30,000 total jobs, up from a 7,000 increase in 1992 and a tiny 2,700 jump in 1991. An increase of 30,000 jobs in a single year might at first glance seem a bit optimistic after the dismal performance of the last few years, but for the 17 years preceding 1993 the metro added an average of 37,000 jobs each year. With continued strengthening in the national economy, as is forecast for the rest of 1993 and on through the next year, total metro employment is forecast to rise by 2.6 percent in 1994. A rebound in the Japanese economy and in the major European economies would add strength to this out-year forecast.

The manufacturing sector remains an important source of wealth and employment for the Dallas area. But because of technological improvements in capital equipment and the competitive pressures to reduce production costs, employment growth in this sector has been and will remain restricted. The current attention upon interactive voice, data and video media products will keep the metro's manufacturing sector in a prominent national position, with its concentration in high-technology electronics and electronic equipment. But these positive forces are mixed with downsizing and cutbacks in defense procurement, so manufacturing employment is expected to increase only 0.8 percent in 1993. Sector employment will grow at a rate slightly above 1 percent for the years beyond.

Mining employment in the metro is expected to be down 9 percent in 1993, continuing a trend that began in 1985. Typical of what has been happening in this sector is the restructuring that Halliburton began in 1991. So far, the company has cut 5,000 employees worldwide, with further cuts to come. Halliburton's restructuring typifies the mining sector and the long-term trend is successively downward as state and national oil and gas activities continue to contract. A substantial rise in the world oil price might stall or reverse this downward drift, but given the current Middle East oil supply situation and the re-emergence of Kuwait as a very large producer, such a rise is not likely. These forces are reflected in the 9.5 percent decline predicted for this sector in 1994.

The number of banking enterprises operating in Texas has declined by 45 percent since 1985. Extreme caution currently pervading bank lending activities continues to constrict the banking portion of the finance, insurance and real estate sector. Furthermore, the penetration and spread of computer technology into finance, insurance and real estate, and the consolidation of firms through acquisitions and mergers, have increased worker productivity in these firms. As these influences spread, employment in this sector is expected to drop by 0.8 percent in 1993, but this is some relief from the 3.7 percent decrease experienced in 1992. In 1994, a small turnaround is expected, with an 800-employee or 0.7 percent increase.

The services sector continues to dominate metro employment growth, both in absolute magnitude and in percentage terms. This continuation emphasizes the metro's strength as a regional center for health services and as a regional, national and international center for business services. Dallas's role as an international player in this sector has been enhanced by the build-up in business services in anticipation of the North American Free Trade Agreement (NAFTA) and by expanded trade with Mexico (apart from NAFTA). For 1993, services sector employment is expected to increase by almost 17,000, a 4.3 percent rise. This increase accounts for over one-half of the increase in total employment expected for the metro in 1993. Like the state and national economies, growth in the service sector will be the mainstay of employment growth in the metro economy, increasing 4.1 percent in 1994.

In percentage terms, growth in the transportation and utilities sector in 1993 will nearly match that of services and will exceed the rate for services in 1994. Even with its smaller size, employment in the transportation and utility sector is projected to grow by about 3,000 in 1993. The strength of this sector is concentrated in several areas—air and surface transportation and telecommunications—all of which are related to the trading of goods and to the services-related side of trade. Local and long-distance trucking, surface courier services, air couriers and scheduled air transportation are segments of this sector that have had net employment growth in recent years. Radiotelephone service, an especially dynamic segment of telecommunications, also has realized recent employment growth, and likely will continue to expand as digital communications facilities and media increase in availability and versatility.

Government employment in the metro continues to rise, at a 2.1 percent rate for 1993, but at a somewhat slower rate than for the state as a whole. For 1994 the expected rate of growth in government is 2.4 percent. This growth, coupled with the strong rise of employment in services, transportation and utilities and the modest rise in manufacturing employment, are propelling a rise in trade and construction employment along with a rise in retail sales activity.

Construction employment shows an eye-popping 5.9 percent increase for 1993, but this number needs to be put into perspective: This rate of increase represents fewer than 3,000 new jobs, and total sector employment, even after this rise, still is not two-thirds of the peak level reached in the mid-1980s. Much of the construction activity is in facilities other than commercial buildings, since Dallas still ranks high in the national office vacancy listings. The housing market is becoming more of a seller's market, however, with the inventory of homes for sale having dropped below a ten-month supply. For 1994, construction employment growth settles back to 3.9 percent, but growth would sag if the Superconducting Super Collider project is halted.

Personal income and retail sales in the Dallas metro will reflect the improved employment picture for 1993. Total personal income is projected to grow by 7.0 percent and retail trade by 6.3 percent. The growth in personal income is an impressive gain, exceeding the rate of income growth for the state as a whole, and is especially impressive in real terms, since inflation in 1993 should be in the 3 percent range. Per capita income growth for 1993, nominally 5.3 percent, also represents a strong gain in real terms. Total personal income and per capita personal income in 1994 are projected to grow by 6.2 percent and 4.6 percent, respectively.

The economic strength of the Dallas metropolitan area will translate into a growing population. For 1993, the increase is expected to be 1.6 percent, the same rate as for the state, for a total metro population of just over 2.7 million persons. In 1994 the rate of increase slows slightly, to 1.5 percent, or a population of nearly 2.75 million.

HOUSTON

Faced with a sluggish national economy and continued cutbacks in domestic oil industry activity, the metropolitan Houston economy slowed dramatically in 1992. After leading the nation in job growth during 1991, total wage and salary employment in Houston fell by 0.2 percent during 1992 to 1.627 million jobs—a net year-to-year loss of 3,000 positions. In comparison, employment in the nation increased by 0.1 percent, and statewide the increase was a substantially stronger 1.4 percent.

The 3.1 percent employment decline in the mining sector from 1991 to 1992 was the largest percentage drop of any sector, underscoring the effect of the low level of domestic drilling activity. Halliburton's layoff of 2,400 announced in late 1991 began showing up in local employment figures in 1992. In July 1992, Amoco also announced a major restructuring, which affected employment in the metro.

Other parts of the oil & gas processing stream showed mixed trends during 1992. Phibro Energy slashed production at their Texas City plant by 50 percent late in the year. Marathon also cut production at Texas City by 10,000 barrels per day. While not causing layoffs, these moves dampen any need for additional hiring. Refiners are being squeezed as refining margins shrink, while simultaneously facing increased cash needs to meet clean air act requirements.

But some parts of Houston's petrocomplex economy are showing positive signs. Phillips Petroleum completed construction on a new polyethylene plant to restore capacity destroyed in a 1989 fire and explosion. Shell announced the impending construction of a new $400 million petroleum processing plant in Deer Park, as part of a joint venture with Pemex, Mexico's national oil company. The plant will use thick, high-sulfur Mayan crude and could create 100 jobs.

The Houston-Mexico connection should serve as a strong link to the future in many parts of the metro's economy. Of 25,000 international patients treated at the Texas Medical Center each year, nearly half are from Latin America, including Mexico. Houston has 53 foreign consulates or trade offices versus 26 in Dallas and 6 in San Antonio. Houston has 15 subsidiaries or branches of major Mexican companies, as compared to 8 in Dallas and 5 in San Antonio.

Growth generated by increased trade with Mexico, along with some likely stability for non-oil–related metro employers such as Compaq Computer and Continental Airlines, should spell slow, but positive, employment growth in 1993. Overall, employment in the metro should increase 1 percent in 1993 over 1992 levels, reaching 1.64 million. With the exception of some continued weakness in both mining and construction, all other sectors of the metro's economy should expand in 1993.

As the nation continues its slow recovery from recession, employment in Houston should also follow a slow, but positive, growth trend, rising 1.6 percent in 1994.

In line with the prospect of slow employment growth, total personal income in the metro should post only moderate gains through 1994. The growth in total personal income should edge up from an annual increase of 4.6 percent from 1992 to 1993, to a 4.9 percent rise in 1994, but will remain slower than the rates of increase in both the state and the nation. The slower forecasted rates for income growth stem, in part, from the likelihood that much of Houston's employment growth will occur in industries which do not pay as highly as manufacturing and mining.

Like expected trends in the growth of total income in the metropolitan area, retail sales should display moderate growth into the mid-point of the decade. Retail sales are expected to post a 7 percent rise in 1993, up slightly from a 6.1 percent rise in 1992, but down from the strong 9.9 percent rise seen in 1990. Lower interest rates will continue to have a positive impact on retail sales. For those with a mortgage, refinancing at lower rates increases disposable income for spending on other items.

Lower interest rates also mean more families can qualify for mortgages, thereby increasing the demand for less expensive "starter" homes. This is undoubtedly a prime factor in the observed trend in local housing of a strong market in low-to-middle cost housing but weak demand in "high end" housing. Improvement for all housing segments must await stronger overall economic growth.

As in-migration slows in line with improving economic conditions elsewhere in the country, the rate of population growth in the metro should also slow, falling from 1.5 percent in 1993 to 1.4 percent in 1994. By 1994, the metro population should reach 3.6 million, up by nearly 250,000 from 1990.

SAN ANTONIO

Building on a competitive, bilingual labor force and its telecommunications infrastructure, metropolitan San Antonio's economic growth should accelerate slightly in 1993 before slowing somewhat in 1994, as torrid employment growth in the construction sector decreases to more normal levels. After posting a strong 3.4 percent job growth rate in 1992 over 1991 levels, San Antonio should add another 19,500 jobs in 1993, representing a 3.6 percent growth rate. In 1994, employment growth will slow to 15,800 jobs or 2.8 percent, reaching a total of 582,900 jobs.

Leading the rapid growth in 1993 is the construction sector, expected to grow by 9.0 percent. San Antonio's good economic performance over the past two years is serving as a magnet for migration into the area. As such, residential construction activity is expected to pick up significantly in 1993, aided by low interest rates. Together with an improving commercial and multi-family market, construction activity should drive substantial job growth in the metro during 1993, even though construction of the Alamodome is largely complete. Construction employment growth will slow to a moderate 2.9 percent in 1994, more in line with past trends.

Underlying much of the recent strength of the metro economy is a growing telecommunications industry which capitalizes on two of San Antonio's strengths—a competitive, bilingual labor force and the availability of a state-of-the-art fiber optics network. In 1993, the U.S. Long Distance Corporation, which provides billing and collection services for many telephone companies, joined West Telemarketing Corporation, Sears Telecatalog Center, QVC Network, American Airlines's Teleservice Resources, AT&T's customer service centers and nearly twenty other telemarketing and telecommunications firms located in San Antonio.

Moreover, the metro's role as a telecommunications center will be strengthened in the future as Southwestern Bell completes its corporate headquarters relocation to San Antonio. The area's cultural and geographical proximity to Mexico surely will prove an important asset to SW Bell as the company strives to strengthen ties with Mexico's telephone company, Teléfonos de Mexico or Telmex, in which SW Bell now holds a 10 percent stake.

In addition to the metro economy's gains from telecommunications and telemarketing attractions, the tourism economy was augmented by the opening of the $100 million Hyatt Resort, golf course and water park. Together with the metro's other tourist attractions, including the Alamo, the Riverwalk, Sea World, and Fiesta Texas, the service economy should continue to flourish during the next two years.

These positive developments will generate growth in a number of economic sectors. Job growth in telecommunications will help the transportation and public utilities sector add 800 jobs in 1993 and another 1,000 in 1994. Telemarketing jobs and some parts of the tourism industry will help generate the 7,800 new jobs expected in services in 1993, along with an additional 6,300 in 1994. Finally, some aspects of the growth in tourism will serve to push employment in the wholesale and retail trade sector up 3.9 percent in 1993 and an additional 2.6 percent in 1994.

To serve an expanding population, government employment is expected to rise by 2.3 percent in 1993 and by 2.2 percent in 1994. In addition, after nearly a decade-long decline, manufacturing employment in the San Antonio area is expected to climb for the second consecutive year, rising 1.9 percent in 1993, followed by a 1.6 percent rise in 1994. Besides mining, the other sector which continues to display some weakness is finance, insurance, and real estate, which is expected to post small job losses in 1993 followed by modest growth in 1994.

In line with increasing employment opportunities, total personal income and population should rise in the San Antonio metro during the next two years while the unemployment rate should fall. Total personal income is expected to grow by 6.7 percent in 1993 and 6.8 percent in 1994. An additional 20,700 people should call the San Antonio metro their home in 1993, followed by a further increase of 22,600 in 1994. The rate of population growth should accelerate slowly during the next couple of years, increasing from a 1.4 percent rate of annual growth in 1992, to 1.5 percent in 1993, to 1.7 percent in 1994. The metro's unemployment rate should decline from 6.7 percent in 1992 to 6.3 percent in 1993 and 1994.

After a very strong year in retail sales in 1992, rising 9.8 percent from 1991 levels, the growth in retail sales will subside somewhat in 1993, but remain strong. Retail sales are expected to climb 7.8 percent in 1993 and an additional 6.1 percent in 1994.

Reprinted from *Texas Economic Outlook*, July 1993, Texas Comptroller's Office, with opening material by Jon Hockenyos.

A LIST-LOVER'S COMPENDIUM

The Texas 500 Companies Ranked by Sales

Rank	Company	Sales ($ mil.)
1	Exxon Corporation	103,160
2	Shell Oil Company	21,702
3	J. C. Penney Company, Inc.	19,085
4	AMR Corporation	14,396
5	Tenneco Inc.	13,139
6	Marathon Group	12,782
7	Coastal Corporation, The	10,063
8	SYSCO Corporation	10,022
9	Southwestern Bell Corporation	10,015
10	Electronic Data Systems Corporation	8,155
11	Texas Instruments Incorporated	7,440
12	Kimberly-Clark Corporation	7,091
13	Halliburton Company	6,525
14	Southland Corporation, The	6,439
15	Enron Corp.	6,325
16	Cooper Industries, Inc.	6,119
17	Continental Airlines Holdings, Inc.	5,575
18	USAA	5,434
19	Texas Utilities Company	4,908
20	Lyondell Petrochemical Company	4,805
21	Tandy Corporation	4,743
22	Burlington Northern Inc.	4,630
23	American General Corporation	4,602
24	Houston Industries Incorporated	4,596
25	Compaq Computer Corporation	4,100
26	HEB Grocery	3,800
27	Dresser Industries, Inc.	3,797
28	National Intergroup, Inc.	3,411
29	FINA, Inc.	3,398
30	Central and South West Corp.	3,289
31	Browning-Ferris Industries, Inc.	3,288
32	Randall's Food Markets, Inc.	3,200
33	Philp Co.	2,910
34	Associated Milk Producers, Inc.	2,835
35	ENSERCH Corp.	2,826
36	Transco Energy Co.	2,724
37	Temple-Inland Inc.	2,713
38	Diamond Shamrock, Inc.	2,612
39	Baker Hughes Incorporated	2,539
40	Centex Corp.	2,503
41	Panhandle Eastern Corp.	2,434
42	Sammons Enterprises	2,400
43	Pennzoil Company	2,357
44	American Medical Holdings, Inc.	2,238
45	MAXXAM Inc.	2,203
46	E-Systems, Inc.	2,099
47	Dell Computer Corporation	2,014
48	Southwest Airlines Co.	1,685
49	Trinity Industries, Inc.	1,540
50	Oryx Energy Co.	1,392

Rank	Company	Sales ($ mil.)
51	CompUSA, Inc.	1,342
52	American National Insurance Co.	1,318
53	Grocers Supply Co.	1,300
54	Blue Cross and Blue Shield of Texas Inc.	1,251
55	Valero Energy Corp.	1,235
56	Lincoln Property Co.	1,173
57	Commercial Metals Co.	1,166
58	Contran Corp.	1,128
59	Lennox International Inc.	1,050
60	Wingate Partners LP	1,000
61	Zale Holding Corporation	981
62	National Convenience Stores	959
63	Tesoro Petroleum Corp.	954
64	Epic Holdings, Inc.	941
65	NL Industries, Inc.	914
66	Mitchell Energy & Development Corp.	903
67	Pilgrim's Pride Corporation	887
68	ClubCorp International	870
69	Maxus Energy Corp.	851
70	Stewart & Stevenson Services, Inc.	813
71	AmeriServ Food Co.	806
72	El Paso Natural Gas Co.	803
73	SnyderGeneral Corp.	800
74	White Swan Inc.	780
75	Service Corporation International	772
76	HB Zachry Co.	750
77	Southwestern Public Service Co.	749
78	Tauber Oil Co.	747
79	Hunt Oil Company Inc.	720
80	Union Texas Petroleum Holdings, Inc.	714
81	CompuCom Systems, Inc.	713
82	Vista Chemical Inc.	700
83	GSC Enterprises, Inc.	699
84	Greyhound Lines, Inc.	682
85	NCH Corp.	680
86	U.S. Home Corp.	679
87	Pride Companies, LP	668
88	Dr Pepper/Seven-Up Companies, Inc.	659
89	Brinker International, Inc.	653
90	Imperial Holly Corp.	648
91	Medical Care America Inc.	641
92	Brookshire Grocery Co.	640
93	Pier 1 Imports, Inc.	629
94	Baroid Corp.	628
95	Texas Industries, Inc.	614
96	Mary Kay Cosmetics Inc.	613
97	Fiesta Mart Inc.	600
98	Gulf States Toyota	600
99	AppleTree Markets Inc.	597
100	Color Tile Inc.	586

The Texas 500 Companies Ranked by Sales (continued)

Rank	Company	Sales ($ mil.)	Rank	Company	Sales ($ mil.)
101	Quanex Corp.	572	151	National Western Life Insurance Co.	401
102	Minyard Food Stores Inc.	550	152	Petro Inc.	400
103	Paragon Group	550	153	Goodman Manufacturing Corporation	400
104	Affiliated Foods Incorporated	550	154	Eljer Industries, Inc.	397
105	Adams Resources & Energy, Inc.	550	155	Edisto Resources Corp.	386
106	CRSS, Inc.	546	156	Glazer's Wholesale Drug Company Inc.	385
107	Brookshire Brothers Incorporated	542	157	Wyndham Hotel Company Ltd.	384
108	Ben E. Keith	540	158	Anadarko Petroleum Corp.	375
109	DSC Communications Corp.	536	159	Vanguard Energy Corp.	375
110	Keystone International, Inc.	528	160	United Insurance Companies, Inc.	371
111	AFG Industries Inc.	525	161	Offshore Pipelines, Inc.	370
112	CompuAdd, Inc.	525	162	McCoy Corporation	370
113	El Paso Electric Co.	525	163	Intertrans Corp.	367
114	Tejas Gas Corp.	524	164	Redman Industries Inc.	365
115	A. H. Belo Corp.	516	165	National-Oilwell	360
116	Austin Industries Inc.	510	166	Coca-Cola Bottling Group-Southwest	356
117	Super Club North America Corporation	510	167	Living Centers of America, Inc.	351
118	Southdown, Inc.	508	168	MorningStar Group, Inc.	351
119	Destec Energy, Inc.	508	169	Southern Foods Groups Incorporated	350
120	Holly Corp.	507	170	Truman Arnold Companies	348
121	Specialty Retailers Inc.	505	171	Luby's Cafeterias, Inc.	346
122	Capstead Mortgage Corp.	504	172	Atmos Energy Corp.	340
123	Darling-Delaware Company Inc.	500	173	United Supermarkets Incorporated	330
124	Plains Cotton Cooperative Association	500	174	BJ Services Co.	330
125	Michaels Stores, Inc.	493	175	King Ranch, Inc.	330
126	Enterprise Products Company	491	176	Weekley Homes Inc.	330
127	First USA, Inc.	480	177	Cactus Feeders Incorporated	325
128	Chief Auto Parts Incorporated	473	178	Quintana Petroleum Corp.	325
129	ElectroCom Automation, Inc.	470	179	Weiners Enterprises	320
130	Sky Chefs, Inc.	467	180	Keystone Consolidated Industries, Inc.	316
131	Placid Oil Co.	464	181	Western Co. of North America	315
132	Howell Corp.	461	182	Oshman's Sporting Goods, Inc.	313
133	Apache Corporation	454	183	Darr Equipment Company	310
134	Justin Industries, Inc.	453	184	Haggar Apparel	300
135	MediaNews Group	450	185	Wyatt Cafeterias Inc.	300
136	Riviana Foods Inc.	450	186	Williamson-Dickie Manufacturing Co.	300
137	East Texas Distributing Inc.	445	187	Overhead Door Corp.	300
138	TNP Enterprises, Inc.	444	188	TIC United Corp.	300
139	Sound Warehouse Incorporated	440	189	Rice Food Markets Inc.	300
140	E-Z Serve Corp.	434	190	Wilson Industries Incorporated	300
141	Sterling Chemicals, Inc.	431	191	Tri-State Wholesale Associated Grocers Inc.	300
142	American Oil and Gas Corp.	431	192	Texas Olefins Co.	300
143	Santa Fe Energy Resources, Inc.	428	193	Reliable Chevrolet Inc.	300
144	Harte-Hanks Communications Holdings Incorporated	427	194	Triangle Pacific Corp.	293
145	Home Interiors & Gifts, Inc.	425	195	Stewart Information Services Corp.	290
146	Chaparral Steel Co.	420	196	E Z Mart Stores Incorporated	290
147	Rexene Corp.	415	197	Tyler Corp.	286
148	Lone Star Technologies, Inc.	411	198	Nabors Industries, Inc.	286
149	Administaff Inc.	410	199	Lomas Financial Corp.	282
150	APS Holding Corporation	404	200	Owen Healthcare Inc.	280

The Texas 500 Companies Ranked by Sales (continued)

Rank	Company	Sales ($ mil.)
201	FFP Partners, L.P.	279
202	Kinetic Concepts, Inc.	278
203	Associated Materials Incorporated	277
204	Bank United of Texas FSB	276
205	Hollywood Casino Corp.	275
206	AMRE, Inc.	274
207	Pillowtex Corp.	273
208	Kirby Corp.	269
209	Furr's/Bishop's, Incorporated	268
210	Tracor Inc.	262
211	Global Marine, Inc.	260
212	Sterling Software, Inc.	259
213	Paging Network, Inc.	258
214	La Quinta Motor Inns, Inc.	256
215	ShowBiz Pizza Time, Inc.	253
216	Cullen/Frost Bankers, Inc.	252
217	Heritage Media Corporation	251
218	Dunlap Co.	250
219	Rowan Companies, Inc.	250
220	Pioneer Concrete of America	250
221	Rip Griffin Truck/Travel Centers Inc.	250
222	HCB Contractors	250
223	Perot Systems Corp.	247
224	Freeman Companies, The	245
225	Endevco, Inc.	245
226	BMC Software, Inc.	239
227	Seagull Energy Corp.	239
228	Mesa Inc.	237
229	Allwaste, Inc.	234
230	Southwest Research Institute Inc.	234
231	BancTec, Inc.	234
232	Gillman Companies, Inc.	234
233	Curtis C. Gunn Inc.	233
234	Bombay Company, Inc., The	232
235	CONVEX Computer Corp.	232
236	Whataburger Systems	230
237	Winn's Stores Incorporated	221
238	Dal-Tile Group Inc.	220
239	Stanley Stores Inc.	220
240	Software Spectrum, Inc.	220
241	Oceaneering International, Inc.	216
242	Fulbright and Jaworski	214
243	Pool Energy Services Co.	213
244	Sematech, Inc.	213
245	Smith International, Inc.	211
246	Daniel Industries, Inc.	210
247	Gerland's Food Fair Inc.	210
248	Babbage's, Inc.	209
249	Datapoint Corp.	208
250	Parker & Parsley Petroleum Co.	208

Rank	Company	Sales ($ mil.)
251	Weatherford International Inc.	206
252	Mundy Cos.	200
253	UETA Inc.	200
254	SLM Power Group Inc.	200
255	Dallas Auto Auction Inc.	200
256	Behrens Inc.	200
257	Vinmar Inc.	200
258	Recognition Equipment Inc.	199
259	Brazos Electric Power Cooperative Inc.	199
260	Life Insurance Company of the Southwest	199
261	Frozen Food Express Industries, Inc.	195
262	Moorco International, Inc.	195
263	George Grubbs Enterprises Inc.	195
264	Vinson & Elkins L.L.P.	194
265	Energy Ventures, Inc.	192
266	Southern Union Co.	192
267	MacGregor Medical Association	190
268	Newell Recycling Company Inc.	190
269	Vista Oil Co.	190
270	Martin Gas Corp.	189
271	Hi-Lo Auto Supply, Inc.	187
272	Cash America International, Inc.	185
273	Tejas Power Corp.	184
274	D. R. Horton, Inc.	183
275	Battle Mountain Gold Co.	182
276	50-Off Stores, Inc.	181
277	W. O. Bankston Enterprises Inc.	181
278	Tech-Sym Corp.	180
279	Blue Bell Creameries	180
280	Foxworth-Galbraith Lumber Company	180
281	Pioneer Chlor Alkali Investments Inc.	180
282	Tarrant Distributors Inc.	180
283	Richards Group Inc.	180
284	Kaneb Services, Inc.	177
285	American Rice, Inc.	176
286	Palm Harbor Homes Inc.	175
287	Vallen Corp.	175
288	American Income Holding, Inc.	175
289	E.R. Fant, Inc.	175
290	Eastex Energy Inc.	175
291	Bass Enterprises Production Co.	174
292	Elcor Corp.	173
293	Remington Hotel Corporation	170
294	Trammell Crow Company	170
295	Men's Wearhouse, Inc., The	170
296	Dr Pepper Bottling Company of Texas	170
297	SPI Holding, Inc.	170
298	R Corp.	170
299	Ancira Enterprises Inc.	169
300	Teppco Partners, L.P.	166

The Texas 500 Companies Ranked by Sales (continued)

Rank	Company	Sales ($ mil.)	Rank	Company	Sales ($ mil.)
301	Mrs. Baird's Bakeries Inc.	165	351	Igloo Holdings Inc.	130
302	Tuboscope Vetco International Inc.	165	352	Brenham Wholesale Grocery Co.	130
303	Pearce Industries Inc.	164	353	Lawrence Marshall Chevrolet-Olds, Inc.	130
304	Allright Corp.	163	354	Gulf Coast Sportswear Inc.	130
305	Xeron Inc.	163	355	Ennis Business Forms, Inc.	129
306	Energy Service Co., Inc.	162	356	Friona Industries LP	129
307	Alliance Employee Leasing Corp. I	161	357	Lufkin Industries, Inc.	127
308	International Bancshares	161	358	Friendly Chevrolet	125
309	Tuesday Morning Corporation	160	359	Miller and Miller Auctioneers Inc.	125
310	Harborage Inc.	160	360	Continuum Company, Inc., The	124
311	RSR Corp.	160	361	Victoria Bankshares, Inc.	123
312	Periodical Management Group Inc.	160	362	Lee Lewis Construction, Inc.	123
313	L&H Packing Company Inc.	160	363	Strafco Inc.	122
314	Mustang Tractor and Equipment Co.	160	364	Hunt Building Corporation	122
315	Hunt Petroleum Corp.	160	365	Whole Foods Market, Inc.	120
316	Houston Peterbilt Inc.	160	366	Dallas Semiconductor Corp.	120
317	Reading & Bates Corp.	157	367	Bracewell and Patterson	120
318	Kent Electronics Corp.	155	368	Thompson and Knight PC	120
319	Intellicall, Inc.	155	369	TTI Inc.	120
320	Academy Corp.	154	370	Rayco	120
321	Solo Serv Corp.	154	371	Locke Purnell Rain Harrell	120
322	Baker and Botts, L.L.P.	154	372	Snyder Oil Corporation	120
323	Farah Inc.	152	373	Pace Entertainment Corporation	120
324	Enterra Corp.	150	374	Hallwood Group Inc.	116
325	MMI Products Inc.	150	375	Gundle Environmental Systems, Inc.	115
326	Chemical Lime Co.	150	376	Park Place Motor Cars	115
327	Sterling Electronics Corp.	150	377	Texas Stadium Corporation	112
328	Handy Andy Supermarkets	148	378	Digicon, Inc.	111
329	Serv-Tech, Inc.	148	379	Computer Language Research, Inc.	111
330	Cabot Oil & Gas Corp.	148	380	Gal-Tex Hotel Corp.	110
331	Frank Parra Chevrolet Inc.	147	381	U.S. Contractors Inc.	110
332	K.S.A. Industries Inc.	141	382	CJC Holdings Inc.	110
333	Pogo Producing Company	141	383	Sunbelt Corp.	110
334	Noble Drilling Corp.	140	384	Voluntary Hospitals of America Inc.	110
335	H and C Communications Inc.	140	385	Triton Energy Corp.	110
336	Supertravel	140	386	Maverick Markets Inc.	110
337	Veragon Corp.	140	387	Hollywood Marine Inc.	110
338	Sunbelt Nursery Group, Inc.	139	388	Farb Companies Ltd.	110
339	TCA Cable TV, Inc.	139	389	Lott Group Inc., The	110
340	TeleCheck Services, Inc.	138	390	Anderson Grain Corp.	110
341	Royal International Optical Corp.	137	391	Linbeck Construction Corp.	110
342	Powell Industries, Inc.	137	392	Wright Brand Foods Inc.	108
343	Helen of Troy Corp.	137	393	Dalfort Corp.	107
344	Plains Resources Inc.	133	394	Zapata Corp.	106
345	Greiner Engineering, Inc.	132	395	Grant Geophysical, Inc.	105
346	Akin, Gump, Strauss, Hauer & Feld	132	396	Independent Grocers Inc.	105
347	Tandycrafts, Inc.	131	397	Intelogic Trace, Inc.	104
348	Southwest Toyota, Inc.	131	398	Pride Petroleum Services, Inc.	101
349	Fish Engineering & Construction Partners Ltd.	130	399	Galveston-Houston Co.	101
350	Plantation Foods Inc.	130	400	Pay 'N Save Inc.	101

The Texas 500 Companies Ranked by Sales (continued)

Rank	Company	Sales ($ mil.)
401	Hydril Co.	100
402	York Group Inc., The	100
403	Fojtasek Companies Inc.	100
404	Davis Food City Inc.	100
405	Jackson and Walker LP	100
406	Strasburger and Price	100
407	Pedernales Electric Cooperative Inc.	100
408	Block Distributing Company Inc.	100
409	Merichem Co.	100
410	Warren Electric Co.	100
411	Hartnett, C.D. Company, The	100
412	Wholesale Electric Supply Company of Houston, Inc.	100
413	AZTX Cattle Co.	100
414	Spectrum Information Technologies, Inc.	100
415	Cap Rock Electric Cooperative	100
416	Walsh-Lumpkin Drug Co.	100
417	Barrett & Crofoot, LLP	98
418	EZCORP, Inc.	96
419	Schultz Industries Inc.	96
420	Dupey Management Corp.	95
421	Clear Channel Communications, Inc.	95
422	JaGee Corp	95
423	W.S. Bellows Construction Corp.	95
424	Barnett Brothers Brokerage Company Inc.	95
425	Tetco Inc.	94
426	WellTech Inc.	94
427	Houston McLane Company, Inc.	93
428	Pannell Kerr Forster	93
429	Andrews and Kurth	93
430	American Produce and Vegetable Co.	92
431	Port City Automotive Partners	92
432	Kinsel Motors Inc.	92
433	New Process Steel Corp.	92
434	Wagner and Brown, Ltd.	91
435	Sewell Village Cadillac	90
436	Southwestern Irrigated Cotton Growers Association	90
437	Weingarten Realty Investors	90
438	Hart Graphics Inc.	88
439	Julius Schepps Co.	88
440	Bay Houston Towing Co.	86
441	GAINSCO, INC.	86
442	Sun Coast Resources Inc.	86
443	Business Records Corporation Holding Co.	85
444	U.S. Long Distance Corp.	85
445	Berry-Barnett Grocery Co.	85
446	Old America Stores Inc.	84
447	Helena Laboratories	84
448	Stevens Graphics Corp.	84
449	Sanifill, Inc.	82
450	Landmark Graphics Corp.	82

Rank	Company	Sales ($ mil.)
451	Taylor Medical	81
452	Gulf Met Holdings Corp.	81
453	Handy Hardware Wholesale Inc.	81
454	Gulf States Inc.	80
455	David's Supermarkets Inc.	80
456	Sid Richardson Carbon and Gasoline Co.	80
457	Ohmstede Inc.	80
458	Delta Industrial Offices Inc.	80
459	Vaughan and Sons Inc.	80
460	Plains Cooperative Oil Mill Inc.	80
461	Jones Blair Co.	78
462	Lone Star Plywood and Door Corp.	78
463	Texas Mill Supply Inc.	78
464	Team, Inc.	77
465	Wainoco Oil Corp.	77
466	Cliffs Drilling Co.	77
467	Coburn Supply Company Inc.	77
468	Cantey & Hanger LLP	76
469	MAXXIM Medical, Inc.	75
470	CCC Group Inc.	75
471	Border Steel Mills Inc.	75
472	Tri-Gas Inc.	75
473	Production Operators Corp	75
474	Standard Fruit and Vegetable Company Inc.	75
475	West Texas Equipment Co.	75
476	Texas Pipe and Supply Company Inc.	75
477	Economy Cash and Carry Inc.	75
478	Texas United Corp	74
479	Fossil Inc.	74
480	Denton County Electric Cooperative	74
481	Pancho's Mexican Buffet, Inc.	73
482	U.S. Intec, Inc.	73
483	Cyrix Corporation	73
484	Gambrinus Company, The	72
485	Tecnol Inc.	71
486	Middleberg, Riddle and Gianna	71
487	American Ecology Corp.	71
488	Sigel Liquor Stores Inc.	71
489	Leif Johnson Ford Inc.	71
490	Emergency Network Inc.	70
491	Texas Kenworth Co.	70
492	Steakley Chevrolet Inc.	70
493	H.T. Ardinger and Son Co.	70
494	Associated Pipeline Contractors Inc.	69
495	TDIndustries Inc.	69
496	Wing Industries Inc.	69
497	American Indemnity Financial Corp.	68
498	Southwest Securities Group Inc.	68
499	M/A/R/C Group, The	67
500	H and H Meat Products Company Inc.	67

The Texas 500 Companies Ranked by Employees

Rank	Company	Employees
1	J. C. Penney Company, Inc.	192,000
2	AMR Corporation	119,300
3	Exxon Corporation	95,000
4	Tenneco Inc.	79,000
5	Electronic Data Systems Corporation	70,500
6	Halliburton Company	69,200
7	Texas Instruments Incorporated	60,577
8	Southwestern Bell Corporation	59,500
9	Cooper Industries, Inc.	52,900
10	Continental Airlines Holdings, Inc.	44,430
11	Kimberly-Clark Corporation	42,902
12	HEB Grocery	42,000
13	Tandy Corporation	39,000
14	Southland Corporation, The	35,646
15	Burlington Northern Inc.	31,204
16	Browning-Ferris Industries, Inc.	29,400
17	Brinker International, Inc.	28,000
18	American Medical Holdings, Inc.	27,500
19	Dresser Industries, Inc.	27,400
20	Shell Oil Company	25,308
21	SYSCO Corporation	24,000
22	Marathon Group	22,810
23	Randall's Food Markets, Inc.	20,000
24	Contran Corp.	19,950
25	Baker Hughes Incorporated	19,600
26	E-Systems, Inc.	18,600
27	Living Centers of America, Inc.	17,000
28	Coastal Corporation, The	16,570
29	ClubCorp International	15,869
30	Heritage Media Corporation	15,300
31	Temple-Inland Inc.	15,000
32	USAA	14,667
33	Texas Utilities Company	14,023
34	Trinity Industries, Inc.	13,000
35	Administaff Inc.	12,800
36	MAXXAM Inc.	12,379
37	ShowBiz Pizza Time, Inc.	12,000
38	Service Corporation International	11,818
39	American General Corporation	11,600
40	Houston Industries Incorporated	11,576
41	Southwest Airlines Co.	11,397
42	Pilgrim's Pride Corporation	10,500
43	NCH Corp.	10,477
44	Epic Holdings, Inc.	10,420
45	ENSERCH Corp.	10,400
46	Michaels Stores, Inc.	10,147
47	Greyhound Lines, Inc.	9,700
48	Compaq Computer Corporation	9,500
49	HB Zachry Co.	9,500
50	Luby's Cafeterias, Inc.	9,200
51	Pennzoil Company	9,125
52	Zale Holding Corporation	9,000
53	Wingate Partners LP	8,800
54	Furr's/Bishop's, Incorporated	8,600
55	Central and South West Corp.	8,595
56	Whataburger Systems	8,500
57	Alliance Employee Leasing Corp. I	8,000
58	Lennox International Inc.	8,000
59	MediaNews Group	8,000
60	Enron Corp.	7,780
61	Pier 1 Imports, Inc.	7,600
62	Specialty Retailers Inc.	7,500
63	Brookshire Grocery Co.	7,300
64	Sky Chefs, Inc.	7,300
65	Centex Corp.	6,500
66	Haggar Apparel	6,500
67	SnyderGeneral Corp.	6,300
68	Minyard Food Stores Inc.	6,100
69	Diamond Shamrock, Inc.	6,000
70	La Quinta Motor Inns, Inc.	6,000
71	Wyndham Hotel Company Ltd.	6,000
72	Harte-Hanks Communications Holdings Incorporated	5,825
73	Chief Auto Parts Incorporated	5,800
74	CompUSA, Inc.	5,679
75	Austin Industries Inc.	5,500
76	Fiesta Mart Inc.	5,500
77	Weiners Enterprises	5,500
78	Wyatt Cafeterias Inc.	5,500
79	Baroid Corp.	5,450
80	Justin Industries, Inc.	5,102
81	Brookshire Brothers Incorporated	5,000
82	Panhandle Eastern Corp.	5,000
83	Sammons Enterprises	5,000
84	Philp Co.	4,820
85	Transco Energy Co.	4,708
86	Dell Computer Corporation	4,650
87	Pool Energy Services Co.	4,519
88	Mundy Cos.	4,500
89	National Convenience Stores	4,500
90	Associated Milk Producers, Inc.	4,364
91	Medical Care America Inc.	4,300
92	Farah Inc.	4,100
93	Keystone International, Inc.	4,100
94	Color Tile Inc.	4,081
95	Lincoln Property Co.	4,059
96	AppleTree Markets Inc.	4,000
97	Williamson-Dickie Manufacturing Co.	4,000
98	Blue Cross and Blue Shield of Texas Inc.	3,900
99	Commercial Metals Co.	3,793
100	Eljer Industries, Inc.	3,750

The Texas 500 Companies Ranked by Employees (continued)

Rank	Company	Employees
101	Oshman's Sporting Goods, Inc.	3,700
102	NL Industries, Inc.	3,600
103	AFG Industries Inc.	3,500
104	Redman Industries Inc.	3,500
105	Super Club North America Corporation	3,500
106	Stewart Information Services Corp.	3,471
107	Tyler Corp.	3,470
108	National-Oilwell	3,400
109	Tracor Inc.	3,400
110	Triangle Pacific Corp.	3,400
111	FINA, Inc.	3,369
112	DSC Communications Corp.	3,301
113	Allwaste, Inc.	3,263
114	AMRE, Inc.	3,250
115	Hollywood Casino Corp.	3,200
116	Royal International Optical Corp.	3,200
117	Winn's Stores Incorporated	3,200
118	Nabors Industries, Inc.	3,168
119	National Intergroup, Inc.	3,138
120	Pancho's Mexican Buffet, Inc.	3,109
121	E-Z Serve Corp.	3,016
122	Allright Corp.	3,000
123	Dunlap Co.	3,000
124	E Z Mart Stores Incorporated	3,000
125	Mrs. Baird's Bakeries Inc.	3,000
126	Remington Hotel Corporation	3,000
127	Bombay Company, Inc., The	2,900
128	Tuesday Morning Corporation	2,877
129	Stewart & Stevenson Services, Inc.	2,850
130	50-Off Stores, Inc.	2,849
131	Emergency Network Inc.	2,800
132	Mitchell Energy & Development Corp.	2,800
133	Sound Warehouse Incorporated	2,800
134	A. H. Belo Corp.	2,788
135	Weatherford International Inc.	2,763
136	Texas Industries, Inc.	2,700
137	Western Co. of North America	2,700
138	Quanex Corp.	2,697
139	Paging Network, Inc.	2,670
140	Southwest Research Institute Inc.	2,606
141	Southdown, Inc.	2,600
142	United Supermarkets Incorporated	2,600
143	BJ Services Co.	2,579
144	Petro Inc.	2,572
145	Dal-Tile Group Inc.	2,500
146	Gal-Tex Hotel Corp.	2,500
147	Overhead Door Corp.	2,500
148	U.S. Contractors Inc.	2,500
149	El Paso Natural Gas Co.	2,499
150	Kinetic Concepts, Inc.	2,460
151	Associated Materials Incorporated	2,400
152	Riviana Foods Inc.	2,400
153	Trammell Crow Company	2,400
154	Hi-Lo Auto Supply, Inc.	2,383
155	Whole Foods Market, Inc.	2,350
156	Rowan Companies, Inc.	2,333
157	Lyondell Petrochemical Company	2,312
158	CRSS, Inc.	2,276
159	APS Holding Corporation	2,225
160	Babbage's, Inc.	2,200
161	Bank United of Texas FSB	2,200
162	Fish Engineering & Construction Partners Ltd.	2,200
163	Maxus Energy Corp.	2,190
164	Grant Geophysical, Inc.	2,178
165	Lomas Financial Corp.	2,163
166	Sterling Software, Inc.	2,150
167	Sunbelt Nursery Group, Inc.	2,150
168	Men's Wearhouse, Inc., The	2,125
169	Lufkin Industries, Inc.	2,098
170	Lone Star Technologies, Inc.	2,070
171	Southwestern Public Service Co.	2,030
172	Kaneb Services, Inc.	2,026
173	Energy Ventures, Inc.	2,000
174	Keystone Consolidated Industries, Inc.	2,000
175	Mary Kay Cosmetics Inc.	2,000
176	Tandycrafts, Inc.	2,000
177	TIC United Corp.	2,000
178	BancTec, Inc.	1,940
179	Imperial Holly Corp.	1,940
180	Tuboscope Vetco International Inc.	1,918
181	Dupey Management Corp.	1,900
182	Grocers Supply Co.	1,900
183	Hunt Oil Company Inc.	1,900
184	Kirby Corp.	1,875
185	Pride Petroleum Services, Inc.	1,875
186	Frozen Food Express Industries, Inc.	1,822
187	Tech-Sym Corp.	1,812
188	MAXXIM Medical, Inc.	1,800
189	Oceaneering International, Inc.	1,800
190	Smith International, Inc.	1,800
191	Datapoint Corp.	1,777
192	Offshore Pipelines, Inc.	1,762
193	Cullen/Frost Bankers, Inc.	1,754
194	Hydril Co.	1,750
195	Vista Chemical Inc.	1,750
196	Valero Energy Corp.	1,735
197	Handy Andy Supermarkets	1,705
198	Academy Corp.	1,700
199	Cash America International, Inc.	1,700
200	Daniel Industries, Inc.	1,700

The Texas 500 Companies Ranked by Employees (continued)

Rank	Company	Employees
201	Palm Harbor Homes Inc.	1,700
202	Pillowtex Corp.	1,700
203	Reading & Bates Corp.	1,700
204	Recognition Equipment Inc.	1,695
205	ElectroCom Automation, Inc.	1,650
206	Paragon Group	1,646
207	Pioneer Concrete of America	1,625
208	CompuCom Systems, Inc.	1,600
209	Gulf States Inc.	1,600
210	Harborage Inc.	1,600
211	Oryx Energy Co.	1,600
212	Owen Healthcare Inc.	1,600
213	Rice Food Markets Inc.	1,600
214	Fulbright and Jaworski	1,590
215	Noble Drilling Corp.	1,580
216	Darling-Delaware Company Inc.	1,550
217	Ben E. Keith	1,500
218	Blue Bell Creameries	1,500
219	Gerland's Food Fair Inc.	1,500
220	Global Marine, Inc.	1,500
221	Goodman Manufacturing Corporation	1,500
222	Perot Systems Corp.	1,500
223	Plantation Foods Inc.	1,500
224	Solo Serv Corp.	1,500
225	Southern Foods Groups Incorporated	1,500
226	TeleCheck Services, Inc.	1,500
227	Vinson & Elkins L.L.P.	1,500
228	White Swan Inc.	1,500
229	Battle Mountain Gold Co.	1,482
230	Moorco International, Inc.	1,472
231	Greiner Engineering, Inc.	1,425
232	Stanley Stores Inc.	1,425
233	FFP Partners, L.P.	1,400
234	First USA, Inc.	1,400
235	Atmos Energy Corp.	1,383
236	Ennis Business Forms, Inc.	1,354
237	Freeman Companies, The	1,325
238	Baker and Botts, L.L.P.	1,307
239	CompuAdd, Inc.	1,300
240	McCoy Corporation	1,300
241	Rexene Corp.	1,300
242	MorningStar Group, Inc.	1,280
243	Old America Stores Inc.	1,275
244	American National Insurance Co.	1,266
245	Strafco Inc.	1,260
246	Dalfort Corp.	1,250
247	Enterra Corp.	1,250
248	GSC Enterprises, Inc.	1,250
249	Home Interiors & Gifts, Inc.	1,250
250	Igloo Holdings Inc.	1,250

Rank	Company	Employees
251	Sterling Chemicals, Inc.	1,225
252	Intelogic Trace, Inc.	1,216
253	AmeriServ Food Co.	1,200
254	Dr Pepper Bottling Company of Texas	1,200
255	Houston McLane Company, Inc.	1,200
256	Rip Griffin Truck/Travel Centers Inc.	1,200
257	Tetco Inc.	1,200
258	WellTech Inc.	1,200
259	Zapata Corp.	1,200
260	CONVEX Computer Corp.	1,164
261	Digicon, Inc.	1,140
262	Intertrans Corp.	1,108
263	El Paso Electric Co.	1,100
264	Foxworth-Galbraith Lumber Company	1,100
265	Gulf States Toyota	1,100
266	TNP Enterprises, Inc.	1,086
267	Continuum Company, Inc., The	1,080
268	Team, Inc.	1,076
269	CJC Holdings Inc.	1,061
270	Clear Channel Communications, Inc.	1,061
271	Glazer's Wholesale Drug Company Inc.	1,050
272	Sunbelt Corp.	1,050
273	Computer Language Research, Inc.	1,031
274	Galveston-Houston Co.	1,013
275	Akin, Gump, Strauss, Hauer & Feld	1,000
276	Coca-Cola Bottling Group-Southwest	1,000
277	Darr Equipment Company	1,000
278	MacGregor Medical Association	1,000
279	MMI Products Inc.	1,000
280	Pannell Kerr Forster	1,000
281	Union Texas Petroleum Holdings, Inc.	1,000
282	York Group Inc., The	1,000
283	Chaparral Steel Co.	985
284	Victoria Bankshares, Inc.	981
285	Anadarko Petroleum Corp.	970
286	U.S. Home Corp.	970
287	Voluntary Hospitals of America Inc.	950
288	Dr Pepper/Seven-Up Companies, Inc.	930
289	BMC Software, Inc.	921
290	EZCORP, Inc.	919
291	Affiliated Foods Incorporated	900
292	Enterprise Products Company	900
293	Fojtasek Companies Inc.	900
294	H and C Communications Inc.	900
295	Pay 'N Save Inc.	900
296	Southern Union Co.	900
297	Tesoro Petroleum Corp.	900
298	Energy Service Co., Inc.	890
299	Tecnol Inc.	861
300	CCC Group Inc.	850

The Texas 500 Companies Ranked by Employees (continued)

Rank	Company	Employees
301	Apache Corporation	844
302	Santa Fe Energy Resources, Inc.	839
303	Gundle Environmental Systems, Inc.	830
304	Serv-Tech, Inc.	817
305	Chemical Lime Co.	800
306	East Texas Distributing Inc.	800
307	Gillman Companies, Inc.	800
308	Plains Cotton Cooperative Association	800
309	Elcor Corp.	796
310	Powell Industries, Inc.	783
311	Business Records Corporation Holding Co.	782
312	TCA Cable TV, Inc.	772
313	Hart Graphics Inc.	750
314	Pearce Industries Inc.	750
315	RSR Corp.	750
316	SPI Holding, Inc.	747
317	Wilson Industries Incorporated	736
318	Vallen Corp.	720
319	Seagull Energy Corp.	704
320	Bass Enterprises Production Co.	700
321	Curtis C. Gunn Inc.	700
322	David's Supermarkets Inc.	700
323	King Ranch, Inc.	700
324	Sematech, Inc.	700
325	Hallwood Group Inc.	697
326	Dallas Semiconductor Corp.	696
327	Parker & Parsley Petroleum Co.	674
328	Davis Food City Inc.	650
329	Helena Laboratories	650
330	Periodical Management Group Inc.	650
331	Sanifill, Inc.	650
332	United Insurance Companies, Inc.	650
333	Triton Energy Corp.	628
334	Stevens Graphics Corp.	624
335	Kent Electronics Corp.	612
336	Placid Oil Co.	611
337	Destec Energy, Inc.	606
338	Associated Pipeline Contractors Inc.	600
339	L&H Packing Company Inc.	600
340	Mustang Tractor and Equipment Co.	600
341	Pioneer Chlor Alkali Investments Inc.	600
342	UETA Inc.	600
343	Martin Gas Corp.	590
344	K.S.A. Industries Inc.	587
345	American Produce and Vegetable Co.	580
346	Maverick Markets Inc.	580
347	TDIndustries Inc.	579
348	U.S. Long Distance Corp.	572
349	Hollywood Marine Inc.	550
350	Pride Companies, LP	550
351	Taylor Medical	550
352	Landmark Graphics Corp.	534
353	W. O. Bankston Enterprises Inc.	530
354	Andrews and Kurth	515
355	Wright Brand Foods Inc.	510
356	R Corp.	508
357	Border Steel Mills Inc.	500
358	Bracewell and Patterson	500
359	Sid Richardson Carbon and Gasoline Co.	500
360	Teppco Partners, L.P.	500
361	Thompson and Knight PC	500
362	TTI Inc.	500
363	Weekley Homes Inc.	500
364	M/A/R/C Group, The	497
365	Jones Blair Co.	480
366	Sterling Electronics Corp.	473
367	Ohmstede Inc.	463
368	Schultz Industries Inc.	450
369	Holly Corp.	438
370	Wainoco Oil Corp.	434
371	George Grubbs Enterprises Inc.	425
372	American Oil and Gas Corp.	416
373	Cabot Oil & Gas Corp.	410
374	Delta Industrial Offices Inc.	400
375	Gulf Met Holdings Corp.	400
376	Jackson and Walker LP	400
377	Rayco	400
378	SLM Power Group Inc.	400
379	Strasburger and Price	400
380	Texas United Corp	400
381	Wing Industries Inc.	400
382	Tri-Gas Inc.	390
383	Locke Purnell Rain Harrell	387
384	Production Operators Corp	383
385	Mesa Inc.	382
386	Dallas Auto Auction Inc.	380
387	Hunt Petroleum Corp.	380
388	Southwest Securities Group Inc.	376
389	Cactus Feeders Incorporated	375
390	Pedernales Electric Cooperative Inc.	370
391	Cliffs Drilling Co.	352
392	Lone Star Plywood and Door Corp.	350
393	Helen of Troy Corp.	348
394	Block Distributing Company Inc.	340
395	Coburn Supply Company Inc.	330
396	Newell Recycling Company Inc.	330
397	Intellicall, Inc.	325
398	Port City Automotive Partners	325
399	Quintana Petroleum Corp.	325
400	Tri-State Wholesale Associated Grocers Inc.	325

The Texas 500 Companies Ranked by Employees (continued)

Rank	Company	Employees
401	U.S. Intec, Inc.	320
402	Bay Houston Towing Co.	318
403	Adams Resources & Energy, Inc.	309
404	Software Spectrum, Inc.	303
405	Ancira Enterprises Inc.	300
406	Farb Companies Ltd.	300
407	H and H Meat Products Company Inc.	300
408	Houston Peterbilt Inc.	300
409	Lee Lewis Construction, Inc.	300
410	Lott Group Inc., The	300
411	Merichem Co.	300
412	Sewell Village Cadillac	300
413	Supertravel	300
414	Vaughan and Sons Inc.	300
415	Kinsel Motors Inc.	299
416	International Bancshares	295
417	Brazos Electric Power Cooperative Inc.	290
418	Snyder Oil Corporation	289
419	Frank Parra Chevrolet Inc.	284
420	Middleberg, Riddle and Gianna	280
421	Texas Olefins Co.	280
422	Wagner and Brown, Ltd.	280
423	Julius Schepps Co.	275
424	Tejas Gas Corp.	273
425	D. R. Horton, Inc.	268
426	Reliable Chevrolet Inc.	265
427	Texas Mill Supply Inc.	265
428	JaGee Corp	255
429	New Process Steel Corp.	250
430	Plains Cooperative Oil Mill Inc.	250
431	Standard Fruit and Vegetable Company Inc.	250
432	Tarrant Distributors Inc.	250
433	Texas Kenworth Co.	250
434	Warren Electric Co.	250
435	West Texas Equipment Co.	250
436	American Ecology Corp.	249
437	American Indemnity Financial Corp.	248
438	Howell Corp.	246
439	Richards Group Inc.	242
440	American Income Holding, Inc.	235
441	American Rice, Inc.	230
442	E.R. Fant, Inc.	230
443	Friona Industries LP	230
444	Sigel Liquor Stores Inc.	230
445	National Western Life Insurance Co.	225
446	Hartnett, C.D. Company, The	220
447	Brenham Wholesale Grocery Co.	217
448	Lawrence Marshall Chevrolet-Olds, Inc.	215
449	Wholesale Electric Supply Company of Houston, Inc.	215
450	Plains Resources Inc.	214

Rank	Company	Employees
451	HCB Contractors	210
452	Cantey & Hanger LLP	200
453	Gulf Coast Sportswear Inc.	200
454	Hunt Building Corporation	200
455	Leif Johnson Ford Inc.	200
456	Southwest Toyota, Inc.	200
457	Steakley Chevrolet Inc.	200
458	Park Place Motor Cars	192
459	Truman Arnold Companies	180
460	Endevco, Inc.	175
461	Behrens Inc.	170
462	Fossil Inc.	164
463	Anderson Grain Corp.	150
464	Berry-Barnett Grocery Co.	150
465	GAINSCO, INC.	149
466	Linbeck Construction Corp.	145
467	AZTX Cattle Co.	140
468	Cyrix Corporation	140
469	Handy Hardware Wholesale Inc.	140
470	Independent Grocers Inc.	140
471	Spectrum Information Technologies, Inc.	129
472	Southwestern Irrigated Cotton Growers Association	125
473	Life Insurance Company of the Southwest	115
474	Texas Pipe and Supply Company Inc.	115
475	Veragon Corp.	110
476	Denton County Electric Cooperative	102
477	Barrett & Crofoot, LLP	100
478	Cap Rock Electric Cooperative	100
479	Gambrinus Company, The	100
480	Pogo Producing Company	100
481	W.S. Bellows Construction Corp.	100
482	Walsh-Lumpkin Drug Co.	100
483	H.T. Ardinger and Son Co.	94
484	Tejas Power Corp.	90
485	Pace Entertainment Corporation	83
486	Friendly Chevrolet	76
487	Economy Cash and Carry Inc.	69
488	Barnett Brothers Brokerage Company Inc.	55
489	Tauber Oil Co.	52
490	Texas Stadium Corporation	50
491	Edisto Resources Corp.	45
492	Miller and Miller Auctioneers Inc.	41
493	Eastex Energy Inc.	34
494	Vinmar Inc.	30
495	Vista Oil Co.	20
496	Vanguard Energy Corp.	19
497	Sun Coast Resources Inc.	17
498	Weingarten Realty Investors	13
499	Xeron Inc.	8
500	Capstead Mortgage Corp.	6

The Largest Employers in Texas — Publicly Traded Companies

Rank	Company Name	Headquarters State	No. of Texas Employees
1	General Motors	Michigan	47,466
2	Halliburton	Texas	41,708
3	Texas Instruments	Texas	38,996
4	AMR	Texas	36,743
5	Wal-Mart Stores	Arkansas	35,971
6	Lockheed	California	27,826
7	Kroger	Ohio	24,692
8	Kmart	Michigan	23,278
9	Texas Utilities	Texas	21,525
10	Sears Roebuck	Illinois	20,354
11	J.C. Penney	Texas	18,510
12	Dow Chemical	Michigan	18,223
13	Southwestern Bell	Texas	16,675
14	Du Pont	Delaware	16,646
15	Exxon	Texas	16,210
16	Amoco	Illinois	15,951
17	Mobil	Virginia	15,079
18	GTE	Connecticut	14,950
19	Tandy	Texas	14,908
20	Litton Industries	California	14,784
21	NationsBank	North Carolina	14,645
22	Dayton Hudson	Minnesota	13,921
23	Chemical Banking	New York	13,839
24	Ford Motor	Michigan	12,226
25	PepsiCo	New York	12,000
26	May Department	Missouri	11,957
27	Phillips Petroleum	Oklahoma	11,912
28	Abbott Laboratories	Illinois	11,866
29	Loral Corporation	New York	11,840
30	Dillard Department Stores	Arkansas	11,437
31	Albertson's	Idaho	11,306
32	Banc One	Ohio	11,211
33	AT&T	New York	10,259
34	Houston Industries	Texas	9,954
35	Dresser Industries	Texas	9,900
36	E-Systems Inc.	Texas	9,398
37	Texaco	New York	9,277
38	Chevron	California	9,251
39	Motorola	Illinois	9,914
40	Rockwell International	California	9,115
41	Marriott	Washington, D.C.	9,011
42	General Electric	Connecticut	8,721
43	IBM	New York	8,664
44	Ryder System	Florida	8,339
45	Occidental Petroleum	California	7,885
46	Compaq Computer	Texas	7,845
47	Tenneco	Texas	7,729
48	Textron	Rhode Island	7,720
49	Humana	Kentucky	7,517
50	Enserch	Texas	7,257

The Largest Employers in Texas — Publicly Traded Companies

Rank	Company Name	Headquarters State	No. of Texas Employees
51	Atlantic Richfield	California	7,172
52	Healthtrust Inc. - Hospital Co.	Tennessee	7,060
53	Beverly Enterprises	Arkansas	6,970
54	Enron Corp	Texas	6,968
55	Baker Hughes	Texas	6,590
56	National Medical Enterprises	California	6,583
57	ConAgra	Nebraska	6,430
58	Harcourt General	Massachusetts	6,351
59	Temple-Inland	Texas	6,258
60	Schlumberger	New York	6,148
61	Coca-Cola Enterprises	Georgia	5,833
62	American Medical Holdings	Texas	5,720
63	Pilgrims Pride	Texas	5,708
64	Minnesota Mining & Mfg	Minnesota	5,706
65	Cooper Industries	Texas	5,494
66	Chrysler	Michigan	5,328
67	General Mills	Minnesota	5,312
68	American General	Texas	5,188
69	Philip Morris	New York	5,115
70	American Building Maint.	California	4,960
71	Goodyear Tire & Rubber	Ohio	4,934
72	Mitchell Energy & Develop.	Texas	4,778
73	Tyler	Texas	4,764
74	Southwest Airlines	Texas	4,736
75	Roadway Services	Ohio	4,592
76	USX	Pennsylvania	4,357
77	Pinkerton's	California	4,304
78	Winn-Dixie Stores	Florida	4,258
79	A.H. Belo	Texas	4,198
80	Central & South West	Texas	4,166
81	Trinity Industries	Texas	4,146
82	Diamond Shamrock	Texas	4,065
83	Champion International	Connecticut	4,021
84	American National Insurance	Texas	4,006
85	Johnson & Johnson	New Jersey	3,985
86	Union Pacific	Pennsylvania	3,982
87	Pool Energy Services	Texas	3,895
88	Anheuser-Busch	Missouri	3,888
89	Union Carbide	Connecticut	3,867
90	Foodmaker	California	3,762
91	Walgreen	Illinois	3,752
92	La Quinta Motor Inns	Texas	3,690
93	Boeing	Washington	3,670
94	Tyson	Arkansas	3,655
95	Eastman Kodak	New York	3,607
96	W. R. Grace	Florida	3,567
97	Primerica	New York	3,536
98	Burlington Northern	Texas	3,472
99	MCI	Washington, D.C.	3,452
100	Fluor	California	3,338

Source: Texas Comptroller of Public Accounts; Dun & Bradstreet Data Services. Published in *The Wall Street Journal*, October 6, 1993.

Largest Companies in Austin, Dallas–Ft. Worth, Houston, and San Antonio

Austin	Sales ($ mil.)
Dell Computer Corporation	2,014
CompuAdd, Inc.	525
National Western Life Insurance Co.	401
Tracor Inc.	262
Sematech, Inc.	213
Southern Union Co.	192
Continuum Company, Inc., The	124
Whole Foods Market, Inc.	120
CJC Holdings Inc.	110
EZCORP, Inc.	96

Dallas–Ft. Worth	Sales ($ mil.)
Exxon Corporation	103,160
J. C. Penney Company, Inc.	19,085
AMR Corporation	14,396
Electronic Data Systems Corporation	8,155
Texas Instruments Incorporated	7,440
Kimberly-Clark Corporation	7,091
Halliburton Company	6,525
Southland Corporation, The	6,439
Texas Utilities Company	4,908
Tandy Corporation	4,743
Burlington Northern Inc.	4,630
Dresser Industries, Inc.	3,797
National Intergroup, Inc.	3,411
FINA, Inc.	3,398
Central and South West Corp.	3,289
Philp Co.	2,910
ENSERCH Corp.	2,826
Centex Corp.	2,503
Sammons Enterprises	2,400
American Medical Holdings, Inc.	2,238
E-Systems, Inc.	2,099
Southwest Airlines Co.	1,685
Trinity Industries, Inc.	1,540
Oryx Energy Co.	1,392
CompUSA, Inc.	1,342
Blue Cross and Blue Shield of Texas Inc.	1,251
Lincoln Property Co.	1,173
Commercial Metals Co.	1,166
Contran Corp.	1,128
Lennox International Inc.	1,050
Wingate Partners LP	1,000
Zale Holding Corporation	981
Epic Holdings, Inc.	941
ClubCorp International	870
Maxus Energy Corp.	851
AmeriServ Food Co.	806
SnyderGeneral Corp.	800
White Swan Inc.	780
Hunt Oil Company Inc.	720
CompuCom Systems, Inc.	713
Greyhound Lines, Inc.	682
NCH Corp.	680
Dr Pepper/Seven-Up Companies, Inc.	659
Brinker International, Inc.	653
Medical Care America Inc.	641
Pier 1 Imports, Inc.	629
Texas Industries, Inc.	614
Mary Kay Cosmetics Inc.	613
Color Tile Inc.	586
Minyard Food Stores Inc.	550

Houston	Sales ($ mil.)
Shell Oil Company	21,702
Tenneco Inc.	13,139
Marathon Group	12,782
Coastal Corporation, The	10,063
SYSCO Corporation	10,022
Enron Corp.	6,325
Cooper Industries, Inc.	6,119
Continental Airlines Holdings, Inc.	5,575
Lyondell Petrochemical Company	4,805
American General Corporation	4,602
Houston Industries Incorporated	4,596
Compaq Computer Corporation	4,100
Browning-Ferris Industries, Inc.	3,288
Randall's Food Markets, Inc.	3,200
Transco Energy Co.	2,724

Largest Companies in Austin, Dallas–Ft. Worth, Houston, and San Antonio

Houston (continued)

Baker Hughes Incorporated	2,539
Panhandle Eastern Corp.	2,434
Pennzoil Company	2,357
MAXXAM Inc.	2,203
American National Insurance Co.	1,318
Grocers Supply Co.	1,300
National Convenience Stores	959
NL Industries, Inc.	914
Mitchell Energy & Development Corp.	903
Stewart & Stevenson Services, Inc.	813
Service Corporation International	772
Tauber Oil Co.	747
Union Texas Petroleum Holdings, Inc.	714
Vista Chemical Inc.	700
U.S. Home Corp.	679
Imperial Holly Corp.	648
Baroid Corp.	628
Fiesta Mart Inc.	600
Gulf States Toyota	600
AppleTree Markets Inc.	597
Quanex Corp.	572
Adams Resources & Energy, Inc.	550
CRSS, Inc.	546
Keystone International, Inc.	528
Tejas Gas Corp.	524
Destec Energy, Inc.	508
Southdown, Inc.	508
Specialty Retailers Inc.	505
Enterprise Products Company	491
Howell Corp.	461
Apache Corporation	454
MediaNews Group	450
Riviana Foods Inc.	450
East Texas Distributing Inc.	445
E-Z Serve Corp.	434

San Antonio

	Sales ($ mil.)
Southwestern Bell Corporation	10,015
USAA	5,434
HEB Grocery	3,800
Associated Milk Producers, Inc.	2,835
Diamond Shamrock, Inc.	2,612
Valero Energy Corp.	1,235
Tesoro Petroleum Corp.	954
HB Zachry Co.	750
Harte-Hanks Communications Holdings Incorporated	427
Luby's Cafeterias, Inc.	346
Kinetic Concepts, Inc.	278
La Quinta Motor Inns, Inc.	256
Cullen/Frost Bankers, Inc.	252
Southwest Research Institute Inc.	234
Curtis C. Gunn Inc.	233
Winn's Stores Incorporated	221
Datapoint Corp.	208
UETA Inc.	200
Newell Recycling Company Inc.	190
50-Off Stores, Inc.	181
Ancira Enterprises Inc.	169
L&H Packing Company Inc.	160
Periodical Management Group Inc.	160
Solo Serv Corp.	154
Handy Andy Supermarkets	148

Inc. 500 Fastest-Growing Private Companies in Texas

Inc. Rank	Company	City	Sales Growth 1988–1992 (% increase)	1992 Sales ($ mil.)
1	Drypers	Houston	49,101	140.2
26	Saber Software	Dallas	4,427	7.2
56	Bergaila & Associates	Houston	3,029	4.8
68	Forum Financial Group	Richardson	2,604	7.5
77	Operator Service	Lubbock	2,449	18.4
83	Waste Reduction Systems	Houston	2,327	10.4
86	Looney & Co.	Houston	2,293	6.5
133	D&K Enterprises	Carrollton	1,666	3.3
173	MJD Investments	Irving	1,405	41.6
207	Daydots Label	Fort Worth	1,255	2.3
229	Di-Mark Group	Houston	1,148	1.6
243	HCFS	Dallas	1,070	1.2
249	Collins/Reisenbichler Architects	Dallas	1,048	1.3
255	Digital Print	Fort Worth	1,020	2.6
269	AnTel	Plano	972	2.1
270	Mustang Engineering	Houston	972	25.0
278	JRL Systems	Austin	956	4.2
309	Jungle Jim's Playlands	San Antonio	874	6.6
313	American Fastsigns	Dallas	854	3.9
321	Watsonrise Business Systems	Arlington	837	1.4
324	Mytech	Austin	825	1.4
325	Govind & Associates	Corpus Christi	824	9.6
331	Item Products	Houston	806	6.4
350	Pest Control Technologies	Dallas	767	1.3
365	DCS Software & Consulting	Richardson	736	6.2
391	Print Mailers	Houston	686	1.7
424	Hernandez Engineering	Houston	648	19.7
429	Triton Marine Construction	Houston	643	25.6
452	Sai Software Consultants	Kingwood	608	5.2
463	Sterling Information Group	Austin	594	1.9
485	Merritt, Hawkins & Associates	Irving	572	7.6
500	ACS Dataline	Austin	551	12.4

Source: *Inc.*; October 1993

THE 100 RICHEST TEXANS

The 100 Richest Texans

Rank	Name	City	Source of Wealth	Age	Net Worth ($ mil.)
1	Henry Ross Perot	Dallas	Data processing systs.	63	3,350
2–6	Perry Richardson Bass	Fort Worth	Investments	78	
	Sid Richardson Bass	Fort Worth	Investments	51	
	Edward Perry Bass	Fort Worth	Investments	47	
	Robert Muse Bass	Fort Worth	Investments	45	7,000
	Lee Marshall Bass	Fort Worth	Investments	37	(1,400 avg.)
7	Robert Henry Dedman	Dallas	Private clubs	67	1,000
8	Robert Lee Moody	Galveston	Insurance	58	790
9	Jerry J. Moore	Houston	Shopping centers	65	775
10	George Phydias Mitchell	Houston	Oil & gas	74	750
11	Charles Clarence Butt	San Antonio	H.E.B. Grocery	55	650
12	Harold Clark Simmons	Dallas	Financier	62	625
13–15	Margaret Hunt Hill	Dallas	Inheritance (oil & gas)	77	
	Haroldson Lafayette "Hassie" Hunt III	Dallas	Inheritance (oil & gas)	75	1,700
	Caroline Rose Hunt	Dallas	Inheritance (oil & gas)	70	(567 avg.)
16	Elizabeth Hall Reid	Denton	Hallmark Cards	71	470
17	Joseph Dahr Jamail	Houston	Law	67	450
18	Richard Edward Rainwater	Fort Worth	Financier	49	450
19	Albert Billy Alkek	Houston	Oil & gas	83	430
20	Anne Windfohr Marion	Fort Worth	Inheritance (oil & gas)	54	430
21	Robert Drayton McLane, Jr.	Temple	Grocery distribution, Wal-Mart	57	410
22–24	Ruth Ray Hunt	Dallas	Inheritance (oil & gas)	76	
	Ray Lee Hunt	Dallas	Inheritance (oil & gas)	50	
	Ruth June Hunt	Dallas	Inheritance (oil & gas)	48	
	Helen Hendrix	out of state			2,000
	Swanee Hunt	out of state			(400 avg.)
25	Fayez Shalaby Sarofim	Houston	Money managment	64	390
26	Robert Brittingham, Sr.	Dallas	Ceramic tile	79	350
27	Fred Trammell Crow	Dallas	Real estate	79	350
28	Edwin Lochridge Cox, Sr.	Dallas	Oil & gas	71	300

The 100 Richest Texans (continued)

Rank	Name	City	Source of Wealth	Age	Net Worth ($ mil.)
29	John Lee Cox	Midland	Oil & gas	68	300
30	Roy Michael Huffington	Houston	Oil & gas	75	300
31–32	Margaret Cullen Marshall	Barksdale	Inheritance (oil & gas)	72*	600
	Wilhelmina Cullen Robertson	Houston	Inheritance (oil & gas)	70	(300 avg.)
33	William Alvin "Tex" Moncrief, Jr.	Fort Worth	Oil & gas	73	300
34	Robert Randall Onstead	Houston	Randall's Food Markets	62	300
35–36	Dennis Martin O'Connor	Refugio	Inheritance (oil & gas)	86	580
	Tom O'Connor, Jr.	Victoria	Inheritance (oil & gas)	78	(290 avg.)
37	Clarence Scharbauer, Jr.	Midland	Inheritance (oil & gas)	68	280
38	James Howard Marshall II	Houston	Oil & gas	88	525
	E. Pierce Marshall	out of state			(262 avg.)
39–40	Jack Eugene Brown	Midland	Oil & gas	68	500
	Cyril Wagner	Midland	Oil & gas	59	(250 avg.)
41	Thomas Milton Benson	San Antonio	New Orleans Saints, investments	66	250
42	Louisa Stude Sarofim	Houston	Divorce	50s	250
43–44	Reese McIntosh Rowling	Corpus Christi	Oil & gas	65	500
	Robert Brian Rowling	Corpus Christi	Oil & gas	39	(250 avg.)
45	John Jay Moores	Sugar Land	BMC Software	49	240
46	Michael Saul Dell	Austin	Dell Computer Corp.	28	240
47	Kenneth Stanley "Bud" Adams, Jr.	Houston	Houston Oilers	70	240
48	Gerald Douglas Hines	Houston	Real estate	68	240
49	George Kozmetsky	Austin	Electronics	75	230
50	Donald Joseph Carter	Coppell	Inheritance (Home Interiors & Gifts), Dallas Mavericks	60	230
51	Henry Bartell Zachry, Jr.	San Antonio	Inheritance (construction)	60	225
52	Harold Viterbo Goodman	Houston	Air conditioning	67	225

*Recently deceased

The 100 Richest Texans (continued)

Rank	Name	City	Source of Wealth	Age	Net Worth ($ mil.)
53	Jerral Wayne Jones	Dallas	Dallas Cowboys, oil & gas	50	220
54	Arthur Temple, Jr.	Diboll	Inheritance (timber)	73	220
55	Grace Williams Dobson	Corpus Christi	Whataburger	67	210
56	William Seldon Davis	Fort Worth	Inheritance (oil & gas)	57	200
57	Harvey Roberts "Bum" Bright	Dallas	Oil & gas, real estate	72	200
58	Dominique de Menil	Houston	Inheritance (oil-field service)	85	200
59	Richard Lynn Scott	Fort Worth	Columbia Hospital Corporation	40	185
60–61	Jamie Abercrombie Robinson	Houston	Inheritance (Cameron Iron Works)	36	360 (180 avg.)
	George Anderson Robinson	Houston	Inheritance (Cameron Iron Works)	34	
62	Donald Adrian Adam	Bryan	Cable TV	58	180
63	Richard Wesley Snyder	Dallas	Air conditioning	55	180
64	Mayer Billy "Duke" Rudman	Dallas	Oil & gas	83	175
65	Gay Alspaugh Roane	Houston	Investments	49	175
66	Billy Joe "Red" McCombs	San Antonio	Investments, car dealerships	65	175
67	Lamar Hunt	Dallas	Inheritance (oil & gas), Kansas City Chiefs	65	170
68–69	Mary Kay Ash	Dallas	Mary Kay Cosmetics	75	320 (160 avg.)
	Richard Raymond Rogers	Dallas	Mary Kay Cosmetics	50	
70	James Richard Leiniger	San Antonio	Kinetic Concepts	49	160
71	Pauline Gill Sullivan	Dallas	Divorce	70s	160
72	Gordon Arbuthnot Cain	Houston	Chemicals	81	150
73	Thomas O. Hicks	Dallas	Financier	47	150
74	Lonnie Alfred "Bo" Pilgrim	Pittsburg	Poultry	65	150
75	Nelda Childers Stark	Orange	Inheritance (oil & timber)	84	150

THE TEXAS 500

The 100 Richest Texans (continued)

Rank	Name	City	Source of Wealth	Age	Net Worth ($ mil.)
76	Dolph Briscoe, Jr.	Uvalde	Ranching	70	150
77	Randall Dee Hubbard	Fort Worth	Glass	58	140
78	Charles Edwin Hurwitz	Houston	Financier	53	140
79	Christopher Bancroft	Denton	Inheritance (Dow Jones and Co.)	42	135
80–81	Oveta Culp Hobby William Pettus Hobby, Jr. Jessica Hobby Catto	Houston Houston out of state	Broadcasting Broadcasting	88 61	400 (133 avg.)
82	William Stamps Farish III	Houston	Inheritance (oil & gas)	54	130
83	Oscar Sherman Wyatt, Jr.	Houston	Coastal Corporation	69	130
84	Belton Kleberg "B" Johnson	San Antonio	Inheritance (King Ranch)	63	130
85	Floyd Alvin Cailloux	Kerrville	Industrial manufacturing	80	130
86	Kit Goldsbury	San Antonio	Pace Foods	50	130
87	Nancy Blackburn Hamon	Dallas	Inheritance (oil & gas)	74	130
88	James Aubrey Cardwell	El Paso	Truck stops	61	130
89	Sybil Buckingham Harrington	Amarillo	Inheritance (oil & gas)	70s	130
90	Sam Wyly	Dallas	Investments	58	130
91–93	Lester Arnold Levy Milton Philip Levy Irvin Louis Levy	Dallas Dallas Dallas	Industrial solvents Industrial solvents Industrial solvents	70 68 64	380 (127 avg.)
94–95	Electra Waggoner Biggs Albert Buckman "Bucky" Wharton III	Vernon Vernon	Inheritance (ranching, oil & gas) Inheritance (ranching, oil & gas)	80 45	240 (120 avg.)
96	Mary Ralph Lowe	Houston	Inheritance (oil & gas)	46	120
97–98	Dan J. Harrison III Bruce Finch Harrison	Houston Houston	Inheritance (oil & gas) Inheritance (oil & gas)	40s 40s	240 (120 avg.)
99	Robert McDonald Rogers	Tyler	Cable TV	66	110
100	Arturo Gregorio Torres	San Antonio	Pizza	56	110

Source: Reprinted with permission. Copyright *TexasMonthly*, "The Texas 100," September 1993

Selected Profiles from *TexasMonthly*'s 100 Richest Texans List

THE BASS FAMILY

Perry Richardson Bass; Sid Richardson Bass; Edward Perry Bass; Robert Muse Bass; Lee Marshall Bass

$7 billion, UP $400 million from 1992. The Basses' money machine rolls on.

When wildcatter Sid Richardson died in 1959, he left $2 million to each of the sons of his nephew and only partner, Perry. A year later Perry pooled their resources to form Bass Brothers Enterprises. By 1969, the inheritance had grown to $50 million, which Perry then turned over to his four sons. With the help of savvy financial advisors like Richard Rainwater, the family fortune continued to swell, diversifying from oil and gas to real estate, banking, and stock in public companies such as Walt Disney. In Fort Worth the Basses maintain a high profile, thanks to both business and personal interests. Last year Alamo Partners, led by Sid, bought the vacant T. Cullen Davis mansion and adjacent undeveloped acreage in southwest Fort Worth. Construction of Sid and wife Mercedes' new home—with its $3 million wall, $12 million in landscaping, and helipad—snarled traffic for months in their tony neighborhood. Ed's Biosphere 2 near Tucson has been plagued with problems, but his Sundance West condominium project and Caravan of Dreams jazz club have reinvigorated downtown Fort Worth. Robert's American Savings Bank in California won praise for its $1 million donation to riot-torn Los Angeles; his investment arm Keystone, Inc., poured another $1 million into L.A.'s largest black-owned bank. Recently Keystone agreed to pay a Dutch conglomerate some $1 billion in a leveraged buyout for a collection of food companies. Lee works closely with Sid and manages the family's oil interests. But everything the Basses touch does not turn to gold. After Bass Enterprises Production pumped $17 million into Harken Energy's two high-risk wildcat wells in Bahrain (both wells were dry), the Basses forged a new agreement to end the partnership.

FRED TRAMMELL CROW

$350 million, DOWN $50 million from 1992. A floundering real estate market takes its toll.

For decades Crow seemed to have a crystal ball that showed him exactly the kind of buildings Dallas needed. Then he built them—warehouses, merchandising marts, office towers, and luxury hotels. Crow has struggled through the bust, losing properties to lenders, selling others, and finally, evolving from the world's largest developer into the world's largest property manager.

MICHAEL SAUL DELL

$240 million, UP $20 million from 1992. Despite difficulties, Dell Computer stock bounces back.

The volatile personal computer market has forced the industry's wunderkind to do some growing up. Dell's stock price, which peaked in January at $49 a share, has been rocked lately because of the company's potentially risky strategy of speculating in foreign currency options and its depressed earnings brought on by the scrapping of Dell's notebook computer projects, which led to Dell Computer's recent announcement of its first-ever quarterly loss. Dell is also facing at least ten lawsuits alleging the company protected its stock price by failing to give investors accurate information. A year shy of a decade in business, the man who began his company in a University of Texas dorm room still has his fans. "I never underestimate Michael Dell," says an analyst.

THE HUNT FAMILY I

Margaret Hunt Hill; Haroldson Lafayette "Hassie" Hunt III; Caroline Rose Hunt

$1.7 billion.

Whether he was producing oil and gas or children, legendary oil magnate H. L. Hunt did not subscribe to the theory that less is more. Daughters Margaret and Caroline and son Hassie are half of Hunt's first family. Sons Bunker and Herbert's financial empire collapsed after a disastrous attempt to corner the silver market; yet another son, Texas 100 member Lamar, is profiled separately. Caroline, Margaret, and Hassie dodged silver bullet by severing ties to the family enterprises in 1983. Former Cub Scout leader Caroline says empty nest syndrome pushed her into hotel business in 1979; today her Rosewood Hotels manages posh properties and owns Dallas' Mansion on Turtle Creek and Crescent Court. Broke ground this year for thirteen-story condominium tower adjacent to the Mansion. Margaret learned oil business from father in the thirties; today oversees her and Hassie's interests. Hassie inherited H. L.'s nose for finding oil; made several discoveries before suffering mental problems in the forties, which left him delusional. Spends time walking and following sports statistics.

THE HUNT FAMILY II

Ruth Ray Hunt; Ray Lee Hunt; Ruth June Hunt

$2 billion, UP $100 million from 1992. Acquisition of new oil and gas reserves increases estimate.

Renowned wildcatter H. L. Hunt fathered his second family with Ruth Ray while married to his first wife. Two years after his wife's death, Hunt married Ruth and adopted their four children. (Out-of-state siblings Swanee Hunt and Helen Hendrix share in this fortune.) The bulk of Hunt Oil and Hunt Realty was left to this clan on Hunt's death in 1974, and Ray took over the family businesses. H. L. never drilled overseas, but Ray went international, making huge finds in the North Sea in 1976 and in Yemen in 1984. Now concentrating again on domestic drilling; also real estate development. As chairman of Southern Methodist University's board of trustees, led cleanup of athletic department after Bill Clements had sanctioned the paying of players. Ruth backs Dallas First Baptist pastor W. A. Criswell's college; June lives quietly in Dallas.

LAMAR HUNT

$170 million, UP $15 million from 1992. Sports franchise values are up.

The youngest of legendary wildcatter H. L. Hunt's first brood, Lamar emerged relatively unscathed from brothers Bunker and Herbert's silver debacle. Rather than oil, Lamar's big financial plays have come through his ownership of the Chiefs, 11 percent of the Chicago Bulls, and two Kansas City, Missouri, amusement parks. Founded Chiefs franchise as the Dallas Texans in 1960; spends night before home games in one of four bedrooms above owner's box.

JOSEPH DAHR JAMAIL

$450 million, UP $20 million from 1992. Settlements and verdicts continue to add up.

"I'm interested in representing injured people and children." Since winning the landmark Texaco-Pennzoil case (he pocketed at least $300 million), plaintiff's lawyer Jamail has the luxury of choosing among the three hundred cases a year that he is offered, and he often opts for the courtroom bashing of corporate America. Recently won a settlement of more than $100 million for 28 clients injured in Pasadena's Phillips Petroleum refinery explosion. Lead counsel for Northwest Airlines, which, along with Continental Airlines, sued American Airlines for predatory pricing.

BELTON KLEBERG "B" JOHNSON

$130 million, DOWN $20 million from 1992. Distribution of proceeds to heirs following sale of Chaparrosa Ranch decreases net worth.

Although Johnson is the great-grandson of King Ranch founder Richard King, he traded in his piece of the family legacy for $70 million in 1976 after being passed over for the position of ranch boss. Johnson invested his inheritance in real estate, hotels (including San Antonio's Hyatt Regency), and the 65,000-acre Chaparrosa Ranch, which he nurtured for some three decades before selling it this spring. But Johnson already has plans. "A good rancher doesn't stay without a ranch for long."

GEORGE PHYDIAS MITCHELL

$750 million, UP $230 million from 1992. The value of Mitchell Energy and Development stock soars, courtesy of higher natural gas prices.

In 1952 George, with brother Johnny, followed a tip from a Chicago bookie to check out eleven dry wildcat wells northwest of Fort Worth. George, an A&M-educated petroleum engineer, saw promising geology but bad engineering. The brothers nabbed the drilling leases in the area and hit the mammoth Boonsville gas field. George has spent some $65 million restoring Galveston's historic Strand district. Owns a handful of Island hotels and Pirate's Beach subdivision. Built North Houston's 25,000-acre Woodlands; recently began construction on Woodlands Mall and accompanying 1.5-mile canal and 20-acre lake.

JOHN JAY MOORES

$240 million, DOWN $30 million from 1992. BMC stock sales shrink Moores's fortune.

At 49, Moores is an anomaly among the Texas 100, mostly a group of driven workaholic people who loathe the mere suggestion of slowing down or giving up control of businesses painstakingly nurtured over decades. In 1992 he retired from BMC Software, which he founded in 1980 with $1,000 and built into a company that now has sales of $238 million.

But Moores is no stranger to hard work. His introduction came from his father, a man who supported his family of four by working as a newspaper photographer, a life insurance salesman, and a jazz musician. Moores kept up the family tradition, marrying his high school sweetheart while still in college, then juggling a full-time computer-programming job, children, and law school classes. Yet after his first year of law school, Moores knew he would never practice. "You have to be extremely cautious to be a lawyer. I'm more of a shoot-from-the-hip type person," he says.

While working at Shell Oil, Moores was struck by an idea that would enable the company's IBM mainframes to run more efficiently. In his spare hours, he wrote two software programs that sped response time from the hulking mainframes to the terminals by three to five seconds—a minuscule difference for one computation, but a huge cumulative time-saver over the course of a workday.

Moores used his programs to launch BMC. "It was startling," marvels Moores of the software's reception. When Moores took BMC public just eight years after its founding, it was the first time the man who started his own business for the sole purpose of making his mortgage payment realized the value of his BMC holdings. "It hit like a ton of bricks," says Moores. He left BMC, he says, because "there wasn't anything I could add to the equation. I'm not well suited to a public company."

Now, five years later, Moores has found something else he is suited for: He is a Santa Claus, handing out sackfuls of money to various business and charitable endeavors. Though John and his wife, Becky, live a kind of modern nomadic life, dividing their time between homes in three states, there is one constant at each location: an office where Moores spends at least four hours a day overseeing his interests and contributions.

Over the years, the Mooreses had quietly donated at least $25 million to various causes, but in 1991 their generosity burst on the public scene. An ecstatic University of Houston received $51.4 million—earmarked for the music department, creative writing programs, and athletics—at the time, the largest private gift ever bestowed on a public university.

Like many philanthropists, the Mooreses are inundated with requests for contributions, which they choose to ignore. "We've got our own causes figured out," Moores says, adding, "My dad worked so hard. That's why I have a problem with holding money to the grave."

HENRY ROSS PEROT

$3.35 billion, UP $100 million from 1992. The cash-based fortune continues to grow.

"I don't spend much time thinking about it," Perot says of his megafortune. That's probably true, considering the time he has devoted in the past year to being a thorn in the side of the nation's political parties. Perot's presidential campaign may have fallen short, but through books, infomercials, appearances on the *Tonight* show with Jay Leno, and the United We Stand America organization, he's still applying pressure to politics-as-usual. Perot's opposition to the North American Free Trade Agreement continues to be strident despite the potential boon to the family-owned Alliance Airport. Perot's billions stem from Electronic Data Systems, the company he founded in 1962, took public in 1968, then sold to General Motors in 1984 for cash and stock. Today Perot's investments include high-tech start-ups and devalued California real estate. Revenues at five-year-old EDS competitor Perot Systems are up, even with glitches like last year's computer crash at NationsBank, which lost account balances for four days.

Source: Reprinted with permission. Copyright *TexasMonthly*, "The Texas 100," September 1993

STATE OF TEXAS PROFILE

STATE OF TEXAS

OVERVIEW

Texas is the 2nd largest US state in land area (after Alaska) and in population and gross state product (after California and New York), with over 17 million people and an economy worth over $400 billion. Its geographic characteristics range from wide plains to "hill country," from desert to lush greenery. In 1992 Houston and Austin made *Money*'s list of the top 10 places to live in the US.

Although Texas may still be synonymous with oil to many, its economy has diversified widely since the 1980s. Hard lessons learned in that decade have resulted in a decreased dependency on petroleum industries, from 27% of GSP in 1981 to about 15% presently. Texas now has a wide range of important industries. Its main economic regions are East Texas, rich in natural resources, including oil, gas, coal, and timber; Central Texas, the center of government and education, as well as the headquarters of many high-tech businesses; the Dallas/Fort Worth metroplex, a concentration of manufacturing, air transportation, distribution, and finance concerns; Houston, housing oil and shipping firms; and the border area, where, naturally, trade and transportation figure prominently.

Texas, about 80% urbanized, boasts 3 of the nation's 10 most populated cities — Houston, Dallas, and San Antonio. Spanish speakers, mostly Mexican-American, make up about 1/4 of the population.

WHEN

Prehistoric peoples are known to have hunted in Texas at least 10,000 years ago. Spaniards were the first Europeans to reach the area, searching for legendary cities said to be rich in gold, in the 1500s. The area was called *Tejas*, meaning "friendly." The Spanish began missionary activities that spread across Texas until the early 1700s. Crops were grown and livestock kept in the missions.

Mexican independence from Spain (1821) heralded the first wave of English-speaking settlers. Mexico offered generous land packages to anyone who would settle in its northern territory. In 1835 Anglo settlers revolted, in part to keep their slaves (Mexican law prohibited slavery). The next year the republic gained independence after numerous battles, including the infamous siege at the Alamo.

Texas was annexed to the US in 1845 despite misgivings concerning its massive debt and pro-slavery views. The stability of statehood and a liberal land policy lured settlers, many from Europe. By 1860 Texas had over 600,000 citizens, 3/4 of whom were foreign-born. Most residents were farmers, growing only enough to sustain themselves. However, the advent of a railroad system, begun in 1856, prompted many to begin selling crops (almost wholly, cotton) for profit, as the railroads provided cheap transportation.

Texas, with over 180,000 slaves in 1860, sided with the Confederacy during the Civil War, providing the only passage out of the US for Confederate goods (all eastern ports had been blockaded) — through Mexico. When the war ended, sharecropping helped farmers cope with the abolition of slavery.

In 1866 the first of the legendary cattle drives up the Chisholm Trail, which led to Kansas and beyond, began. The cotton industry grew quickly as well, and textile mills began dotting the landscape. In 1873 thousands of farmers banded to form the Grange, an organization that fought the monopolistic practices of railroads and banks.

In 1901 oil was discovered at Spindletop, near Beaumont. News of the gusher spread, and in just 2 years oil production in Texas increased tenfold, to about 17 million barrels. In the 1920s manufacturing replaced agriculture as the state's chief industry, and in the 1950s oil production topped one billion barrels per year. Like the rest of the nation, Texas enjoyed an economic boom after WWII.

The 1973 OPEC oil embargo caused oil prices to skyrocket. Although the embargo ended in 1974, prices continued to rise, and Texas's economy, closely tied to oil, was buoyed as well. A collapse in oil prices, ill-considered and sometimes fraudulent lending policies by banks, and tremendous overbuilding led to recession in the 1980s, when most Texas banks and S&Ls folded. Unemployment rose sharply in the 1980s.

In the 1990s the Texas economy turned around (well ahead of the rest of the nation), aided by diversification, especially into high-tech industries. The state's leading companies now include Dell Computer, Texas Instruments, and Compaq Computer.

Official name: State of Texas
Admitted as state: December 29, 1845
State capital: Austin
Motto: "Friendship"

WHO

Governor: Ann W. Richards (D)
Lieutenant Governor: Bob Bullock (D)
Attorney General: Dan Morales (D)
Comptroller: John Sharp (D)
Treasurer: Martha Whitehead
Auditor: Lawrence F. Alwin
Supreme Court Chief Justice: Tom Phillips (R)
Senators: Phil Gramm (R), Kay Bailey Hutchison (R)
Commissioner of Agriculture: Rick Perry (R)
Commissioner of Education: Lionel R. Meno
Commissioner of the General Land Office: Garry Mauro (D)

WHERE

HQ: Office of the Governor, Capitol Building, Austin, TX 78701
Phone: 512-463-2300
Fax: 512-463-1849
Department of Commerce: 816 Congress Ave., Austin, TX 78701
Phone: 512-472-5059
University of Texas at Austin (administrative offices): Main Building, Austin, TX 78705
Phone: 512-471-3434

Texas is the US's 2nd largest state (after Alaska), approximately the same size as Kenya. The state has 254 counties. Total land area is 266,807 square miles.

Largest Cities	1990 Population
Houston	2,735,766
Dallas	1,957,378
San Antonio	1,071,954
Fort Worth–Arlington	973,138
Austin	536,688
El Paso	479,899
Beaumont–Port Arthur	375,497
Corpus Christi	326,228
McAllen-Edinburg-Mission	283,229
Killeen-Temple	214,656
Lubbock	211,651

WHAT

1989 GSP Distribution

	$ bil.	% of total
Manufacturing	57	17
Services	57	17
Finance, insurance & real estate	51	15
Government	39	11
Transportation & public utilities	38	11
Retail trade	30	9
Wholesale trade	23	7
Construction	14	4
Farms, forestry & fisheries	7	2
Other	24	7
Total	**340**	**100**

Exports
Agricultural exports
 Cotton
 Feed grains
 Hides and skins
 Meat and meat products
Minerals
 Cement
 Coal
Petroleum products

HOW MUCH

	Annual Growth	1983	1984	1985	1986	1987	1988	1989	1990	1991	1992
Population (mil.)	1.3%	15,753	16,009	16,275	16,563	16,624	16,669	16,807	16,987	17,349	17,656
Gross state product ($ bil.)	4.3%	—	289	308	295	303	322	340	366	387	406
GSP per capita (constant $)	(0.1%)	—	—	17,819	17,026	16,963	17,338	17,443	19,115	19,010	19,098
GSP ($ bil., constant $)	2.2%	—	—	290	282	282	289	293	325	330	337
Personal income per capita	5.1%	11,686	12,575	13,494	13,489	13,843	14,590	15,702	16,668	17,325	18,333
Employment growth (annual percentage change)	—	(1.1)	4.8	2.6	(1.5)	(0.7)	2.5	2.4	2.8	0.9	1.2

GSP per capita 1985–92 ($)

THE TEXAS 500

Texas Statistics

Category	Statistic	Rank Among All States
Population and Housing		
Total persons:		
1992 (July 1)	17,656,000	3
Percent increase, 1990–92	3.9%	13
65 years old and over, 1992	10.2%	46
Foreign-born, 1990	9.0%	8
Persons 5 years old and over speaking		
a language other than English, 1992	25.4%	3
Residing in a metro area, 1990	83.4%	13
One-parent families, percent of all families		
with children, 1990	22.6%	28
Housing units:		
Built between 1980 and 1990	29.7%	6
With no telephone, 1990	8.6%	9
Vital Statistics and Health		
Infant deaths per 1,000 live births, 1990	8.1	37
Community hospitals, 1991:		
Beds per 100,000 people	340	30
Occupancy rate	56.6%	45
Average cost per patient per day	$846	10
Physicians per 100,000 people, 1990	175	31
Education		
Public elementary and secondary schools:		
Enrollment, percent increase, 1990–93	1.5%	34
Teachers' average salaries, 1992	$29,000	34
High school graduates, percent		
increase, 1990–94	0.3%	12
Educational attainment, persons 25 years old		
and over, 1990:		
High school or higher	72.1%	39
Bachelor's degree or higher	20.3%	22
College enrollment, 1991:		
Full-time students	54.5%	38
Minority students	29.9%	4
Crime		
Violent crime rate per 100,000 people, 1991	840	9
Criminal justice expenditures per person, 1991	$237	27
Federal and state prisoners, percent		
increase, 1980–91	72.9	45

Texas Statistics

Category	Statistic	Rank Among All States
Federal Funds and Social Insurance		
Federal funds, 1992:		
Funds for defense	$15.6 billion	3
Grants to state and local governments per person:		
Total	$546	46
Highway trust fund	$50	40
Percent of population receiving, 1991:		
Social Security	13.0%	45
Aid to Families with Dependent Children and/or Supplemental Security Income	5.8%	27
Labor Force		
Civilian labor force, 1992:		
Employment/population ratio	63.7	24
Female participation rate	59.2	29
Unemployment rate	7.5%	12
Income and Poverty		
Median household income, 1989:		
All races	$27,016	32
White	$29,728	26
Black	$17,853	36
Persons below poverty level, 1989:		
All races	18.1%	8
White	13.9%	6
Black	31.0%	18
Business		
Business failure rate per 10,000 concerns, 1992	108	16
Manufacturing, 1991:		
Value added	$78 billion	4
Value of shipments	$204 billion	2
Retail sales per household, percent change, 1990–91	3.3%	6
U.S. exports by state of origin	$43.6 billion	2
Miscellaneous		
Voting-age population casting votes for president, 1992	49.1%	46
Energy expenditures per person, 1990	$2,549	4
Motor vehicles:		
State gasoline tax per gallon, 1992	20¢	18
Miles of travel per 1,000 miles of road, 1991	540	24
Deaths per 100 million vehicle miles, 1991	1.9	24
Farm land, percent increase in average value per acre, 1990–92	-5.8%	37
Hazardous waste sites, 1992	29	13

Source: U.S. Bureau of the Census, *Statistical Abstract of the United States*, 1993

THE TOP 25

AMERICAN GENERAL CORPORATION

RANK: 23

OVERVIEW

American General is one of the largest financial services companies in the US. The Houston-based company provides retirement annuities and consumer loans and is the nation's #1 seller of life insurance policies among publicly owned life insurance companies.

American General's operating companies are divided among 4 business units (Retirement Annuities, Consumer Finance, Insurance — Special Markets, and Insurance — Home Service) and offer everything from retirement plans to home equity loans. American General's net income rose 11% in 1992, helped by strong growth in its consumer finance and annuities businesses.

American General has grown rapidly through acquisitions, a strategy that has set it apart from its insurance industry competitors, who have generally avoided acquisitions for growth. CEO Harold Hook owns his own management school, and his executives use a program developed by Hook, called Main Event Management, to run the company.

WHEN

In 1925 the Commission of Appeals of Texas ruled that insurers could underwrite more than one line of insurance, allowing companies that had previously provided only one type of insurance to provide a variety of products. One of the first to take advantage of the ruling was Gus Wortham, who formed American General Insurance Company in 1926. Providing both fire and casualty insurance, American General was one of the first multi-line insurance companies in the US.

In 1939 the company established The American General Investment Corporation — its first subsidiary and its first move beyond fire and casualty insurance.

The company's first acquisition came in 1945, when it bought Houston-based Seaboard Life Insurance, but American General didn't really take off until Benjamin Woodson joined the company in 1953. Woodson, who had been managing director of the National Association of Life Underwriters, used his contacts to find acquisitions to expand American General's life and health business. Woodson and the company bought life and health companies in Hawaii, Nebraska, Oklahoma, and Pennsylvania.

After concentrating on strengthening its life and health business through the 1950s, American General turned its attention to property and casualty insurance. Instead of building up its business through a series of small acquisitions, American General swung for the fences. In 1964 it doubled its size when it acquired Maryland Casualty Company in a stock swap. The move made American General a major property and casualty insurer with a presence across the US and in Canada.

In 1968 American General began an acquisition that would bring not only a large life insurer, California-Western States Life Insurance (Cal-West), into the fold but also a future CEO, Harold Hook. It purchased 1/3 of Cal-West in 1968 and increased its stake to 100% by 1975. Hook came to Houston that same year to become president, and in 1978 he succeeded Woodson as chairman.

During the 1980s the company changed its name (to American General Corporation in 1980) and diversified into financial services. It also continued to make big acquisitions, buying NLT Corporation for $1.5 billion (1982) and Gulf United's insurance business for $1.2 billion (1984). American General also began to shift its emphasis away from its more cyclical operations, selling its property and casualty business to Zurich Insurance Company for $740 million in 1989.

Although American General had spent the better part of 30 years as the acquisitor, the tables were turned in 1990 when Torchmark Corporation came knocking. Torchmark's $50-a-share offer set off a proxy fight. Hook won that battle and then turned around and announced that American General was for sale. When no buyers turned up, he took the company off the market later that year. Hook set out to cut costs and boost earnings, consolidating operations and laying off over 500 employees in 1991.

In 1993 a company subsidiary, American General Investment, was ordered to pay $310 million in compensatory and punitive damages to Avia Development Group for allegedly reneging on a joint venture agreement to build cargo facilities in 2 airports. The award was later reduced to $176.5 million.

NYSE symbol: AGC
Fiscal year ends: December 31

WHO

Chairman and CEO: Harold S. Hook, age 61, $1,715,000 pay
VC: Robert M. Devlin, age 52
President: James R. Tuerff, age 52, $428,308 pay (prior to promotion)
SVP and CFO: Austin P. Young, age 52
SVP and General Counsel: Jon P. Newton, age 51
SVP, Group Executive: Nicholas Rasmussen, age 46
SVP and Corporate Secretary: Kurt G. Schreiber, age 46
SVP, Investments: Peter V. Tuters, age 40
SVP, Group Executive: Ronald W. Wuensch, age 50
VP and Treasurer: James L. Gleaves, age 41
Human Resources Director: Tom Pulliam
Auditors: Ernst & Young

WHERE

HQ: 2929 Allen Pkwy., Houston, TX 77019
Phone: 713-522-1111
Fax: 713-831-3028

American General provides insurance and other financial services to over 14 million customers in all 50 US states, the District of Columbia, Canada, Puerto Rico, and the Virgin Islands.

WHAT

	1992 Assets $ mil.	% of total	1992 Pretax Income $ mil.	% of total
Retirement Annuities	17,673	44	188	24
Consumer Finance	7,192	18	248	32
Insurance — Special Markets	5,315	13	103	13
Insurance — Home Service	8,014	20	360	46
Other	1,859	5	(126)	(15)
Adjustments	(311)	—	2	—
Total	**39,742**	**100**	**775**	**100**

Retirement Annuities
Fixed and variable annuities
Retirement counseling services
Tax-deferred retirement plans

Consumer Finance
Consumer loans
Home equity loans
Life and credit-related insurance
Private label credit cards
Retail financing
VISA and MasterCard

Insurance — Special Markets
Annuities
Interest-sensitive life insurance
Payroll deduction services
Traditional life insurance

Insurance — Home Service
Annuities
Fire insurance
Health insurance
Interest-sensitive life insurance
Traditional life insurance

KEY COMPETITORS

Aetna
AIG
Blue Cross
Chubb
CIGNA
Citicorp
Countrywide Credit
Equitable
GEICO
General Re
John Hancock
Household International
Kemper
Marsh & McLennan
MassMutual
MetLife
New York Life
Northwestern Mutual
Prudential
State Farm
Teachers Insurance
Travelers
USAA

HOW MUCH

	Annual Growth	1983	1984	1985	1986	1987	1988	1989	1990	1991	1992
Assets ($ mil.)	11.2%	15,252	19,674	21,515	23,447	25,432	30,422	32,062	33,808	36,105	39,742
Net income ($ mil.)	6.0%	316	439	477	648	540	442	464	562	480	533
Income as % of assets	—	2.1%	2.2%	2.2%	2.8%	2.1%	1.5%	1.4%	1.7%	1.3%	1.3%
Earnings per share ($)	5.2%	1.55	1.50	1.60	2.17	1.86	1.72	1.88	2.35	2.13	2.45
Stock price – high ($)	—	13.13	13.13	18.13	23.38	22.38	18.44	19.25	25.32	22.50	29.38
Stock price – low ($)	—	9.13	9.69	12.38	16.69	13.63	13.69	14.75	11.75	14.00	20.13
Stock price – close ($)	10.7%	11.38	13.07	17.44	18.44	15.88	14.82	15.63	15.38	22.25	28.50
P/E – high	—	8	9	11	11	12	11	10	11	11	12
P/E – low	—	6	6	8	8	7	8	8	5	7	8
Dividends per share ($)	11.2%	0.40	0.45	0.50	0.56	0.63	0.70	0.75	0.79	1.00	1.04
Book value per share ($)	8.0%	10.65	11.90	13.58	15.32	16.15	17.18	18.53	18.57	19.86	21.33
Employees	(6.2%)	—	—	—	—	16,000	18,300	12,500	12,000	11,000	11,600

1992 Year-end:
Equity as % of assets: 8.6%
Return on equity: 11.9%
Cash (mil.): $17
Long-term debt (mil.): $1,371
No. of shares (mil.): 218
Dividends:
  1992 average yield: 3.5%
  1992 payout: 42.4%
Market value (mil.): $6,210
Sales (mil.): $4,602

Stock Price History High/Low 1983–92

THE TEXAS 500

AMR CORPORATION

RANK: 4

OVERVIEW

Fort Worth–based AMR, a holding company for the world's largest airline (American Airlines) and a group of regional airlines (American Eagle), set a new record in 1992. After reporting a $240 million loss in 1991, AMR topped that mark with a $475 million loss in 1992. Company forecasts predict a difficult 1993 as well, owing to fare wars, excess capacity, and a sluggish economy.

The company tried to stabilize air fares by introducing "Value Pricing" (a simplified 4-tier fare structure) in 1992. When other carriers began discounting, AMR initiated a price war during the summer that led to an explosion in traffic.

AMR has canceled or postponed $8.5 billion in capital spending. With 18% of US air travel controlled by bankrupt carriers and with numerous small airlines taking off, competition is expected to keep fares low. To reduce annual operating expenses by $300 million, CEO Bob Crandall is laying off employees, cutting service to less profitable markets, reducing the number of airplanes to 661 (from 672) by the end of 1993, and building ground operations (non-airline operations such as network management, data-processing, information services, management consulting, and groundhandling) to help weather the current storms in the air.

One ace that AMR can rely on is its SABRE Travel Information Network, the leading computer reservation system among travel agents.

WHEN

In 1929 Sherman Fairchild's Fairchild Aviation Corporation created a New York City holding company called The Aviation Corporation (AVCO). By 1930 AVCO owned about 85 small airlines, which together formed an unconnected coast-to-coast network. Hoping to consolidate this route structure, AVCO created American Airways in 1930.

In 1934 new postal regulations forced AVCO to split up its aircraft-making and transportation concerns. American Airlines was formed as a result and, through an exchange of stock, it bought American Airways.

With former AVCO manager C. R. Smith at the helm, American surpassed United as the leading US airline in the late 1930s. The Douglas DC-3, built to Smith's specifications, was introduced into service by American in 1936 and became the first commercial airliner to pay its way on passenger revenues alone.

After WWII, American bought American Export Airlines (renamed American Overseas Airlines), with flights to northern Europe, but sold this division to Pan Am in 1950. American formed subsidiary Americana Hotels in 1963 and introduced SABRE, the industry's first automated reservations system, in 1964. In 1968 Smith left American to serve President Johnson as secretary of commerce.

American bought Trans Caribbean Airlines in 1971, gaining routes to the Caribbean. In 1977 Americana Hotels bought the Howard Corporation's hotel properties and by 1978 operated 21 hotels and resorts in the US, Latin America, and Korea. American had sold all of its hotels by 1987 except the Inn of the Six Flags at Arlington, Texas.

In 1979 American moved its headquarters from New York to Dallas/Fort Worth. Former CFO Bob Crandall became president in 1980 and, using SABRE to keep track of mileage, introduced the industry's first frequent flyer program (AAdvantage) in 1981. In 1982 American created AMR Corporation as its holding company. After acquiring Nashville Eagle (commuter airline) in 1987, AMR established AMR Eagle to operate commuter services as American Eagle, buying 4 new commuters in 1988 and 1989.

In 1989 AMR weathered an unsolicited takeover bid by Donald Trump and bought Eastern Air Lines's Latin American routes from Texas Air (now Continental Airlines Holdings). In 1991 AMR bought TWA's US-London routes for $445 million. The company also won DOT approval to fly to Manchester, England. AMR spent $140 million to buy Continental's Seattle-Tokyo route and $21.3 million for Midway Airlines's gates at LaGuardia and Washington National airports. The new routes did not bring the expected financial results, and AMR scaled back its expansion.

Late in 1992 AMR agreed to invest $192 million in PWA, owner of Canadian Airlines, in exchange for a 25% voting interest and a 20-year services contract. In 1993 AMR announced the layoff of up to 450 pilots.

THE TEXAS 500

NYSE symbol: AMR
Fiscal year ends: December 31

WHO

Chairman, President, and CEO: Robert L. Crandall, age 57, $900,000 pay
EVP and CFO: Donald J. Carty, age 46, $618,750 pay
SVP; SVP Marketing, American Airlines, Inc.: Michael W. Gunn, age 47, $368,750 pay
SVP and General Counsel: Anne H. McNamara, age 45
VP Employee Relations, American Airlines, Inc.: Thomas J. Kiernan
Auditors: Ernst & Young

WHERE

HQ: 4333 Amon Carter Blvd., Fort Worth, TX 76155
Phone: 817-963-1234
Fax: 817-967-9641
Reservations: 800-433-7300

American serves 192 worldwide destinations. American Eagle serves 173 cities in the US, the Caribbean, and the Bahamas.

Hub Locations
Chicago, IL
Dallas/Fort Worth, TX
Miami, FL
Nashville, TN
Raleigh/Durham, NC
San Jose, CA
San Juan, Puerto Rico

	1992 Sales % of total
US & Canada	73
Central & South America	12
Europe	12
Pacific	3
Total	**100**

WHAT

	1992 Sales $ mil.	% of total
Passenger	12,390	86
Cargo	581	4
Other	1,425	10
Total	**14,396**	**100**

Selected Subsidiaries and Affiliates
American Airlines, Inc.
AMR Eagle, Inc. (commuter services)
  Command Airways, Inc.
  Executive Airlines, Inc.
  Nashville Eagle, Inc.
  Simmons Airlines, Inc.
  West Wings Airlines, Inc.
AMR Services, Inc. (ground services)
SABRE Travel Information Network (markets SABRE computer reservations system)

Flight Equipment	No.	Orders
A300	34	1
Boeing 727	142	—
Boeing 757	69	22
Boeing 767	58	13
Fokker 100	39	36
DC-10	59	—
MD-11	11	8
MD-80	260	—
Other	277	27
Total	**949**	**107**

KEY COMPETITORS

Alaska Air
All Nippon Airways
America West
British Airways
Continental Airlines
Delta
HAL
JAL
KLM
Lufthansa
Mesa Airlines
NWA
Qantas
SAS
Singapore Airlines
Southwest
TWA
UAL
USAir
Virgin Group

HOW MUCH

	9-Year Growth	1983	1984	1985	1986	1987	1988	1989	1990	1991	1992
Sales ($ mil.)	13.1%	4,763	5,354	6,131	6,018	7,198	8,824	10,480	11,720	12,887	14,396
Net income ($ mil.)	—	228	234	346	279	198	477	455	(40)	(240)	(475)
Income as % of sales	—	4.8%	4.4%	5.6%	4.6%	2.8%	5.4%	4.3%	(0.3%)	(1.9%)	(3.3%)
Earnings per share ($)	—	4.48	4.16	5.88	4.63	3.28	7.66	7.15	(0.64)	(3.54)	(6.35)
Stock price – high ($)	—	39.13	41.25	50.75	62.13	65.50	55.00	107.50	70.25	71.13	80.25
Stock price – low ($)	—	18.50	24.25	33.50	39.25	26.75	32.63	52.13	39.75	44.25	54.38
Stock price – close ($)	7.2%	36.13	36.13	41.38	53.63	35.25	53.63	58.00	48.38	70.50	67.50
P/E – high	—	9	10	9	13	20	7	15	—	—	—
P/E – low	—	4	6	6	8	8	4	7	—	—	—
Dividends per share ($)	0.0%	0.00	0.00	0.00	0.00	0.00	0.00	0.00	0.00	0.00	0.00
Book value per share ($)	5.8%	26.87	31.23	37.17	42.30	45.58	53.54	60.54	59.83	55.79	44.65
Employees	12.2%	42,500	46,900	52,100	54,300	65,100	77,100	89,000	102,809	116,264	119,300

1992 Year-end:
Debt ratio: 71.7%
Return on equity: —
Cash (mil.): $858
Current ratio: 0.61
Long-term debt (mil.): $7,838
No. of shares (mil.): 75
Dividends:
  1992 average yield: 0.0%
  1992 payout: 0.0%
Market value (mil.): $5,063

Stock Price History High/Low 1983–92

THE TEXAS 500

BURLINGTON NORTHERN INC.

RANK: 22

OVERVIEW

Burlington Northern (BN) operates the longest rail system in North America, a 25,000-mile system spanning 25 states and 2 Canadian provinces.

With track stretching from the Florida Panhandle to British Columbia, Fort Worth–based BN serves some of the continent's richest coal, grain, and timber-producing regions. But heavy debt, high labor and injury costs, poor operating ratios, and aging equipment have hurt BN's performance. The railroad is working to cut costs while improving customer service, but it could lose a big chunk of coal business (33% of revenues) in 1994 to rival Union Pacific, which charges lower rates.

CEO Gerald Grinstein, who had no former railroad experience, has been criticized for failing to turn the company around. Revenues have been flat since he took charge in 1989, but earnings recovered in 1992 after plunging in 1991 because of a $708 million charge for severance pay and personal injury and environmental cleanup costs. And Grinstein has nearly halved BN's debt, upgraded its technology, and resolved a costly labor dispute over train crew reductions. By 1995, he says, BN's turnaround should be on track.

WHEN

Burlington Northern is largely the creation of James J. Hill, who began his railroad empire in 1878 by acquiring the St. Paul & Pacific Railroad in Minnesota. By 1893 Hill had completed the Great Northern Railway, which extended from St. Paul to Seattle. The following year he gained control of Northern Pacific (chartered in 1864), which had been constructed between Duluth, Minnesota, and Tacoma, Washington, with extensions to Portland, Oregon, and St. Paul. With the help of J. P. Morgan, in 1901 Hill acquired the Chicago, Burlington & Quincy (Burlington), whose routes included Chicago–St. Paul, Chicago–Denver, Omaha–Billings, and Billings–Denver–Fort Worth–Houston. To give Great Northern an entrance to Oregon, Hill created the Spokane, Portland & Seattle Railway (SP&S), completed in 1908.

Hill intended to merge Great Northern, Northern Pacific, SP&S, and Burlington under his Morgan-backed Northern Securities Company, but in 1904 the Supreme Court found that Northern Securities had violated the Sherman Anti-Trust Act. Although the Court dissolved the holding company, Hill kept control of the individual railroads, remaining a director of Great Northern until his death in 1916.

Meanwhile, Jim Hill's railroads produced some of America's best-known passenger trains. Great Northern's Empire Builder began service between Chicago and Seattle in 1929; it is operated today by Amtrak. The 1934 Burlington Zephyr was the nation's first streamlined passenger diesel.

After several years of deliberation by the ICC, Great Northern and Northern Pacific were allowed to merge in 1970 along with jointly owned subsidiaries Burlington and SP&S. The new company, Burlington Northern (BN), acquired the St. Louis–San Francisco Railway (Frisco) in 1980. The Frisco, with lines stretching from St. Louis to such cities as Dallas, Oklahoma City, Kansas City, and Pensacola, added more than 4,650 miles to the BN rail network.

The company formed Burlington Motor Carriers (BMC) in 1985 to manage 5 trucking companies it had acquired. Later (in 1988), as a result of its decision to focus only on railroads, BN sold BMC and spun off Burlington Resources, an independent holding company for its nonrailroad businesses (primarily natural gas, oil, minerals, construction, and forest products, including 1.8 million acres of land), leaving Burlington Northern Railroad and BN Leasing as its principal subsidiaries.

In 1989 BN hired an outsider as CEO: Gerald Grinstein, a former Western Airlines CEO with a knack for labor relations.

In 1991 BN built a link into Mexico through a rail-barge joint venture with Mexican industrial firm Grupo Protexa. In 1992 it cut 4 levels of field management; a system-wide control center was opened in Fort Worth the same year.

In 1993 BN made one of the biggest locomotive purchases in history by agreeing to spend $675 million for 350 locomotives from 1993 to 1997. BN's service was disrupted by midwestern summer flooding, one of the worst natural disasters to affect US railroads.

NYSE symbol: BNI
Fiscal year ends: December 31

WHO

Chairman and CEO: Gerald Grinstein, age 60, $1,156,250 pay
EVP Law and Secretary: Edmund W. Burke, age 44, $406,800 pay
COO, Burlington Northern Railroad Co.: William E. Greenwood, age 54, $595,583 pay
EVP Safety and Corporate Support, Burlington Northern Railroad Co.: John T. Chain, Jr., age 58, $618,780 pay
EVP Marketing and Sales, Burlington Northern Railroad Co.: John Q. Anderson, age 41
EVP and CFO: David C. Anderson, age 51, $482,917 pay
EVP Employee Relations: James B. Dagnon, age 52
Auditors: Coopers & Lybrand

WHERE

HQ: 3800 Continental Plaza, 777 Main St., Fort Worth, TX 76102-5384
Phone: 817-878-2000
Fax: 817-878-2377

Selected Cities Served

Billings, MT	Memphis, TN
Birmingham, AL	Minneapolis–St. Paul, MN
Cheyenne, WY	Omaha, NE
Chicago, IL	Pensacola, FL
Dallas, TX	Portland, OR
Denver, CO	Seattle, WA
Fargo, ND	St. Louis, MO
Fort Worth, TX	Tulsa, OK
Houston, TX	Vancouver, BC
Kansas City, MO	Winnipeg, MB

WHAT

1992 Sales

Items transported	$ mil.	% of total
Coal	1,520	33
Agricultural commodities	776	17
Industrial products	1,049	23
Intermodal	711	15
Merchandise	585	12
Automotive products	134	3
Other	(145)	(3)
Total	**4,630**	**100**

Equipment	No.
Locomotives	2,251
Freight cars	59,548
Total	**61,799**

Subsidiaries
BN Leasing Corp. (acquires rail cars and other equipment)
Burlington Northern Railroad Co.

KEY COMPETITORS

American Freightways
American President
Canadian Pacific
Chicago and North Western
Consolidated Freightways
Consolidated Rail
Heartland Express
Norfolk Southern
Roadway
Santa Fe Pacific
Southern Pacific Rail
Union Pacific
UPS
Yellow Corporation

HOW MUCH

	9-Year Growth	1983	1984	1985	1986	1987	1988	1989	1990	1991	1992
Sales ($ mil.)	0.3%	4,508	9,156	8,651	6,941	6,621	4,700	4,606	4,674	4,559	4,630
Net income ($ mil.)	(3.5%)	413	579	633	(529)	367	207	243	222	(306)	299
Income as % of sales	—	9.2%	6.3%	7.3%	(7.6%)	5.5%	4.4%	5.3%	4.8%	(6.7%)	6.5%
Earnings per share ($)	(5.1%)	5.39	7.15	7.96	(7.53)	4.91	2.76	3.18	2.89	(3.96)	3.35
Stock price – high ($)	—	54.75	50.00	72.63	82.38	84.25	80.38	32.38	39.25	41.88	47.38
Stock price – low ($)	—	25.50	35.00	46.25	46.50	35.00	56.00	21.38	22.25	26.25	33.25
Stock price – close ($)	(1.4%)	49.50	47.00	68.25	53.25	62.75	79.00	31.50	28.75	40.50	43.50
P/E – high	—	10	7	9	—	17	29	10	14	—	14
P/E – low	—	5	5	6	—	7	20	7	8	—	10
Dividends per share ($)	3.7%	0.87	1.00	1.40	1.70	2.05	2.20	1.20	1.20	1.20	1.20
Book value per share ($)	(12.2%)	50.76	56.98	63.13	47.90	50.80	12.31	14.33	16.29	13.76	15.80
Employees	(4.9%)	49,486	48,076	45,022	44,200	42,300	32,700	32,900	32,900	31,760	31,204

1992 Year-end:
Debt ratio: 47.6%
Return on equity: 22.7%
Cash (mil.): $57
Current ratio: 0.57
Long-term debt (mil.): $1,527
No. of shares (mil.): 88
Dividends:
 1992 average yield: 2.8%
 1992 payout: 35.8%
Market value (mil.): $3,829

Stock Price History
High/Low 1983–92

THE TEXAS 500

THE COASTAL CORPORATION

RANK: 7

OVERVIEW

Based in Houston, Coastal is a diversified energy company with operations in a variety of industries, including natural gas gathering, marketing, and transmission; petroleum refining, marketing, and distribution; oil and gas exploration; coal mining; chemicals; independent power production; and trucking.

Coastal subsidiaries operate 7 refineries; own a fleet of tank cars and trucks, tankers, and barges; and market retail products, including Next Generation gasoline and diesel fuels in Coastal branded outlets.

Coastal's Natural Gas group, which operates 20,000 miles of pipelines in the US and Canada, generated more profits than any other group in 1992. In 1993 Coastal formed Coastal Gas Services Company in order to take advantage of recent regulatory changes intended to foster greater competition in the natural gas industry. Coastal plans to expand its products and services.

While the Natural Gas group may be able to brag at the company picnic, Coastal's Refining and Marketing group might want to stay home. The group posted an operating loss of $192 million in 1992. In response Coastal took a $125 million charge against earnings in the 4th quarter of 1992, cut staff and inventory, and closed a Kansas refinery.

Besides trying to revive its Refining and Marketing group, Coastal also plans to reduce its long-term debt, hoping to shrink it to 60% of total capitalization by the end of 1995.

WHEN

After spending boyhood summers working in the oil fields, serving as a bomber pilot in WWII, and earning a mechanical engineering degree from Texas A&M, Oscar Wyatt started a small natural gas gathering business in Corpus Christi, Texas. It was 1951.

In 1955 the company became Coastal States Gas Producing Company. It collected and distributed natural gas from South Texas oil fields. In 1962 Coastal purchased Sinclair Oil's Corpus Christi refinery and pipeline network. Also in the early 1960s, a Coastal subsidiary, Lo-Vaca Gathering, supplied natural gas to Texas cities and utilities. During the energy crisis of the early 1970s, Lo-Vaca curtailed its natural gas supplies and then raised prices. Unhappy customers sued Coastal, and regulators in 1977 ordered Lo-Vaca to refund $1.6 billion. To finance the settlement, Coastal spun off Lo-Vaca as Valero Energy.

Meanwhile the combative Wyatt, who would earn a reputation as one of the swashbuckling corporate raiders of the 1980s, had been expanding Coastal through a series of deals. Coastal won Rio Grande Valley Gas, a small South Texas pipeline (1968), and then in 1973 mounted a successful $182 million hostile bid for Colorado Interstate Gas and changed its name to Coastal States Gas Corporation. With aggressive acquisitions, Coastal moved into low-sulfur Utah coal (Southern Utah Fuel, 1973), New England pipelines (Union Petroleum, 1973), California refining (Pacific Refining, 1976), and Florida petroleum marketing and transportation (Belcher Oil, 1977; renamed in 1990). In 1980 Coastal adopted its present name.

Wyatt tried to snare Texas Gas Resources (1983) and Houston Natural Gas (1984). These bids were thwarted, but when the companies bought back stock owned by Coastal to defend themselves, Coastal made money.

In 1985 Coastal purchased American Natural Resources in a $2.45 billion hostile takeover. In 1989, just before Wyatt stepped down as CEO, Coastal bid $2.6 billion for Texas Eastern, but that company sold out to "white knight" Panhandle Eastern.

Before the 1991 Gulf War, Wyatt courted the Iraqis, attempting to trade Coastal's refining and marketing assets for a steady supply of Iraq's crude oil. Wyatt and Coastal director John B. Connally, former US secretary of the treasury, met with Saddam Hussein and flew hostages out of Baghdad. Wyatt's statements against Operation Desert Storm drew harsh US criticism.

In 1993 Coastal announced plans to build the 600-mile SunShine Pipeline in Florida. Coastal also signed contracts with Peoples Gas System and Florida Power Corporation to supply Florida with natural gas. Construction is scheduled to begin in 1994, with service beginning in 1995. Also in 1993 James Paul resigned as president and CEO. His duties were taken over by Wyatt.

THE TEXAS 500

NYSE symbol: CGP
Fiscal year ends: December 31

WHO

Chairman, President, and CEO: Oscar S. Wyatt, Jr., age 68, $1,038,178 pay (prior to promotion)
EVP Natural Gas: James F. Cordes, age 52, $663,721 pay
EVP and CFO: David A. Arledge, age 48, $542,983 pay
EVP Refining, Engineering, and Marine Operations: James A. King, age 53
SVP and General Counsel: Carl A. Corrallo
SVP Exploration and Production: Jerry D. Bullock, age 63
SVP Marketing: Dan J. Hill, age 52
SVP Coal, Chemicals, and Power: James L. Van Lanen, age 48
VP Corporate Communications and Employee Relations: E. C. Simpson
Auditors: Deloitte & Touche

WHERE

HQ: Coastal Tower, Nine Greenway Plaza, Houston, TX 77046-0995
Phone: 713-877-1400
Fax: 713-877-6754

Coastal has operations in the US, Germany, Singapore, the UK, Aruba, Bahrain, Cyprus, the Netherlands, Argentina, and Bermuda. The company and its branded marketers operate 1,243 Coastal outlets in 36 states.

WHAT

	1992 Sales $ mil.	% of total	1992 Operating Income $ mil.	% of total
Natural gas	2,747	27	403	122
Refining & marketing	6,561	65	(192)	(58)
Exploration & production	111	1	46	14
Coal	447	5	93	28
Other	197	2	(20)	(6)
Adjustments	—	—	26	—
Total	**10,063**	**100**	**356**	**100**

Selected Subsidiaries

Natural Gas
ANR Pipeline Co.
ANR Storage Co.
Coastal Gas Services Co.
Colorado Interstate Gas Co.

Refining, Marketing, and Distribution
Coastal Fuels Marketing, Inc.
Coastal Refining & Marketing, Inc.

Exploration and Production
ANR Production Co.
CIG Exploration, Inc.
Coastal Oil & Gas Corp.

Coal
ANR Coal Co.
Coastal States Energy Co.

Other
Coastal Chem, Inc.
Coastal Power Production Co.

KEY COMPETITORS

AMAX	DuPont	Petrobrás
Amerada Hess	Elf Aquitaine	Petrofina
Amoco	Enron	Phillips Petroleum
Ashland	Exxon	Repsol
Associated Natural Gas	Ingram	Royal Dutch/Shell
Atlantic Richfield	Koch	Southland
British Petroleum	Mobil	Sun
Broken Hill	Norsk Hydro	Tenneco
Chevron	Oryx	Texaco
Columbia Gas	PDVSA	Total
Cyprus Minerals	PEMEX	Unocal
	Pennzoil	USX

HOW MUCH

	9-Year Growth	1983	1984	1985	1986	1987	1988	1989	1990	1991	1992
Sales ($ mil.)	6.0%	5,963	6,260	7,275	6,668	7,429	8,187	8,271	9,381	9,549	10,063
Net income ($ mil.)	—	94	102	142	72	113	157	178	226	96	(127)
Income as % of sales	—	1.6%	1.6%	2.0%	1.1%	1.5%	1.9%	2.2%	2.4%	1.0%	(1.3%)
Earnings per share ($)	—	1.07	1.31	1.56	0.56	1.39	1.79	1.89	2.14	0.91	(1.23)
Stock price – high ($)	—	9.76	10.57	17.44	17.78	26.92	23.67	33.08	39.63	36.75	30.00
Stock price – low ($)	—	4.95	6.96	8.19	10.44	14.00	17.58	22.00	29.25	23.75	22.00
Stock price – close ($)	11.4%	9.02	8.37	17.39	15.56	17.33	22.83	33.08	32.25	24.63	23.88
P/E – high	—	9	8	11	32	19	13	17	19	40	—
P/E – low	—	5	5	5	19	10	10	12	14	26	—
Dividends per share ($)	15.7%	0.11	0.22	0.16	0.18	0.24	0.27	0.30	0.40	0.40	0.40
Book value per share ($)	11.2%	7.43	8.45	11.40	11.58	12.67	14.24	17.36	19.12	19.67	19.33
Employees	13.1%	5,484	5,324	16,200	16,500	17,800	19,000	13,100	13,900	16,500	16,570

1992 Year-end:
Debt ratio: 69.8%
Return on equity: —
Cash (mil.): $44
Current ratio: 1.16
Long-term debt (mil.): $4,306
No. of shares (mil.): 104
Dividends:
  1992 average yield: 1.7%
  1992 payout: —
Market value (mil.): $2,483

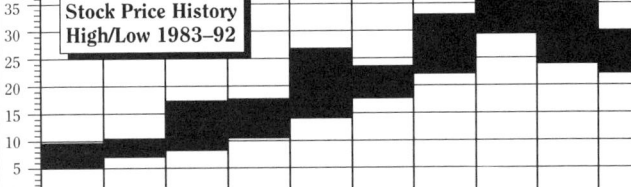

Stock Price History High/Low 1983–92

COMPAQ COMPUTER CORPORATION

RANK: 25

OVERVIEW

Compaq is back. The maker of IBM-compatible laptop and desktop personal computers ranks #3 (after IBM and Apple) in the world market, with a 6.6% market share in 1992.

At the end of 1991, Compaq was watching Dell eat away its market share the way Compaq had once feasted on IBM's PC markets. Cofounder and CEO Rod Canion was forced to resign after Compaq reported its first layoffs and quarterly loss, and the company's COO, German-born Eckhard Pfeiffer, was tapped to lead Compaq back. Determining that the company's PCs were overengineered and overpriced, Pfeiffer cut costs and slashed prices. About 2,000 workers have left the company since 1990, and another 1,000 are expected to leave in 1993.

Traditionally, the company has sold its products through computer dealers, but now Compaq's machines are available through superstores and other resellers as well as through catalogs and telemarketing. Compaq introduced a line of printers in 1992 and continues to roll out new products, with 39 in March 1993 alone. To differentiate itself from other PC makers, Compaq is emphasizing service by providing free, 24-hour technical assistance service by telephone and a 3-year warranty. With profit margins shrinking, Compaq plans to make money by increasing sales volume. For 1992 Compaq reported a record $4.1 billion in revenues (up 25% over 1991) and $213 million in net income (up 63% over 1991, but still less than half 1990's $455 million profit).

WHEN

Joseph R. (Rod) Canion and 2 other ex–Texas Instruments engineers started Compaq in Houston in 1982 to manufacture and sell portable IBM-compatible computers. Compaq's first portable was developed from a prototype the 3 sketched on a paper place mat when they first discussed the product idea.

Compaq shipped its first computer in 1982 and in 1983 (the year it went public) recorded sales of $111 million — unprecedented growth for a computer start-up. Compaq's success was due in part to emphasis on leading-edge technology. In 1983 Compaq introduced a portable computer 18 months before IBM did, and in 1986 it was first out with a computer based on Intel's 386 chip.

However, Compaq delayed introduction of its laptop until the prototype's display and battery technologies were satisfactorily developed to engineering specifications. Although introduced late (1988), Compaq's SLT/286 laptop with its crisp display screen became an immediate success.

To sell its products Compaq capitalized on the extensive base of dealers and suppliers built up around the IBM PC. Rather than establish a large sales force, Compaq gave exclusive rights to dealers for sales and service of its products and by 1990 had a network of 3,800 retailers in 152 countries. The dealer channel has proved to be effective. In 1988 Compaq became the first company to exceed the $2 billion sales mark in only 6 years from its first product introduction (1982–88). Sales in 1989 rose to $2.9 billion.

In 1989 the company dropped Businessland, its 2nd largest reseller (after ComputerLand), as an authorized dealer after Businessland demanded preferential discounts. Compaq reauthorized Businessland as a dealer in 1990 after it agreed to abide by Compaq's policies. In 1991 Compaq bought a 13% interest in engineering workstation maker Silicon Graphics and paid $50 million for access to its graphics technology. Compaq also took a lead role in creating a 21-company alliance, Advanced Computer Environment (ACE), set up to establish a standard for Reduced Instruction Set Computing (RISC) computers to compete with those of Sun and IBM.

But the turbulence of 1991 proved too much for Compaq's board of directors. Founder and CEO Rod Canion (an engineer) was forced to resign and was replaced with Eckhard Pfeiffer (a salesman). The next year Compaq withdrew from ACE and sold back its stake in Silicon Graphics, and its 20% interest in Conner Peripherals (bought in 1986) for an $80 million profit. Late in 1992 Compaq introduced the world's fastest PC server, the Compaq SYSTEMPRO/XL.

Early in 1993 Compaq and Microsoft announced a joint venture to develop pen-based PCs, mobile computing, and multiprocessor computers and servers. The company also announced plans to make PCs in China.

62   THE TEXAS 500

NYSE symbol: CPQ
Fiscal year ends: December 31

WHO

Chairman: Benjamin M. Rosen, age 60
President and CEO: Eckhard Pfeiffer, age 51, $1,721,400 pay
SVP, General Counsel, and Secretary: Wilson D. Fargo, age 48
SVP Systems: Gary Stimac, age 41, $660,000 pay
SVP Europe: Andreas Barth, age 48, $599,851 pay
SVP PC Division: H. Douglas Johns, age 44, $650,000 pay
SVP Finance and CFO: Daryl J. White, age 45, $595,000 pay
VP Human Resources: Jerry G. Welch, age 54
Auditors: Price Waterhouse

WHERE

HQ: 20555 SH 249, Houston, TX 77070
Phone: 713-370-0670
Fax: 713-374-1740

The company does business in 85 countries and has manufacturing facilities in Houston, Scotland, and Singapore.

	1992 Sales $ mil.	1992 Sales % of total	1992 Operating Income $ mil.	1992 Operating Income % of total
US & Canada	1,833	45	37	15
Europe	1,886	46	74	29
Other countries	381	9	143	56
Adjustments	—	—	69	—
Total	**4,100**	**100**	**323**	**100**

WHAT

	1992 Distribution % of Outlets
Dealers	69
Retail	16
Value-added resellers/ systems integrators	15
Total	**100**

Laptops
COMPAQ LTE Series

Portables

Desktop PCs
COMPAQ DESKPRO Series
COMPAQ PROLINEA Series

PC Systems
COMPAQ ProSignia
COMPAQ SYSTEMPRO
COMPAQ SYSTEMPRO/LT
COMPAQ SYSTEMPRO/XL
COMPAQ SYSTEMPRO Model 486

Printers
PAGEMARQ 15
PAGEMARQ 20

Computer Peripherals
COMPAQ ProLiant

KEY COMPETITORS

Apple	Fujitsu	Oki
AST	Gateway 2000	Olivetti
AT&T	Hewlett-Packard	Philips
Atari	Hitachi	Sharp
Canon	Hyundai	Siemens
Casio	IBM	Sun Microsystems
Commodore	Intel	Tandy
Data General	Machines Bull	Toshiba
DEC	Matsushita	Unisys
Dell	NEC	Wang

HOW MUCH

	9-Year Growth	1983	1984	1985	1986	1987	1988	1989	1990	1991	1992
Sales ($ mil.)	49.3%	111	329	504	625	1,224	2,066	2,876	3,599	3,271	4,100
Net income ($ mil.)	63.2%	3	13	27	43	136	255	333	455	131	213
Income as % of sales	—	2.3%	3.9%	5.3%	6.9%	11.1%	12.4%	11.6%	12.6%	4.0%	5.2%
Earnings per share ($)	50.1%	0.07	0.24	0.45	0.67	1.79	3.14	3.88	5.12	1.49	2.52
Stock price – high ($)	—	6.25	7.31	7.13	10.81	39.25	32.88	56.25	67.88	74.25	49.88
Stock price – low ($)	—	5.50	1.75	3.06	5.81	9.63	21.00	29.63	35.50	22.13	22.25
Stock price – close ($)	25.6%	6.25	3.31	6.63	9.63	27.69	29.81	39.75	56.38	26.38	48.75
P/E – high	—	96	31	16	16	22	10	15	13	50	20
P/E – low	—	85	7	7	9	5	7	8	7	15	9
Dividends per share ($)	0.0%	0.00	0.00	0.00	0.00	0.00	0.00	0.00	0.00	0.00	0.00
Book value per share ($)	34.1%	1.79	2.08	2.58	3.39	5.85	10.57	14.92	21.59	22.93	25.14
Employees	35.5%	615	1,318	1,860	2,200	4,000	6,900	9,500	11,400	10,000	9,500

1992 Year-end:
Debt ratio: 0.0%
Return on equity: 10.5%
Cash (mil.): $357
Current ratio: 2.42
Long-term debt (mil.): —
No. of shares (mil.): 80
Dividends:
  1992 average yield: 0.0%
  1991 payout: 0.0%
Market value (mil.): $3,892

Stock Price History High/Low 1983–92

THE TEXAS 500

CONTINENTAL AIRLINES HOLDINGS, INC.

RANK: 17

OVERVIEW

After 6 years of losses and a 2-year sojourn in bankruptcy, Continental Airlines, the #5 air carrier in the US, emerged in April 1993 with a new color scheme (mainly blue and gray), new wings (in the form of $600 million in cash), and new owners. The new owners include Air Canada and Air Partners (an association of Texas investors), who acquired around 60% of the company by investing $450 million, and Continental's unsecured creditors, who ended up with the rest of the company in settlement of their claims.

Continental was forced into bankruptcy in December 1990 by large debts and rising fuel expenses. This latest trip was its 2nd excursion to bankruptcy court in the past 10 years. Despite its financial woes, the company remains the dominant carrier at 3 of its 6 hubs (Houston, Newark, and Cleveland). However, deep fare discounts, initiated by American Airlines, threatened to complicate Continental's recovery. In response the company filed an antitrust action against American in June 1992, accusing the latter of predatory pricing tactics. Continental must also overcome the problems of an aging airline fleet and its poor reputation with business travelers.

Continental's reemergence has not been without turbulence at the top: the company has had 10 CEOs in the past 11 years. Current president and CEO Robert Ferguson took over in 1991 and brought the company out of bankruptcy.

WHEN

Houston-based Trans Texas Airways began serving Texas communities in 1947. It became Texas International in 1968 and was serving the West Coast and Mexico by 1970. However, the company was unable to compete with major airlines on interstate routes or with commuter airlines in Texas and faced bankruptcy by 1972, when Frank Lorenzo's Jet Capital Corporation gained control. With Lorenzo at the helm, Texas International had netted over $3 million by 1976. In 1980 Lorenzo formed Texas Air, a holding company for Texas International and a newly created New York–to–Washington, DC, shuttle, New York Air.

In 1981 Texas Air bought 50% of Continental Airlines (founded as Varney Speed Lines in 1934), which operated in the western US, Mexico, and the Pacific. Continental's employees tried to block the takeover, but Texas Air bought the rest of the company in 1982. Continental had lost over $500 million between 1978 and 1983. In 1983, when Lorenzo's efforts to wrest wage concessions from the airline's unions resulted in a strike, Lorenzo maneuvered the airline into Chapter 11, abrogating union contracts. Continental emerged from bankruptcy in 1986 as a nonunion, low-fare carrier with the industry's lowest labor costs.

That year Texas Air bought Eastern Air Lines (founded as Pitcairn Aviation in 1927). WWI ace Eddie Rickenbacker had run Eastern from 1935 until his retirement in 1963. Losses and union disputes in the 1960s and 1970s forced Eastern's CEO Frank Borman (a former astronaut) to sell in 1986. Texas Air also bought People Express Airlines and Frontier Airlines in 1986, becoming the #1 US airline in passenger miles flown.

In 1988 Lorenzo sold Eastern's Air Shuttle to Donald Trump, but in 1989 mounting losses and a machinists' strike forced Eastern into bankruptcy. In 1990 the bankruptcy court removed Texas Air from Eastern's management, appointing Martin Shugrue as trustee. Texas Air then changed its name to Continental Airlines Holdings. Lorenzo resigned as chairman, president, and CEO after selling his stake in the company to SAS for a substantial premium plus $19.7 million in salary and severance pay. Following Lorenzo's resignation, Hollis L. Harris, former president of Delta Air Lines, was named CEO.

With fuel prices up and traffic down, Continental followed Eastern into bankruptcy late in 1990. Eastern held on until January 1991, when mounting losses forced it to liquidate. Harris, who opposed new cost-cutting efforts, left Continental in 1991 and was replaced by former CFO Robert Ferguson.

In 1991 Continental sold its Seattle-Tokyo route to AMR for $145 million. After emerging from bankruptcy in 1993, Continental placed a $4.5 billion order with Boeing for 92 new jets.

NYSE Symbols: CAIA; CAIB
Fiscal year ends: December 31

WHO

Chairman: David Bonderman, age 50
President and CEO; VC and CEO, Continental Airlines, Inc.: Robert R. Ferguson III, age 44, $512,294 pay
EVP and COO; EVP, Continental Airlines, Inc.: Charles T. Goolsbee, age 58, $279,043 pay
EVP Marketing, Continental Airlines, Inc.: John W. Nelson, age 50, $249,359 pay
SVP and CFO: Daniel P. Garton, age 35
SVP Human Resources, Continental Airlines, Inc.: Robert F. Allen, age 46
Auditors: Arthur Andersen & Co.

WHERE

HQ: 2929 Allen Pkwy., Ste. 2010, Houston, TX 77019
Phone: 713-834-5000
Fax: 713-834-2087
Reservations: 800-525-0280

Continental flies to 136 cities in the US and to 57 foreign destinations.

Hub Locations
Cleveland
Denver
Guam
Honolulu
Houston
Newark

WHAT

	1992 Sales	
	$ mil.	% of total
Passengers	4,637	83
Cargo, mail & other	938	17
Total	**5,575**	**100**

Major Subsidiaries and Affiliates
Continental Airlines, Inc.
  Britt Airways, Inc. (commuter airline)
  New York Airlines, Inc. (commuter airline)
  Rocky Mountain Airways, Inc. (commuter airline)
System One Holdings, Inc. (computer reservation system)
Chelsea Catering Corp. (airline catering services)

Flight Equipment	No.
A300	21
Boeing 727	85
Boeing 737	88
Boeing 747	7
DC-9	34
DC-10	20
MD-80	64
Total	**319**

KEY COMPETITORS

Alaska Air	Mesa Airlines
All Nippon Airways	NWA
America West	Ogden
AMR	Qantas
British Airways	SAS
Delta	Singapore Airlines
HAL	Southwest
JAL	Swire Pacific
Kimberly-Clark	TWA
KLM	UAL
Lufthansa	USAir
Marriott	Virgin Group

HOW MUCH

	Annual Growth	1983	1984	1985	1986	1987	1988	1989	1990	1991	1992
Sales ($ mil.)	18.1%	1,246	1,372	1,944	4,407	8,475	8,573	6,685	6,231	5,551	5,575
Net income ($ mil.)	—	(180)	28	49	42	(466)	(719)	(886)	(2,403)	(306)	(125)
Income as % of sales	—	(14.4%)	2.0%	2.5%	1.0%	(5.5%)	(8.4%)	(13.2%)	(38.6%)	(5.5%)	(2.2%)
Earnings per share ($)	—	(14.74)	1.20	1.81	0.68	(12.58)	(18.88)	(22.71)	(58.96)	(6.74)	(2.70)
Stock price – high ($)	—	12.38	9.88	20.00	40.88	51.50	17.13	23.38	12.13	5.00	2.25
Stock price – low ($)	—	4.75	5.63	8.88	14.13	9.00	8.88	11.13	1.00	0.25	0.13
Stock price – close ($)	(30.5%)	6.63	9.13	15.00	33.75	10.88	11.88	11.50	1.75	0.44	0.25
P/E – high	—	—	8	11	60	—	—	—	—	—	—
P/E – low	—	—	5	5	21	—	—	—	—	—	—
Dividends per share ($)	(100%)	0.08	0.00	0.00	0.00	0.00	0.00	0.00	0.00	0.00	0.00
Book value per share ($)	—	(8.88)	(5.24)	5.48	22.00	12.53	(5.47)	(26.80)	(80.18)	(81.05)	(83.31)
Employees	15.8%	—	—	15,900	65,820	69,431	67,937	53,055	41,300	42,450	44,430

1992 Year-end:
Debt ratio: —
Return on equity: 3.3%
Cash (mil.): $358
Current ratio: 0.66
Long-term debt (mil.): $228
No. of shares (mil.): 46
Dividends:
  1992 average yield: —
  1992 payout: —
Market value (mil.): $12

Stock Price History High/Low 1983–92

THE TEXAS 500

COOPER INDUSTRIES, INC.

RANK: 16

OVERVIEW

After 8 years of rising profits, Houston-based Cooper Industries reported a decline in net income for 1992 owing to depressed markets for electrical power and petroleum equipment. Sales remained flat as a result of weak Canadian and European markets. Net income continued to fall through the middle of 1993, without any significant increase in sales.

In order to focus on its core businesses (automotive parts, hand tools, hardware, electrical equipment, and petroleum industrial equipment), the 150-year-old company announced that it was selling its Belden Division (electrical wires and cables) in a public offering to be completed by the fall of 1993.

Over the past 20 years Cooper has acquired a diversified portfolio of products, including Champion spark plugs, Crescent wrenches, Wiss shears, Lufkin measuring tapes, and Moog steering and suspension systems. Cooper's electrical products range from massive power transformers to tiny fuses used on circuit boards. Its engines and compressors serve the oil and gas industry, and the Cooper-Bessemer engine division owns half of a joint venture with Rolls-Royce. The company's automotive products include windshield wipers, brakes, lights, wires and cables, and temperature-control products.

The company believes that its process of "Cooperization" (its ability to improve acquired properties), rather than technological innovation, is the key to its success. Management emphasizes diversified operations and strong cash flow while seeking to improve manufacturing facilities and methods.

WHEN

In 1833 Charles Cooper sold a horse for $50 and borrowed money to open a foundry with his brother Elias in Mount Vernon, Ohio. Known as C. & E. Cooper, the company made plows, hog troughs, maple syrup kettles, stoves, and wagon boxes.

In the 1840s Cooper began making steam engines for use in mills and on farms and later adapted the engines for wood-burning locomotives. In 1868 the company built its first Corliss steam engine and in 1875 introduced the first steam-powered farm tractor. By 1900 Cooper's steam engines were sold in the US and overseas. In 1909 Cooper introduced an internal combustion engine-compressor for natural-gas pipelines.

In the 1920s Cooper became the biggest seller of compression engines for oil and gas pipeline transmission. A 1929 merger with Bessemer (small gas and diesel engines) created Cooper-Bessemer, whose diesel engines powered marine vessels. Cooper was hurt badly by the Depression; sales fell 90% in 1931. The success of a new turbocharged diesel to power locomotives revived revenues.

Diversification began in the late 1950s with the purchase of Rotor Tools (1959). Cooper adopted its current name in 1965 and moved its headquarters to Houston in 1967. The company went on to acquire 20 other companies, including its "tool basket": Lufkin Rule (measuring tapes, 1967), Crescent (wrenches, 1968), and Weller (soldering tools, 1970).

The purchase of Gardner-Denver in 1979 gave Cooper a strong position in oil-drilling and mining equipment, and the 1981 acquisition of Crouse-Hinds was a significant diversification into electrical materials. Another 1981 purchase was Kirsch (drapery hardware). The decline in oil prices in the early 1980s caused sales to drop more than 35% between 1981 and 1983, but Cooper remained profitable because of its diversification into tools and electrical products.

The electrical segment expanded further with the 1985 purchase of McGraw-Edison, maker of both consumer products (Buss fuses) and heavy transmission gear for electrical utilities. Cooper bought RTE (electrical equipment, 1988), Champion Spark Plug (1989), and Cameron Iron Works (oil-drilling equipment, 1989). In 1991 Cooper bought 3 Canadian operations and in 1992 it bought the Brazilian hand-tool maker, Ferramentas Belzer do Brasil. Also in 1992 Cooper acquired Moog Automotive for $612 million, making the company the largest supplier of automobile replacement parts.

In 1993 Cooper sold the mining and construction business of its petroleum and industrial equipment division. That same year the company acquired Hawker Fusegear (electrical fuses) of the UK.

66 THE TEXAS 500

NYSE symbol: CBE
Fiscal year ends: December 31

WHO

Chairman and CEO: Robert Cizik, age 62, $798,750 pay
VC: Alan E. Riedel, age 62, $440,000 pay
President and COO: H. John Riley, Jr., age 52, $343,333 pay
EVP Operations: Michael J. Sebastian, age 62, $335,000 pay
SVP Finance: Dewain K. Cross, age 55, $295,500 pay
VP and General Counsel: James A. Chokey, age 49
VP Human Resources and Environmental Affairs: Carl J. Plesnicher, Jr., age 55
Auditors: Ernst & Young

WHERE

HQ: PO Box 4446, First City Tower, 1001 Fannin St., Ste. 4000, Houston, TX 77002
Phone: 713-739-5400
Fax: 713-739-5555

Cooper operates 170 plants in 36 countries.

	1992 Sales $ mil.	% of total	1992 Operating Income $ mil.	% of total
US	4,831	75	562	76
Europe	961	15	113	15
Canada	375	5	3	—
Other regions	312	5	63	9
Adjustments	(360)	—	(85)	—
Total	**6,119**	**100**	**656**	**100**

WHAT

	1992 Sales $ mil.	% of total	1992 Operating Income $ mil.	% of total
Petroleum & industrial equip.	1,831	30	202	27
Electrical products	1,572	26	285	38
Elec. power equip.	618	10	58	8
Tools & hardware	812	13	63	8
Automotive prods.	1,286	21	132	19
Adjustments	—	—	(84)	—
Total	**6,119**	**100**	**656**	**100**

Electrical Products
Buss fuses
Crouse-Hinds industrial lighting
Halo lighting
McGraw-Edison and Edison lighting
Metalux fluorescent lighting

Electrical Power Equipment
McGraw-Edison transformers
RTE power system components

Tools and Hardware
Crescent wrenches
Gardner-Denver pneumatic tools
Kirsch drapery hardware
Lufkin measuring tapes
Plumb hammers
Turner torches

Wiss scissors and shears
Xcelite screwdrivers

Automotive Products
Anco windshield wipers
Champion spark plugs
Wagner brakes and lights

Industrial Equipment
Ajax engine-compressors
Cameron oil field equipment
Coberra turbines (50%, joint venture with Rolls-Royce)
Cooper-Bessemer engines and turbines
Gardner-Denver drilling equipment
OPI pumps

KEY COMPETITORS

ABB	Emerson	Philips
Baker Hughes	General Electric	Robert Bosch
Black & Decker	General Signal	Siemens
Borg-Warner	Illinois Tool Works	Snap-on Tools
Dana	Ingersoll-Rand	Stanley Works
Dresser	Masco	Textron
Eaton	PACCAR	Westinghouse

HOW MUCH

	9-Year Growth	1983	1984	1985	1986	1987	1988	1989	1990	1991	1992
Sales ($ mil.)	14.3%	1,842	2,028	3,062	3,421	3,575	4,250	5,115	6,206	6,155	6,119
Net income ($ mil.)	19.8%	71	107	135	148	174	224	268	361	393	361
Income as % of sales	—	3.9%	5.3%	4.4%	4.3%	4.9%	5.3%	5.2%	5.8%	6.4%	5.9%
Earnings per share ($)	17.4%	0.64	1.06	1.39	1.52	1.73	2.20	2.49	2.81	3.01	2.71
Stock price – high ($)	—	19.00	18.94	21.19	25.75	37.25	31.38	40.00	46.00	58.00	59.38
Stock price – low ($)	—	13.50	13.00	14.00	17.81	19.50	25.06	26.88	31.25	38.50	41.75
Stock price – close ($)	11.8%	17.38	14.19	21.00	20.69	27.75	27.00	40.00	41.13	57.25	47.38
P/E – high	—	30	18	15	17	22	14	16	16	19	22
P/E – low	—	21	12	10	12	11	11	11	11	13	15
Dividends per share ($)	5.6%	0.76	0.76	0.76	0.76	0.80	0.84	0.90	1.00	1.08	1.24
Book value per share ($)	6.2%	14.49	14.65	14.58	14.66	15.91	17.47	24.75	27.66	29.96	24.99
Employees	6.6%	29,838	30,370	46,000	40,200	43,200	46,300	58,100	57,500	53,900	52,900

1992 Year-end:
Debt ratio: 42.0%
Return on equity: 9.9%
Cash (mil.): $18
Current ratio: 1.72
Long-term debt (mil.): $1,816
No. of shares (mil.): 113
Dividends:
 1992 average yield: 2.6%
 1992 payout: 45.8%
Market value (mil.): $5,272

Stock Price History High/Low 1983–92

THE TEXAS 500

ELECTRONIC DATA SYSTEMS CORP.

RANK: 10

OVERVIEW

Electronic Data Systems (EDS), based in Plano, Texas, and a wholly owned subsidiary of General Motors since 1984, is the largest data processing corporation in the US. EDS operates, installs, and designs data management systems for businesses in many fields, including the insurance, automotive, financial, and communications industries, as well as the government. Founded by H. Ross Perot, EDS had over $8 billion in 1992 sales.

The outsourcing boom in the US is working in EDS's favor, as companies discover that EDS can run their computer systems more efficiently and cheaply than they can. The company measures its own success by evaluating the successes of its customers. A mix of entrepreneurial spirit and a military-like sense of discipline and loyalty (a legacy left by Perot) exists among EDS's ranks. In keeping with this, the company's state-of-the-art communications headquarters, the I.M.C. (Information Management Center), in Plano, Texas, is known by employees as the "Impossible Mission Center."

EDS is looking for a telephone company with which to form an alliance to further extend its communications network. Talks between the company and British Telecommunications fell through in 1993. The communications market is one of EDS's fastest growing. In 1993 EDS announced joint venture plans with Fujitsu (on a product data management system), Canon (on Canon's optical card business), and Amdahl (to help companies move from mainframes to smaller computers).

WHEN

After 10 years with Big Blue, disgruntled salesman H. Ross Perot founded Electronic Data Systems in 1962. IBM executives had pooh-poohed Perot's idea to provide companies with electronic data processing management services, taking computer and data management worries off clients' hands.

It took Perot 5 months to find his first customer, Collins Radio of Cedar Rapids, Iowa. EDS pioneered the long-term fixed-price contract with Frito-Lay in 1963, writing a 5-year contract instead of the 60- to 90-day contracts usually offered by service companies.

The company entered Medicare and Medicaid claims processing (mid-1960s), insurance company data processing (1963), and data management for banks (1968). EDS would become the #1 provider of data management services in all 3 of these markets.

The company went public in 1968. EDS bought Wall Street Leasing (computer services) and established Regional Data Centers and central data processing stations, pioneering the concept of distributed processing in the early 1970s.

In 1976 EDS signed its first offshore contract, in Saudi Arabia. The company also signed a contract with the government of Iran that year, but by 1978 Iran had fallen 6 months behind in its payments, and EDS halted operations. When 2 EDS employees were later arrested, amid the disorder of the Khomeini revolution, Perot assembled a rescue team to get them out of the country. The 2 employees were eventually released, and the team aided in their flight from Iran.

In the mid-1970s EDS began moving toward the installation of computer systems and away from the management of them.

In 1984, on its 22nd anniversary (and Perot's birthday), EDS was bought by General Motors for $2.5 billion. GM promised EDS its independence as well as contract work managing its lumbering data processing system. EDS prospered, but the differing managerial styles of Perot and GM chairman Roger B. Smith resulted in an uneasy alliance that ended in divorce. GM bought Perot's EDS shares in 1986 for over $700 million. Perot formed competitor Perot Systems Corporation in 1988. After 5 years in operation Perot's company has barely dented EDS's sales.

Lester Alberthal became CEO, and through the rest of the 1980s, he lessened EDS's dependence on GM, diversifying widely. GM-generated revenues accounted for about 70% of EDS's net sales in the mid-1980s, but by 1992 this percentage had decreased to 41%.

In 1990 EDS bought the UK's SD-Scicon. The next year IBM, facing declining profits (and looking more green than blue), entered the profitable data management industry.

In 1992 EDS won an FAA contract worth $508 million. The next year EDS announced that it would begin, on a small scale, selling new house-brand personal computers.

NYSE symbol: GME
Fiscal year ends: December 31

WHO

Chairman, President, and CEO: Lester M. Alberthal, Jr., age 49
SVP and Secretary: John R. Castle, Jr.
SVP and CFO: Joseph M. Grant
SVP: Paul J. Chiapparone
SVP: Gary J. Fernandes
SVP: J. Davis Hamlin
SVP: Jeffrey M. Heller
SVP: Dean Linderman
SVP Personnel: G. Stuart Reeves
VP, General Counsel, and Assistant Secretary: D. Gilbert Friedlander
Auditors: KPMG Peat Marwick

WHERE

HQ: Electronic Data Systems Corporation, 5400 Legacy Dr., Plano, TX 75024-3199
Phone: 214-604-6000
Fax: 214-392-8790 (Investor Relations)

EDS has operations in 30 countries.

	1992 Sales		1992 Operating Income	
	$ mil.	% of total	$ mil.	% of total
US	6,256	77	773	79
Europe	1,375	17	131	13
Other	524	6	76	8
Total	**8,155**	**100**	**980**	**100**

WHAT

	1992 Sales	
	$ mil.	% of total
GM and subsidiaries	3,348	41
Outside customers	4,807	59
Total	**8,155**	**100**

Notable Customers
Apple Computer
Benetton
Blue Cross/Blue Shield of Massachusetts
Bruno's
Caterpillar
City of Chicago
Connaught Laboratories
Del Monte Foods
General Electric
General Motors
Heineken
Kmart
McKesson Drug Company
3M
Montgomery Ward
Motorola
National Car Rental
U.S. Postal Service
Virgin Group
Warsaw Stock Exchange

KEY COMPETITORS

ADP
American Software
Arthur Andersen
CompuCom
Continuum
Coopers & Lybrand
Deloitte & Touche
IBM
Intelligent Electronics
Knowledgeware
Policy Management Systems
System Software Associates

HOW MUCH

	9-Year Growth	1983	1984	1985	1986	1987	1988	1989	1990	1991	1992
Sales ($ mil.)	32.9%	630	775	3,406	4,321	4,324	4,745	5,374	6,022	7,029	8,155
Net income ($ mil.)	30.3%	59	71	190	261	323	384	435	497	563	636
Income as % of sales	—	9.3%	9.2%	5.6%	6.0%	7.5%	8.1%	8.1%	8.3%	8.0%	7.8%
Earnings per share ($)	29.6%	0.13	0.16	0.39	0.53	0.66	0.79	0.91	1.04	1.17	1.33
Stock price – high ($)	—	5.27	5.78	11.63	12.41	12.75	11.22	14.41	20.06	33.06	34.00
Stock price – low ($)	—	2.72	3.06	5.16	6.19	6.00	8.38	10.63	12.19	17.50	25.25
Stock price – close ($)	26.4%	3.98	5.30	10.22	6.22	9.63	11.22	13.66	19.31	31.50	32.88
P/E – high	—	41	37	30	23	19	14	16	19	28	26
P/E – low	—	21	20	13	12	9	11	12	12	15	19
Dividends per share ($)	27.7%	0.04	0.04	0.05	0.10	0.13	0.17	0.24	0.28	0.32	0.36
Book value per share ($)	41.4%	0.56	1.32	2.00	3.75	5.10	6.93	9.03	10.89	12.57	12.65
Employees	20.7%	13,000	14,100	40,000	45,000	44,000	47,500	55,000	59,900	65,800	70,500

1992 Year-end:
Debt ratio: 21.3%
Return on equity: 10.5%
Cash (mil.): $588
Current ratio: 1.13
Long-term debt (mil.): $561
No. of shares (mil.): 242
Dividends:
　1992 average yield: 1.1%
　1992 payout: 27.1%
Market value (mil.): $7,961

Stock Price History
High/Low 1983–92

THE TEXAS 500

ENRON CORP.

RANK: 15

OVERVIEW

Enron's CEO, Kenneth Lay, is serious about natural gas. So serious that in 1992 Enron announced it would spin off its oil trading and transportation business to its stockholders, cutting Enron's sales in half. However, the move shouldn't hurt earnings too much. Without the trading and transportation business, Enron's profits were up 39% in 1992.

Based in Houston, Enron is North America's #1 buyer and seller of natural gas, handling about 1/5 the natural gas consumed in the US. Its integrated, diversified approach includes the production, transportation and marketing of natural gas and liquid fuels, and the construction and management of independent power projects. Enron operates nearly 40,000 miles of natural gas pipelines in the US and is part owner of 4 US power plants (3 in Texas and one in Virginia).

Lay sees natural gas as the fuel of the 21st century, and he wants Enron to be the world's first major natural gas company. As part of that goal, Enron plans a strong focus on global expansion. In 1993 the company completed construction of a 1,875-MW power plant at Teesside, UK (of which it owns 50%).

Enron has also entered discussions to build another 3 or 4 power plants in the UK, discussed a joint venture in China to build a 2,000–4,000-MW power station, and is looking at power development projects in India, Germany, Turkey, Kuwait, and Russia.

WHEN

Enron traces its history through 2 well-established natural gas companies — InterNorth and Houston Natural Gas (HNG).

InterNorth started out in 1930 as Northern Natural Gas, an Omaha, Nebraska, gas pipeline company. By 1950 Northern had doubled its capacity and in 1960 started processing and transporting natural gas liquids. The company changed its name to InterNorth in 1980. In 1983 it spent $768 million to buy Belco Petroleum, adding 821 billion cubic feet of natural gas and 67 million barrels of oil to its reserves. At the same time the company (with 4 partners) was building the Northern Border Pipeline to link Canadian producing fields with US markets.

HNG, formed in 1925 as a South Texas natural gas distributor, served more than 55,000 customers by the early 1940s. It started developing oil and gas properties in 1953 and bought Houston Pipe Line Company in 1956. Other major acquisitions included Valley Gas Production, a South Texas natural gas company (1963), and Houston's Bammel Gas Storage Field (1965). In the 1970s the company started developing offshore fields in the Gulf of Mexico, and in 1976 it sold its original gas distribution properties to Entex. In 1984 HNG, faced with a hostile takeover attempt by Coastal Corporation, brought in former Exxon executive Kenneth Lay as CEO. Lay refocused Enron on natural gas, selling $632 million worth of unrelated assets. He added Transwestern Pipeline (California) and Florida Gas Transmission, and by 1985 Enron operated the only transcontinental gas pipeline.

In 1985 InterNorth bought HNG for $2.4 billion, creating the US's largest natural gas pipeline system (38,000 miles). Soon after, Kenneth Lay became chairman/CEO of newly named Enron (1986), and the company moved its headquarters from Omaha to Houston.

Laden with $3.3 billion of debt (most related to the HNG acquisition), Enron sold 50% of Citrus Corporation (operates Florida Gas Transmission, 1986), 50% of Enron Cogeneration (1988), and 16% of Enron Oil & Gas (1989). In the meantime the company paid $31 million for Tesoro Petroleum's gathering and transportation businesses in 1988.

In 1990 the company bought CSX Energy's Louisiana production facilities, which helped to increase Enron's production of natural gas liquids by nearly 33%. In 1991 Enron closed a deal with Tenneco to buy that company's natural gas liquids/petrochemical operations for $632 million.

In 1992 Enron signed a contract with Sithe Energies Group to supply $4 billion worth of natural gas over 20 years to a planned upstate New York cogeneration plant. Also in 1992, Enron and three partners acquired a 70% interest in the 3,800-mile Transportadora de Gas del Sur pipeline in Argentina.

In 1993 Enron acquired the Louisiana Resources Company and several other gas businesses, including a 540-mile pipeline, from the Williams Companies for $170 million.

70   THE TEXAS 500

NYSE symbol: ENE
Fiscal year ends: December 31

WHO

Chairman and CEO: Kenneth L. Lay, age 50, $1,975,000 pay
President and COO: Richard D. Kinder, age 48, $1,333,377 pay
Chairman and CEO, Enron Gas Pipeline and Liquids Group: Ronald J. Burns, age 39, $693,021 pay
Chairman and CEO, Enron Gas Services Group: Jeffrey K. Skilling, age 39
Chairman and CEO, Enron Power Corp.: Thomas E. White, age 49
SVP and Chief Information, Administrative, and Accounting Officer: Jack I. Tompkins, age 47, $580,337 pay
SVP and General Counsel: James V. Derrick, Jr., $448,337 pay, age 48
VP Human Resources: James E. Street
Auditors: Arthur Andersen & Co.

WHERE

HQ: 1400 Smith St., Houston, TX 77002-7369
Phone: 713-853-6161
Fax: 713-853-3129

Enron operates more than 43,000 miles of natural gas pipelines in North and South America and is engaged in oil and gas exploration, principally in the US. The company also has interests in power plants in the US, the UK, the Philippines, and Guatemala.

WHAT

	1992 Sales		1992 Operating Income	
	$ mil.	% of total	$ mil.	% of total
Natural gas	3,957	62	412	65
Power	70	1	59	9
Exploration & production	291	5	100	16
Liquid fuels	2,007	32	59	10
Adjustments	—	—	(10)	—
Total	**6,325**	**100**	**620**	**100**

Natural Gas
Enron Gas Services Corp. (natural gas services)
Major pipeline companies
  Florida Gas Transmission Co. (50% owned)
  Houston Pipe Line Co.
  Northern Natural Gas Co.
  Transportadora de Gas del Sur (Argentina, 25% interest in a consortium that owns 70% of the pipeline)
  Transwestern Pipeline Co.

Power
Enron Development
Enron Power Corp.
Enron Power Management Ventures

Exploration and Production
Enron Exploration
Enron Gas & Oil Trinidad

Enron Oil & Gas Co. (80%)
Enron Oil Canada

Liquid Fuels
Enron Field Producer Services
EGP Fuels
Enron Liquids Pipeline

KEY COMPETITORS

Associated Natural Gas
Coastal
Columbia Gas
Consolidated Edison
Koch
Occidental
Panhandle Eastern
Public Service Enterprise
Tenneco

HOW MUCH

	9-Year Growth	1983	1984	1985	1986	1987	1988	1989	1990	1991	1992
Sales ($ mil.)	2.7%	4,997	7,510	10,253	7,453	5,916	5,708	9,836	13,165	5,563	6,325
Net income ($ mil.)	3.1%	255	297	125	(108)	54	130	226	202	241	336
Income as % of sales	—	5.1%	4.0%	1.2%	(1.4%)	0.9%	2.3%	2.3%	1.5%	1.8%	5.3%
Earnings per share ($)	0.4%	2.56	2.60	0.87	(1.77)	0.32	1.07	1.93	1.72	2.04	2.66
Stock price – high ($)	—	20.50	21.25	27.31	25.31	26.75	21.50	30.50	31.38	38.44	50.13
Stock price – low ($)	—	12.06	16.38	19.50	16.88	15.50	17.44	17.75	25.13	24.81	30.63
Stock price – close ($)	9.9%	19.75	21.13	22.50	19.75	19.56	18.31	28.81	27.38	35.00	46.38
P/E – high	—	8	8	31	—	85	20	16	18	19	19
P/E – low	—	5	6	22	—	49	16	9	15	12	12
Dividends per share ($)	2.0%	1.11	1.20	1.24	1.24	1.24	1.24	1.24	1.24	1.26	1.33
Book value per share ($)	2.0%	16.64	17.80	14.01	10.84	14.66	14.77	15.38	16.04	16.86	19.93
Employees	(2.4%)	9,741	10,551	11,911	7,200	6,900	6,300	6,300	6,962	7,400	7,780

1992 Year-end:
Debt ratio: 49.1%
Return on equity: 14.5%
Cash (mil.): $142
Current ratio: 0.80
Long-term debt (mil.): $2,459
No. of shares (mil.): 119
Dividends:
  1992 average yield: 2.9%
  1992 payout: 49.8%
Market value (mil.): $5,500

Stock Price History High/Low 1983–92

THE TEXAS 500

EXXON CORPORATION

RANK: 1

OVERVIEW

Exxon, the largest US oil company and the US's 2nd largest industrial company (after General Motors), is a diversified petroleum business. Its "upstream" activities (exploration and production in its oil and gas properties) are balanced by its major "downstream" (refining and marketing) operations.

The Irving, Texas–based company also makes and sells petrochemicals, mines coal and other minerals, and owns 60% of an electric power generating station in Hong Kong. Exxon's net income was down 14% in 1992, as the company's refining and chemical businesses suffered through downturns in their respective industries.

Exxon continues to shift its exploration and production business overseas. In 1992, 80% of the company's exploration budget went to projects outside North America. In 1993 Exxon signed an agreement with Royal Dutch Shell, Mitsubishi, and PDVSA, Venezuela's national oil company, to develop a $3 billion gas project in eastern Venezuela.

Also in 1993, Lee R. Raymond replaced Lawrence Rawl as CEO following Rawl's retirement.

WHEN

John D. Rockefeller, a commodity trader, started his first oil refinery in 1863 in Cleveland. Realizing that the price of oil at the well would shrink with each new strike, Rockefeller chose to monopolize oil refining and transportation. He raised $1 million in loans and investments and in 1870 formed the Standard Oil Company. In 1882 Rockefeller and his associates created the Standard Oil Trust, which allowed Rockefeller and 8 others to dissolve existing Standard Oil affiliates and set up new, ostensibly independent companies in different states, including the Standard Oil Company of New Jersey (Jersey Standard).

Initially capitalized at $70 million, the Standard Oil Trust controlled 90% of the petroleum industry. In 1911, after 2 decades of political and legal wrangling, the Supreme Court disbanded the trust into 34 companies, the largest of which was Jersey Standard. In that year John D. Archbold took over as president of Jersey Standard and commenced more active exploration efforts.

Walter Teagle took over the presidency in 1917, secretly bought half of Humble Oil of Texas (1919), and expanded into South America. In 1928 Jersey Standard joined in the Red Line Agreement, which reserved most Middle East oil for a handful of companies. Congressional investigation of a prewar research pact giving Farben of Germany patents for a lead essential to the development of aviation fuel in exchange for a formula for synthetic rubber (never received) led to Teagle's resignation in 1942.

The 1948 purchase of a 30% interest in Arabian American Oil Company for $74 million, combined with a 7% share of Iranian production acquired in 1954, made Jersey Standard the world's largest oil company.

Other US companies still using the Standard Oil name objected to Jersey Standard marketing in their territories as Esso (derived from the initials S.O. for Standard Oil). To end the confusion, Jersey Standard became Exxon in 1972. The name change cost $100 million.

In the 1970s nationalization of oil assets by producing countries reduced Exxon's access to oil. Despite increased exploration in the 1970s and 1980s, Exxon's reserves shrank faster than new reserves could be found.

The oil tanker *Exxon Valdez* spilled nearly 11 million gallons of oil into Alaska's Prince William Sound in 1989. The resulting legal and public relations damage to the company has threatened its ability to gain rights to drill in other US coastal areas.

In late 1991 Exxon agreed to settlement of lawsuits resulting from the *Valdez* spill. Payments to the US government and the state of Alaska will total $900 million over a 10-year period, plus $125 million in fines. Exxon has already spent over $2 billion for cleanup of the Alaskan coast.

In 1992 Exxon announced a $900 million expansion of its Sriracha refinery in Thailand and announced an agreement with Mobil to develop an 86-million-acre area in Russia's West Siberia basin. Also in 1992, Sidney Reso, president of Exxon's international division, was kidnapped. After Reso's body was found in southern New Jersey, Arthur Seale, a former security official with the company, pleaded guilty to the kidnapping and murder.

NYSE symbol: XON
Fiscal year ends: December 31

WHO

Chairman and CEO: Lee R. Raymond, age 54, $1,362,000 pay (prior to promotion)
President: Charles R. Sitter, age 62, $1,002,500 pay
SVP: Robert E. Wilhelm, $713,000 pay
SVP: C. M. Harrison, age 62
SVP: E. J. Hess, age 59
VP and Treasurer (Principal Financial Officer): E. A. Robinson, age 59
VP and General Counsel: C. K. Roberts, age 63
VP Human Resources: M. E. Gillis, age 62
Auditors: Price Waterhouse

WHERE

HQ: 225 E. John W. Carpenter Freeway, Irving, TX 75062-2298
Phone: 214-444-1000
Fax: 214-444-1505

Exxon conducts operations in the US and in more than 80 foreign countries.

	1992 Sales $ mil.	% of total	1992 Net Income $ mil.	% of total
US	24,028	21	1,192	22
Other North America	17,810	16	275	5
Other countries	71,578	63	3,932	73
Adjustments	(10,256)	—	(589)	—
Total	**103,160**	**100**	**4,810**	**100**

WHAT

	1992 Sales $ mil.	% of total	1992 Operating Income $ mil.	% of total
Petroleum	104,282	92	6,538	91
Chemicals	9,131	8	660	9
Adjustments	(10,253)	—	(314)	—
Total	**103,160**	**100**	**6,884**	**100**

Petroleum
Upstream operations
 Oil and gas exploration
 Oil and gas production
Downstream operations
 Convenience stores
 Lubricants
 Refining
 Service stations
 Transportation

Other
 Coal mining
 Power generation
 Mineral mining

Chemicals
 Fertilizers
 Fuel and lubricant additives
 Performance chemicals for oilfield operations
 Plasticizers
 Polyethylene and polypropylene plastics
 Specialty and commodity solvents
 Specialty resins

KEY COMPETITORS

Amerada Hess
Amoco
Ashland
Associated Natural Gas
Atlantic Richfield
British Petroleum
Broken Hill
Chevron
Circle K
Coastal
DuPont
Elf Aquitaine
Imperial Oil
Koch
Lyondell Petrochemical
Mobil
Norsk Hydro
Occidental
Oryx
PDVSA
PEMEX
Pennzoil
Petrobrás
Petrofina
Phillips Petroleum
Repsol
Royal Dutch/Shell
Southland
Sun
Texaco
Total
Unocal
USX

HOW MUCH

	9-Year Growth	1983	1984	1985	1986	1987	1988	1989	1990	1991	1992
Sales ($ mil.)	1.7%	88,561	90,854	86,673	69,888	76,416	79,557	86,656	105,519	102,847	103,160
Net income ($ mil.)	(0.4%)	4,978	5,528	4,870	5,360	4,840	5,260	2,975	5,010	5,600	4,810
Income as % of sales	—	5.6%	6.1%	5.6%	7.7%	6.3%	6.6%	3.4%	4.7%	5.4%	4.7%
Earnings per share ($)	3.1%	2.89	3.39	3.23	3.71	3.43	3.95	2.32	3.96	4.45	3.82
Stock price – high ($)	—	19.88	22.75	27.94	37.06	50.38	47.75	51.63	55.13	61.88	65.50
Stock price – low ($)	—	14.25	18.06	22.06	24.19	30.88	32.00	40.50	44.88	49.63	53.75
Stock price – close ($)	14.1%	18.69	22.50	27.56	35.06	38.13	44.00	50.00	51.75	60.88	61.13
P/E – high	—	7	7	9	10	15	12	22	14	14	17
P/E – low	—	5	5	7	7	9	8	17	11	11	14
Dividends per share ($)	6.9%	1.55	1.68	1.73	1.80	1.90	2.15	2.30	2.47	2.68	2.83
Book value per share ($)	5.1%	17.40	18.42	19.91	22.30	24.38	24.65	23.39	25.78	27.42	27.19
Employees	(5.3%)	156,000	150,000	146,000	102,000	100,000	101,000	104,000	104,000	101,000	95,000

1992 Year-end:
Debt ratio: 28.4%
Return on equity: 13.8%
Cash (mil.): $1,515
Current ratio: 0.84
Long-term debt (mil.): $8,637
No. of shares (mil.): 1,242
Dividends:
 1992 average yield: 4.6%
 1992 payout: 74.1%
Market value (mil.): $75,917

Stock Price History High/Low 1983–92

THE TEXAS 500

HALLIBURTON COMPANY

RANK: 13

OVERVIEW

These are not easy times for Halliburton. The Dallas-based company, one of the world's largest oil field and construction services companies and the 2nd largest driller (measured by sales, after Schlumberger), posted a loss of $124 million in 1992.

Halliburton's Engineering and Construction Services Group, which includes construction firm Brown & Root, faced a slowdown in construction and engineering activity because of weak US and European economies. And its Insurance Services Group has been hurt by underwriting losses linked to Hurricanes Andrew and Iniki and to increases in claim loss reserves in the UK.

The company's energy services business hasn't fared much better. The group, which provides a wide range of equipment, products, and services for oil and gas production, saw US oil field activity fall to a post–World War II low in 1992. Previously made up of 10 separate divisions, it was combined into a single unit, called Halliburton Energy Services.

Besides reorganizing its energy services business, Halliburton is taking a number of steps to right itself. In the 4th quarter of 1992, the company took a $265 million restructuring charge. It also cut its US work force by over 4,000 in 1992.

In 1993 Halliburton acquired Smith International's directional drilling and services business for $240 million in stock. The acquisition is part of Halliburton's strategy to provide a one-stop shop of drilling services for its Big Oil customers.

WHEN

Erle Halliburton began his oil career in 1916, when he went to work for Perkins Oil Well Cementing. Discharged for suggesting too many new ideas, Halliburton left for Burkburnett, Texas, in 1919 and started his Better Method Oil Well Cementing Company. Halliburton used cement to hold a steel pipe in a well, which kept oil out of the water table; although his contribution is widely recognized today, it was considered nonessential then. In 1921, the same year he moved to Duncan, Oklahoma, he recorded his first profit — of $.50. In 1924 he incorporated as Halliburton Oil Well Cementing Company.

Between the 1950s and 1970s, Halliburton built up its present-day, Dallas-based oil service business by buying companies with expertise throughout the oil and gas market.

Halliburton acquired Welex, a well-logging company (1957), and Houston-based Brown & Root construction company (1966), which had expertise in offshore platforms. The company bought Ebasco Services, an electric utility engineering company with expertise in nuclear plants (1973), but the Justice Department forced its sale (1976), fearing that Halliburton's 20% share of the utility engineering market would limit competition.

The investments in Welex and Brown & Root left Halliburton well positioned to benefit from the oil boom of the 1970s. Later that decade, as drilling costs surged, Halliburton became the leader in stimulating old and abandoned wells by developing new techniques for fracturing deep formations.

When the oil industry slumped in 1982, Halliburton avoided further energy investments, instead cutting employment by more than half, while rivals Schlumberger and Dresser bought distressed companies at bargain prices. Another Halliburton business was not faring well either: in 1985 Brown & Root, already suffering a scarcity of new construction projects, settled out of court for $750 million for mismanagement of the South Texas Nuclear Project.

Halliburton began reinvesting in oil and gas services, buying 60% of Texas Instruments's Geophysical Services (GSI) and Geosource, another geophysical service company (1988). Halliburton also bought Gearhart Industries (wireline services) and merged it with Welex to form Halliburton Logging Services. It purchased the remaining interest in GSI in 1991.

Halliburton opened an office in Moscow in 1991 and has established joint enterprises throughout the former Soviet Union. Later that same year Brown & Root was chosen by Tokyo-based Sanpo Land Industrial as the prime contractor for an $8 billion luxury resort to be located near Nagoya, Japan.

In 1993 the company signed a joint venture agreement with China National Petroleum Corporation to provide oil and gas field equipment and services.

THE TEXAS 500

NYSE symbol: HAL
Fiscal year ends: December 31

WHO

Chairman and CEO: Thomas H. Cruikshank, age 61, $800,000 pay
President: Dale P. Jones, age 56, $500,000 pay
VC: W. Bernard Pieper, age 61, $487,956 pay
Chairman and CEO, Halliburton Energy Services: Alan A. Baker, age 60, $435,000 pay
President and CEO, Brown & Root, Inc.: Tommy E. Knight, age 54, $419,391
VP Finance: Jerry H. Blurton, age 48
VP Administration (Personnel): Karen S. Stuart
VP Legal: Robert M. Kennedy
Auditors: Arthur Andersen & Co.

WHERE

HQ: 3600 Lincoln Plaza, Dallas, TX 75201
Phone: 214-978-2600
Fax: 214-978-2611

Halliburton conducts business in the US and in over 100 foreign countries.

	1992 Sales $ mil.	% of total	1992 Operating Income $ mil.	% of total
US	4,017	61	(22)	—
Europe	1,090	17	(5)	—
Other countries	1,459	22	(53)	—
Adjustments	(41)	—	203	—
Total	**6,525**	**100**	**123**	**100**

WHAT

	1992 Sales $ mil.	% of total	1992 Operating Income $ mil.	% of total
Energy services	2,726	42	119	64
Engineering & construction	3,564	54	71	38
Insurance services	276	4	(5)	(2)
Adjustments	(41)	—	(62)	—
Total	**6,525**	**100**	**123**	**100**

Selected Businesses

Halliburton Energy Services
Halliburton Geodata, Ltd. (measurement-while-drilling and surface data logging)
Halliburton Geophysical Services, Inc. (seismic data collection and data processing services)
Halliburton Reservoir Services (well testing and reservoir evaluation)
Halliburton Resource Management (rental equipment for compression, processing, and conditioning)
Halliburton Services (cementing, stimulation, and water control)
Jet Research Center (explosive charges for well perforation)

Engineering and Construction Services
Brown & Root, Inc.

Insurance Services
Highlands Insurance Co. (casualty, property, surety, and marine insurance)

KEY COMPETITORS

ABB	FMC	Schlumberger
Ashland	General Electric	Siemens
Baker Hughes	Litton Industries	Union Pacific
Bechtel	McDermott	Westinghouse
CSX	Ogden	WMX Technologies
Duke Power	Peter Kiewit Sons'	Other insurance
Fluor	Raytheon	companies

HOW MUCH

	9-Year Growth	1983	1984	1985	1986	1987	1988	1989	1990	1991	1992
Sales ($ mil.)	1.9%	5,511	5,428	4,781	3,527	3,836	4,826	5,660	6,905	6,976	6,525
Net income ($ mil.)	—	315	330	29	(515)	48	85	134	197	27	(124)
Income as % of sales	—	5.7%	6.1%	0.6%	(14.6%)	1.3%	1.8%	2.4%	2.9%	0.4%	(1.9%)
Earnings per share ($)	—	2.66	2.87	0.27	(4.85)	0.45	0.81	1.26	1.8	0.33	(1.02)
Stock price – high ($)	—	47.25	44.00	33.88	28.00	43.13	36.50	44.50	58.75	55.25	36.88
Stock price – low ($)	—	29.25	27.13	24.50	17.38	20.13	24.38	27.50	38.75	25.50	21.75
Stock price – close ($)	(3.7%)	40.38	28.50	27.50	24.38	24.75	28.00	42.75	45.63	28.50	28.75
P/E – high	—	18	15	125	—	96	45	35	32	167	—
P/E – low	—	11	9	91	—	45	30	22	21	77	—
Dividends per share ($)	(5.4%)	1.65	1.80	1.80	1.20	1.00	1.00	1.00	1.00	1.00	1.00
Book value per share ($)	(5.7%)	30.18	31.19	26.30	20.30	19.76	19.80	19.90	21.04	20.23	17.79
Employees	(0.6%)	73,165	67,540	64,955	46,909	48,600	61,400	65,500	77,000	73,400	69,200

1992 Year-end:
Debt ratio: 25.6%
Return on equity: —
Cash (mil.): $256
Current ratio: —
Long-term debt (mil.): $603
No. of shares (mil.): 107
Dividends:
  1992 average yield: 3.5%
  1992 payout: —
Market value (mil.): $3,082

Stock Price History High/Low 1983–92

THE TEXAS 500

HOUSTON INDUSTRIES INCORPORATED

RANK: 24

OVERVIEW

Electricity is what runs the engine at Houston Industries, but the company pours a mixture of cable television and utility services into the tank as well. The company's largest operation, Houston Lighting & Power (HL&P), provides electric service to over 1.4 million customers in a 5,000-square-mile area on the Texas Gulf Coast. With milder-than-normal temperatures in HL&P's operating areas, Houston Industries net income was down 18% in 1992.

KBLCOM, the company's cable television subsidiary, serves nearly 1.5 million customers through KBL Cable and through Paragon Communications, a partnership with Time Warner Entertainment. KBLCOM narrowed its losses in 1992 (losses related to the costs of its 1986 start-up) and expects to show its first profit in 1994. Utility Fuels, which operates the 2nd largest private fleet of coal-carrying rail cars in the US, provides coal supply services to HL&P and railcar leasing and power plant services to other customers.

Houston Industries made its first foray into the international power market in 1992 as part of a consortium that bought 51% of an electric distribution system in Argentina. In 1993 the company formed a new subsidiary, Houston Industries Energy, to handle its Argentine operations and to pursue domestic and international independent natural gas power projects.

WHEN

Houston Industries was formed as a holding company in 1976, but its history, through HL&P, goes back to the 19th century. The company's earliest predecessor, Houston Electric Lighting and Power, was formed in 1882 by a group including Emanuel Raphael, cashier at Houston Savings Bank, and Mayor William R. Baker.

Faced with financial difficulties, the company changed hands a number of times, with affiliates of General Electric owning the company twice. GE's financial arm, United Electric Securities Company, took control of the company in 1901. That same year the company became Houston Lighting and Power. United Electric sold HL&P in 1906. In 1922 National Power & Light Company bought HL&P. NP&L was a subsidiary of Electric Bond & Share Company, which in turn was a public utility holding company that had been spun off by General Electric.

HL&P became an independent company in 1942 when National Power & Light was forced to sell it in order to comply with the 1935 Public Utility Holding Company Act.

Following WWII, HL&P began a major expansion of its power supply to meet the growing demands of the booming petroleum industry. The company continued its expansion during the 1950s and 1960s. HL&P also built a "power highway" connecting it with other Texas utilities from the Red River to the Gulf of Mexico.

Beginning in the 1970s HL&P began looking into nuclear energy as a way to meet its growing power needs. In 1973 HL&P became managing partner (with 30.8% ownership) in a joint venture to build a nuclear power plant on the Texas Gulf Coast. Construction on the South Texas Project, with partners Central Power and Light Company and the cities of Austin and San Antonio, began in 1975 and was scheduled for completion in 1982. Its price tag was estimated at under $1 billion.

By 1980 the plant was 4 years behind schedule, and soon the lawsuits began flying. In 1982 HL&P and its partners sued construction company Brown & Root, receiving a $700 million settlement in 1985. In 1983 the city of Austin sued HL&P for $419 million in damages. HL&P won that suit in 1989. The power plant finally began commercial operation in 1988, with final cost estimated at $5.8 billion.

In the meantime the company had to tend to other business. In 1986 it diversified into cable television, forming The Enrcom (later Paragon Communications) in a joint venture with American Television and Communications Corp., a subsidiary of Time Inc. In 1988 Houston Industries bought Canadian cable company Rogers Communications for $1.27 billion.

In 1993 the Nuclear Regulatory Commission put the South Texas Project on its "Watch List" of troubled plants (which calls for increased inspections) after both units at the plant went out of service because of technical problems. HL&P plans to have the units back on line in early 1994.

NYSE symbol: HOU
Fiscal year ends: December 31

WHO

Chairman and CEO: Don D. Jordan, age 60, $785,125 pay
President and COO: Don D. Sykora, age 62, $523,417 pay (prior to promotion)
President and COO, HL&P: R. Steve Ledbetter, age 44
VP; President and COO, KBLCOM: Gary G. Weik, age 47, $325,000 pay
VP, General Counsel, and Corporate Secretary: Hugh Rice Kelly, age 50, $297,583 pay
VP and Treasurer: William A. Cropper, age 53
VP Human Resources: Susan D. Fabre, age 37
Auditors: Deloitte & Touche

WHERE

HQ: 5 Post Oak Park, 4400 Post Oak Parkway, Houston, TX 77027
Phone: 713-629-3000
Fax: 713-629-3129

Houston Lighting & Power has 11 electric generating stations serving its Houston-area customers. Utility Fuels buys and transports coal primarily from the Powder River Basin of Wyoming. KBLCOM operates cable systems in San Antonio and Laredo, Texas; Minneapolis, Minnesota; Portland, Oregon; and Orange County, California. Through Paragon it serves cable customers in Arizona, California, Florida, Maine, New Hampshire, New York, and Texas.

WHAT

	1992 Sales $ mil.	% of total	1992 Operating Income $ mil.	% of total
Electricity sales & utility services	4,359	95	924	98
Cable television	237	5	19	2
Adjustments	—	—	(1)	—
Total	**4,596**	**100**	**942**	**100**

1992 Electricity Sales	$ mil.	% of total
Residential	1,466	40
Commercial	926	25
Industrial	1,135	31
Street lighting	23	—
Sales to other utilities	27	—
Other	133	4
Total	**3,710**	**100**

1992 Fuel Sources	% of total
Coal and lignite	39
Natural gas	34
Nuclear	9
Other, including purchased power	18
Total	**100**

KEY COMPETITORS

Capital Cities/ABC
Cox
Duke Power
FPL
General Electric
Hallmark
Knight-Ridder
Pacific Enterprises

Pacific Gas and Electric
Southern Co.
SCEcorp
TCI
Time Warner
Times Mirror
Viacom
Westinghouse

HOW MUCH

	Annual Growth	1983	1984	1985	1986	1987	1988	1989	1990	1991	1992
Sales ($ mil.)	1.6%	3,993	4,182	4,062	3,536	3,628	3,650	3,790	4,179	4,444	4,596
Net income ($ mil.)	1.8%	324	391	461	452	466	431	458	387	464	380
Income as % of sales	—	8.1%	9.3%	11.3%	12.8%	12.9%	11.8%	12.1%	9.3%	10.4%	8.3%
Earnings per share ($)	(3.0%)	3.49	3.80	4.13	3.81	3.74	3.34	3.32	2.67	3.28	2.63
Stock price – high ($)	—	24.25	22.50	29.50	37.00	39.38	33.88	35.88	37.13	44.38	46.88
Stock price – low ($)	—	19.00	17.63	21.75	27.25	26.50	26.63	26.75	30.63	34.63	40.13
Stock price – close ($)	10.1%	19.38	22.50	28.00	34.75	30.00	28.00	35.00	36.75	44.25	45.88
P/E – high	—	7	6	7	10	11	10	11	14	14	18
P/E – low	—	5	5	5	7	7	8	8	11	11	15
Dividends per share ($)	3.0%	2.28	2.44	2.60	2.76	2.86	2.94	2.96	2.96	2.96	2.98
Book value per share ($)	0.7%	23.79	24.95	25.88	27.19	28.33	28.75	29.05	28.45	26.63	25.36
Employees	0.1%	—	—	—	—	11,506	11,599	12,878	13,084	13,289	11,576

1992 Year-end:
Debt ratio: 59.4%
Return on equity: 10.1%
Cash (mil.): $71
Current ratio: 0.42
Long-term debt (mil.): $4,441
No. of shares (mil.): 130
Dividends:
  1992 average yield: 6.5%
  1992 payout: 113.3%
Market value (mil.): $5,942

Stock Price History High/Low 1983–92

THE TEXAS 500

KIMBERLY-CLARK CORPORATION

RANK: 12

OVERVIEW

In the diaper world, #2 has never been too popular, but that's where Kimberly-Clark stands in market share (29% to Procter & Gamble's 43%) in the $4 billion US diaper market these days. Huggies disposable diapers are the Dallas-based company's best-selling product, but in the US Kimberly-Clark is also known for its Kleenex and Kotex brand consumer products, controlling 46% of the US facial tissue market and 37% of the feminine pad market in 1992. The company also makes Depend incontinence care products and Pull-Ups training pants.

Besides personal products, Kimberly-Clark also makes and markets health care products, including disposable surgical gowns, masks, and related products. The company's commercial products include Neenah business paper, cigarette papers, and newsprint. Through K-C Aviation the company also operates Milwaukee-based airline Midwest Express and 2 aircraft maintenance facilities.

The company introduced UltraTrim, a super-absorbent diaper, in 1992, well ahead of Procter & Gamble, which was still test marketing its version in 1993. But Kimberly-Clark also must look over its shoulder at cheaper, private-label diaper brands that continue to carve out market share.

In 1993 Kimberly-Clark announced plans to enter the disposable diaper and training pants market in Europe. However, the company has faced toubles in Europe recently. In 1992, as part of streamlining, it cut 800 jobs in Europe (and another 100 in North America) and took a $172 million restructuring charge, putting a serious dent in its net income. Also, a proposed consumer paper products joint venture with Germany's VP-Schickedanz fell through in 1992.

WHEN

In 1872 John Kimberly, Charles Clark, Havilah Babcock, and Frank Shattuck founded Kimberly, Clark & Company in Neenah, Wisconsin, to manufacture newsprint from rags. After incorporating as Kimberly & Clark Company (1880), the company built a pulp and paper plant on the Fox River (1889). The town of Kimberly, Wisconsin, formed as a result of the plant and was named in John Kimberly's honor.

In 1914 the company developed cellucotton, a cotton substitute used by the US army as surgical cotton during WWI. Army nurses began using cellucotton pads as disposable sanitary napkins, and in 1920 the company introduced Kotex, the first disposable feminine hygiene product. Kleenex, the first throw-away handkerchief, followed in 1924, and soon many Americans were referring to all sanitary napkins and facial tissues as Kotex and Kleenex, respectively. In 1926, the company joined with the New York Times Company to build a newsprint mill (now Spruce Falls Power and Paper) in Ontario. In 1928 the company adopted its present name and was listed on the NYSE.

Kimberly-Clark expanded internationally during the 1950s, opening plants in Mexico, Germany, and the UK. During the 1960s the company began operations in 17 more foreign locations.

Before retiring in 1971, Guy Minard (CEO since 1968) sold the 4 mills that handled Kimberly-Clark's unprofitable coated-paper business and entered the paper towel and disposable diaper markets. Minard's successor, Darwin Smith, introduced Kimbies diapers in 1968, but they leaked and were withdrawn from the market. An improved version of Kimbies came out in 1976, followed by Huggies, a premium-priced diaper with elastic leg bands, in 1978.

From its corporate flight department, the company formed Midwest Express Airlines in 1984. Smith moved Kimberly-Clark's headquarters from Neenah to Dallas in 1985. From 1988 to 1989 he served as chairman and president of the King Ranch while still acting as chief executive of Kimberly-Clark.

In 1991 Kimberly-Clark, along with the New York Times Company, sold Spruce Falls Power and Paper. Smith retired as chairman in 1992. Wayne Sanders, who was largely responsible for designing Huggies Pull-Ups (introduced in 1989) succeeded Smith. Also in 1992 Procter & Gamble settled out of court with Kimberly-Clark for an undisclosed sum. P&G had been charged with trying to illegally dominate the US diaper market. In 1993 Midwest Express Airlines added service from Milwaukee to Cleveland and Columbus, Ohio, and Las Vegas, Nevada.

78 THE TEXAS 500

NYSE symbol: KMB
Fiscal year ends: December 31

WHO

Chairman and CEO: Wayne R. Sanders, age 45, $987,400 pay
EVP: James G. Grosklaus, age 58, $524,000 pay
EVP: James D. Bernd, age 60, $521,500 pay
EVP: James P. McCauley, age 54, $455,000 pay
EVP, Infant and Child Care: Thomas J. Falk, age 34
SVP Law and Government Affairs: O. George Everbach, age 54
SVP and Principal Finance Officer: John W. Donehower
Auditors: Deloitte & Touche

WHERE

HQ: PO Box 619100, DFW Airport Station, Dallas, TX 75261-9100
Phone: 214-830-1200
Fax: 214-830-1289

Kimberly-Clark has manufacturing plants in 19 US states and 19 foreign countries. Kleenex is sold in 150 countries.

	1992 Sales $ mil.	% of total	1992 Operating Income $ mil.	% of total
US	5,297	72	720	89
Canada	587	8	(3)	—
Europe	1,017	14	25	3
Other countries	444	6	66	8
Adjustments	(254)	—	(15)	—
Total	**7,091**	**100**	**793**	**100**

WHAT

	1992 Sales $ mil.	% of total	1992 Operating Income $ mil.	% of total
Consumer & service products	5,782	81	650	80
Newsprint & paper	1,061	15	143	18
Air transportation	299	4	15	2
Adjustments	(51)	—	(15)	—
Total	**7,091**	**100**	**793**	**100**

Consumer and Service Products
Baby wipes (Huggies)
Bathroom tissue (Delsey, Kleenex)
Commercial wipes (Kimwipes)
Disposable diapers and training pants (Huggies, Pull-Ups, UltraTrim)
Disposable surgical gowns and accessories (Kimguard)
Facial tissue (Kleenex)
Feminine hygiene products (Kotex, New Freedom, Lightdays, Anyday)
Incontinence products (Depend, Poise)
Paper napkins (Kleenex)
Paper towels (Hi-Dri)
Pulp

Newsprint and Paper
Business and writing papers (Neenah)
Newsprint
Printing papers
Technical papers
Tobacco industry papers

Air Transportation
Midwest Express Airlines

KEY COMPETITORS

Alco Standard
America West
American Cyanamid
AMR
Boise Cascade
Canadian Pacific
Champion International
Fletcher Challenge
Georgia-Pacific
Gerber
International Paper
ITT
James River
Johnson & Johnson
Mead
Procter & Gamble
Scott
Southwest
Stone Container
Weyerhaeuser

HOW MUCH

	9-Year Growth	1983	1984	1985	1986	1987	1988	1989	1990	1991	1992
Sales ($ mil.)	9.0%	3,274	3,616	4,073	4,303	4,885	5,394	5,734	6,407	6,777	7,091
Net income ($ mil.)	6.9%	189	218	267	269	325	379	424	432	508	345
Income as % of sales	—	5.8%	6.0%	6.6%	6.3%	6.7%	7.0%	7.4%	6.7%	7.5%	4.9%
Earnings per share ($)	8.3%	1.05	1.19	1.45	1.47	1.87	2.36	2.63	2.70	3.18	2.15
Stock price – high ($)	—	12.38	12.19	17.50	23.16	31.63	32.88	37.69	42.88	52.25	63.25
Stock price – low ($)	—	8.22	9.84	11.25	15.84	19.69	23.06	28.69	30.75	38.00	46.25
Stock price – close ($)	19.9%	11.50	11.91	16.75	19.97	25.00	29.13	36.75	42.00	50.69	59.00
P/E – high	—	12	10	12	16	17	14	14	16	16	29
P/E – low	—	8	8	8	11	11	10	11	11	12	22
Dividends per share ($)	13.5%	0.53	0.55	0.58	0.62	0.72	0.80	1.30	1.36	1.52	1.64
Book value per share ($)	5.8%	8.20	8.60	9.52	10.44	9.80	11.58	12.93	14.14	15.74	13.63
Employees	2.7%	33,836	35,284	36,648	36,490	37,357	38,328	39,664	39,954	41,286	42,902

1992 Year-end:
Debt ratio: 39.7%
Return on equity: 14.6%
Cash (mil.): $41
Current ratio: 0.92
Long-term debt (mil.): $995
No. of shares (mil.): 161
Dividends:
  1992 average yield: 2.8%
  1992 payout: 76.3%
Market value (mil.): $9,485

Stock Price History High/Low 1983–92

THE TEXAS 500

LYONDELL PETROCHEMICAL COMPANY

RANK: 20

OVERVIEW

Lyondell, one of the US's largest chemical companies, is an integrated petrochemical and petroleum processor and manufacturer. Its petrochemical products are used in a variety of applications, including trash bags, upholstery, and adhesives. Lyondell's petroleum products include gasoline and jet fuel. The company, a former subsidiary of Atlantic Richfield, was spun off to the public in 1989. ARCO still owns 49.9% of Lyondell.

Lyondell has built a reputation for flexibility, taking maximum advantage of the open market for crude supply and for petrochemical demand. CEO Bob Gower also has a reputation for listening to his workers' input, and employee ideas have saved the company an estimated $40 million annually.

As part of its strategy of upgrading its facilities, in 1993 Lyondell signed a joint venture agreement with Citgo Petroleum, a subsidiary of Petróleos de Venezuela. The deal calls for Citgo to provide most of the money needed for a $500 million upgrade of Lyondell's refinery in exchange for an interest in the plant.

Lyondell's sales dropped 16% in 1992, as both the refining and petrochemical industries faced lower prices and oversupply.

WHEN

It wasn't exactly a model of efficiency. Located 16 miles apart on the Texas Gulf Coast, Atlantic Richfield's Houston refinery and its Channelview petrochemical complex were run by offices in Los Angeles and Philadelphia, respectively.

The operations were losing ground in the competitive Gulf Coast market, and ARCO Chemical was contemplating selling the petrochemical complex. However, Bob Gower, a senior vice-president of planning, convinced the company that the 2 Houston-area properties could be run together. In 1985 ARCO set up Lyondell Petrochemical Corporation (soon changed to Lyondell Petrochemical Company) as a wholly owned division, with Bob Gower as CEO.

The refining facility that Gower and Lyondell got dated back to 1919, when Sinclair Oil & Refining Company had built a crude oil refinery in Houston. What was to become Lyondell's petrochemical complex was a petrochemical plant built on the Lyondell Country Club in Channelview by Texas Butadiene and Chemical Corporation in 1955. Sinclair Petrochemical, a subsidiary of Sinclair Oil, which had become a subsidiary of Richfield Oil Corporation in 1936, bought the petrochemical plant in 1962.

In 1966 Richfield and Atlantic Refining Company merged. Following the merger, the refinery became part of ARCO Products Company and the petrochemicals plant joined ARCO Chemical Company.

Like the facilities that were to make up Lyondell, Bob Gower's roots were in Sinclair Oil, where he had started as a research scientist. When ARCO Chemical was considering selling the petrochemical complex, Gower argued that there were synergies between the refinery and the petrochemical plant that could be exploited. The plant used inputs such as gas oil produced at the refinery, and the refinery used by-products such as gasoline produced by the plant.

Gower proved to be right. By the 4th quarter of its first year Lyondell was showing a profit. From the beginning Gower focused on making Lyondell flexible and efficient. The company upgraded its refinery so it could handle any kind of crude oil in the world. Also, following the spinoff, Gower reduced Lyondell's work force by over 1,000 workers (including 75% of management) through voluntary layoffs. The move cut layers of management, allowing the company to react more quickly to changes in market prices.

With Lyondell's profits jumping 341% between 1987 and 1988, ARCO decided to sell the company to the public. In 1989 ARCO sold 50% of Lyondell in an IPO worth $1.4 billion. However, before the sale ARCO had Lyondell pay it $500 million, leaving the fledgling company saddled with debt.

Lyondell persevered, and during 1989 the company upgraded its petrochemicals facilities to increase capacity. In 1990 the company acquired 2 chemical plants from Rexene Products Company.

In 1992 Lyondell became the first major US refiner to recycle used motor oil into gasoline. In 1993 the company entered into an agreement with CDTECH to develop its petrochemical technologies.

THE TEXAS 500

NYSE symbol: LYO
Fiscal year ends: December 31

WHO

Chairman: Robert E. Wycoff, age 62
President and CEO: Bob G. Gower, age 55, $527,215 pay
SVP Manufacturing and Supply: William E. Haynes, age 49, $208,800 pay
SVP, CFO, and Treasurer: Russell S. Young, age 44, $186,722 pay
VP, General Counsel, and Secretary: Jeffrey R. Pendergraft, age 44, $213,277 pay
VP Marketing and Sales, Polymers and Petroleum Products: Robert H. Isé, age 58, $193,519 pay
VP Petrochemicals Marketing and Business Services: David C. Vaughan, age 55
VP Refining Operations: John P. Yoars, age 49
VP Human Resources: Richard W. Park, age 53
Auditor: Coopers & Lybrand

WHERE

HQ: 1221 McKinney St., Ste. 1600, Houston, TX 77010
Phone: 713-652-7200
Fax: 713-652-7430

Lyondell operates a petrochemical complex in Channelview, Texas, and a refinery on the Houston Ship Channel.

WHAT

	1992 Sales	
	$ mil.	% of total
Refined products	2,837	52
Petrochemicals	1,658	31
Crude oil resales	893	17
Adjustments	(583)	—
Total	**4,805**	**100**

Refined Products
Aromatics
Coke
Diesel fuel
Gasoline
Heating oil
Industrial lubricants
Jet fuel
Motor oils

Petrochemicals
Aromatics
Olefins
Oxygenated products
Polymers
Specialty products

KEY COMPETITORS

Amerada Hess
Amoco
Ashland
Atlantic Richfield
British Petroleum
Broken Hill
Chevron
Coastal
DuPont
Elf Aquitaine
Exxon
Hauser Chemical
Imperial Oil
Koch
Mobil
Norsk Hydro

Occidental
Oryx
PDVSA
PEMEX
Pennzoil
Petrobrás
Petrofina
Phillips Petroleum
Repsol
Royal Dutch/Shell
Sun
Texaco
Total
Unocal
USX

HOW MUCH

	Annual Growth	1983	1984	1985	1986	1987	1988	1989	1990	1991	1992
Sales ($ mil.)	8.1%	—	—	—	3,010	3,931	4,696	5,358	6,495	5,729	4,805
Net income ($ mil.)	(23.3%)	—	—	—	128	123	543	374	356	222	26
Income as % of sales	—	—	—	—	4.2%	3.1%	11.6%	7.0%	5.5%	3.9%	0.5%
Earnings per share ($)	(59.1%)	—	—	—	—	—	—	4.67	4.45	2.78	0.32
Stock price – high ($)	—	—	—	—	—	—	—	33.50	21.50	26.13	25.88
Stock price – low ($)	—	—	—	—	—	—	—	16.75	13.13	14.63	21.13
Stock price – close ($)	4.6%	—	—	—	—	—	—	21.50	14.63	22.63	24.63
P/E – high	—	—	—	—	—	—	—	7	5	9	81
P/E – low	—	—	—	—	—	—	—	4	3	5	66
Dividends per share ($)	—	—	—	—	—	—	0.00	1.20	4.10	1.75	1.80
Book value per share ($)	—	—	—	—	—	—	2.98	0.11	0.48	1.53	(0.08)
Employees	3.2%	—	—	—	1,911	1,874	2,000	2,200	2,250	2,270	2,312

1992 Year-end:
Debt ratio: 100.8%
Return on equity: 44.1%
Cash (mil.): $121
Current ratio: 1.65
Long-term debt (mil.): $725
No. of shares (mil.): 80
Dividends:
  1992 average yield: 7.3%
  1992 payout: —
Market value (mil.): $1,970

Stock Price History High/Low 1989–92

THE TEXAS 500

MARATHON GROUP

RANK: 6

OVERVIEW

USX-Marathon Group is one of 3 groups (along with USX-US Steel Group and USX-Delhi Group) that were created by USX when it split its holdings into separate stock offerings. The Marathon Group's largest holding is Houston-based Marathon Oil, the nation's 11th largest oil and gas company. Other group companies include Emro Marketing and Carnegie Natural Gas.

Marathon Oil is an integrated energy company with operations ranging from exploration to marketing. It sells its products through Marathon-brand retailers and other outlets. The group's companies are also involved in natural gas transportation and liquefied natural gas operations. Marathon also owns 32% of the US's only deep-water oil port, off the coast of Louisiana.

Marathon has focused on increasing production recently. One of its most important developments is the East Brae field in the UK's North Sea, where it is scheduled to begin oil production in late 1993. Major oil and gas discoveries in the Gulf of Mexico are slated to start producing in 1995. Marathon is also negotiating a production agreement with the Russian government for oil and natural gas off the coast of Sakhalin Island.

Like most of its competitors in the slumping US petroleum industry, Marathon has faced hard times recently. Net income has fallen more than 73% over the past 2 years.

WHEN

Marathon was founded in 1887, as The Ohio Oil Company, by a group of 14 independent Ohio oil producers who joined together to better compete with the dominant purchaser of the time, Standard Oil. The partnership worked so well that within 2 years Ohio Oil was the largest producer in the state, a fact that did not go unnoticed at Standard Oil headquarters. Standard Oil bought out Ohio Oil in 1889.

When Standard Oil was ordered broken up by the US Supreme Court in 1911, Ohio Oil became independent once again. Led by new president James Donnell, the company soon began to expand its exploration activities to Wyoming, Kansas, Louisiana, and Texas.

One major discovery in Texas almost never happened. In 1924 Ohio Oil agreed to drill 3 wells on leases west of the Pecos River. By mistake, it drilled 3 dry holes on leases east of the river. Ohio Oil planned to abandon the properties, until a geologist reported the error. Drilled in the right place, the wells flowed voluminously. Also in 1924 the company acquired Lincoln Oil Refining — its first venture outside crude oil production.

O. D. Donnell became president of the company following his father's death in 1927 and continued the company's expansion into refining and marketing operations.

Following WWII a 3rd generation of Donnells took the helm of the company. J. C. Donnell II led Ohio Oil's foray into international exploration. Through Conorada Petroleum Corporation, a partnership with Continental Oil (now Conoco) and Amerada Hess, the company explored Africa and South and Central America. Conorada's biggest overseas deal came in 1955 when it acquired concessions on over 60 million acres in Libya.

In 1962 Ohio Oil acquired Plymouth Oil, including its producing properties, a refinery in Texas City, and transportation, distribution, and marketing facilities, for over $100 million. Also in 1962 the company changed its name to Marathon Oil Company, although it had been using the Marathon name in its marketing activities since the late 1930s.

In 1976 Marathon added a 200,000-barrel-a-day refinery in Louisiana to its operations when it acquired ECOL Ltd. for $403 million.

Following a battle with Mobil, US Steel acquired Marathon in 1982 for $6.5 billion. In 1986 US Steel changed its name to USX and acquired Texas Oil & Gas for $3.6 billion. Also that year the US government introduced economic sanctions against Libya, putting Marathon's Libyan holdings in suspension.

In 1990 USX consolidated Texas Oil with Marathon. Following a protracted battle with corporate raider Carl Icahn, USX split Marathon and US Steel into 2 separate stock classes in 1991. In 1992 USX created a 3rd offering, USX-Dehli Group. The pipeline operator had previously been a part of the Marathon Group.

In 1993 the UK Department of Trade & Industry awarded Marathon Oil 2 licenses to explore off the coast of Wales.

82   THE TEXAS 500

NYSE symbol: MRO
Fiscal year ends: December 31

WHO

VC, Marathon Group; President, Marathon Oil:
Victor G. Beghini, age 58, $698,167 pay
EVP Refining, Marketing, and Transportation, Marathon Oil: J. Louis Frank, age 56
EVP Exploration and Production, Marathon Oil:
Carl P. Giardini, age 57
SVP Finance and Accounting, Marathon Oil:
Jimmy D. Low, age 55
SVP Administration and Services, Marathon Oil:
James H. Brannigan, age 60
General Counsel and Secretary, Marathon Oil:
William F. Schwind, Jr., age 48
Director Human Resources, Marathon Oil:
Kenneth L. Matheny
Auditors: Price Waterhouse

WHERE

HQ: Marathon Oil Company, 5555 San Felipe Rd., Houston, TX 77253-3128
Phone: 713-629-6600
Fax: 713-871-0728

Marathon conducts exploration and development activities in 14 countries. The group also operates 5 refineries in the US and sells petroleum products in 2,290 Marathon-brand retail outlets and in 1,541 retail outlets operated by Emro Marketing Company.

WHAT

	1992 Sales $ mil.	% of total
Refined products & merchandise	6,629	52
Liquid hydrocarbons	832	6
Crude oil & refined products buy/sell agreements	2,537	20
Natural gas	581	5
Excise taxes	1,655	13
Other	548	4
Total	**12,782**	**100**

Selected Subsidiaries and Affiliates
Carnegie Natural Gas Company
CLAM Petroleum Company (the Netherlands, 50%)
Emro Marketing Company
FWA Drilling Company, Inc.
LOCAP INC. (pipeline & storage facilities, 37%)
LOOP INC. (offshore oil port, 32%)
Kenai LNG Corporation (30%)
Marathon Oil UK, Ltd.
Marathon Pipe Line Company

Selected Brand Names
Bonded
Cheker
Ecol
Gastown
Marathon
Speedway
Starvin' Marvin
United

KEY COMPETITORS

Amerada Hess	Elf Aquitaine	Pennzoil
Amoco	Exxon	Phillips
Ashland	Koch	Petroleum
Associated Natural Gas	Mobil	Royal Dutch/ Shell
British Petroleum	Norsk Hydro	
Chevron	Occidental	Southland
Circle K	Oryx	Sun
Coastal	PDVSA	Texaco
	PEMEX	Total

HOW MUCH

	Annual Growth	1983	1984	1985	1986	1987	1988	1989	1990	1991	1992
Sales ($ mil.)	6.5%	—	—	—	—	—	9,949	12,264	14,616	13,975	12,782
Net income ($ mil.)	19.8%	—	—	—	—	—	53	425	508	(71)	109
Income as % of sales	—	—	—	—	—	—	5.3%	3.5%	3.5%	(0.5%)	0.9%
Earnings per share ($)	—	—	—	—	—	—	—	—	—	(0.31)	0.37
Stock price – high ($)	—	—	—	—	—	—	—	—	—	33.13	24.75
Stock price – low ($)	—	—	—	—	—	—	—	—	—	20.88	15.75
Stock price – close ($)	—	—	—	—	—	—	—	—	—	20.50	17.25
P/E – high	—	—	—	—	—	—	—	—	—	—	67
P/E – low	—	—	—	—	—	—	—	—	—	—	43
Dividends per share ($)	—	—	—	—	—	—	—	—	—	1.31	1.22
Book value per share ($)	—	—	—	—	—	—	—	—	—	12.45	11.37
Employees	1.0%	—	—	—	—	—	23,772	25,762	26,200	24,762	22,810

1992 Year-end:
Debt ratio: 54.9%
Return on equity: 33.7%
Cash (mil.): $35
Current ratio: 0.85
Long-term debt (mil.): $3743
No. of shares (mil.): 283
Dividends:
  1992 average yield: 0.7%
  1992 payout: 329.7%
Market value (mil.): $4,890

Stock Price History
High/Low 1991–92

THE TEXAS 500

J. C. PENNEY COMPANY, INC.

RANK: 3

OVERVIEW

Sears's loss is J. C. Penney's gain. The closure of Sears's catalog operations will force millions of loyal catalog shoppers to turn elsewhere for mail-order purchases, and Penney, which published over 70 catalogs in 1992, is prepared to take up the slack. Penney is the 4th largest retailer in the US (after Wal-Mart, Kmart, and Sears), operating over 1,200 department stores and more than 500 Thrift Drug and Treasury Drug stores throughout all 50 states and Puerto Rico. Catalog sales accounted for 17% of 1992 revenues.

The company has been changing its historical image as a discount dime store, targeting upper-middle-class consumers by adding brand-name apparel and dropping many hard goods (appliances, furniture, and automotive products). Today's stores emphasize apparel, shoes, jewelry, and home furnishings. Lately, a focus on developing proprietary brands has produced favorable results, notably in the women's apparel division — which, as other clothing retailers moved toward casual wear, nimbly filled the career-wear gap with its Worthington brands — and in its home soft-goods and hard-goods lines. Unlike many competitors, Penney purchases all materials for each such line from the same supplier to ensure color and texture coordination.

In 1990 and 1991 the recession contributed to flat sales. But when other retailers adopted discount merchandising tactics, Penney stayed on course, pricing its products moderately and even introducing a bit of upscale flair to its mix. Sales rebounded by 10% in 1992 over 1991, and same-store sales climbed 11%.

Penney also operates an insurance company and a credit bank.

WHEN

In 1902 James Cash Penney (1875–1971) and 2 former employers opened The Golden Rule, a dry goods store, in Kemmerer, Wyoming. Buying out his partners in 1907, Penney opened stores in small communities and sold high-demand soft goods. He based customer service policy on his Baptist heritage, holding employees (called "associates") to a high moral code. Managers, usually former sales clerks, were offered 1/3 partnerships in the stores.

The company incorporated in Utah in 1913 as the J. C. Penney Company, with headquarters in Salt Lake City, but moved to New York City in 1914 to aid buying and financial operations. During the 1920s the company expanded to nearly 1,400 stores and publicly offered stock in 1929. By 1951 sales in the more than 1,600 stores had surpassed $1 billion. A company study of consumer trends led the chain to introduce credit plans (1958; in all stores, 1962) and hard goods (1963).

Through the purchase of General Merchandise Company (1962, Milwaukee, mail-order catalog and Treasure Island discount stores; renamed The Treasury; sold 1981), the company established a catalog service (1963). JCPenney Insurance started from companies bought in the mid-1960s. The company bought Thrift Drug in 1969 and in 1968 began expanding overseas. In the 1970s Penney bought Sarma, a retail and supermarket chain in Belgium (1968; sold 1987).

The company bought First National Bank (Harrington, Delaware; 1983), renamed JCPenney National Bank (1984), to issue MasterCard and VISA cards. In the 1980s Penney discontinued automotive services and hard goods in stores and closed many downtown locations or moved them to suburban malls. Stores were classified as metropolitan or geographic (outside metropolitan areas).

The company entered the cable television shopping market (1987) through Telaction, an interactive home-shopping program (discontinued in 1989). Penney also established a joint venture with Shop Television Network (1987; purchased and renamed JCPenney Television Network, 1989; sold 1991). In 1988 JCPenney Telemarketing was started to take catalog phone orders and provide telemarketing services for other companies; the network is the largest privately owned telemarketing system in the US.

To cut expenses the company sold its 45-story headquarters in New York City and relocated to Dallas (1988), renting office space there until 1992, when it moved into its new headquarters in Plano, Texas. In 1993 Penney plans to add 25-30 new department stores and acquire additional national brands.

NYSE symbol: JCP
Fiscal year ends: Last Saturday in January

WHO

Chairman and CEO: William R. Howell, age 57, $1,526,402 pay
President, JCPenney Stores and Catalog: James E. Oesterreicher, age 51, $453,344 pay
EVP and CFO: Robert E. Northam, age 62, $547,526 pay
SEVP; Director Merchandising, Quality Assurance, and Distribution: W. Barger Tygart, age 57, $431,355 pay
EVP; Director Personnel and Administration: Richard T. Erickson, age 61, $406,383 pay
EVP; Director Support Services: Terry S. Prindiville, age 57
EVP; Director Merchandising: Thomas D. Hutchens, age 52
SVP, Secretary, and General Counsel: Charles R. Lotter, age 55
Auditors: KPMG Peat Marwick

WHERE

HQ: 6501 Legacy Dr., Plano, TX 75024-3698
Phone: 214-431-1000
Fax: 214-431-2212

J. C. Penney operates 1,266 JCPenney retail stores (totalling over 114 million square feet of selling space), 548 Thrift and Treasury drugstores (totalling over 5 million square feet of selling space), 640 freestanding catalog sales centers, and 6 catalog distribution centers throughout all 50 states and Puerto Rico.

WHAT

	1992 Sales	
	$ mil.	% of total
JCPenney stores	13,460	71
Catalog	3,166	17
Drug stores	1,383	7
Other	1,076	5
Total	**19,085**	**100**

	No. of Stores	% of Total
JCPenney stores	1,266	52
Drugstores	548	22
Catalog stores	640	26
Total	**2,454**	**100**

Subsidiaries and Operations
J. C. Penney Funding Corporation
J. C. Global Finance N. V. (Netherlands Antilles)
J. C. Penney Properties, Inc.
JCPenney Insurance Company, Inc.
JCPenney National Bank (VISA and MasterCard)
JCP Realty, Inc. (shopping center ventures)
JCP Receivables, Inc.
Thrift Drug, Inc.

KEY COMPETITORS

American Stores	Harcourt General	Merck
Ames	Jack Eckerd	Montgomery Ward
Carter Hawley Hale	Kmart	Nordstrom
Circuit City	Lands' End	Rite Aid
Costco Wholesale	The Limited	Sears
Dayton Hudson	Longs	Service Merchandise
Dillard	Macy	Spiegel
Federated	May	TJX
Fred Meyer	Melville	Walgreen
	Mercantile Stores	Wal-Mart

HOW MUCH

	9-Year Growth	1983	1984	1985	1986	1987	1988	1989	1990	1991	1992
Sales ($ mil.)	4.7%	12,647	14,038	14,418	15,443	16,008	15,938	17,045	17,410	17,295	19,085
Net income ($ mil.)	5.8%	467	435	397	530	608	807	802	577	264	777
Income as % of sales	—	3.7%	3.1%	2.8%	3.4%	3.8%	5.1%	4.7%	3.3%	1.5%	4.1%
Earnings per share ($)	7.3%	1.56	1.45	1.33	1.77	2.06	2.96	2.93	2.17	0.99	2.95
Stock price – high ($)	—	16.97	14.28	14.44	22.09	33.00	27.88	36.63	37.81	29.13	40.19
Stock price – low ($)	—	10.44	11.50	11.16	13.16	17.81	19.00	25.19	18.69	21.25	25.38
Stock price – close ($)	11.9%	14.16	11.59	13.88	18.06	21.69	25.31	36.38	22.13	27.50	38.88
P/E – high	—	11	10	11	13	16	9	13	17	30	14
P/E – low	—	7	8	8	7	9	6	9	9	22	9
Dividends per share ($)	10.4%	0.54	0.59	0.59	0.62	0.74	1.00	1.12	1.37	1.32	1.32
Book value per share ($)	5.3%	11.98	12.81	13.58	14.50	15.08	15.95	17.73	18.29	17.20	19.11
Employees	1.0%	175,000	180,000	177,000	176,000	181,000	190,000	198,000	196,000	185,000	192,000

1992 Year-end:
Debt ratio: 46.4%
Return on equity: 16.3%
Cash (mil.): $397
Current ratio: 2.27
Long-term debt (mil.): $3,171
No. of shares (mil.): 235
Dividends:
  1992 average yield: 3.4%
  1992 payout: 44.7%
Market value (mil.): $9,127

Stock Price History High/Low 1983–92

SHELL OIL COMPANY

RANK: 2

OVERVIEW

In the US, Shell Oil Company is the #3 seller of refined petroleum products, the #4 producer of crude oil and natural gas liquids, the #4 refinery processor, and the #6 producer of natural gas. The Houston-based company is a subsidiary of the world's leading petroleum and natural gas company (Royal Dutch/Shell Group). Shell Oil is 100% owned by Shell Petroleum, which is owned 60% by Royal Dutch Petroleum of the Netherlands and 40% by The "Shell" Transport and Trading Company of the UK.

Ranked #18 on *Fortune* magazine's 1993 list of the largest industrial companies in the US, Shell Oil is in the midst of a major restructuring aimed at making it the lowest-cost producer in the US. The company reduced the number of its employees from roughly 32,000 in 1990 to almost 25,000 by the end of 1992. As a result of this restructuring, debt has been reduced and net income has risen from $20 million in 1991 to $445 million in 1992. Results continued to improve in 1993, as the company reported that the first half of that year was the best since 1989.

Shell Oil searches for, develops, produces, purchases, transports, and markets crude oil and natural gas. It also manufactures, purchases, markets, and transports oil and chemical products. Although Shell Oil operates primarily in the US, its exploration and production activities also extend outside the country, sometimes in joint ventures with other subsidiaries of the Royal Dutch/Shell Group. Most of Shell Oil's US production of crude oil is in the Gulf of Mexico, California, West Texas, and along the Gulf Coast. Natural gas production is concentrated in South Texas, Michigan, and along the Gulf Coast.

At the end of 1992, Shell Oil had international reserves of 337 million crude oil equivalent barrels plus US reserves of more than 3 billion equivalent barrels.

WHEN

The Royal Dutch/Shell Group began importing gasoline from Sumatra to the US in 1912 to take advantage of the breakup of the Standard Oil trust and the expanding automobile industry. That year it formed American Gasoline in Seattle and Roxana Petroleum in Oklahoma. Refineries were established in New Orleans in 1916 and Wood River, Illinois, in 1918.

In 1922 Royal Dutch/Shell consolidated all of its US operations into a 65%-owned holding company, Shell Union Oil Co. Shell products were available in every state by 1929. That same year the company built a refinery in Houston.

During WWII the company shared its aviation fuel technology and produced chemicals used to make synthetic rubber. Shell Oil adopted its present corporate name in 1949.

Shell Oil moved its headquarters to Houston in 1970. In 1979 the company substantially boosted its oil reserves by acquiring Belridge Oil. The Royal Dutch/Shell Group acquired 100% of Shell Oil in 1985, but shareholders sued, claiming Shell Oil's assets were undervalued in the deal. In 1990 a judge awarded the shareholders $110 million.

An explosion in 1991 at Shell Oil's Norco, Louisiana, refinery crippled production and contributed to a 39% drop in profits. In mid-1991 the company announced cuts of 10–15% in its US work force, to be made over the next year. Stricter US environmental regulations have caused Shell Oil to reduce its activities in the US while looking overseas for new sources of oil. The company sold its 125,000-barrels-per-day refinery in Wilmington, California, in 1991 and is increasing its production in Syria and pursuing exploration efforts in Yemen and China.

Shell Oil exchanged its coal mining subsidiary for a 25% interest in the purchaser, Zeigler Coal Holding, in 1992. That same year the company entered a joint venture with PEMEX, the Mexican national oil company, concerning Shell Oil's Deer Park, Texas, refinery, in which Shell Oil will operate the facility while PEMEX will provide supplies of crude oil. Late in 1992 Shell Oil acquired the polyester resins business of Goodyear Tire and Rubber, including its principal product, polyethylene terephthalate (PET), used in the manufacture of food containers, beverage bottles, and other packaging materials.

In 1993 Frank Richardson retired as president and was succeeded by Philip Carroll, a 32-year Shell Oil veteran.

Wholly owned subsidiary
Fiscal year ends: December 31

WHO

President and CEO: Philip J. Carroll
President, Shell Chemical Company: Michael H. Grasley, age 56
President, Shell Oil Products: James M. Morgan, age 45
EVP Exploration and Production: Jack E. Little
VP and General Counsel: S. A. Lackey
VP Finance and Business Services and CFO: P. G. Turberville
VP Marketing: J. W. Schutzenhofer
VP Operations: R. L. Howard
VP Technology: B. E. Bernard
VP Human Resources: B. W. Levan
Auditors: Price Waterhouse

WHERE

HQ: One Shell Plaza, Houston, TX 77002
Phone: 713-241-6161
Fax: 713-241-6781 (Communications)

Shell Oil operates in the US and around the world, including Brazil, China, Syria, and Yemen. The company has 6 operating refining facilities in Martinez, California; Wood River, Illinois; Norco, Louisiana; Deer Park and Odessa, Texas; and Anacortes, Washington.

	Sources of Crude Oil	
	(thou. of barrels daily)	% of total
US	591	64
Other countries	334	36
Total	**925**	**100**

WHAT

	1992 Sales		1992 Operating Income	
	$ mil.	% of total	$ mil.	% of total
Oil & gas exploration & production	1,280	6	482	92
Oil	15,650	74	59	11
Chemical	3,354	16	50	10
Other	869	4	(67)	(13)
Adjustments	549	—	—	—
Total	**21,702**	**100**	**524**	**100**

Selected Subsidiaries and Affiliates
Saudi Petrochemical Company (minority interest, Saudi Arabia)
Shell Chemical Company
Shell Oil Products
Shell Pipe Line Corporation
Zeigler Coal Holding Company (25%, domestic coal mining)

Selected Brand Names
EPON (epoxy resin systems)
ETD (franchise convenience stores)
KRATON (thermoplastic elastomers)
NONATEL (pulp and paper surfactants for recycled paper)
REPETE (polyester resin)
SHELLVIS 260 (lubricant viscosity improver)

KEY COMPETITORS

Amoco	Oryx
Ashland	PDVSA
Atlantic Richfield	PEMEX
British Petroleum	Pennzoil
Broken Hill	Petrobrás
Chevron	Petrofina
Coastal	Phillips Petroleum
DuPont	Repsol
Elf Aquitaine	Sun
ENI	Texaco
Exxon	Total
Imperial Oil	Unocal
Koch	USX
Mobil	Other chemical companies
Norsk Hydro	Other mining companies
Occidental	

HOW MUCH

	Annual Growth	1983	1984	1985	1986	1987	1988	1989	1990	1991	1992
Sales ($ mil.)	1.0%	19,883	20,898	20,474	17,338	21,199	21,399	21,948	24,790	22,411	21,702
Net income ($ mil.)	(13.5%)	1,633	1,772	1,650	883	1,230	1,204	1,405	1,036	20	445
Income as % of sales	—	8.2%	8.5%	8.1%	5.1%	5.8%	5.6%	6.4%	4.2%	0.1%	2.1%
Employees	(3.6%)	35,185	34,699	35,167	32,641	33,184	32,432	31,338	31,637	29,437	25,308

1992 Year-end:
Debt ratio: 20.2%
Return on equity: 2.9%
Cash (mil.): $734
Current ratio: 1.02
Long-term debt (mil.): $2,507

Net Income ($ mil.) 1983–92

THE TEXAS 500

THE SOUTHLAND CORPORATION

RANK: 14

OVERVIEW

The Southland Corporation is the owner of 7-Eleven, the world's largest convenience store chain, with over 6,000 stores in the US and Canada. Since 1991 Southland has been controlled by Japan's #1 retailer, Ito-Yokado, which now owns 64% of the company's stock.

While 7-Elevens in Japan have been growing rapidly, Southland's US stores have been struggling. The company filed for bankruptcy protection in 1990, but was rescued the next year by Ito-Yokado. In 1991 and 1992 more than 270 underperforming 7-Elevens were shut down, and total revenues and same-store sales fell in 1992, by 14.9% and 3.9%, respectively. Ito-Yokado blamed its 1992 slide in profits on Southland's $131 million pretax loss for the year.

A much-needed restructuring of Southland's stores seems imminent. Fifty 7-Elevens in Austin, Texas, recorded double-digit sales growth for the first half of fiscal 1993, a result of operational reforms that began in 1991. Southland will now extend these reforms, which include a wider product mix (including fresh food products), store remodeling, and lower gas prices, to 7-Elevens around the country and hope for the same outcome.

WHEN

Claude Dawley, son of an ice company pioneer, formed the Southland Ice Company in Dallas in 1927 to buy 4 other Texas ice plant operations. Ice was both a rare commodity and a basic necessity during Texas summers for storing and transporting food and, especially, beer. Dawley was backed in his bid by Chicago utility magnate Martin Insull.

One of the ice operations Dawley bought was Consumers Ice, where a young employee, Joe C. Thompson, Jr., had made the firm some money with his idea of selling chilled watermelons off the truck docks.

After the Dawley enterprise was under way, an ice dock manager in Dallas began stocking a few food items for customers. He demonstrated the idea to Thompson, who was by then running the ice operation, and the practice was adopted at all company locations.

Thompson promoted the grocery operations by calling them Tote'm Stores and erecting Alaska-made totem poles by the docks. In 1928 he arranged for the construction of gas stations at some stores.

Insull bought out Dawley in 1930, and Thompson became president. He expanded Southland's operations even as the Depression-hurt company operated briefly under the direction of the bankruptcy court (1932–34). The company began a dairy, Oak Farms, to meet its needs as the largest dairy retailer in the Dallas–Fort Worth area (1936). By 1946 the company had bought other ice-retail operations in Texas, changed its name to the Southland Corporation, and adopted the name 7-Eleven, a reference to the store hours, for its stores.

When Thompson died in 1961, his eldest son, John, became president and opened new stores in Colorado, New Jersey, and Arizona in 1962 and in Utah, California, and Missouri in 1963. The company purchased Gristede Brothers (1968), a New York grocer; Baricini Stores (1969), a candy chain; and Hudgins Truck Rental (1971, sold in 1980).

Southland franchised the 7-Eleven format in the UK (1971), and in Japan (1973) through one of that country's largest retailers, Ito-Yokado. In 1983 the company purchased Citgo, a gasoline refining and marketing business, later selling 50% of the company to Petroleos de Venezuela, a Venezuelan oil company (1986).

In 1988 John Thompson and his 2 brothers borrowed heavily to buy 70% of Southland's stock in an LBO. The company defaulted on $1.8 billion in publicly traded debt in mid-1990. Southland persuaded bondholders to restructure the debt and take 25% of the company stock, clearing the way for the purchase of 70% of Southland, a deal completed in March 1991, by its Japanese partner, Ito-Yokado.

In 1992 the company contracted Wal-Mart's McLane subsidiary to provide wholesale distribution services to its stores. Southland also sold McLane 2 of its 5 distribution centers and 3 food processing plants.

Although same-store sales fell, the company recorded its first profitable quarter in 2 years in August 1993.

NASDAQ symbol: SLCMC
Fiscal year ends: December 31

WHO

Chairman: Masatoshi Ito, age 68
VC: Toshifumi Suzuki, age 60
President and CEO: Clark J. Matthews II, age 56, $551,850 pay
SVP Operations: Stephen B. Krumholz, age 43, $332,950 pay
SVP, Chief Administrative Officer, and Secretary: John H. Rodgers, age 49, $412,905 pay
VP and General Counsel: Bryan F. Smith, Jr., age 40
VP Merchandising: Rodney A. Brehm, age 45
VP Human Resources: David M. Finley, age 52
Auditors: Coopers & Lybrand

WHERE

HQ: 2711 N. Haskell Ave., Dallas, TX 75204-2906
Phone: 214-828-7011
Fax: 214-828-7848

	1992 Stores	
	No. of stores	% of total
California	1,229	20
Colorado	256	4
Florida	521	8
Maryland	374	6
New Jersey	211	3
New York	217	4
Texas	480	8
Virginia	696	11
Washington	275	5
Other states	1,414	23
Canada	494	8
Total	**6,167**	**100**

WHAT

	1992 Stores	
	No. of stores	% of total
Franchised	3,011	49
Company-operated	3,156	51
Total	**6,167**	**100**

	1992 Stores	
	No. of stores	% of total
7-Eleven	5,997	97
High's Dairy Stores	112	2
Quik Mart/Super-7s	58	1
Total	**6,167**	**100**

	1992 Sales
	% of total
Gasoline	23
Tobacco products	19
Beer/wine	10
Soft drinks	10
Groceries	9
Food service	8
Nonfoods	6
Dairy products	5
Candy	4
Baked goods	3
Customer services	2
Health/beauty aids	1
Total	**100**

KEY COMPETITORS

Albertson's	Exxon	Texaco
Ashland	Kroger	Vons
Atlantic Richfield	Meijer	Winn-Dixie
British Petroleum	Mobil	Other gasoline
Chevron	Royal Dutch/Shell	and grocery
Circle K	Safeway	retailers
Coastal	Sun	

HOW MUCH

	9-Year Growth	1983	1984	1985	1986	1987	1988	1989	1990	1991	1992
Sales ($ mil.)	(3.1%)	8,512	11,661	12,377	8,187	7,629	7,602	7,916	7,975	7,566	6,439
Net income ($ mil.)	—	132	160	213	200	(756)	(216)	(1,320)	(302)	(74)	(131)
Income as % of sales	—	1.5%	1.4%	1.7%	2.4%	(1.0%)	(2.8%)	(16.7%)	(3.8%)	(1.0%)	(2.0%)
Earnings per share ($)	—	32.10	33.80	43.70	39.10	(7.30)	(12.20)	(65.40)	(15.10)	(0.22)	(0.32)
Stock price – high ($)	—	—	—	—	—	—	—	—	—	3.03	4.25
Stock price – low ($)	—	—	—	—	—	—	—	—	—	0.94	1.19
Stock price – close ($)	(40.4%)	—	—	—	—	—	—	—	—	1.88	3.03
P/E – high	—	15	11	11	15	—	—	—	—	—	—
P/E – low	—	8	7	6	10	—	—	—	—	—	—
Dividends per share ($)	(100.0%)	8.40	9.20	10.00	11.20	618.80	0.00	0.00	0.00	0.00	0.00
Book value per share ($)	—	229.44	253.92	288.40	319.07	(7.52)	(18.90)	(83.68)	(97.58)	(2.95)	(3.22)
Employees	(5.7%)	60,834	61,800	63,548	67,174	65,800	50,724	48,114	45,665	42,616	35,646

1992 Year-end:
Debt ratio: —
Return on equity: 10.4%
Cash (mil.): $14
Current ratio: 0.46
Long-term debt (mil.): $2,408
No. of shares (mil.): 410
Dividends:
 1992 average yield: 0.0%
 1992 payout: 0.0%
Market value (mil.): $1,243

Stock Price History
High/Low 1991–92

THE TEXAS 500

SOUTHWESTERN BELL CORPORATION

RANK: 9

OVERVIEW

Southwestern Bell is an offspring any mother would be proud of. Since it left Ma Bell's nest as part of the 1984 dissolution of AT&T, the company has delivered a 389% return to its shareholders, better than any other regional Bell operating company. Southwestern Bell has not cut all of its apron strings, however. About 12% of 1992 revenues came from AT&T.

Through its Southwestern Bell Telephone subsidiary, the company provides local phone service, access to long distance carriers, and PBX and data communications systems. In cellular and mobile communications, Southwestern Bell increased its customer base by 47% in 1992 and has the highest penetration rate (a measure of how many potential customers become actual customers) of all the major US cellular providers. Internationally the company has investments in Telmex (the Mexican phone company, which is one of the fastest-growing telecommunication concerns in the world), cable TV in Israel, and directories in Israel and Australia. Southwestern Bell is also one of the 3 largest cable providers in the UK.

Southwestern Bell's success has stemmed from diversification and increasing productivity. About 25% of net income comes from nontraditional telephone services. Since the dissolution of AT&T, Southwestern Bell has reduced the number of employees required to serve access lines by 43%. The company recently relocated to San Antonio from St. Louis. About 60% of its revenues come from Texas, and the company will be able to keep a close eye on the value of its investment in Telmex, which has grown from $953 million to $2.5 billion.

WHEN

Southwestern Bell was once an arm of AT&T, providing local communications services in its present region. Telephone service first arrived in Southwestern Bell territory in 1878, just 2 years after the telephone was invented. One man responsible for early growth of telephony in this region was George Durant, who located 12 customers for St. Louis's first telephone exchange. This grew into Bell Telephone Company of Missouri.

Meanwhile the Missouri and Kansas Telephone Company had also been established. The first president of Southwestern Bell, Eugene Nims, negotiated the merger of Missouri and Kansas and Southwestern Bell into the Southwestern Telephone System around 1912. Southwestern Bell became part of AT&T in 1917; Nims served as president from 1919 to 1929. After WWII demand for new telephone lines grew rapidly. By 1945 Southwestern Bell was providing service to one million telephones; by the 1980s this number had grown nearly tenfold.

In 1983 AT&T was split from the Bell Operating Companies, and Southwestern Bell became a separate legal entity; it began operations in 1984. At the time of the breakup, Southwestern Bell received local phone service rights in 5 states; Southwestern Bell Mobile Systems (cellular service provider); the directory advertising business; and a 1/7 share in Bell Communications Research (Bellcore), the R&D arm shared by the Bell companies. The company set up its telecommunications and publishing groups later.

Southwestern Bell has concentrated much of its diversification effort in mobile communications. The company purchased operations from Metromedia (1987), which included paging in 19 cities and 6 major cellular franchises. Southwestern Bell also bought paging assets from Omni Communications (1988).

By 1988 Southwestern Bell had deployed more lines than any other company for an integrated voice and data phone service known as ISDN.

In 1990 Southwestern Bell joined with France Télécom and Grupo Carso (mining, manufacturing, and tobacco) to purchase 20.4% of Teléfonos de México (Telmex), the previously state-owned telephone monopoly, for a total of $1.76 billion. Southwestern Bell's stake in the venture represents about 10% of Telmex.

In 1993 Southwestern Bell sold a 25% interest in its UK cable television and telephone operations to Cox Cable. That same year Southwestern Bell announced its intention to acquire 2 Washington, DC–area cable systems from Hauser Communications if it could obtain regulatory approval. Also in 1993 Southwestern Bell and Panasonic offered a new wireless telephone called Freedom Link, which can be used as a cellular phone outside of an office and as a cordless phone inside the office.

NYSE symbol: SBC
Fiscal year ends: December 31

WHO

Chairman and CEO: Edward E. Whitacre, Jr., age 51, $1,528,050 pay
VC and CFO: Robert G. Pope, age 57, $1,001,000 pay
Group President: James R. Adams, age 54, $815,000 pay
Group President: Charles E. Foster, age 56
President, Southwestern Bell Telephone Co. of Texas: William E. Dreyer, age 54, $562,000 pay
President, Southwestern Bell Telephone Co. of the Midwest: J. Cliff Eason, age 45
President, Southwestern Bell Services: Royce S. Caldwell, age 54
SEVP and General Counsel: James D. Ellis, age 50
SEVP Human Resources: Richard A. Harris, age 52
SVP Strategic Planning: Edward A. Mueller, age 45
Auditors: Ernst & Young

WHERE

HQ: 175 E. Houston, San Antonio, TX 78299-2933
Phone: 210-821-4105
Fax: 210-351-2071 (Investor Relations)

Southwestern Bell Telephone provides telephone services in Texas, Kansas, Oklahoma, Arkansas, and Missouri. Other divisions operate nationally or internationally.

WHAT

	1992 Sales	
	$ mil.	% of total
Local telephone service	4,668	47
Network access	2,548	25
Long-distance service	1,012	10
Directory advertising	848	8
Other	939	10
Total	**10,015**	**100**

Subsidiaries and Affiliates
Associated Directory Services, Inc.
Bell Communications Research (14.28%)
Metromedia Paging Services, Inc.
Southwestern Bell International Holdings Corporation (international business development)
Southwestern Bell Mobile Systems, Inc. (cellular phone services)
Southwestern Bell Printing Company
Southwestern Bell Telecommunications, Inc. (communications equipment)
Southwestern Bell Telephone Company
Southwestern Bell Yellow Pages, Inc. (directory advertising and publishing)
Teléfonos de México, SA de CV (Telmex, 10%)

KEY COMPETITORS

Alcatel Alsthom	Ericsson
American Business Information	GTE
	MCI
Ameritech	Metromedia
AT&T	Motorola
Bell Atlantic	NYNEX
BellSouth	Pacific Telesis
BT	Sprint
Cable & Wireless	Telefónica de España
Century Telephone	Telephone and Data Systems
Contel Cellular	U.S. Long Distance
R. R. Donnelley	U S WEST
Dun & Bradstreet	

HOW MUCH

	Annual Growth	1983	1984	1985	1986	1987	1988	1989	1990	1991	1992
Sales ($ mil.)	4.2%	—	7,191	7,925	7,902	8,003	8,453	8,730	9,113	9,332	10,015
Net income ($ mil.)	5.0%	—	883	996	1,023	1,047	1,060	1,093	1,101	1,157	1,302
Income as % of sales	—	—	12.3%	12.6%	12.9%	13.1%	12.5%	12.5%	12.1%	12.4%	13.0%
Earnings per share ($)	(4.0%)	—	1.51	1.67	1.71	1.74	1.77	1.82	1.84	1.93	2.17
Stock price – high ($)	—	—	11.92	14.75	19.40	22.75	21.31	32.19	32.38	32.94	37.38
Stock price – low ($)	—	—	9.17	11.40	13.17	14.13	16.50	19.44	23.63	24.50	28.31
Stock price – close ($)	5.8%	—	11.79	14.25	18.71	17.19	20.19	31.94	28.00	32.31	37.00
P/E – high	—	—	8	9	11	13	12	18	18	17	17
P/E – low	—	—	6	7	8	8	9	11	13	13	13
Dividends per share ($)	(0.4%)	—	0.70	0.98	1.05	1.14	1.22	1.29	1.36	1.41	1.45
Book value per share ($)	(5.0%)	—	11.71	12.38	13.04	13.63	14.15	13.92	14.31	14.76	15.51
Employees	(2.3%)	—	71,900	71,400	67,500	67,100	64,930	66,200	66,690	61,230	59,500

1992 Year-end:
Debt ratio: 42.9%
Return on equity: 14.3%
Cash (mil.): $505
Current ratio: 0.78
Long-term debt (mil.): $5,716
No. of shares (mil.): 600
Dividends:
 1992 average yield: 3.9%
 1992 payout: 66.8%
Market value (mil.): $22,191

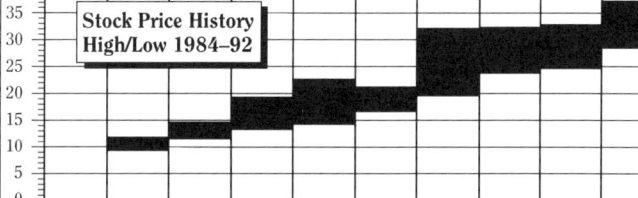

Stock Price History High/Low 1984–92

SYSCO CORPORATION

RANK: 8

OVERVIEW

SYSCO is the US's largest marketer and distributor of foodservice products. With an 8% share of the highly fragmented foodservice distribution market, the company is larger than its 5 biggest competitors combined. SYSCO had another good year in 1992 as its sales rose 9% and its net income was up 12%.

Based in Houston, SYSCO serves a variety of away-from-home eating establishments including restaurants, hotels, schools, hospitals, and fast-food outlets. Through its 69 operating companies, SYSCO serves approximately 230,000 customers across the US (including the 150 largest metropolitan areas in the country) and the Pacific Coast region of Canada.

SYSCO buys goods from about 3,000 independent sources in several countries. The company sells about 150,000 products, including fully prepared frozen entrees; frozen fruits, vegetables, and desserts; and a full line of canned and dry goods. Other SYSCO products include fresh meat, imported specialties, and fresh produce. The company also sells disposable napkins, plates, and cups; china and silverware; restaurant and kitchen equipment and supplies; and cleaning supplies.

SYSCO continues to expand its sales force. It plans to add 300 sales people in fiscal 1993. The company has also recently been adding medical and surgical supplies as well as personal care products to its mix, for sale to its nursing home and hospital customers.

The company expanded through nearly 50 acquisitions between its founding in 1969 and the end of 1992.

WHEN

SYSCO was founded in 1969 when John Baugh, a Houston wholesale foods distributor, convinced the owners of 8 other US wholesalers that they should combine and form a national distribution company. Joining Baugh's Zero Foods of Houston to form SYSCO were Frost-Pack Distributing (Grand Rapids, Michigan), Louisville Grocery (Louisville, Kentucky), Plantation Foods (Miami), Thomas Foods and its Justrite subsidiary (Cincinnati), Wicker (Dallas), Houston's Food Service Company (Houston), Global Frozen Foods (New York), and Texas Wholesale Grocery (Dallas). SYSCO, which derives its name from Systems and Services Company, benefited from Baugh's recognition of the trend toward dining out in American society. Until SYSCO was formed, food distribution to restaurants, hotels, and other nongrocers was provided almost exclusively by thousands of small, independent, regional operators.

During the 2 decades since its inception, SYSCO has expanded to 70 times its original size through internal growth and the acquisition of strong local distributors. SYSCO has ensured the success of its acquisitions through buyout agreements requiring the seller to continue managing the company and earn a portion of the sale price with future profits.

In 1988, when SYSCO was already the largest food service distributor, it purchased Olewine's, a Harrisburg, Pennsylvania, distributor. It also acquired CFS Continental, the food distribution unit of Staley Continental and the 3rd largest food distributor at the time, for $750 million. Following the transaction, SYSCO sold CFS's manufacturing units. The CFS acquisition added several warehouses and a large truck fleet and increased the company's penetration along the West Coast of the US and Canada. In 1990 SYSCO acquired the Oklahoma City–based foodservice distribution business of Scrivner (renamed SYSCO Food Services of Oklahoma). SYSCO plans to continue expanding through deeper penetration of existing markets and by buying smaller competitors.

In 1991 SYSCO's Houston subsidiary, SYSCO Food Services, pleaded guilty to one count of conspiring to rig contract bids for wholesale groceries to public schools in southeastern Texas. SYSCO reorganized its school-bid department and added controls to prevent any recurrences.

SYSCO acquired Collin's Foodservice and Benjamin Polakoff & Son in 1992. It also acquired Philadelphia-based Perloff Brothers, which operated Tartan Foods, and created a new subsidiary, Tartan Sysco Food Services. SYSCO also sold its last remaining retail business, consumer-size frozen food distributor Global Sysco, in 1992.

In 1993 SYSCO acquired St. Louis–based Clark Foodservice and New Jersey's Ritter Food Corporation.

NYSE symbol: SYY
Fiscal year ends: Saturday closest to June 30

WHO

Chairman and CEO: John F. Woodhouse, age 61, $835,875 pay
President and COO: Bill M. Lindig, age 55, $718,781 pay
EVP and President, Foodservice Operations: Charles H. Cotros, age 55, $529,947 pay
EVP Finance and Administration: E. James Lowrey, age 64, $533,673 pay
Auditors: Arthur Andersen & Co.

WHERE

HQ: 1390 Enclave Pkwy., Houston, TX 77077-2099
Phone: 713-584-1390
Fax: 713-584-1188

SYSCO has 103 facilities in 37 states and Canada.

State	No. of Facilities
California	9
Colorado	5
Florida	3
Georgia	3
Kentucky	3
Maryland	4
Michigan	5
New York	11
Ohio	7
Pennsylvania	3
Tennessee	5
Texas	9
Other states	34
Canada	2
Total	**103**

WHAT

Customers	1992 Sales % of total
Hospitals & nursing homes	13
Hotels & motels	6
Restaurants	60
Schools & colleges	8
Other	13
Total	**100**

Products	1992 Sales % of total
Beverage products	3
Canned & dry products	26
Dairy products	8
Equipment & smallwares	3
Fresh & frozen meats	17
Fresh produce	5
Janitorial products	2
Other frozen products	15
Paper & disposable products	7
Poultry	8
Seafoods	6
Total	**100**

KEY COMPETITORS

Amway
Heinz
Philip Morris
Quaker Oats
Sara Lee
Scott
Wal-Mart

HOW MUCH

	9-Year Growth	1983	1984	1985	1986	1987	1988	1989	1990	1991	1992
Sales ($ mil.)	18.4%	1,950	2,312	2,628	3,172	3,656	4,385	6,851	7,591	8,150	8,893
Net income ($ mil.)	17.6%	40	45	50	58	62	80	108	132	154	172
Income as % of sales	—	2.1%	2.0%	1.9%	1.8%	1.7%	1.8%	1.6%	1.7%	1.9%	1.9%
Earnings per share ($)	16.1%	0.24	0.27	0.29	0.34	0.35	0.45	0.60	0.73	0.84	0.93
Stock price – high ($)	—	5.56	4.80	5.81	8.47	10.38	9.72	16.00	19.19	23.69	27.75
Stock price – low ($)	—	3.91	3.22	3.97	5.59	5.63	6.50	9.16	12.81	15.00	20.56
Stock price – close ($)	21.5%	4.56	4.22	5.59	7.50	6.78	9.63	15.81	16.81	23.31	26.38
P/E – high	—	23	18	20	25	30	22	27	26	28	30
P/E – low	—	16	12	14	17	16	15	15	18	18	22
Dividends per share ($)	18.3%	0.04	0.04	0.05	0.05	0.07	0.08	0.09	0.10	0.12	0.17
Book value per share ($)	16.5%	1.44	1.71	1.96	2.25	2.55	3.01	3.54	4.20	4.96	5.69
Employees	13.0%	7,500	8,300	9,100	10,700	12,000	13,000	18,700	19,600	21,000	22,500

1992 Year-end:
Debt ratio: 32.2%
Return on equity: 17.5%
Cash (mil.): $74
Current ratio: 1.89
Long-term debt (mil.): $489
No. of shares (mil.): 186
Dividends:
  1992 average yield: 0.6%
  1992 payout: 18.3%
Market value (mil.): $4,900

Stock Price History High/Low 1983–92

THE TEXAS 500

TANDY CORPORATION

RANK: 21

OVERVIEW

At Tandy Corporation the motto lately has been "sell, sell, sell." That might not seem so surprising since the Fort Worth–based company is the US's #1 retailer of consumer electronics, but Tandy has also taken the motto to heart in its effort to overcome sagging earnings by selling off most of its manufacturing businesses.

In 1993 Tandy announced it would sell its personal computer manufacturing business to AST Research for $175 million. Also on the block are most of the other pieces of its TE Electronics manufacturing subsidiary, including O'Sullivan Industries (office furniture), Lika (printed circuit boards), and Memtek Products (Memorex tapes).

Tandy's move away from manufacturing allows the company to focus on its retailing operations, including its 4,558 company-owned and 2,056 franchised Radio Shack stores, which have faced slowing sales recently. As part of its efforts to boost its retail business, Tandy plans to close more than 100 of its 432 Name Brand Retail Group stores, primarily in larger markets. The group includes McDuff (electronics), VideoConcepts (audio and video), and The Edge in Electronics (upscale mall boutiques).

With its new focus on retailing, Tandy is not hesitating to try new ideas. In late 1992 the company opened the first 2 units of its new retailing concept, Incredible Universe, a gigantic electronics superstore with a sales floor as large as 3 football fields; it plans to add several new units in 1993 and 1994. Tandy also plans to open 16 new Computer City computer warehouse stores in 1993, and in mid-1993 the company said it will try 4 new retailing concepts, including smaller versions of Radio Shack and Computer City.

WHEN

During the 1950s Charles Tandy expanded his family's small Fort Worth leather business (founded in 1919) into a nationwide chain of leathercraft and hobby stores. By 1960 Tandy Corporation stock was being traded on the NYSE. In the early 1960s Tandy began to expand into other retail areas, buying Leonard's, a Fort Worth department store.

In 1963 Tandy purchased Radio Shack, a nearly bankrupt electronic parts supplier with a mail-order business and 9 retail stores in the Boston area. Tandy collected part of the $800,000 owed the company and began expansion, stocking the stores with quick turnover items and putting 8–9% of sales revenue into advertising. Between 1961 and 1969 Tandy sales grew from $16 million to $180 million, and earnings rose from $720,000 to $7.7 million, with the bulk of the growth due to the expansion of Radio Shack. Between 1968 and 1973 Tandy expanded from 172 to 2,294 stores; Radio Shack provided over 50% of Tandy's sales and 80% of earnings in 1973.

In 1974 the company sold its department store operations to Dillard. In 1975 Tandy spun off to shareholders its leather products business as Tandy Brands and its hobby and handicraft business as Tandycrafts, focusing Tandy Corporation on the consumer electronics business. During 1976 the boom in CB radio sales pushed income up 125% as Tandy opened 1,200 stores. In 1977 Tandy introduced the first mass-marketed personal computer — the TRS-80, which became the #1 PC on the market. In 1979, the year after Charles Tandy died, there were 5,530 McDonald's, 6,805 7-Elevens, and 7,353 Radio Shacks.

In 1984 the company introduced the Tandy 1000, the first IBM-compatible PC priced under $1,000. Since 1984 Tandy has expanded through acquisitions — Scott/McDuff and VideoConcepts in 1985, GRiD Systems in 1988, and Victor Technologies in 1990.

In 1987 Tandy spun off its foreign retail operations as InterTAN. Realizing that Radio Shack had nearly exhausted its expansion possibilities, the company focused on alternate retail formats such as GRiD Systems Centers and in 1991 opened Computer City and The Edge in Electronics. That same year Tandy announced the introduction of name-brand products into Radio Shack stores. The company also increased its manufacturing and R&D capacity and focused on emerging technologies such as digital audio recording and multimedia computing.

In 1993 Tandy and Casio Computer entered the emerging personal digital assistant (PDA) market when they jointly introduced the Zoomer. The device, which weighs less than a pound, can access reference data, save handwritten notes, translate languages, and retrieve electronic mail.

94   THE TEXAS 500

NYSE symbol: TAN
Fiscal year ends: December 31

WHO

Chairman, CEO, and President: John V. Roach, age 54, $856,498 pay
CEO, TE Electronics Inc.: William C. Bousquette, age 56, 520,000 pay (prior to promotion)
President and COO, TE Electronics Inc.: Robert M. McClure, age 57, $358,871 pay
SVP and Secretary: Herschel C. Winn, age 61, $309,600 pay
VP and Treasurer: Dwain H. Hughes, age 45
VP Marketing: Lowell C. Duncan, Jr., age 48
VP Human Resources: George J. Berger
Auditors: Price Waterhouse

WHERE

HQ: 1800 One Tandy Center, Fort Worth, TX 76102
Phone: 817-390-3700
Fax: 817-390-2774

Tandy operates company-owned and dealer/franchise Radio Shack, Name Brand Retail Group, Incredible Universe, and Computer City stores across the US. Radio Shack also has 66 international dealer stores, and Tandy operates 2 Computer City stores in Europe.

	1992 Sales $ mil.	1992 Sales % of total	1992 Operating Income $ mil.	1992 Operating Income % of total
US	4,322	92	326	—
Other countries	359	8	(24)	—
Adjustments	62	—	30	—
Total	**4,743**	**100**	**332**	**—**

WHAT

Divisions
Computer City
Computer City Express
Energy Express Plus
Famous Brand Electronics
Incredible Universe
Radio Shack
Radio Shack Express
Tandy Name Brand Retail
  The Edge in Electronics
  McDuff
  VideoConcepts

Subsidiary
TE Electronics
  Memtek Products (Memorex audio and video tape)
  O'Sullivan Industries (office furniture)
  Lika Corporation (printed circuit boards)

KEY COMPETITORS

Babbage's
BASF
Best Buy
Circuit City
CompuCom Systems
CompUSA
Costco Wholesale
Egghead
Fuji Photo
Good Guys
Matsushita
3M
Montgomery Ward
Office Depot

Philips
Pioneer
Price Co.
Sears
Service Merchandise
Sharp
Sharper Image
Siemens
Software Etc.
Sony
Staples
Toshiba
Wal-Mart

HOW MUCH

	9-Year Growth	1983	1984	1985	1986	1987	1988	1989	1990	1991	1992
Sales ($ mil.)	7.5%	2,475	2,737	2,841	3,036	3,452	3,794	4,181	4,562	4,656	4,743
Net income ($ mil.)	(4.5%)	279	282	189	198	242	316	324	290	206	184
Income as % of sales	—	11.3%	10.3%	6.7%	6.5%	7.0%	8.3%	7.7%	6.4%	4.4%	3.9%
Earnings per share ($)	(2.1%)	2.67	2.75	2.11	2.22	2.70	3.54	3.64	3.54	2.58	2.20
Stock price – high ($)	—	64.50	43.38	42.13	45.00	56.50	48.63	48.75	41.13	36.50	31.75
Stock price – low ($)	—	33.25	23.25	24.00	30.50	28.00	31.50	37.00	23.50	23.38	22.25
Stock price – close ($)	(4.1%)	43.38	24.25	40.75	42.50	33.00	41.00	39.13	29.25	28.88	29.75
P/E – high	—	24	16	20	20	21	14	13	12	14	14
P/E – low	—	12	8	11	14	10	9	10	7	9	10
Dividends per share ($)	—	0.00	0.00	0.00	0.00	0.38	0.58	0.60	0.60	0.60	0.60
Book value per share ($)	9.1%	10.71	10.64	12.00	14.57	15.38	18.10	20.65	21.78	23.48	23.53
Employees	2.8%	32,000	34,000	35,000	36,000	39,000	37,000	38,000	40,000	40,000	41,000

1992 Year-end:
Debt ratio: 23.4%
Return on equity: 9.4%
Cash (mil.): $107
Current ratio: 2.99
Long-term debt (mil.): $358
No. of shares (mil.): 63
Dividends:
  1992 average yield: 2.0%
  1991 payout: 27.3%
Market value (mil.): $1,880

Stock Price History
High/Low 1983–92

THE TEXAS 500

TENNECO INC.

RANK: 5

OVERVIEW

Houston-based Tenneco, best known for its profit-leading natural gas pipelines, is trying to plug losses at its largest subsidiary, Case Corporation, maker of farm and construction equipment. Tenneco's other operations are in the black. Its Newport News Shipbuilding and Dry Dock Co. is the US's #1 privately owned shipbuilder, specializing in nuclear submarines. Other businesses include Monroe Auto Equipment and Walker Manufacturing (automotive parts), Packaging Corporation of America (corrugated shipping containers, paperboard, and disposable plastic and aluminum containers), and Albright & Wilson (UK-based chemical production).

A shake-up by President Michael Walsh has swept Tenneco, from its factories (many of which he has closed or redesigned) to the executive dining room (which he has eliminated, along with the company yacht). Since joining Tenneco in 1991 Walsh has cut 10,000 jobs, sold more than $1 billion in assets, and issued more than $1 billion of stock. He is using the stock proceeds to pay down debt, which he has already cut by 28%. In 1993 Walsh revealed he has brain cancer but said he would retain his post indefinitely.

Walsh hopes to reverse Tenneco's losses by focusing on Case, which lost $1.2 billion in 1992 (included is a $920 million restructuring charge). Sales of combines and bulldozers have suffered from the recession and poor management. Walsh plans to eliminate more Case factories in the US and Europe, privatize the company's 150 retail outlets, and cease production of low-horsepower tractors.

WHEN

Tennessee Gas and Transmission began in 1943 as a division of The Chicago Corporation, headed by Gardiner Symonds and authorized to construct a 1,265-mile pipeline between the Gulf of Mexico and West Virginia. As the US faced WWII fuel shortages, the fledgling group completed the project in a record 11 months, obtaining right-of-way from thousands of landowners and crossing 67 rivers.

Just after WWII, Tennessee Gas went public; Symonds became president. While expanding the pipeline, the company merged its oil and gas exploration interests into Tennessee Production Company (1954), which, with Bay Petroleum (bought 1955), formed subsidiary Tenneco Oil (1961). Symonds entered the chemical industry by acquiring 50% of Petro-Tex Chemical (1955), now Tenneco Chemicals.

In 1963 Tennessee Gas moved to its present Houston headquarters and in 1966 adopted the Tenneco name. In 1967 Tenneco bought Kern County Land Company, which owned 2.5 million acres of California farmland and mineral rights. The purchase thrust Tenneco into the farming business; by 1984 Tenneco was the US's largest grower/shipper of table grapes and 2nd largest almond processor. The Kern purchase also included 2 Racine, Wisconsin–based manufacturers: J. I. Case, known for tractors and construction digging equipment, and Walker Manufacturing, which entered the automotive field in 1912 by producing jacks.

Symonds bought Packaging Corporation of America, a maker of shipping containers, pulp, and paperboard products, in 1965. In 1968 he acquired Newport News Shipbuilding, founded by Collis Huntington in 1886. Newport News began building submarines and nuclear-powered aircraft carriers in the 1960s.

Following Symonds's death in 1971, Tenneco bought shock absorber manufacturer Monroe of Monroe, Michigan (1977) and Philadelphia Life Insurance Company (1977; sold to ICH Corporation in 1986). In 1985 Case bought major competitor International Harvester's agricultural equipment operations. Tenneco sold its agricultural operations in 1987 and its oil operations in 1988.

As part of its 1991 restructuring plan, Tenneco sold its natural gas liquids business to Enron ($632 million, 1991), its pulp chemicals business to Sterling Chemicals ($202 million, 1992), and a US soda ash plant to Belgium's Solvay ($500 million, 1992). Tenneco Gas's 20,200 miles of pipeline delivered 14% of the nation's natural gas in 1992. Also that year the company purchased EnTrade Corp., a gas marketing company.

In 1993 Tenneco agreed to pursue joint ventures in South America with British Gas, which started a subsidiary in Argentina that year. Also in 1993 Newport News Shipbuilding said it would lay off 1,000 more workers.

NYSE symbol: TGT
Fiscal year ends: December 31

WHO

Chairman and CEO: Michael H. Walsh, age 50, $2,503,272 pay
President and COO: Dana G. Mead, age 56, $1,055,208 pay
SVP Strategy: Stacy S. Dick, age 36, $275,000 pay
General Counsel: Theodore R. Tetzlaff, age 48
President, Case Corp.: Edward J. Campbell
President, Tenneco Gas: Stephen D. Chesebro'
President, Newport News Shipbuilding: W.R. Phillips, Jr.
President, Tenneco Automotive: J.P. Reilly
SVP and CFO: Robert T. Blakely, age 51, $494,672 pay
SVP Human Resources: Barry R. Schuman, age 51
Auditors: Arthur Andersen & Co.

WHERE

HQ: Tenneco Bldg., PO Box 2511, Houston, TX 77252-2511
Phone: 713-757-2131
Fax: 713-757-1410

	1992 Sales		1992 Operating Income	
	$ mil.	% of total	$ mil.	% of total
US	9,507	72	568	—
Canada	605	5	67	—
Europe	2,599	20	(666)	—
Other countries	428	3	28	—
Adjustments	—	—	772	—
Total	**13,139**	**100**	**769**	**—**

WHAT

	1992 Sales		1992 Operating Income	
	$ mil.	% of total	$ mil.	% of total
Nat. gas pipelines	2,183	17	374	—
Farm & const. equip.	3,829	29	(1,160)	—
Automotive parts	1,808	14	237	—
Shipbuilding	2,265	17	262	—
Packaging	2,078	16	229	—
Chemicals	951	7	78	—
Other	25	—	(23)	—
Adjustments	—	—	772	—
Total	**13,139**	**100**	**769**	**—**

Pipeline Operations
Altamont Gas Transmission Co. (52%)
Channel Industries Gas Co.
Creole Gas Pipeline Corp.
East Tennessee Natural Gas Co.
Iroquois Gas Transmission Co. (13.2%)
Kern River Gas Transmission Co. (50%)
LHC Pipeline Co.
Midwestern Gas Transmission Co.
State Gas Pipeline Co.
Tennessee Gas Pipeline Co.
THC Pipeline Co.

Manufacturing Companies
Albright & Wilson Ltd. (chemicals, UK)
Case Corp. (farm and construction equipment)
Monroe Auto Equipment Co. (shock absorbers)
Newport News Shipbuilding and Dry Dock Co.
Packaging Corp. of America
Tenneco Brake (auto brakes)
Tenneco Credit Corp.
Walker Manufacturing Co. (exhaust systems and emissions control)

KEY COMPETITORS

AlliedSignal
American Standard
Borg-Warner
Caterpillar
Coastal
Columbia Gas
Daewoo
Deere
Eaton
Fiat
General Dynamics
Hyundai
Johnson Controls
Litton Industries
Occidental
Owens-Illinois
Reynolds Metals

HOW MUCH

	9-Year Growth	1983	1984	1985	1986	1987	1988	1989	1990	1991	1992
Sales ($ mil.)	(1.1%)	14,449	14,890	15,270	14,529	14,790	13,234	14,083	14,511	13,662	13,139
Net income ($ mil.)	—	716	631	431	139	(132)	(1)	584	561	(674)	(683)
Income as % of sales	—	5.0%	4.2%	2.8%	1.0%	(0.9%)	0.0%	4.1%	3.9%	(4.9%)	(5.2%)
Earnings per share ($)	—	4.74	4.00	2.52	0.50	(1.22)	(0.18)	4.45	4.36	(5.62)	(4.85)
Stock price – high ($)	—	42.38	44.75	45.25	43.13	62.50	51.00	64.25	71.00	52.00	46.00
Stock price – low ($)	—	31.88	32.38	36.50	34.50	36.13	38.25	46.88	40.00	27.38	31.25
Stock price – close ($)	(0.1%)	41.00	37.88	39.75	38.25	39.75	48.88	62.25	47.50	31.38	40.63
P/E – high	—	9	11	18	86	—	—	14	16	—	—
P/E – low	—	7	8	14	69	—	—	11	9	—	—
Dividends per share ($)	(5.8%)	2.74	2.83	2.95	3.04	3.04	3.04	3.04	3.12	2.80	1.60
Book value per share ($)	(15.6%)	41.75	42.24	40.20	30.02	25.66	24.93	26.02	27.60	22.33	9.11
Employees	(2.2%)	97,000	98,000	111,000	101,000	104,000	93,700	90,000	92,000	89,000	79,000

1992 Year-end:
Debt ratio: 85.9%
Return on equity: —
Cash (mil.): $111
Current ratio: 1.11
Long-term debt (mil.): $6,400
No. of shares (mil.): 145
Dividends:
  1992 average yield: 3.9%
  1992 payout: —
Market value (mil.): $5,890

Stock Price History High/Low 1983–92

THE TEXAS 500

TEXAS INSTRUMENTS INCORPORATED

RANK: 11

OVERVIEW

Dallas-based Texas Instruments is the leading producer of DRAM (dynamic random access memory) chips in the US. Known for its technological innovations (integrated circuits, single-chip microcomputers, liquid-crystal displays, and pocket calculators), the company has produced inconsistent financial results, although it moved back into the black in 1992 after 2 years of losses. R&D spending has dropped from $540 million in 1990 (8.2% of revenues) to $470 million in 1992 (6.3% of revenues). To meet growing semiconductor demand, TI plans to raise capital expenditures from $429 million in 1992 to $625 million in 1993, with all of its new manufacturing capacity in Asia except for a single plant in Italy.

In semiconductors the company is shifting its product mix from commodity chips to higher-margin differentiated (proprietary) chips such as digital signal processors (DSPs), analog and digital mixed-signal devices for telecommunications, SuperSPARC microprocessors, and the TI486 microprocessor. TI is now the principal supplier of chips for Sun Microsystems workstations. The TI486 is a toehold in the Intel-dominated PC market. The company's defense electronics division benefited from $500 million in orders in 1992 to replace stocks depleted by the Persian Gulf War as the unit tries to commercialize its expertise in high-density microelectronics packaging, manufacturing technology, and infrared sensor systems. TI is also doing well in Japan as Japanese firms are increasing their orders from American companies.

WHEN

"Doc" Karcher and Eugene McDermott founded Geophysical Service Inc. (GSI) in Newark, New Jersey, in 1930. The company specialized in reflective seismology, a new technology used to explore for oil and gas deposits. In 1934 GSI moved its headquarters to Dallas.

GSI started making defense electronics during WWII, when it made submarine detectors for the US Navy, and established a defense division in 1946. The company changed its name to Texas Instruments in 1951 and was listed on the NYSE in 1953.

TI started manufacturing transistors in 1952 after buying a license from Western Electric. In an effort to reduce the price of the germanium transistor, TI invested about $2 million, which expanded the market for its uses and made possible the pocket transistor radio (1954). TI produced the first commercial silicon transistor in 1954, and TI engineer Jack Kilby (with Intel founder Bob Noyce) invented the integrated circuit in 1958. By 1959 TI's semiconductor manufacturing division accounted for half of the company's total sales.

TI's technological know-how led to other firsts in microelectronics, including terrain-following airborne radar (1958), forward-looking infrared (FLIR) systems (1964), hand-held calculators (1967), single-chip microcomputers (1971), and the LISP chip, a 32-bit microcomputer for artificial intelligence applications (1987). GSI, now TI's oil exploration subsidiary, introduced equipment capable of digitally recording seismic data in 1961.

TI moved from defense and semiconductors into consumer products in the 1970s with calculators, digital watches, and home computers. Although TI had developed the basic technologies for these products, its inability to follow through in the face of low-cost foreign competition led it to lose money and then abandon both its digital watch and PC businesses. Attempts to meet competitors' prices, as well as plunging semiconductor prices, led to TI's first annual loss in 1983.

In 1988 TI sold 60% of GSI to Halliburton, the balance in 1991. TI's Kilby patent for the integrated circuit (named after the TI engineer who co-invented the IC) was upheld in Japan in 1989, and all major Japanese electronics firms except Fujitsu pay royalties to TI. The company took a $130-million charge and announced the elimination of 3,200 jobs in the second quarter of 1991; it also sold its industrial controls business (1991) and its computer business (to Hewlett-Packard, 1992). Through a cross-licensing agreement with privately held Cyrix Corporation of Richardson, Texas, TI is turning up the heat on rival Intel by offering a PC chip to compete with Intel's 486.

In 1992 TI set up a joint venture with Peter Kiewit Sons' (construction) to develop an electronic toll-tag system. The next year TI and Hitachi formed a joint venture to research and develop 256-megabit DRAM chips.

98 THE TEXAS 500

NYSE symbol: TXN
Fiscal year ends: December 31

WHO

Chairman, President, and CEO: Jerry R. Junkins, age 55, $900,000 pay
EVP: William P. Weber, age 52, $517,600 pay
EVP: William B. Mitchell, age 57, $483,500 pay
SVP, Treasurer, and CFO: William A. Aylesworth, age 50, $383,900 pay
SVP, Secretary, and General Counsel: Richard J. Agnich, age 49, $386,900 pay
VP Human Resources: Charles F. Nielson
Auditors: Ernst & Young

WHERE

HQ: 13500 N. Central Expressway,
PO Box 655474, Dallas, TX 75365-5474
Phone: 214-995-2551
Fax: 214-995-3340 (Public Relations)

TI has sales and manufacturing operations in more than 30 countries.

	1992 Sales $ mil.	% of total	1992 Operating Income $ mil.	% of total
US	4,829	65	581	—
Europe	1,249	17	(24)	—
East Asia	1,307	17	(28)	—
Other countries	62	1	(5)	—
Adjustments	(7)	—	(104)	—
Total	**7,440**	**100**	**420**	**—**

WHAT

	1992 Sales $ mil.	% of total	1992 Operating Income $ mil.	% of total
Components	3,982	53	340	60
Defense electronics	1,990	27	194	34
Digital products	1,345	18	27	5
Metallurgical matls.	116	2	3	1
Adjustments	7	—	(144)	—
Total	**7,440**	**100**	**420**	**100**

Selected Products and Services
Calculators and learning aids
Custom engineering and manufacturing services
Defense suppression missiles and other weapon systems
Electrical and electronic control devices
Electronic connectors
Electronic warfare systems
Integrated enterprise information systems
Missile guidance and control systems
Navigation systems
Notebook computers
Printers
Radio-frequency identification systems
Radar and infrared surveillance systems
Semiconductors
Software-development tools

KEY COMPETITORS

AMD	Harris	NEC
Apple	Hewlett-Packard	Oki
Canon	Hitachi	Raytheon
Casio	Honeywell	Rockwell
Chips and Technologies	Hyundai	Samsung
	IBM	Sharp
Compaq	Intel	Siemens
EG&G	Lucky-Goldstar	Thomson SA
Emerson	Micron Technology	Thorn EMI
Fujitsu	Motorola	Toshiba
General Dynamics	National Semiconductor	Other electronics companies
General Electric		

HOW MUCH

	9-Year Growth	1983	1984	1985	1986	1987	1988	1989	1990	1991	1992
Sales ($ mil.)	5.5%	4,580	5,742	4,925	4,974	5,595	6,295	6,522	6,567	6,784	7,440
Net income ($ mil.)	—	(145)	316	(119)	40	257	366	292	(39)	(409)	247
Income as % of sales	—	(3.2%)	5.5%	(2.4%)	0.8%	4.6%	5.8%	4.5%	(0.6%)	(6.0%)	3.3%
Earnings per share ($)	—	(2.01)	4.32	(1.58)	0.38	2.95	4.05	3.04	(0.92)	(5.40)	2.49
Stock price – high ($)	—	58.67	49.83	43.92	49.42	80.25	60.00	46.75	44.00	47.63	52.25
Stock price – low ($)	—	33.67	37.25	28.75	34.25	36.25	34.50	28.13	22.50	26.00	30.00
Stock price – close ($)	0.1%	46.21	39.83	35.17	39.38	55.75	41.00	35.88	38.00	30.75	46.63
P/E – high	—	—	12	—	130	27	15	15	—	—	21
P/E – low	—	—	9	—	90	12	9	9	—	—	12
Dividends per share ($)	0.9%	0.67	0.67	0.67	0.67	0.71	0.72	0.72	0.72	0.72	0.72
Book value per share ($)	2.5%	16.69	20.86	18.91	22.51	21.95	21.36	24.10	22.46	19.36	20.92
Employees	(3.1%)	80,696	86,563	77,872	77,270	77,984	75,685	73,854	70,318	62,939	60,577

1992 Year-end:
Debt ratio: 33.1%
Return on equity: 12.4%
Cash (mil.): $859
Current ratio: 1.58
Long-term debt (mil.): $909
No. of shares (mil.): 83
Dividends:
  1992 average yield: 1.5%
  1992 payout: 28.9%
Market value (mil.): $3,851

Stock Price History High/Low 1983–92

THE TEXAS 500

TEXAS UTILITIES COMPANY

RANK: 19

OVERVIEW

Dallas-based Texas Utilities is one of the nation's largest electric utilities and is the #1 utility consumer of natural gas in the US. Through its principal subsidiary, Texas Utilities Electric Company (TU Electric), the company provides electric service to nearly 5.6 million people (roughly 1/3 of the state's population) in 372 cities and towns (including the Dallas–Fort Worth metroplex) in north central, eastern, and western Texas.

Other TU subsidiaries support TU Electric by providing the lignite coal (Texas Utilities Mining Company) and natural gas and oil (Texas Utilities Fuel Company) necessary to fuel the company's generating plants. In addition, TU Fuel Company owns a 50% interest in a 395-mile natural gas pipeline, linking the Dallas–Fort Worth area to West Texas producing fields. Chaco Energy owns coal reserves totaling some 120 million recoverable tons. Another subsidiary, Texas Utilities Services, furnishes administrative services to the system's other companies.

Although Texas Utilities had a 1.7% increase in customers in 1992, energy sales were down 2.5% because of milder temperatures and a slow economy. It also undertook a major restructuring program in 1992 in order to increase efficiency, including voluntary reductions in work force. Nevertheless, Texas Utilities raised its dividend, as it has every year since 1948.

Texas Utilities applied for a 15.3% rate increase in early 1993, but the Public Utility Commission of Texas (PUC) recommended an 11.7% increase and questioned $462 million of costs related to the Comanche Peak nuclear plant.

WHEN

The first electric power company in North Texas was founded in Dallas in 1883. Another was built in 1885 in Fort Worth. From these and other small power plants grew 3 companies that developed to serve the north-central, western, and eastern regions of the state: Texas Power and Light (1912), Dallas Power and Light (1917), and Texas Electric Service Company (1929). By 1932 a network of transmission lines connecting these 3 utilities was virtually complete. Texas Utilities Company was formed in 1945 as a holding company to enable the 3 utilities to raise capital and obtain construction financing at lower cost.

Beginning in the 1940s TU moved away from strict dependence on natural gas, which was cheap and abundant, and began to lease large lignite coal reserves. In 1952 it formed Industrial Generating Company to mine lignite and operate an early coal-fired generating plant. It pioneered new lignite coal–burning technology during the 1960s, building larger boilers than had ever been used in the US. The first of 9 large lignite plants went into use in 1971, and TU began construction of the Comanche Peak nuclear plant, 45 miles southwest of Fort Worth, in 1974.

In 1984 Dallas Power and Light, Texas Electric Service, Texas Power and Light, and Texas Utilities Generating Company were combined as Texas Utilities Electric. The mining company was renamed Texas Utilities Mining.

In 1985 the Nuclear Regulatory Commission suspended licensing of the Comanche Peak nuclear plant, citing both design and construction faults. Further negotiations with the NRC resulted in the granting of a license to operate the plant at 5% of capacity in 1990, followed by a full-power license in the spring of that year. In the interim TU lost its 3 construction partners over the issue of multibillion-dollar cost overruns and bought their interests for $984.5 million.

In 1990 Santa Fe Pacific Corporation agreed to settle an antitrust suit brought by TU in 1981 over a 1977 lease agreement granting TU the right to mine about 228 million tons of coal owned by Santa Fe. TU, the 4th largest coal producer in the US in 1988, won substantial royalty and lease agreement concessions from Santa Fe in a new agreement, running from 1990 through 2017.

In 1991 the PUC authorized a 10.2% rate increase (worth about $442 million in revenues) but disallowed $1.4 billion in costs related to the construction of its Comanche Peak nuclear facility and the buyout of a former minority interest in the project.

In 1993 Texas Utilities announced plans to acquire Southwestern Electric Service Company for approximately $65 million in stock and cash. That company serves about 40,000 customers in central and eastern Texas. Also in 1993 TU Electric received a low-power license for Unit 2 at Comanche Peak.

NYSE symbol: TXU
Fiscal year ends: December 31

WHO

Chairman and CEO: Jerry S. Farrington, age 58, $700,000 pay
President: Erle Nye, age 55, $525,000 pay
VP and Principal Financial Officer: H. Jarrell Gibbs, age 55
Auditors: Deloitte & Touche

WHERE

HQ: 2001 Bryan Tower, Dallas, TX 75201
Phone: 214-812-4600
Fax: 214-812-4079

Principal Cities Served

Arlington	Irving	Plano
Carrollton	Killeen	Richardson
Dallas	Mesquite	Tyler
Fort Worth	Midland	Waco
Grand Prairie	Odessa	Wichita Falls

Generating Facilities

Oil and Gas
Collin	River Crest
Dallas	Stryker Creek
Decordova	Tradinghouse Creek
Eagle Mountain	Trinidad
Forest Grove	Twin Oak
Graham	Valley
Handley	
Lake Creek	**Lignite**
Lake Hubbard	Big Brown
Morgan Creek	Martin Lake
Mountain Creek	Monticello
North Lake	Sandow
North Main	
Parkdale	**Nuclear**
Permian Basin	Comanche Peak

WHAT

	1992 Sales	
	$ mil.	% of total
Residential	1,996	41
Commercial	1,406	29
Industrial	849	17
Government & municipal	304	6
Other utilities	209	4
Other	144	3
Total	**4,908**	**100**

	1992 Fuel Sources
	% of total
Lignite	44
Oil & gas	35
Purchased power	13
Nuclear	8
Total	**100**

Subsidiaries
Basic Resources Inc. (resource development and related technology and services)
Chaco Energy Company (coal production, sale, and delivery)
Southwestern Electric Service Company (SESCO, electric utility serving customers in eastern and central Texas)
Texas Utilities Electric Company
Texas Utilities Fuel Company (natural gas pipeline; acquires, stores, and delivers gas fuel)
Texas Utilities Mining Company (surface mining for lignite)
Texas Utilities Services Inc. (accounting and administrative services)

HOW MUCH

	9-Year Growth	1983	1984	1985	1986	1987	1988	1989	1990	1991	1992
Sales ($ mil.)	3.9%	3,488	3,932	4,170	3,932	4,083	4,154	4,321	4,543	4,893	4,908
Net income ($ mil.)	4.1%	513	587	654	705	769	738	888	969	(288)	738
Income as % of sales	—	14.7%	14.9%	15.7%	17.9%	18.8%	17.8%	20.5%	21.3%	(5.9%)	15.0%
Earnings per share ($)	(3.3%)	3.90	4.15	4.35	4.45	4.55	4.00	4.44	4.40	(1.98)	2.88
Stock price – high ($)	—	27.38	28.13	31.88	37.50	36.63	30.63	37.50	39.00	43.00	43.75
Stock price – low ($)	—	22.25	20.75	25.13	29.50	25.50	24.63	27.75	32.00	34.13	37.00
Stock price – close ($)	6.9%	23.25	26.38	29.88	31.50	27.00	28.13	35.13	36.63	41.75	42.50
P/E – high	—	7	7	7	8	8	8	8	9	—	15
P/E – low	—	6	5	6	7	6	6	6	7	—	13
Dividends per share ($)	3.7%	2.20	2.36	2.52	2.68	2.80	2.88	2.92	2.96	3.00	3.04
Book value per share ($)	1.7%	26.16	27.79	29.46	31.24	33.02	33.38	34.56	34.66	29.82	30.33
Employees	(1.6%)	16,324	16,208	16,528	16,927	16,086	16,237	15,775	15,502	15,239	14,023

1992 Year-end:
Debt ratio: 52.8%
Return on equity: 9.6%
Cash (mil.): $106
Current ratio: 0.43
Long-term debt (mil.): $7,932
No. of shares (mil.): 217
Dividends:
  1992 average yield: 7.2%
  1992 payout: 105.6%
Market value (mil.): $9,236

Stock Price History High/Low 1983–92

THE TEXAS 500

USAA

RANK: 18

OVERVIEW

If you want to get insurance from San Antonio–based USAA, the nation's 4th largest homeowners insurer and 5th largest automobile insurer, you don't have to let an insurance agent into your home; the company doesn't have any. However, there is one catch: USAA's membership is confined to active and retired military officers, Secret Service and FBI agents, other selected government officials, and their families. It has over 2.5 million members, including more than 95% of active-duty US military officers.

The company, which has dropped its full name, United Services Automobile Association, as its scope of activities has grown, provides a wide variety of products and services, including property, casualty, life, and health insurance; discount brokerage; banking; mutual funds; credit cards; a travel agency; and a buying service that allows members to buy discount merchandise. The property and casualty insurance and the buying service are sold only to members, but most of USAA's other products are available to nonmembers.

USAA's headquarters (at 5 million square feet) is billed as the largest private office building in the world. The company, which has become known for its customer service and its use of high technology, conducts almost all of its business by telephone or mail.

USAA continues to add new services. A new card introduced in 1993 allows members access to a number of perks, including long distance service through Sprint.

The company's net income dropped 66% in 1992, as it felt the effects of Hurricane Andrew, which helped to push its claims to more than $750 million for the year. USAA also faces shrinking military budgets that could cut into its potential membership base.

WHEN

In 1922 a group of US Army officers gathered in a San Antonio hotel and formed their own automobile insurance association. The reason? As military officers they often moved from one post to another, and they had a hard time getting insurance because they were considered "transient." So the 26 officers who met that day decided to insure each other. Led by Major William Garrison, who became the company's first president, they formed the United States Army Automobile Insurance Association.

In 1924, when Navy and Marine Corps officers were allowed to join, the company changed its name to United Services Automobile Association. By the mid-1950s the company had over 200,000 members.

During the 1960s the company added to its insurance lines when it formed USAA Life Insurance Company (1963) and USAA Casualty Insurance Coampany (1968).

In 1969 Robert McDermott, a retired Air Force brigadier general and a former dean of the Air Force Academy, took over as president. McDermott cut employment through attrition (USAA has never had a layoff since its founding), established education and training seminars for employees, and invested heavily in computers and telecommunications. A computer system McDermott installed cut automobile policy processing time from 13 days to 3 days.

McDermott also added new products and services, such as mutual funds, real estate investments, and banking services. Under McDermott, USAA's membership grew from 653,000 in 1969 to over 2.5 million in 1993.

In 1974 USAA began its move into its huge new headquarters facilities on a 286-acre campus, featuring subsidized cafeterias, 2 walk-in medical clinics, and 2 physical fitness centers.

During the 1970s, as part of McDermott's goal to make USAA a completely paperless company, USAA switched most of its business from mail to toll-free telephone, becoming one of the insurance industry's first companies to use 800 numbers.

In the early 1980s the company introduced USAA Buying Services, allowing members to buy merchandise at a discount. In 1985 it opened the USAA Federal Savings Bank next door to its headquarters. In the late 1980s USAA began installing an optical storage system, automating some customer service operations.

In 1993 McDermott retired as chairman and CEO and was succeeded by Robert Herres, a former vice-chairman of the Joint Chiefs of Staff.

Mutual company
Fiscal year ends: December 31

WHO

Chairman and CEO: Robert T. Herres, age 60
VC: H. T. Johnson
EVP and Chief Administrative Officer: Herb Emanuel
EVP and CFO: Staser Holcomb
SVP and Chief Communications Officer: John R. Cook
SVP Human Resources: Bill Tracy
President, Property and Casualty Division: Charles Bishop
President, Life Company: Ed Rosane
President, Investment Management Division: Mickey Roth
President, Information Services Division: Don Lasher
Auditors: KPMG Peat Marwick

WHERE

HQ: 9800 Fredericksburg Rd., USAA Building, San Antonio, TX 78288-0001
Phone: 210-498-2211
Fax: 210-498-9940

USAA provides services worldwide.

Regional Offices
Colorado Springs, CO   Tampa, FL
Norfolk, VA   London, England
Sacramento, CA   Frankfurt, Germany

WHAT

	1992 Revenues	
	$ mil.	% of total
Property & casualty	4,115	76
Life insurance	618	11
Investment management	64	1
Other	637	12
Total	**5,434**	**100**

Products and Services
Alliance Services
   USAA Floral Service
   USAA Road & Travel Plan
   USAA/Sprint Long-Distance Program
Annuities
Auto insurance
Banking
Car rental discounts
Credit card services
Health insurance
Homeowners/property insurance
Investments
   Brokerage services
   Mutual funds
   Tax deferred retirement plans
Life insurance
Merchandise
   Electronics
   Jewelry
   Furnishings
Real estate limited partnerships
Retirement services
   USAA Parklane West (health care facility)
   USAA Towers (retirement community)
Travel services

KEY COMPETITORS

Aetna	Merrill Lynch
AIG	MetLife
American Express	New York Life
American Financial	Northwestern Mutual
American General	Paine Webber
Carlson	J. C. Penney
Charles Schwab	Primerica
Chubb	Prudential
CIGNA	Raymond James Financial
Damark International	Sears
Equitable	Service Merchandise
GEICO	Sharper Image
General Re	Spiegel
John Hancock	Teachers Insurance
ITT	Transamerica
Kemper	Travelers
Loews	USF&G
MassMutual	

HOW MUCH

	Annual Growth	1983	1984	1985	1986	1987	1988	1989	1990	1991	1992
Assets ($ mil.)	20.8%	2,962	3,455	4,121	5,740	7,168	8,866	10,562	12,258	14,520	16,235
Net income ($ mil.)	(6.0%)	—	230	207	294	482	430	424	321	413	140
Income as % of assets	—	—	6.7%	5.0%	5.1%	6.7%	4.8%	4.0%	2.6%	2.8%	0.9%
Employees	10.0%	6,227	7,020	7,896	8,355	9,274	11,226	12,515	13,884	14,222	14,667

1992 Year-end:
Revenues ($ mil.): 5,434

Net income ($ mil.) 1984–92

THE TEXAS 500

THE BUBBA 10

BAKER HUGHES INCORPORATED

RANK: 39

OVERVIEW

If the number of oil and gas exploration rigs is rising, so are Baker Hughes's prospects. The Houston-based company has kept track of the rig count in the US since 1940, and the count is crucial to Baker Hughes's business. The company, which is the world's #1 manufacturer of rock drilling bits, provides a broad range of services for the oil well and mining industries. So the most important news to Baker Hughes has been the steady rise in rig counts it has charted during 1993.

Baker Hughes is organized into 3 major operating groups — Baker Hughes Drilling Technologies (drill bits, drilling fluids, and other equipment used in the drilling process), Baker Hughes Production Tools (equipment and services involved in the completion and repair of oil and gas wells, including hanger and fishing tools), and EnviroTech (equipment and instruments used in industries ranging from mining to wastewater treatment).

Baker Hughes's sales were down 10% and its profits fell sharply in 1992 as US drilling activity hit a 50-year low. In addition, the company's process technology business was hurt by the economic slowdown in the industrialized countries. In response, the company consolidated a number of its operations in order to increase efficiency. The company is also looking to the former Soviet Union for new opportunities.

WHEN

Howard R. Hughes, Sr., developed the first oil well drill bit for rock in 1909. Hughes and partner Walter Sharp opened a plant in Houston, and Sharp & Hughes soon had a near monopoly on rock bits. When Sharp died in 1912, Hughes bought his half of the company, incorporating as Hughes Tool. Hughes held 73 patents when he died in 1924, and the company passed to Howard R. Hughes, Jr.

It is estimated that the tool company provided Hughes, Jr., with $745 million in pretax profits between 1924 and 1972, which he used to diversify into movies (RKO), airlines (TWA), and Las Vegas casinos. In 1972 Hughes sold the tool division of Hughes Tool to the public for $150 million. After 1972 the company expanded into above-ground oil production tools.

In 1913 oil well drilling contractor Carl Baker organized the Baker Casing Shoe Company in California to collect royalties on his 3 oil tool inventions. In 1918 Baker began to manufacture his own products. During the 1920s Baker expanded nationwide, began international sales, and formed Baker Oil Tools (1928). Sales increased sixfold between 1933 and 1941. In the late 1940s and the 1950s, Baker grew as oil drilling boomed.

During the 1960s Baker prospered despite fewer US well completions. Foreign sales increased from 19% to 33% of total revenues. Baker bought Kobe (oil field pumping equipment) in 1963 and diversified into mining equipment with the purchase of Galigher (1969) and Ramsey Engineering (1974). The company bought Reed Tool (oil well drill bits) in 1975. In 1979 revenues topped $1 billion for the first time.

Between 1982 and 1986 US expenditures for oil services fell from $40 billion to $9 billion. In 1987, when both Baker and Hughes faced declining revenues and Hughes had large debts from expansion, the 2 companies merged to form Baker Hughes. By closing plants and combining operations, the company cut annual expenses by $80 million and was profitable by the end of fiscal 1988. Several small acquisitions in 1989 included Bird Machine (process centrifuges) and EDECO Petroleum Services (pumps). The company bought Eastman Christensen (world leader in directional and horizontal drilling equipment) and added the instrumentation unit of Tracor Holdings to its Process Technologies group (1990).

In 1991 Baker Hughes spun off BJ Services (pumping services) to the public. Also in 1991 the company sold the Eastern Hemisphere operations of Baker Hughes Tubular Services (BHTS) to Tuboscope. It sold Western Hemisphere operations of BHTS to ICO in 1992.

Also in 1992 Baker Hughes bought Teleco Oilfield Services, a pioneer in sophisticated directional drilling techniques, from Sonat Inc. for $350 million. In 1993 the company consolidated its drilling technologies businesses into a single unit, named Baker Hughes INTEC, to package services more efficiently for its clients.

NYSE symbol: BHI
Fiscal year ends: September 30

WHO

Chairman, President, and CEO: James D. Woods, age 61, $715,385 pay
SVP; President, Baker Hughes Drilling Technologies: Joel V. Staff, age 48, $417,000 pay
SVP; President, Baker Hughes Production Tools: Max L. Lukens, age 44, $356,153 pay
SVP; President, EnviroTech: Stephen T. Harcrow, age 46, $277,791 pay
VP and General Counsel: Franklin Myers, age 40, $279,110 pay
VP and Treasurer: Eric L. Mattson, age 41
VP Human Resources: Phillip A. Rice, age 57
VP and Controller (Principal Accounting Officer): George S. Finley, age 41
Auditors: Deloitte & Touche

WHERE

HQ: 3900 Essex Ln., Houston, TX 77027-5177
Phone: 713-439-8600
Fax: 713-439-8699

	1992 Sales $ mil.	% of total	1992 Operating Income $ mil.	% of total
US	1,125	45	(87)	(73)
Other Western Hemisphere	695	27	139	117
Europe	286	11	13	11
Other countries	433	17	54	45
Adjustments	—	—	54	—
Total	**2,539**	**100**	**173**	**100**

WHAT

	1992 Sales $ mil.	% of total	1992 Operating Income $ mil.	% of total
Drilling	885	35	(3)	(2)
Production	1,005	40	103	86
Process	649	25	26	22
Disposed businesses	—	—	(7)	(6)
Adjustments	—	—	54	—
Total	**2,539**	**100**	**173**	**100**

Divisions and Selected Subsidiaries

Baker Hughes Drilling Technologies
Develco
Eastman Teleco Company
EXLOG, Inc.
Hughes Christensen Company
Milpark Drilling Fluids

Baker Hughes Production Tools
Baker Oil Tools
Baker Performance Chemicals, Inc.
Baker Sand Control
Centrilift

EnviroTech
EnviroTech Pumps
EnviroTech Process Equipment
EnviroTech Measurement & Controls

KEY COMPETITORS

Bechtel
Cooper Industries
Dresser
Fluor
FMC
Halliburton
Ingersoll-Rand
Ingram
Kaneb Services
LTV
McDermott
Michael Baker Corp.
Nabors Industries
Pearson
Schlumberger

HOW MUCH

	9-Year Growth	1983	1984	1985	1986	1987	1988	1989	1990	1991	1992
Sales ($ mil.)	3.7%	1,838	1,834	1,904	1,557	1,924	2,316	2,328	2,614	2,828	2,539
Net income ($ mil.)	—	(64)	71	88	(362)	(255)	59	83	142	173	5
Income as % of sales	—	(3.5%)	3.9%	4.6%	(23.2%)	(13.2%)	2.6%	3.6%	5.4%	6.1%	0.2%
Earnings per share ($)	—	(0.91)	1.00	1.25	(5.15)	(2.22)	0.45	0.64	1.06	1.26	0.00
Stock price – high ($)	—	26.63	23.50	18.88	17.88	27.38	19.88	27.63	34.75	31.00	25.38
Stock price – low ($)	—	16.00	15.00	14.13	8.88	11.13	12.13	13.63	21.75	17.88	15.88
Stock price – close ($)	0.2%	19.25	16.63	17.88	11.88	13.63	14.00	25.50	25.63	19.25	19.63
P/E – high	—	—	24	15	—	—	44	43	33	25	—
P/E – low	—	—	15	11	—	—	27	21	21	14	—
Dividends per share ($)	(7.4%)	0.92	0.92	0.92	0.81	0.46	0.46	0.46	0.46	0.46	0.46
Book value per share ($)	(2.4%)	14.78	14.34	14.43	9.67	7.78	8.10	8.31	10.36	11.17	11.84
Employees	(0.5%)	20,552	20,131	20,578	14,908	21,191	21,492	20,400	20,900	21,300	19,600

1992 Year-end:
Debt ratio: 33.8%
Return on equity: —
Cash (mil.): $7
Current ratio: 2.11
Long-term debt (mil.): $813
No. of shares (mil.): 139
Dividends:
 1992 average yield: 2.3%
 1992 payout: —
Market value (mil.): $2,721

Stock Price History
High/Low 1983–92

Note: 1982–86 figures for Baker International Corporation only

BROWNING-FERRIS INDUSTRIES, INC.　　RANK: 31

OVERVIEW

Houston-based Browning-Ferris Industries (BFI) amply illustrates the old British saying, "Where there's muck, there's brass (money)." BFI's main business is the collection and disposal of trash, largely for corporate customers — a business that has helped BFI hold the #2 position in the US waste management market, after WMX Technologies. The company is the largest provider of medical waste services in North America and provides recycling services at 220 of its 360 global locations. American Ref-Fuel, a joint venture with Air Products and Chemicals, builds waste-to-energy conversion plants.

BFI has been down in the dumps in recent years, with net income falling away from its 1989 high, primarily because of intensified competition in the solid-waste collection business, the recession, and an increasing interest in recycling, all of which reduce demands on the core business. BFI's international operations grew modestly in 1992, owing in part to its Italian unit reporting an operating loss of $13.8 million.

BFI was positioning for economic recovery in 1992, with an emphasis on controlling costs. BFI's recycling operations reached profitability, with revenues jumping from $10 million in 1989 to $175 million in 1992. Medical waste revenues also improved.

These improvements, coupled with a slight increase in the volume of business in its core area of waste disposal, were not lost on the stock market: in June 1993 BFI's stock stood 40% higher in price than in June 1992.

WHEN

Accountant Tom Fatjo and Harvard MBA Louis Waters founded American Refuse Systems in 1967 with a single truck, providing garbage collection to a Houston neighborhood. They saw that the 1960s clean-air laws created opportunities for large garbage businesses with the resources to comply with changing environmental regulations. In 1969 the company bought construction equipment distributor Browning-Ferris Machinery and changed its name to Browning-Ferris Industries. Subsequently, BFI bought numerous waste disposal firms, acquiring a total of 157 by 1973.

Revenues and profits fell 18% in 1975, partly because of decreased demand for waste paper, which had previously provided nearly half of the company's revenues. BFI spun off its waste-paper subsidiary (Consolidated Fibres) in 1976. In late 1976 and again in 1977 BFI succeeded in hiking prices across its entire operation 5–5.5%; the result was a 37% rise in earnings in 1977. That year Harry Phillips, who had joined BFI in 1970 when BFI acquired his 5 companies, became CEO, replacing Louis Waters, who became BFI's chairman. Tom Fatjo had left BFI in 1976 to run an investment company.

By 1980 BFI had become the 2nd largest US waste disposal company. Phillips continued to expand BFI, acquiring 508 companies from 1981 to 1988. BFI bought hazardous-waste disposer CECOS International (1983), formed a joint venture to market trash-burning power plants (1984), and entered the medical-waste field by buying 2 small firms (1986).

BFI paid fines of $1.35 million after pleading guilty to price fixing in 1987 and paid $2.5 million in 1988 and $1.55 million in 1990 to settle suits arising from environmental violations at Louisiana hazardous-waste sites. To improve its image BFI recruited William Ruckelshaus, a former EPA administrator, to take over as CEO in 1988.

After the EPA denied BFI permits to restart 2 hazardous-waste operations in 1990, the company discontinued such operations altogether, writing off $295 million in the process. The company reserved another $246.5 million in 1991 for projected landfill closure and post-closure management costs resulting from new EPA regulations.

A bright spot in BFI's otherwise lackluster 1992 was the performance of its medical-waste unit, with revenues up 27% on the 1991 return of $123 million. BFI services about 1,900 of the 6,000 hospitals in the US, and the company's 1992 market share was estimated at between 22% and 27%. Further improvements came in 1993 with new landfill permits and 20 acquisitions, which will allow the company to substantially increase its volume of waste disposal.

NYSE symbol: BFI
Fiscal year ends: September 30

WHO

Chairman and CEO: William D. Ruckelshaus, age 60, $806,000 pay
VC and Chief Marketing Officer: Norman A. Myers, age 57, $459,000 pay
President and COO: Bruce E. Ranck, age 44, $371,100 pay
Chairman of BFI International, Inc.: Louis A. Waters, age 54, $341,500 pay
SVP and CFO: Jeffrey E. Curtiss, age 44, $300,000 pay
VP Human Resources and Employee Relations: Susan J. Piller
Auditors: Arthur Andersen & Co.

WHERE

HQ: 757 N. Eldridge, Houston, TX 77079
Phone: 713-870-8100
Fax: 713-870-7844

BFI operates in 480 locations in North America and Puerto Rico and in Australia, Hong Kong, Italy, the Netherlands, New Zealand, Spain, the UK, and Venezuela.

	1992 Sales $ mil.	% of total	1992 Operating Income $ mil.	% of total
US & Puerto Rico	2,720	83	307	88
Other countries	568	17	43	12
Adjustments	—	—	—	—
Total	**3,288**	**100**	**350**	**100**

WHAT

	1992 Sales % of Total
Solid waste collection	62
Solid waste transfer & disposal	14
Medical waste	4
Recycling	5
Other North American services	3
International	12
Total	**100**

Solid Waste Services
Commercial/industrial/residential collection

Solid Waste Transfer and Disposal
Transfer stations
Sanitary landfills

Medical Waste
Collection and disposal

Recycling
Curbside service/organic waste treatment
Tires-to-energy conversion

Other services
Portable restroom services
Street and parking-lot sweeping

Selected Subsidiaries and Affiliates
American Ref-Fuel Co. (50%, joint venture with Air Products and Chemicals, Inc.)
BFI Services Group, Inc.
Browning-Ferris Industries Europe, Inc.
Browning-Ferris International, Inc.
Swire BFI Waste Services Ltd. (50%, joint venture with Swire Pacific)

KEY COMPETITORS

Bechtel
Canadian Pacific
Consolidated Rail
EnClean
Mid-American Waste Systems
Ogden
Safety-Kleen
TRW
Union Pacific
USA Waste Services
WMX Technologies

HOW MUCH

	9-Year Growth	1983	1984	1985	1986	1987	1988	1989	1990	1991	1992
Sales ($ mil.)	16.3%	844	1,001	1,145	1,328	1,657	2,067	2,551	2,967	3,183	3,288
Net income ($ mil.)	9.2%	80	89	112	137	172	227	263	257	65	176
Income as % of sales	—	9.4%	8.9%	9.8%	10.3%	10.4%	11.0%	10.3%	8.7%	2.0%	5.3%
Earnings per share ($)	7.1%	0.60	0.65	0.80	0.95	1.15	1.51	1.74	1.68	0.42	1.11
Stock price – high ($)	—	11.91	11.13	16.00	23.69	35.75	29.25	42.75	49.25	30.75	27.13
Stock price – low ($)	—	8.19	6.63	9.16	15.13	17.50	20.88	26.88	20.75	16.88	19.50
Stock price – close ($)	10.4%	10.75	9.25	16.00	22.38	28.00	27.38	38.75	22.25	21.75	26.13
P/E – high	—	20	17	20	25	31	19	25	29	73	24
P/E – low	—	14	10	11	16	15	14	15	12	40	18
Dividends per share ($)	14.6%	0.20	0.24	0.27	0.32	0.40	0.48	0.56	0.64	0.68	0.68
Book value per share ($)	12.5%	2.99	3.39	3.95	5.11	5.93	7.05	8.33	7.61	7.29	8.66
Employees	7.4%	15,500	16,800	17,300	18,600	18,200	21,500	25,500	25,200	27,000	29,400

1992 Year-end:
Debt ratio: 43.5%
Return on equity: 13.9%
Cash (mil.): $389
Current ratio: 1.3
Long-term debt (mil.): $1,094
No. of shares (mil.): 168.6
Dividends:
 1992 average yield: 2.6%
 1992 payout: 61.3%
Market value (mil.): $4,405

Stock Price History High/Low 1983–92

DELL COMPUTER CORPORATION

RANK: 47

OVERVIEW

"Slow down" is a new phrase at Dell Computer, which grew in 1992 from the world's #11 PC seller to #5. The Austin, Texas–based company more than doubled its sales, to $2 billion in 1992; earnings doubled to $102 million. But Dell had problems in 1993, including its first quarterly loss ($76 million) since the company went public in 1988. In a major strategy shift, Dell is focusing on restoring profits instead of promoting growth.

Dell is the brainchild of 28-year-old Michael Dell, who pioneered the direct-mail approach to PC marketing and owns 30% of Dell's stock. Salespeople take orders over Dell's toll-free lines 24 hours daily. The company has suffered from price wars with IBM and Compaq, but Dell's own growing pains have created more problems.

In 1992 a prominent Wall Street analyst questioned whether Dell had overstated its earnings to mask losses from currency trading. In 1993 Dell withdrew an equity offering after a sharp drop in its stock and scrapped a poorly designed line of notebook computers. (Dell's entry into the notebook business, the industry's fastest-growing market, has been slow.) Dell's faulty forecasting system caused it to overestimate demand for its PCs, which have had glitches.

Michael Dell is repairing the company on several fronts. He hired John Medica, developer of Apple Computer's PowerBook line, to direct Dell's notebook line. He is unleashing the company's direct sales tactics in Japan, the world's #2 PC market, and is tapping more US retailers to sell Dell computers.

WHEN

At the age of 13, Michael Dell was already a successful businessman. From his parents' home in Houston, Dell ran a mail-order stamp trading business that, within a few months, grossed over $2,000. At 16 he sold subscriptions to the *Houston Post* and at 17 bought his first BMW. When he enrolled at the University of Texas in 1983, he was thoroughly bitten by the business bug.

Although Dell started as a pre-med student, on the side he sold RAM chips and disk drives for IBM PCs. Dell bought his products at cost from IBM dealers, who, at the time, were required to order from IBM large monthly quotas of PCs, which frequently exceeded demand. Dell resold his stock through ads in local papers (and later through national computer magazines) at 10% to 15% below retail.

By April 1984 Michael Dell's dorm room computer components business was grossing about $80,000 a month — enough to convince him to drop out of college. At about that time he started making and selling his own IBM clones under the brand name PC's Limited. Drawing on his previous sales experience, Dell sold his machines directly to end-users rather than through retail computer outlets, as most manufacturers did. By eliminating the retail markup, Dell could sell his PCs at about 40% of the price of an IBM.

The company was plagued by management changes during the mid-1980s. Renamed Dell Computer, it expanded its customer base by adding international sales offices in 1987. In 1988 it started selling to government agencies and added a sales force to serve larger customers. That year Dell went public in a $34.2 million offering.

Dell tripped in 1989, reporting a 64% drop in profits. Sales were growing — but so were costs, mostly because of the company's expensive efforts to design a PC using proprietary components and RISC chips; the project has since been largely abandoned. Also, the company's warehouses were greatly oversupplied. But within a year the company turned itself around by cutting inventories and coming out with 8 new products.

In 1990 Dell entered the retail arena by allowing Soft Warehouse Superstores (now CompUSA) to sell its PCs at mail-order prices. In 1991 it struck a similar deal with Staples, an office supply chain. Dell introduced upgradable processor systems, allowing users to replace slower processors with faster ones as they come out. Also that year, Dell opened a plant in Limerick, Ireland.

In 1992 Xerox agreed to sell Dell machines in 19 Latin American countries. The same year Dell developed a new line of PCs to be sold through Price Club, the warehouse-club subsidiary of Price Company. In 1993 Dell opened subsidiaries in Japan and Austria and began selling PCs through Best Buy Co.'s 117 US stores, located in 16 states.

110 THE TEXAS 500

NASDAQ symbol: DELL
Fiscal year ends: Around January 31
(52/53 week year)

WHO

Chairman and CEO: Michael S. Dell, age 28, $539,383 pay
SVP Product Group: G. Glenn Henry, age 50, $386,016 pay
SVP; President, Dell International: Andrew R. Harris, age 38, $454,746 pay
SVP; President, Dell USA: Joel J. Kocher, age 36, $449,019 pay
VP Portable Products: John K. Medica, age 34
VP, General Counsel, and Secretary: Richard E. Salwen, age 50, $258,890 pay
CFO: Thomas J. Meredith, age 43
VP Human Resources: Savino R. Ferrales, age 42
Auditors: Price Waterhouse

WHERE

HQ: 9505 Arboretum Blvd., Austin, TX 78759
Phone: 512-338-4400
Fax: 512-728-8700

Dell has operations in the US, Canada, Mexico, Australia, Japan, and 15 European countries. It has factories in the US and Ireland and sells its computers in more than 95 countries.

	1992 Sales $ mil.	1992 Sales % of total	1992 Operating Income $ mil.	1992 Operating Income % of total
US & Canada	1,452	72	111	80
Other countries	562	28	28	20
Total	**2,014**	**100**	**139**	**100**

WHAT

	1992 Sales % of total
Major accounts	47
Small & medium businesses & individuals	39
Value-added remarketers	14
Total	**100**

	1992 Sales % of total
Portables	12
High-end systems	14
Standard desktops	74
Total	**100**

Servers
Series 4000/XE
Performance 486/ME series
Performance 486/T series

Workstations
Performance 486/T series
Dimension 486DX2/50

Desktop systems
Dell 333s/L
Dell 425s/L
Dell 433/L
Dell 433s/L
Dell 450/L
Dell 466/L
Dimension 486DX2/50
Dimension DX/33
Dimension 486SX/25

Portable systems
Dimension NL 20
Dimension NL25
Dimension NL25C
Performance 325NC
Performance 325SLi

KEY COMPETITORS

Apple
AST
AT&T
Commodore
Compaq
CompuCom Systems
CompUSA
Data General
DEC
Fujitsu
Gateway 2000
Hewlett-Packard
Hitachi
Honeywell
Hyundai
IBM
Machines Bull
Matsushita
NEC
Oki
Olivetti
Philips
Sharp
Siemens
Software Etc.
Sun Microsystems
Toshiba
Unisys
Wang

HOW MUCH

	Annual Growth	1983	1984	1985	1986	1987	1988	1989	1990	1991	1992
Sales ($ mil.)	79.2%	—	—	34	70	159	258	389	546	890	2,014
Net income ($ mil.)	93.6%	—	—	1	2	9	14	5	27	51	102
Income as % of sales	—	—	—	2.3%	3.1%	5.9%	5.6%	1.3%	5.0%	5.7%	5.0%
Earnings per share ($)	40.1%	—	—	—	—	0.48	0.53	0.18	0.91	1.40	2.59
Stock price – high ($)	—	—	—	—	—	—	8.42	7.08	12.58	24.17	48.38
Stock price – low ($)	—	—	—	—	—	—	5.17	3.33	3.08	10.50	15.00
Stock price – close ($)	63.8%	—	—	—	—	—	6.67	3.67	12.33	17.08	48.00
P/E – high	—	—	—	—	—	—	16	39	14	17	19
P/E – low	—	—	—	—	—	—	10	19	3	8	6
Dividends per share ($)	0.0%	—	—	—	—	0.00	0.00	0.00	0.00	0.00	0.00
Book value per share ($)	77.4%	—	—	—	—	0.57	2.69	2.83	3.86	7.66	10.02
Employees	49.3%	—	—	—	—	627	1,184	1,508	2,050	2,970	4,650

1992 Year-end:
Debt ratio: 11.6%
Return on equity: 29.3%
Cash (mil.): $95
Current ratio: 1.73
Long-term debt (mil.): $48
No. of shares (mil.): 37
Dividends:
  1992 average yield: 0.0%
  1992 payout: 0.0%
Market value (mil.): $1,769

Stock Price History High/Low 1988–92

DR PEPPER/SEVEN-UP COMPANIES, INC.

RANK: 88

OVERVIEW

Once again a public company, Dallas-based Dr Pepper/Seven-Up trails only Coke and Pepsi in the US soft drink market, with an 11.1% share. The holding company's array of beverage brands includes Dr Pepper, 7-Up, Welch's, and IBC. Dr Pepper, the company's flagship product, is the oldest nationwide soft drink and is the 5th most popular soft drink in the country.

Dr Pepper/Seven-Up produces flavoring extracts and markets them to independent bottlers. Most of the company's business comes from the US; although international sales climbed 29% in 1992, foreign business accounted for less than 1% of the company's total. Domestically, Dr Pepper's recent sales growth has far outpaced the industry as a whole. Revamped sales and marketing strategies have produced modest gains for 7-Up, the #2 lemon-lime soft drink.

In January 1993 Dr Pepper/Seven-Up made a public offering, which produced $283.5 million in equity. In August Cadbury Schweppes prepared to raise its stake in the company to 26% by agreeing to buy Prudential's 20% share for $231 million.

WHEN

The Dr Pepper brand was first sold in 1885 in Waco, Texas, at Morrison's Old Corner Drug Store. The pharmacist, Charles Alderton, concocted the unique syrup, and the store's owner, Wade Morrison, named the new drink after an acquaintance in his home state of Virginia. A Waco bottler, Robert Lazenby, began producing the syrup and bottling the drink at his Circle "A" Ginger Ale Bottling Works. Lazenby and Morrison formed a new company, the Artesian Manufacturing and Bottling Company, and in 1923 they moved its headquarters to Dallas. In 1924 the name was changed to the Dr Pepper Company. The drink's popularity continued to grow, and in 1946 the company's stock was listed on the NYSE. Dr Pepper remained a public company until 1984, when its shareholders voted to accept a $22-per-share bid by Forstmann Little & Company, which privatized the company.

Dr Pepper is distinguished by its noncola flavor and its memorable advertising slogans, including the 1930s motto "10, 2 and 4" (the times of day to drink Dr Pepper); the 1960s description as the most "misunderstood" soft drink; the "Be a Pepper" campaign in the 1980s; and the current "Just what the Dr ordered."

The 7-Up soft drink began in 1929 when C. L. Grigg, owner of The Howdy Company in St. Louis (home of Howdy Orange drink), introduced his new lemon-lime soda. The drink's success prompted Grigg to change his company's name to The Seven-Up Company in 1936, and by the late 1940s 7-Up was the world's 3rd best-selling soft drink. The company remained in family hands until it went public in 1967. Sales increased with the "Uncola" marketing campaign and the introduction of Diet 7-Up.

Philip Morris bought Seven-Up in 1978, but profits began to slide. By 1986 Philip Morris was negotiating to sell Seven-Up to PepsiCo. About the same time Coca-Cola was reaching an agreement to buy Dr Pepper. The FTC ruled the sales anticompetitive, and Hicks and Haas, a Dallas investment firm, stepped in to buy both companies in 1986. Dr Pepper sold for $416 million and Seven-Up sold for $240 million. PepsiCo came away with the international rights to 7-Up.

Hicks and Haas merged the 2 companies in 1988 to form Dr Pepper/Seven-Up Companies, Inc. The new company managers (many of them from Dr Pepper) consolidated plant operations at Seven-Up's St. Louis facility, selling other property and trimming Seven-Up staff. While sales of Dr Pepper grew after the company's merger, 7-Up sales diminished. Francis Mullin III took over as Seven-Up COO in 1991 and now serves as president.

Recognizing its appeal to both cola and noncola drinkers, Dr Pepper in 1992 shifted its advertising focus away from cola bashing.

Dr Pepper/Seven-Up's 1993 initial public offering followed a withdrawn offer in 1992, which called for $20 to $23 per share but met disinterest. The asking price in 1993 was $15 per share for 20 million shares.

In 1993 Seven-Up continued lawsuits against Coke for interfering in bottling contracts and against the FTC for preventing a New York bottler from selling 7-Up, while Dr Pepper and Coke settled lawsuits accusing each other of trademark infringement.

NYSE symbol: DPS
Fiscal year ends: December 31

WHO

Chairman, President, and CEO: John R. Albers, age 61, $1,226,983 pay
EVP and CFO: Ira M. Rosenstein, age 53, $612,671 pay
EVP; President, Dr Pepper USA: True H. Knowles, age 55, $455,577 pay
EVP; President, Seven-Up USA: Francis I. Mullin III, age 49, $455,423 pay
VP, General Counsel, and Secretary: Nelson A. Bangs
SVP: Charles P. Grier, age 62, $282,309 pay
VP; SVP, Dr Pepper USA: John G. Clarke, age 47
VP; SVP, Dr Pepper USA: John C. Kilduff, age 46
VP; SVP, Seven-Up USA: Russell B. Klein, age 35
VP; SVP, Seven-Up USA: Robert E. Quirk, age 43
VP, Corporate Communications: James A. Ball III
VP Finance and Treasurer: Michael R. Buiter
VP International: Daniel F. O'Neill
VP Human Resources: John L. Quigley, Jr.
Auditors: KPMG Peat Marwick

WHERE

HQ: 8144 Walnut Hill Ln., Dallas, TX 75231-4372
Phone: 214-360-7000
Fax: 214-360-7981

Dr Pepper/Seven-Up owns a state-of-the-art facility in Overland, Missouri, where it manufactures concentrates, extracts, and fountain syrups. In Dallas the company rents 167,000 square feet of office space for its headquarters and 73,000 square feet of warehouse space.

WHAT

	1992 Sales % of total
Dr Pepper USA	40
Seven-Up USA	32
Dr Pepper/Seven-Up Foodservice	19
Premier Beverages (IBC, Welch's)	8
International	1
Total	**100**

Brands Produced
Dr Pepper
  Caffeine-Free Diet Dr Pepper
  Caffeine-Free Dr Pepper
  Diet Dr Pepper
  Dr Pepper
  IBC Cream Soda
  IBC Root Beer
  Welch's
Seven-Up
  7-Up
  Cherry 7-Up
  Diet 7-Up
  Diet Cherry 7-Up

Brands Distributed
Canada Dry
Sunkist
Tahitian Treat

KEY COMPETITORS

Cable Car Beverage
Coca-Cola
Heineken
PepsiCo
Snapple
Whitman

HOW MUCH

	Annual Growth	1983	1984	1985	1986	1987	1988	1989	1990	1991	1992
Sales ($ mil.)	6.6%	—	—	—	—	—	510	514	540	601	659
Net income ($ mil.)	—	—	—	—	—	—	(68)	(42)	(33)	(20)	(8)
Dr Pepper cases sold (mil.)	8.3%	284.4	301.5	320.5	323.6	355.6	399.5	416.8	460.4	530.5	581.5
Dr Pepper % of market	—	4.9	4.9	4.9	4.8	5.0	5.3	5.4	5.8	6.0	6.4
7-Up cases sold (mil.)	(2.7%)	412.4	417.3	383.8	340.7	374.9	350.5	318.8	315.5	315.3	323.0
7-Up % of market	—	7.2	6.8	5.9	5.0	5.2	4.7	4.1	4.0	3.9	4.0
Total cases sold (mil.)	2.9%	696.8	718.8	704.3	664.3	730.5	750.0	735.6	775.9	845.8	904.5
Total % of market	—	12.1	11.7	10.8	9.8	10.2	10.0	9.5	9.8	10.4	11.1
Employees	2.5%	—	—	—	—	—	842	854	873	905	930

1992 Year-end:
Debt ratio: —
Return on equity: 2.9%
Cash (mil.): $0
Current ratio: 0.46
Long-term debt (mil.): $1,092

Total Cases Sold (mil.) 1983–92

THE TEXAS 500

DRESSER INDUSTRIES, INC.

RANK: 27

OVERVIEW

Dresser, a major global industrial equipment maker based in Dallas, is returning to the oil patch. During the past 10 years the company has shed 26 subsidiaries involved in everything from life insurance to construction equipment to fire hydrants while acquiring over 10 oil and natural gas–related operations. Long-term debt had dropped to less than 3% of book capitalization by the end of 1992.

CEO John Murphy is positioning the company for a global resurgence in demand for hydrocarbon energy sources by making equipment from wellhead to gas pump. Dresser provides oilfield services through Western Atlas International (seismic exploration, core and fluid analysis, workstation software, and wireline logging; a 29.5%-owned joint venture with Litton), M-I Drilling Fluids (a 64%-owned joint venture with Halliburton), Security (roller cone and PDC drill bits), IRI (drilling rigs), and Guiberson AVA (production equipment). In hydrocarbon processing, the company has formed 2 joint ventures with Ingersoll-Rand. One, Dresser-Rand (51% owned by Dresser), makes generators, compressors, gas and steam turbines, and electric motors. The other, Ingersoll-Dresser Pump (49% owned by Dresser), offers the world's broadest selection of pumps and related services. Engineering services are provided through M. W. Kellogg.

WHEN

Solomon Dresser arrived in the oil boom town of Bradford, Pennsylvania, in 1878 with a consumptive wife and 4 children. He eked out a living in oil field jobs. He also tinkered with an invention, and in 1880 Dresser was granted a patent for a cap packer, a device that prevents crude oil from mixing with other fluids in a well. In the 1880s and 1890s he perfected a coupling that used fitted rubber to prevent leaks in pipeline connections.

As the natural gas industry grew, so did demand for the reliable Dresser coupling. The family firm prospered even after Solomon's death in 1911, but his heirs, anxious to pursue other interests, sold the company to W. A. Harriman & Company in 1928, and the investment banker took Dresser public.

Soon after, 3 Harriman executives — including Roland Harriman, son of the founder, and Prescott Bush, father of future US president George Bush — were discussing the vacant Dresser presidency. Just then, an old Yale friend, Neil Mallon, dropped by the office, and Harriman tapped Mallon for the top post.

During Mallon's 41-year career with Dresser, the company grew to an oil field conglomerate. Bryant Heating and Manufacturing was the first acquisition (bought in 1933 and sold in 1949). As Dresser tried to develop a high-speed compressor for gas pipelines, it purchased Clark Brothers (compressors, 1937). It later abandoned its compressor research, but Olean, New York–based Clark became a company cornerstone.

Dresser moved its headquarters to Cleveland in 1945, then to Dallas in 1950. Company acquisitions ranged from Magnet Cove (drilling "mud" lubricant for oil well holes, 1949) to Symington-Wayne (gasoline pumps, 1968).

In 1983, after an oil services boom had peaked, CEO Jack Murphy began refocusing on the petroleum business, balancing upstream and downstream services and products. Dresser bought M. W. Kellogg Company (refinery engineering, 1988) just in time for a petrochemical boom but withdrew a 1989 bid for drill-bit maker Smith International in the face of antitrust problems. In 1990 Dresser bought the diamond drill-bit product line of rival Baker Hughes. Also that year Dresser bought 2 European businesses, Mono Group (pumps) and Peabody (blowers and combustion equipment). The next year the company acquired the fuel dispensing group of Ferranti International, a UK concern.

In 1992 Dresser divested its industrial products and equipment operations by transferring the businesses into a separate company (INDRESCO) and distributing shares of INDRESCO to Dresser's shareholders. That same year Dresser acquired AVA International, a maker of oil field safety valves and well completion equipment. Also in 1992 Dresser pooled its pump operations with Ingersoll-Rand to form a new joint venture, Ingersoll-Dresser Pump.

Dresser acquired Bredero Price Pipe (pipe coating) and TK Valve (ball valves for oil and gas production and transmission) in 1993.

THE TEXAS 500

NYSE symbol: DI
Fiscal year ends: October 31

WHO

Chairman and CEO: John J. Murphy, age 61, $900,000 pay
VC: Bill D. St. John, age 61, $452,004 pay (prior to promotion)
President and COO: William E. Bradford, age 58, $610,546 pay (prior to promotion)
SVP Operations; Chairman, President, and CEO, M. W. Kellogg: Donald C. Vaughn, age 56, $535,259 pay
VP Operations: James L. Bryan, age 56, $260,992 pay
VP and General Counsel: M. Scott Nickson, Jr.
VP Human Resources: Richard E. Hauslein
Auditors: Price Waterhouse

WHERE

HQ: 1600 Pacific, Dallas, TX 75201
Phone: 214-740-6000
Fax: 214-740-6584

The company operates manufacturing and service facilities in 50 countries around the world.

	1992 Sales		1992 Operating Income	
	$ mil.	% of total	$ mil.	% of total
US	2,339	59	90	33
Canada	84	2	7	3
Europe	934	24	78	29
Other countries	577	15	93	35
Adjustments	(137)	—	(153)	—
Total	**3,797**	**100**	**115**	**100**

WHAT

	1992 Sales		1992 Operating Income	
	$ mil.	% of total	$ mil.	% of total
Oil field products & services	565	15	38	14
Hydrocarbon processing	1,679	44	162	61
Engineering services	1,559	41	67	25
Adjustments	(6)	—	(152)	—
Total	**3,797**	**100**	**115**	**100**

Oil Field Products and Services
Drill bits
Drilling fluid systems
Exploration services
Production tools
Rigs and equipment

Energy Processing and Conversion Equipment
Compressors and turbines
Control products
Engineering services
Marketing systems (Wayne gas pumps)
Power systems
Pumps

KEY COMPETITORS

ABB	Friedrich Krupp
Baker Hughes	General Electric
Bechtel	Keystone International
Caterpillar	LTV
Cooper Industries	McDermott
Deere	Peter Kiewit Sons'
Fluor	Schlumberger
FMC	

HOW MUCH

	9-Year Growth	1983	1984	1985	1986	1987	1988	1989	1990	1991	1992
Sales ($ mil.)	1.0%	3,473	3,732	4,111	3,661	3,120	3,942	3,956	4,480	4,670	3,797
Net income ($ mil.)	33.8%	5	97	(196)	1	16	123	163	174	140	70
Income as % of sales	—	0.1%	2.6%	(4.8%)	0.0%	0.5%	3.1%	4.1%	3.9%	3.0%	1.8%
Earnings per share ($)	37.3%	0.03	0.62	(1.29)	0.01	0.11	0.89	1.21	1.29	1.04	0.52
Stock price – high ($)	—	12.75	11.69	12.13	10.19	17.81	17.81	24.00	28.13	28.50	23.63
Stock price – low ($)	—	7.50	7.63	8.38	7.00	8.81	11.25	14.50	16.50	16.25	17.25
Stock price – close ($)	6.3%	10.38	9.13	9.06	9.69	13.13	14.69	22.44	20.88	20.13	18.00
P/E – high	—	—	19	—	—	162	20	20	22	27	45
P/E – low	—	—	12	—	—	80	13	12	13	16	33
Dividends per share ($)	4.6%	0.40	0.40	0.40	0.35	0.20	0.28	0.45	0.55	0.60	0.60
Book value per share ($)	(6.2%)	12.31	12.45	10.80	10.67	10.76	11.19	11.88	13.01	13.11	6.93
Employees	(4.2%)	40,516	42,400	46,200	39,700	30,800	30,700	31,400	33,100	31,800	27,400

1992 Year-end:
Debt ratio: 11.3%
Return on equity: 5.2%
Cash (mil.): $155
Current ratio: 1.07
Long-term debt (mil.): $25
No. of shares (mil.): 137
Dividends:
 1992 average yield: 3.3%
 1992 payout: 115.4%
Market value (mil.): $2,465

Stock Price History High/Low 1983–92

THE TEXAS 500

KING RANCH, INC.

RANK: 175

OVERVIEW

Described as the "birthplace of American ranching," the King Ranch's 825,000-acre expanse, larger than Rhode Island, sprawls across the southern tip of Texas, 500 miles of roads contained within its borders. One of the world's largest private agribusinesses, the ranch inspired Edna Ferber's *Giant* and the Rock Hudson–Elizabeth Taylor–James Dean film that followed. Throughout its history the ranch has been the domain of one family — the heirs of the founder, Capt. Richard King.

The King Ranch operates an oil-and-gas subsidiary that handles royalties — more than $1 billion since WWII — and explores for oil and gas on its own. It runs 60,000 head of cattle (including the King Ranch–developed Santa Gertrudis breed) and other animals. The company also breeds quarter horses and thoroughbreds, owns overseas real estate, and cultivates grain sorghum and cotton in Texas and sugarcane and wildflowers in Florida.

King Ranch is experimenting with crossing Santa Gertrudis cattle with other breeds for leaner meat and is breeding earlier-maturing heifers for increased calf production.

WHEN

As Texas was joining the Union in 1845, steamboat pilot Richard King arrived at the Rio Grande to ferry goods. After crossing the vast plain between the river and Corpus Christi, he and a Texas Ranger friend began running cattle around Santa Gertrudis Creek in 1853.

The Ranger was later killed by a jealous husband, but King continued to build the ranch in the Wild Horse Desert, an area known for the mustangs that roamed free. King went to Mexico in 1854 and relocated the residents of an entire drought-ravaged village to the ranch and employed them as ranch hands, known ever since as *Kineños* ("King's men"). In 1858 King and his wife, Henrietta, built their homestead at a site recommended by friend Robert E. Lee.

King Ranch endured attacks from Union guerrillas during the Civil War and from Mexican bandits after the war. In 1867 the ranch used its famed Running W brand for the first time. After King's death in 1885, a Corpus Christi attorney named Robert Kleberg married King's daughter Alice and managed the ranch for his mother-in-law.

Henrietta King died in 1925, and the Klebergs assembled land through inheritance or purchase from other heirs. Before his death in 1932, Kleberg passed control of the ranch to his sons, Richard and Bob. In 1933 Bob Kleberg negotiated an exclusive and lucrative oil and gas lease through the year 2013 with Humble Oil, later part of Exxon. The ranch was incorporated in 1935.

While Richard Kleberg served in Congress, Bob Kleberg intensified crossbreeding of cattle. British breeds, imported to flesh out the stringy native longhorns, were not suited to dry, hot South Texas. By crossbreeding Indian Brahman cattle, the King Ranch developed the Santa Gertrudis breed, recognized by the US government in 1940 as the first beef breed ever created in America.

Bob Kleberg also made King Ranch a leading quarter horse breeder, the stock used to work cattle. For thoroughbred breeding he bought Kentucky Derby winner Bold Venture (1938) and Idle Hour Stable, a Kentucky breeding farm (1946). In 1946 a King Ranch horse, Assault, won racing's Triple Crown.

Richard died in 1955, and with Bob's death in 1974 the family asked James Clement, husband of one of the founder's great-granddaughters, to become CEO. The corporation formed King Ranch Oil and Gas in 1980 to explore for and produce oil and gas in 5 states and the Gulf of Mexico. King Ranch Oil and Gas sold Louisiana and Oklahoma properties to Presidio Oil for more than $40 million in cash and stock (1988).

When Clement retired in 1988, Darwin Smith became CEO, the first not related by blood or marriage to founder Richard King. Smith left after only a year, and the reins passed to Roger Jarvis, head of the Houston-based oil and gas operation, and corporate headquarters moved to Houston.

In 1992 King Ranch Oil & Gas, along with National Fuel Gas and Holly Petroleum, discovered natural gas off the coast of Louisiana. King Ranch owns 40% of the venture. In 1993 the US Navy announced plans to put transmitter antenna towers on the King Ranch as part of a radar system designed to track drug-carrying aircraft.

Private company
Fiscal year ends: December 31

WHO

Chairman: Leroy G. Denman, Jr.
President and CEO: Roger L. Jarvis, age 39
VP: Stephen J. "Tio" Kleberg, age 48
VP and Treasurer: Mark Kent
VP, General Counsel, and Secretary: Larry Worden
VP, Controller, and Assistant Secretary: James E. Savage
VP Audit: James B. Spear
Director: Thomas W. Keesee, Jr.
Director: Abraham Zaleznik
Director: John H. Duncan
Personnel Manager: Rickey Blackman

WHERE

HQ: Two Greenspoint Plaza, 16825 Northchase, Ste. 1450, Houston, TX 77060
Phone: 713-872-5566
Fax: 713-872-7209

King Ranch operates ranching and farming interests in South Texas, Arizona, Kentucky, Florida, and Brazil.

US Agricultural Operations
Eslabon Feedyard (Kingsville, TX)
King Ranch (Kingsville, TX)
King Ranch — Arizona
King Ranch Farm (Lexington, KY)
King Ranch Farms — Florida (Belle Glade, FL)

WHAT

Ranching Animals
Cattle
Monkey (foundation sire of the Santa Gertrudis breed)
Running W "A" herd

Quarter Horses
Mr San Peppy
Old Sorrel
Peppy
Peppy San Badger
Wimpy

Thoroughbred Horses
Assault (1946 Triple Crown winner)
Bold Venture
Chicaro
Gallant Bloom
High Gun
Middleground

Farming
Cotton
Milo
Sod
Sugar cane
Wildflowers

Subsidiaries
King Ranch Oil and Gas, Inc.
King Ranch Properties, Inc.
King Ranch Properties of Texas, Inc.
King Ranch Saddle Shop (leather products)
King Ranch Texas, Inc.
Kingsville Lumber Co. (retail building material)
Kingsville Publishing Co. (newspaper)
Robstown Hardware (farm equipment)

KEY COMPETITORS

Amerada Hess
Amoco
Ashland
Atlantic Richfield
British Petroleum
Broken Hill
Cargill
Chevron
Coastal
Continental Grain
Enron
Exxon
IBP
Imperial Oil
Koch
Mobil

Norsk Hydro
Occidental
Oryx
PDVSA
PEMEX
Pennzoil
Petrobrás
Petrofina
Phillips Petroleum
Reposol
Royal Dutch/Shell
Sun
Texaco
Total
Unocal
USX

HOW MUCH

	Annual Growth	1983	1984	1985	1986	1987	1988	1989	1990	1991	1992
Estimated Sales ($ mil.)	27.3%	—	—	—	—	—	—	160	160	165	330
Employees	26.0%	—	—	—	—	—	—	350	350	350	700

Sales ($ mil.) 1989–92

THE TEXAS 500

MARY KAY COSMETICS INC.

RANK: 96

OVERVIEW

No, pink is not Mary Kay Ash's favorite color. The 75-year-old matriarch of Mary Kay Cosmetics, the 2nd largest direct seller of cosmetics in the US (after Avon), also likes blues and yellows. Mary Kay's cosmetics are manufactured in Dallas (where the company is headquartered) and shipped to distribution centers located across the US. Total retail sales now surpass $1 billion.

Mary Kay cosmetics are sold only by the company's direct sales consultants, although these are not too difficult to find: they number about 300,000. Upon signing up, consultants purchase a sales case containing sample wares and Mary Kay's autobiography. Most of the consultants work part-time, and turnover hovers around 40% (far below Avon's 100–150% of its annual work force).

Mary Kay, who believes that "Appreciation is the oil that makes things run," still stays up late at night signing birthday cards for her employees. Recognition, not necessarily just money, is the name of the game at Mary Kay. At the company's annual seminars, top saleswomen win diamonds, furs, lavish vacations, and, of course, the trademark pink Cadillacs. (Others win Buick Regals outfitted with a bumper sticker that reads: When I grow up, I'm going to be a Cadillac.)

Mary Kay was included in the 1993 edition of *The 100 Best Companies to Work for in America* and boasts more women making more than $50,000 per year than any other US company. The company has made millionaires of about 50 women to date and is owned almost wholly by Ash and her family.

WHEN

Before founding her own company in 1963, Mary Kay Ash worked as a salesperson for Stanley Home Products. Overcome with envy for the prize awarded the top saleswoman at a Stanley convention — an alligator handbag — Mary Kay determined to win the next year's prize. She succeeded.

Tired of not receiving the recognition she deserved because of her sex, Mary Kay used her life savings, $5,000, to go into business for herself. She bought a cosmetics formula invented years earlier by a hide tanner. (The mixture was originally used to soften leather, but when the hide tanner noticed how young the formula made his hands look, he began applying the mixture to his face, with great results.) Mary Kay kept her first line simple — about 10 products — and enlisted consultants, who were to hold "Beauty Shows" with 5 or 6 women in attendance. The idea was that, with such small numbers, consultants could spend more time with clients individually. With son Richard Roberts handling finances, the company grossed $198,000 in its first year.

In 1966 Mary Kay bought herself a pink Cadillac that was much admired by employees. She began awarding the cars as prizes the following year. By 1981 orders had grown so large (almost 500) that GM dubbed a color "Mary Kay Pink."

When the company went public in 1968, Mary Kay became a millionaire. The same year the company launched its first fragrance, Snare. In 1969 May Kay began foreign operations, in Australia. Over the next 20 years the company entered Argentina, Canada, West Germany, and the UK.

The company grew steadily through the 1970s. Mary Kay published her autobiography in 1981, mainly as a motivational tool, complete with tips on how to save time (eat lunch in your office) and gain your husband's support (don't talk to him too much about your work) and favored words of wisdom ("Flowers leave their fragrance on the hand which bestows them").

In 1985 Mary Kay and Richard reacquired the company in a $315 million LBO. In the late 1980s the company, weighted with debt, lost money. A number of steps were taken to boost sales, income, and public image, including the introduction of recyclable packaging and empowerment groups (called Creative Action Teams). The company also began advertising in women's magazines (after a 5-year hiatus) to counter its old-fashioned image. In 1989 Avon rebuffed a buyout offer by Mary Kay. The company reorganized its debt structure in 1990, buying back much of its publicly held debentures.

Mary Kay introduced a line of bath and body products in 1991, the result of a joint venture with International Flavors & Fragrances. In 1993 the company announced that it was shopping for new headquarters.

Private company
Fiscal year ends: December 31

WHO

Chairman Emeritus: Mary Kay Ash, age 75
Chairman and CEO: Richard R. Rogers, age 50
President and COO: Richard C. Bartlett
SVP, Secretary, and Legal Counsel: Bradley R. Glendening
CFO: John P. Rochon
Auditors: Ernst & Young

WHERE

HQ: 8787 Stemmons Fwy., Dallas, TX 75247
Phone: 214-630-8787
Fax: 214-905-5699
Consultant Directory: 1-800-627-9529 (1-800-MARYKAY)

Mary Kay Cosmetics Inc. employs close to 300,000 direct sales consultants who sell the company's merchandise in the US and 15 other countries. The company conducts research and manufacturing activities at its Dallas headquarters and operates distribution centers in Atlanta, Chicago, Los Angeles, and Piscataway, New Jersey.

WHAT

	Types of Jobs % of total
Distribution	37
Manufacturing & research	35
Administration	12
Sales & marketing	10
Other	6
Total	**100**

Selected Subsidiaries
Business Travel Management Inc.
Mary Kay Cosmeticos Sociedad Anonima
Mary Kay Cosmetics (Taiwan) Inc.
Mary Kay Cosmetics Chile Ltd.
Mary Kay Cosmetics de Mexico SA de CV
Mary Kay Cosmetics GMBH
Mary Kay Cosmetics Guatemala SA
Mary Kay Cosmetics, Ltd.
Mary Kay Cosmetics of Uruguay
Mary Kay Cosmetics Pty. Ltd.
Mary Kay Foreign Sales Corp.
Mary Kay (N.Z.) Limited
New Arrow Corp.
New Arrow Corp. II
Tender Power Inc.

KEY COMPETITORS

Ames	Kmart
Amway	L'Oréal
Avon	Longs
Carter Hawley Hale	Macy
Carter-Wallace	Marks and Spencer
Chattem	May
Colgate-Palmolive	Mercantile Stores
Dayton Hudson	Montgomery Ward
Dillard	Nature's Sunshine
Edison Brothers	Nordstrom
Estée Lauder	J. C. Penney
Gillette	Procter & Gamble
Henkel	Rite Aid
Hudson's Bay	Shiseido
Jack Eckerd	Unilever
Jean Philippe Fragrances	Walgreen
	Wal-Mart
S.C. Johnson	Woolworth

HOW MUCH

	Annual Growth	1983	1984	1985	1986	1987	1988	1989	1990	1991	1992
Sales ($ mil.)	7.3%	324	278	249	255	326	406	450	487	520	613
Net income ($ mil.)	—	37	34	21	(33)	(3)	9	20	0	—	—
Income as % of sales	—	11.4%	12.2%	8.4%	(12.9%)	(9.2%)	2.2%	4.4%	0.0%	—	—
Direct sales consultants	4.9%	195,671	173,101	145,493	141,113	—	—	192,804	208,009	225,000	300,000
Employees	7.9%	—	—	—	1,265	—	—	1,400	1,722	1,900	2,000

Sales ($ mil.) 1983-1992

THE TEXAS 500   119

PENNZOIL COMPANY

RANK: 43

OVERVIEW

Maker of the US's best-selling motor oil, Houston-based Pennzoil has operations in oil and gas exploration, production, and marketing; sulphur mining and production; and real estate management. The company also owns Jiffy Lube International, the world's largest quick-lube operator, and makes and markets Gumout car care products. Pennzoil's net income dropped 57% in 1992, hurt by the company's sulphur and franchise operations.

Pennzoil continues to look overseas for new opportunities. In late 1992 the company signed its biggest international deal ever when it reached an agreement with the Republic of Azerbaijan to develop the Guneshli oil field in the Caspian Sea.

In order to raise cash for the project and as part of a plan to focus more on core operations, CEO James Pate has been playing his own version of "Let's Make a Deal." In late 1992 Pennzoil swapped $1.17 billion of its Chevron stock for 266 of Chevron's oil and gas properties. The properties — located primarily in the Gulf of Mexico and along the Gulf Coast, where Pennzoil's operations are concentrated — nearly double Pennzoil's oil and gas production. The trade also increases Pennzoil's cash flow by about $150 million.

Pennzoil had originally acquired the Chevron shares using the proceeds from a $3 billion settlement (of a $10 billion judgment against Texaco) in 1988.

WHEN

The post-WWII oil boom in West Texas attracted brothers J. Hugh and Bill Liedtke and a Connecticut scion named George Bush. Eager to make their fortunes, they formed Zapata Petroleum. Zapata hit big, with more than 120 producing wells in the Jameson Field in Coke County.

Zapata expanded with a subsidiary that drilled in the Gulf of Mexico. In 1959 Bush bought out the subsidiary and moved to Houston, where he later embarked on a political career that eventually took him to the White House. The Liedtkes set their sights on South Penn Oil of Oil City, Pennsylvania — a rusty relic from the 1911 dissolution of Standard Oil. Enlisting the support of oilman J. Paul Getty, the Liedtkes took control of South Penn in 1963, merged it with Zapata, renamed it Pennzoil in honor of the lubricant it sold, and moved the headquarters to Houston.

In 1965 J. Hugh Liedtke engineered the historic takeover of Shreveport-based United Gas Pipeline, 5 times the size of Pennzoil. Though blessed with a large pipeline system and vast mineral interests, United Gas was hampered by lethargic management. Using a takeover tactic that would break ground for a generation of corporate raiding, Liedtke launched a hostile cash tender offer. Pennzoil invited United Gas shareholders to sell their shares at a price higher than the market price.

Shareholders tendered 5 times the number of shares that Pennzoil wanted to buy. Undaunted, the Liedtkes raised the additional funds to buy 42% of United Gas stock. Pennzoil spun off a scaled-down United in 1974.

In the late 1960s Pennzoil financed speculative drilling by selling, directly to the public, stock in subsidiary companies. Shareholders in the subsidiaries were given some security, with rights to Pennzoil stock if the risky drilling proved unsuccessful.

In 1983 J. Hugh Liedtke hoped to purchase Getty Oil, the company begun by his old benefactor, and thought he had a deal. Texaco bought Getty instead. Pennzoil sued, and in 1985 a Texas jury awarded a record $10.53 billion in damages. Texaco sought refuge in bankruptcy court, emerging after settling with Pennzoil for $3 billion.

Liedtke stepped down as CEO in 1988 but remained chairman as Pennzoil determined how to spend its booty. In 1989 Pennzoil spent $2.1 billion for 8.8% of Chevron, but Liedtke denied that his company had a takeover in mind. Chevron wasn't convinced and filed suit in 1989 to keep him at bay. Much of the suit was dismissed in 1990, and by year's end Pennzoil had increased its stake to 9.4%, just under Chevron's poison pill threshold. However, the 1992 swap agreement ended litigation between the 2 companies.

Also in 1992 Pennzoil spun off filter-maker Purolator to the public, raising about $206 million.

In 1993 the company sold its interests in an Indonesian gold and silver project to Australia's Ashton Mining Limited.

120 THE TEXAS 500

NYSE symbol: PZL
Fiscal year ends: December 31

WHO

Chairman: J. Hugh Liedtke, age 71
President and CEO: James L. Pate, age 57, $820,400 pay
Group VP, Oil and Gas: Thomas M. Hamilton, age 49, $437,100 pay
Group VP Finance and Treasurer: David P. Alderson II, age 43, $298,300 pay
General Counsel: James W. Shaddix, age 46 $319,200 pay
VP Human Resources: Harold C. Mitchell
Auditors: Arthur Andersen & Co.

WHERE

HQ: PO Box 2967, Pennzoil Place, Houston, TX 77252-2967
Phone: 713-546-4000
Fax: 713-546-6639

Exploration and Production: Drilling in the US (primarily in Texas, Louisiana, West Virginia, Pennsylvania, and Utah) and in 4 foreign countries.

Products: 3 refineries — Oil City, PA; Shreveport, LA; and Roosevelt, UT. Pennzoil motor oil is sold in 57 countries.

Sulphur: Mining in Culberson County, TX; processing in Galveston, TX, and in Antwerp, Belgium.

Richland Development: Surface acreage and mineral rights in the Raton Basin of Colorado and New Mexico.

WHAT

	1992 Sales		1992 Operating Income	
	$ mil.	% of total	$ mil.	% of total
Oil & gas	419	18	135	47
Automotive prods.	1,510	64	78	27
Sulphur	148	6	1	—
Franchise ops.	174	7	(13)	(5)
Other	105	5	88	31
Adjustments	(133)	—	(200)	—
Total	**2,223**	**100**	**89**	**100**

Brand Names
Gumout carburetor cleaner and automotive products
Jiffy Lube quick lubrication shops
Pennzoil gasoline (East Coast and upper Midwest)
Pennzoil motor oils, lubricants
Performax synthetic motor oil
Wolf's Head lubricants and related products

KEY COMPETITORS

Amerada Hess	Occidental
Amoco	Oryx
Ashland	PDVSA
Atlantic Richfield	PEMEX
British Petroleum	Pennzoil
Broken Hill	Petrobrás
Chevron	Petrofina
Coastal	Phillips Petroleum
DuPont	Repsol
Elf Aquitaine	Royal Dutch/Shell
Exxon	Sun
Imperial Oil	Texaco
Koch	Total
Mobil	Unocal
Norsk Hydro	USX

HOW MUCH

	9-Year Growth	1983	1984	1985	1986	1987	1988	1989	1990	1991	1992
Sales ($ mil.)	(0.3%)	2,278	2,349	2,239	1,782	1,787	2,088	1,985	2,180	2,158	2,223
Net income ($ mil.)	(22.1%)	164	214	188	69	46	(187)	236	94	40	17
Income as % of sales	—	7.2%	9.1%	8.4%	3.8%	2.5%	(9.0%)	11.9%	4.3%	1.9%	0.8%
Earnings per share ($)	(19.5%)	3.03	3.89	3.96	1.28	0.72	(5.22)	6.06	2.37	0.99	0.43
Stock price – high ($)	—	42.50	45.38	72.00	91.00	95.00	79.13	88.88	89.50	76.50	57.50
Stock price – low ($)	—	31.25	30.75	40.50	48.13	38.50	65.25	71.63	61.75	52.13	43.13
Stock price – close ($)	4.4%	34.00	44.50	64.00	67.00	71.00	71.75	88.63	66.00	56.38	50.00
P/E – high	—	14	12	18	71	132	—	15	38	77	134
P/E – low	—	10	8	10	38	53	—	12	26	53	100
Dividends per share ($)	3.5%	2.20	2.20	2.20	2.20	2.20	2.60	3.00	3.00	3.00	3.00
Book value per share ($)	2.2%	23.88	21.38	18.23	16.79	7.67	35.67	35.23	31.10	28.77	28.99
Employees	0.6%	8,682	8,697	8,320	6,257	6,153	10,021	6,103	7,885	11,694	9,125

1992 Year-end:
Debt ratio: 66.8%
Return on equity: 1.5%
Cash (mil.): $21
Current ratio: 0.83
Long-term debt (mil.): $1,893
No. of shares (mil.): 41
Dividends:
  1992 average yield: 6.0%
  1992 payout: —
Market value (mil.): $2,036

Stock Price History High/Low 1983–92

THE TEXAS 500

SOUTHWEST AIRLINES CO.

RANK: 48

OVERVIEW

Southwest Air knows that the only way an airplane makes money is by flying. By keeping its planes in the air (typical ground time is 1/3 the industry average), Southwest (the #7 domestic carrier, with a 2.6% market share) is the only major US carrier to report both an operating and a net profit from 1990 to 1992. With a system of short hops, Southwest dominates the intrastate markets in California and Texas and is the leading carrier of originating passengers in Phoenix, Las Vegas, and Kansas City.

As other airlines pull out of markets, Southwest is rushing in. The company has rejected standard airline industry practices: hub-and-spoke flying, connecting flights, assigned seating, in-flight meals, and large computer reservation systems. Fares are so low that the company's main competition seems to be automobiles. To keep maintenance costs low, Southwest flies only one type of plane, the fuel-efficient Boeing 737. In 1992 the company claimed the first annual Triple Crown for the airline industry (best customer complaint record, the best baggage handling record, and the best on-time performance), an award no other major carrier has won even for a single month.

Flying also has to be fun for CEO Herb Kelleher. Known as "Uncle Herb" among employees, Kelleher has staged weekly parties at company headquarters, worn a clown suit, and encouraged flight attendants to deliver instructions in rap.

WHEN

Texas businessman Rollin King and lawyer Herb Kelleher founded Air Southwest Company in 1967 as an intrastate airline, linking Dallas, Houston, and San Antonio. Braniff and Texas International sued the company, questioning whether the region needed another airline, but the Texas Supreme Court ruled in Southwest's favor. In 1971 the company (renamed Southwest Airlines) made its first scheduled flight, from Dallas Love Field to San Antonio.

Capitalizing on its home base at Love Field, Southwest adopted love as the theme of its early ad campaigns, complete with stewardesses wearing hot pants and serving love potions (drinks) and love bites (peanuts). When other airlines moved to the Dallas–Fort Worth (D-FW) airport in 1974, Southwest stayed at Love Field, gaining a virtual monopoly at the airfield. This monopoly proved to be limiting, however, when the Wright Amendment became law in 1979, preventing companies operating out of Love Field from providing direct service to states other than those neighboring Texas. Southwest's customers could fly from Love Field to New Mexico, Oklahoma, Arkansas, and Louisiana but had to buy new tickets and board different Southwest flights to points beyond.

When Lamar Muse, Southwest's president, resigned in 1978 because of differences with King, Kelleher became president. Muse later took over his son Michael's nearly bankrupt airline, Muse Air Corporation, and in 1985 sold it to Southwest. Kelleher operated the Houston-based airline as TranStar but liquidated it in 1987 when competition from another Houston-based airline, Continental, caused Southwest's profits to fall.

Kelleher, who is regarded as something of an industry maverick, went on to introduce advance-purchase "Fun Fares" in 1986 and a frequent-flyer program based on the number of flights rather than mileage in 1987. He has often starred in Southwest's unconventional TV commercials, and, when Southwest became the official airline of Sea World (Texas) in 1988, Kelleher painted a 737 to resemble Shamu, the park's killer whale.

Southwest established an operating base at Phoenix Sky Harbor Airport in 1990. The airline continues to develop its route structure, especially on the West Coast, adding service to Oakland and Indianapolis (1989), Burbank and Reno (1990), and Sacramento (1991).

In 1992 Kelleher arm-wrestled Kurt Herwald (the 37-year-old chairman of Stevens Aviation, a California aircraft servicing company) for rights to the ad slogan "plane smart." Herwald won the highly publicized match but ceded the slogan to Southwest. Also in 1992 Southwest assumed the leased operations of Northwest Airlines at Chicago Midway Airport and Detroit Metropolitan Airport. Southwest initiated service to Baltimore in 1993, its first East Coast destination.

NYSE symbol: LUV
Fiscal year ends: December 31

WHO

Chairman, President, and CEO: Herbert D. Kelleher, age 61, $513,042 pay
EVP and COO: Gary A. Barron, age 48, $231,140 pay
VP and General Counsel: James F. Parker, age 46
VP Finance and CFO: Gary C. Kelly, age 37
VP People: Margaret Ann Rhoades
Auditors: Ernst & Young

WHERE

HQ: PO Box 36611, Love Field, Dallas, TX 75235-1611
Phone: 214-904-4000
Fax: 214-904-4200
Reservations: 800-531-5601

Cities Served

Albuquerque, NM	Little Rock, AR
Amarillo, TX	Los Angeles, CA
Austin, TX	Lubbock, TX
Baltimore, MD	Midland, TX
Birmingham, AL	Nashville, TN
Burbank, CA	New Orleans, LA
Chicago, IL	Oakland, CA
Cleveland, OH	Oklahoma City, OK
Columbus, OH	Ontario, CA
Corpus Christi, TX	Phoenix, AZ
Dallas, TX	Reno, NV
Detroit, MI	Sacramento, CA
El Paso, TX	St. Louis, MO
Harlingen, TX	San Antonio, TX
Houston, TX	San Diego, CA
Indianapolis, IN	San Francisco, CA
Kansas City, MO	San Jose, CA
Las Vegas, NV	Tulsa, OK

WHAT

	1992 Sales	
	$ mil.	% of total
Passengers	1,624	96
Freight	33	2
Other	28	2
Total	**1,685**	**100**

Services
The Company Club (frequent-flyer program based on trips rather than mileage)
In-flight beverage services
On-time flights
Quick ticketing and boarding procedures
Superior baggage handling

Flight Equipment	No.	Orders
Boeing 737-200	49	—
Boeing 737-300	67	60
Boeing 737-500	25	—
Total	**141**	**60**

KEY COMPETITORS

America West
AMR
Continental Airlines
Delta
Kimberly-Clark
Mesa Airlines
NWA
TWA
UAL
USAir

HOW MUCH

	9-Year Growth	1983	1984	1985	1986	1987	1988	1989	1990	1991	1992
Sales ($ mil.)	15.9%	448	536	680	769	778	860	1,015	1,187	1,314	1,685
Net income ($ mil.)	9.3%	41	50	47	50	20	58	72	47	27	91
Income as % of sales	—	9.1%	9.3%	7.0%	6.5%	2.6%	6.7%	7.1%	4.0%	2.1%	5.4%
Earnings per share ($)	8.6%	0.46	0.55	0.50	0.52	0.21	0.61	0.78	0.55	0.32	0.97
Stock price – high ($)	—	11.73	9.80	10.33	9.17	8.42	6.96	10.25	10.00	17.50	29.88
Stock price – low ($)	—	6.67	4.92	7.08	6.08	3.92	4.38	6.54	6.38	8.19	16.19
Stock price – close ($)	14.0%	9.07	7.33	8.96	6.88	4.46	6.75	8.00	8.75	17.06	29.50
P/E – high	—	25	18	21	18	40	11	13	18	55	31
P/E – low	—	14	9	14	12	19	7	8	12	26	17
Dividends per share ($)	2.4%	0.04	0.04	0.04	0.04	0.04	0.04	0.05	0.05	0.05	0.05
Book value per share ($)	11.2%	3.56	4.08	4.82	5.29	5.48	6.05	6.70	7.17	7.44	9.24
Employees	14.2%	3,462	3,934	5,271	5,819	5,765	6,467	7,760	8,620	9,778	11,397

1992 Year-end:
Debt ratio: 45.4%
Return on equity: 11.6%
Cash (mil.): $411
Current ratio: 1.37
Long-term debt (mil.): $699
No. of shares (mil.): 93
Dividends:
 1992 average yield: 0.2%
 1992 payout: 5.5%
Market value (mil.): $2,728

Stock Price History
High/Low 1983–92

TRAMMELL CROW COMPANY

RANK: 294

OVERVIEW

Trammell Crow Company's space under construction declined nearly 90% in 1992, and the US's largest property developer in 1991 dropped to 16th in 1992. Although you may think management is reaching for the smelling salts, the drop is actually by design. Facing an unfavorable climate for commercial real estate development in the US, the company has shifted its focus from development to services, including property and construction management and leasing. It is still the US's top property manager, with 242 million square feet under management.

The change in strategy has resulted in the departure of the majority of Trammell Crow's commercial real estate partners. In the past employees became partners by accepting low salaries and equity interests in projects, and at one time the company had a network of over 2,000 partnerships. As part of a restructuring, it spun off most of those projects into a separate asset company. Founder Trammell Crow, his family, CEO J. McDonald "Don" Williams, and 30-odd partners now control a $7.5 billion property portfolio.

Through Trammell Crow Corporate Services (TCCS) the company provides real estate services to corporate clients. TCCS has recently expanded into hospital facilities management.

WHEN

Trammell Crow returned to his native Dallas after WWII. An accountant who earned his degree in night school, he tried the moving business and then went to work for the grain wholesaling firm of his wife's family. When Crow found tenants for vacant warehouse space in the firm's building, he took his first steps to becoming the US's largest landlord.

When Ray-O-Vac, a tenant, outgrew the grain firm's space in 1948, Crow bought land and built a warehouse for the battery firm. Spurred by a booming postwar economy and the emergence of Dallas as a regional business center, Crow and his partners, the Stemmons brothers, built more than 50 warehouses in one section of Dallas alone. Much of Crow's success sprang from his knack of anticipating the needs of his tenants and adding amenities to the workplace.

Crow's methods revolutionized real estate. Ebullient with sunny optimism, he broke with Depression-spawned conventional wisdom and built even when no tenants were signed. He avoided long leases so he could raise rents in an expanding economy. He formed partnerships, often with little more than a handshake and a smile, sharing incentives and rewards with those who would otherwise be employees. Crow partners started at low salaries but earned sales commissions and equity participation in their projects.

Crow developed the Dallas Decorative Center in 1955. Emboldened by success, Crow began to change the face of Dallas with his masterpiece, the Dallas Market Center, a complex of buildings along the Trinity River.

He built the Dallas Homefurnishing Mart (1957) and the Trade Mart (1960), whose atrium became a Trammell Crow signature feature. Crow added Market Hall, the largest privately owned exhibition hall in the US, and combined the buildings' operations in 1963.

In 1972 Crow planned to add the 1.5-million-square-foot World Trade Center to the Market Center, but longtime partner John Stemmons balked and Crow offered to buy him out. Crow valued Stemmons's interests at $8 million, but his friend wouldn't take a penny more than $7 million. Finally Crow "lost" the argument and paid the lower figure.

In the 1960s and 1970s, Crow helped develop Atlanta's Peachtree Center and San Francisco's Embarcadero Center and entered residential real estate development. Struggling with high interest rates and heavy debts, Crow's enterprises faltered in 1975. In 1977 Crow and his partners sold off $100 million in properties to raise money and reorganized the company. The founder's wheeler-dealer instincts were curbed.

In the mid-1980s some longtime Crow partners defected as control became centralized in Dallas. The company formally diversified into investment banking and properties management and put 13 properties into Trammell Crow Real Estate Investors.

In 1993 Trammell Crow Real Estate Investors announced plans to "internalize management" and end its trust advisory agreement with Trammell Crow Ventures, an affiliate of Trammell Crow Company.

124   THE TEXAS 500

Private company
Fiscal year ends: December 31

WHO

Chairman: Trammell Crow, age 79
President and CEO: H. Don Williams, age 52
CFO: Mike Decker
Chief Administrative Officer: Steve Laver
Auditors: Ernst & Young

WHERE

HQ: 3500 Trammell Crow Center, 2001 Ross Ave., Dallas, TX 75201
Phone: 214-979-5100
Fax: 214-979-6058

Trammell Crow Company has offices in 70 US cities and affiliated operations in Mexico, Europe, Brazil, and the Far East.

Regional Headquarters
Midwest – Tulsa, OK
Northeast – Voorhees, NJ
Northwest – San Mateo, CA
Southeast – Memphis, TN
Southern California – Los Angeles
Texas – Dallas; Houston; Austin

WHAT

	1992
	% sq. ft. under development
Office	6
Industrial	84
Retail	10
Total	**100**

	1992
	% sq. ft. under management
Office	22
Industrial	67
Retail	11
Total	**100**

Major 1992 Development Projects
Circuit City (Dallas, TX)
Covenant Life Insurance (Berwyn, PA)
Kent North Industrial Park, Phase I (Kent Valley, WA)
Wadsworth Boulevard Marketplace (Denver, CO)

Major Projects Managed
Market Square (Washington, DC)
Texas Commerce Tower (Dallas, TX)
Travelers Headquarters (Hartford, CT)

National Operating Companies
Trammell Crow Asset Management (portfolio and asset management)
Trammell Crow Corporate Services (real estate services for Fortune 500 companies)

Affiliated Company
Trammell Crow Ventures Ltd.

KEY COMPETITORS

Bass
Canadian Pacific
Carlson
Dial
Edward J. DeBartolo
ITT
Ogden
Promus
Prudential
Rank
Other real estate developers and management companies

HOW MUCH

	Annual Growth	1983	1984	1985	1986	1987	1988	1989	1990	1991	1992
Sales ($ mil.)	(25.6%)	—	—	—	1,000	1,074	1,400	1,628	1,275	1,186	170[1]
Total sq. ft. under construction (thou.)	(53.9%)	—	—	—	—	—	61,383	43,537	26,635	25,200	2,784
Total sq. ft. under management (thou.)	3.0%	—	—	—	—	—	215,000	246,000	—	286,000	242,153
Employees	3.1%	—	—	—	2,000	5,000	7,500	12,324	3,000	2,700	2,400

Sales ($ mil.) 1986–92

[1] Commercial operations only; Trammell Crow residential operations generated 1992 revenues of $895 million.

THE HOT 20

50-OFF STORES, INC.

RANK: 276

OVERVIEW

50-Off Stores operates 110 family apparel shops throughout the southern US. Clothing, which accounts for 72% of sales, is sold at half its suggested retail price; on the price tag of each item in the company's stores is the suggested price and the statement: "You pay one-half of this amount." The company markets name brand label apparel to moderate- and lower-income families and licenses space in most of its stores to shoe sellers. In 1991 50-Off Stores went public and subsequently was named a Hot Growth Company by *Business Week*.

The first 50-Off store was opened in 1986. Formed in 1975 by current chairman Charles Siegel and current VP Joseph Lehrman, the company operated stores under the name Shoppers World. Siegel became president in 1982; the next year the company developed a discount chain called Siegels, which sold apparel and nonapparel items, such as jewelry, appliances, and consumer electronics. However, Siegels wasn't as profitable as hoped; management opened the first 50-Off store to liquidate Siegels merchandise in 1986. 50-Off stores were an immediate triumph, and the company soon changed its existing stores over to the new format; the company name was changed in 1988.

This distinctive marketing approach has led the company to success; in 1991 same-store sales increased by a remarkable 20% (but fell in 1992 by 2%). To grow, management is now relying heavily on new store expansion, especially in the south and southeast. 50-Off Stores usually attempts to saturate a market, peppering it with new stores. Although this is bad for same-store sales in the short term, it keeps competitors at bay and increases company market share in the target area.

The company recently announced plans to open 3 to 5 stores in Mexico in 1993.

WHO

Chairman, President, and CEO: Charles M. Siegel, age 53, $310,340 pay
VP, Secretary, and Treasurer: Joseph Lehrman, age 67, $132,723 pay
VP General Merchandise Manager: Marshall Bernstein, age 51, $118,200 pay
VP Operations: Ray Trevino, age 47, $98,275 pay
VP and CFO: Pat L. Ross, age 55, $87,500 pay
VP Advertising and Public Relations: David Siegel
Director Human Resources: Roy Springer
Auditors: Deloitte & Touche

WHERE

HQ: 8750 Tesoro Dr., San Antonio, TX 78217
Phone: 210-805-9300   **Fax:** 210-805-0067

	1992 Stores % of total
Texas	56
Other states	44
Total	**100**

WHAT

	1992 Sales % of total
Apparel	72
Other	28
Total	**100**

KEY COMPETITORS

Ames
Damark International
Dayton Hudson
Dillard
Edison Brothers
Kmart
Lands' End
May
Mercantile Stores

Montgomery Ward
J. C. Penney
Sears
Service Merchandise
Tuesday Morning
U.S. Shoe
Wal-Mart
Woolworth

HOW MUCH

NASDAQ symbol: FOFF FY ends: last Sun. in Jan.	5-Year Growth	1987	1988	1989	1990	1991	1992
Sales ($ mil.)	41.9%	31.5	43.6	57.8	78.1	130.1	181.0
Net income ($ mil.)	88.8%	0.2	1.0	1.4	2.8	6.5	4.8
Income as % of sales	—	0.7%	2.2%	2.3%	3.6%	5.0%	2.7%
Earnings per share ($)	—	(0.04)	0.16	0.21	0.33	0.63	0.45
Stock price – high ($)	—	2.83	1.33	4.42	4.08	27.50	32.25
Stock price – low ($)	—	0.67	0.33	1.17	2.08	3.58	10.50
Stock price – close ($)	80.8%	0.67	1.33	3.00	3.83	23.25	12.88
P/E – high	—	—	8	21	12	44	72
P/E – low	—	—	2	6	6	6	23
Dividends per share ($)	0.0%	0.00	0.00	0.00	0.00	0.00	0.00
Book value per share ($)	—	—	(0.04)	0.71	1.16	1.57	3.74	4.29
Employees	43.8%	464	664	820	1,249	1,984	2,849

1992 Year-end:
Debt ratio: 3.8%
Return on equity: 11.2%
Cash (mil.): $6.7
Current ratio: 1.85
Long-term debt (mil.): $1.4
No. of shares (mil.): 10.3
Dividends:
    1992 average yield: 0.0%
    1992 payout: 0.0%
Market value (mil.): $133.2
R&D as % of sales: —
Advertising as % of sales: 2.2%

BABBAGE'S, INC.

RANK: 248

OVERVIEW

Kids across the country flock to Babbage's to pick up the latest Super Mario Brothers or WWF Wrestlemania games. The discount home software retailer derives over 70% of its revenues from entertainment system and software sales. Babbage's is the leading specialty software seller in the US, with over 250 mall stores in 37 states. Top management owns over 17% of company stock.

The company, named for 19th-century mathematician Charles Babbage (considered the father of the computer), was founded by James McCurry and Gary Kusin, ex-Harvard Business schoolmates, in 1983. The pair had planned to open 20 stores in their first month of operation but lost steam when the company lost money immediately. When it became evident that more capital was needed for expansion, Kusin's family friend H. Ross Perot stepped in to help. He put up $3 million initially and advised the ambitious team to proceed a little more cautiously. It wasn't until 1987 that the company broke even. The next year Babbage's went public.

The company's secret has been its focus on selling software for home use, especially game software, and its placement of stores mainly in malls, where most of its target consumers hang out. In 1987 Nintendo game systems and software began generating sales. Since then Nintendo and Sega have been major contributors to company income, providing 12% and 18% of inventory purchases, respectively, in 1992. When PC prices fell through the floor in 1991, software sales at Babbage's rose dramatically; year-over-year, same-store sales increased by 15% in 1991 and by 8% in 1992. Sales also surged that year when both Sega and Nintendo introduced their 16-bit game systems.

Sales grew by 24% and net income by 21% in fiscal 1993 over fiscal 1992.

WHO

Chairman: James B. McCurry, age 44, $410,000 pay
President: Gary M. Kusin, age 41, $410,000 pay
CFO, Secretary, and Treasurer: Opal P. Ferraro, age 38, $225,000 pay
VP Stores: Mary P. Evans, age 33, $103,333 pay
VP Merchandising: Terri L. Favell, age 33, $103,333 pay
VP Construction: Barry R. Fehrs
VP Distribution: Ron E. Freeman
VP Personnel: Michael A. Ivanich
Auditors: Ernst & Young

WHERE

HQ: 10741 King William Dr., Dallas, TX 75220
Phone: 214-401-9000   **Fax:** 214-401-9002

	1992 Stores
	No. of stores
Midwest	80
Southeast	70
Northeast	52
Southwest	31
West	25
Total	**258**

WHAT

	1992 Sales
	% of total
Entertainment software & systems	70
Education & productivity software	16
Computer supplies & accessories	14
Total	**100**

KEY COMPETITORS

Best Buy	Kmart
BLOC Development	Montgomery Ward
Circuit City	Office Depot
CompuAdd	Random Access
CompuCom Systems	Sears
CompUSA	Software Etc.
DEC	Software Spectrum
Dell	Staples
Egghead	Tandy
Gateway 2000	Toys "R" Us
Good Guys	Wal-Mart

HOW MUCH

NASDAQ symbol: BBGS FY ends: first Sat. in Feb.	Annual Growth	1987	1988	1989	1990	1991	1992	1992 Year-end: Debt ratio: 0.0%
Sales ($ mil.)	48.2%	29.3	58.8	95.3	132.8	168.4	209.2	Return on equity: 14.7%
Net income ($ mil.)	62.5%	0.6	2.6	2.3	4.1	5.6	6.8	Cash (mil.): $6.4
Income as % of sales	—	2.2%	4.5%	2.4%	3.1%	3.3%	3.2%	Current ratio: 2.42
Earnings per share ($)	55.9%	0.14	0.56	0.44	0.78	1.06	1.29	Long-term debt (mil.): $0.0
Stock price – high ($)	—	—	14.75	15.88	9.75	23.50	30.00	No. of shares (mil.): 5.3
Stock price – low ($)	—	—	10.13	6.63	4.13	6.63	14.25	Dividends:
Stock price – close ($)	14.5%	—	14.38	7.38	8.75	21.50	24.75	1992 average yield: 0.0%
P/E – high	—	—	26	36	13	22	23	1992 payout: 0.0%
P/E – low	—	—	18	15	5	6	11	Market value (mil.): $130.7
Dividends per share ($)	0.0%	0.00	0.00	0.00	0.00	0.00	0.00	R&D as % of sales: —
Book value per share ($)	4.3%	7.66	5.87	6.30	7.08	8.15	9.45	Advertising as % of sales: —
Employees	21.8%	—	1,000	1,200	1,300	1,600	2,200	

THE TEXAS 500

BMC SOFTWARE, INC.

RANK: 226

OVERVIEW

Don't let the shorts and Hawaiian shirts fool you; debt-free BMC is the leading supplier of software utilities for the 2 principal IBM mainframe databases, IMS and DB2. The company's IMS Database Utilities, Masterplan for DB2, and Trimar Fast Path product groups generated 72% of 1992 revenues by making IBM mainframes work smarter and faster. Before BMC commits to developing a product, the product must meet BMC requirements; that is, it must save the customer money, not force the customer to make changes, install easily, and sell over the phone.

BMC was launched in 1979 by John Moores, who still owns 16.6% of the company, with the 3270 SuperOptimizer, a utility that dramatically improved terminal input/output operations when it was introduced.

BMC markets its software to large companies: 87% of *Fortune* 100 and 94% of *Fortune* 50 companies hold at least one BMC license. By selling products almost exclusively by phone, BMC salespersons can make up to 15 contacts a day. Most BMC salespersons have work experience with other software companies or IBM, so they can talk the lingo. The company has a liberal free-trial program, betting that demonstrated savings in time and hardware will end in a sale, which it does about 50% of the time. To develop new products, BMC holds extensive group seminars with customers and then encourages developers with a bonus of up to 6% of the resulting products' sales. BMC has marketed its products creatively, using, for example, a catalog resembling a comic book and a series of posters featuring dinosaurs named after company products.

Despite the decline in mainframe installations, the future for BMC looks bright, as mainframe power and data storage requirements continue to grow. Sales for the first 9 months of fiscal 1993 were up 32% and net income 42% over the same period in the prior year.

WHO

Chairman, President, and CEO: Max P. Watson, Jr., age 46, $888,643 pay
SVP Research and Development: Theodore W. Van Duyn, age 43, $624,643 pay
VP North American Sales and Marketing: Alan Hunt, age 50, $503,384 pay
SVP International Sales and Marketing: F. Joseph Backer, age 54, $479,811 pay
VP and CFO: David A. Farley, age 37, $428,462 pay
Director Human Resources: Johnnie Horn
Auditors: Arthur Andersen

WHERE

HQ: 2101 CityWest Blvd., Houston, TX 77042-2827
Phone: 713-918-8800   **Fax:** 713-918-8000

	1992 Sales $ mil.	1992 Sales % of total	1992 Operating Income $ mil.	1992 Operating Income % of total
North America	103.2	56	12.3	19
Other countries	81.4	44	50.1	81
Total	184.6	100	62.4	100

WHAT

	1992 Sales $ mil.	% of total
Licenses	105.7	57
Maintenance	78.9	43
Total	184.6	100

Products
CICS Integrity Series	IMS/TM Enhancements
DASD Data Compression	LOADPLUS
DB2 Database Utilities	Masterplan
DELTA/IMS	Network Performance
IMS Database Utilities	Trimar Fast Path Series

KEY COMPETITORS

American Software	IBM
Computer Associates	Oracle
Dun & Bradstreet	PLATINUM technology
H&R Block	System Software Associates

HOW MUCH

NASDAQ symbol: BMCS FY ends: March 31	Annual Growth	1987	1988	1989	1990	1991	1992
Sales ($ mil.)	45.8%	28.0	41.6	60.3	93.0	130.1	184.6
Net income ($ mil.)	64.0%	3.9	7.4	12.4	20.3	25.5	46.2
Income as % of sales	—	13.9%	17.8%	20.6%	21.8%	19.6%	25.0%
Earnings per share ($)	53.8%	—	0.32	0.53	0.83	1.02	1.79
Stock price – high ($)	—	—	9.33	20.50	30.25	74.75	79.00
Stock price – low ($)	—	—	5.25	9.08	17.75	27.00	37.25
Stock price – close ($)	67.0%	—	9.33	20.17	30.00	66.00	72.50
P/E – high	—	—	29	38	36	73	44
P/E – low	—	—	16	17	21	26	21
Dividends per share ($)	0.0%	—	0.00	0.00	0.00	0.00	0.00
Book value per share ($)	16.6%	—	2.97	1.39	2.52	3.53	5.49
Employees	27.4%	233	262	330	424	593	782

1992 Year-end:
Debt ratio: 0.0%
Return on equity: 39.7%
Cash (mil.): $137.9
Current ratio: 2.23
Long-term debt (mil.): $0.0
No. of shares (mil.): 25.6
Dividends:
  1992 average yield: 0.0%
  1992 payout: 0.0%
Market value (mil.): $1,859.3
R&D as % of sales: 13.1%
Advertising as % of sales: —

THE TEXAS 500

THE BOMBAY COMPANY, INC.

RANK: 234

OVERVIEW

The Bombay Company and its Alex & Ivy division sell inexpensive English traditional–style and French country–style accent furniture and decorative accessories at 376 locations in Canada and the US (April 1993). It is one of the US's top 20 furniture companies and the fastest-growing home decor retailer.

Husband-and-wife team Robert and Aagje Nourse bought the Canadian rights from the original Bombay Company — a New Orleans–based mail-order house — in 1979. Tandy Brands (men's accessories) bought the US company in 1980 and the Canadian operations in 1981; Robert Nourse became head of both operations in 1984. In 1991 the accessories business was spun off as Tandy Brands Accessories, and the company renamed itself The Bombay Company, Inc.

The emphasis on small, ready-to-assemble pieces at "uncommon values" saves the cost of delivery and allows the stores to locate in small mall sites. The products' portability encourages impulse buying. The company is popular with mall managers and often receives lease discounts.

Bombay emphasizes fashion, with 7 selling seasons in which new products are introduced. This strategy was successful in the 1990s recession, as people sought inexpensive pick-ups for their decor. Bombay merchandise is proprietary, and 64% of it is made in Southeast Asia. The company also has a distribution system that can replenish the inventories of 90% of the stores in 72 hours.

The Bombay Company has no long-term debt. In 1992 its sales growth rate of 26% exceeded its goal of an annual average of 20%. In 1993, after opening 20 superstores (up to 3,800 square feet), the company decided to convert all stores to the larger format. Costs associated with upsizing caused earnings to drop 37% despite a 26% increase in sales for the first 9 months of fiscal 1993.

WHO

President and CEO: Robert E. M. Nourse, age 54, $912,295 pay
EVP Marketing: Aagje M. T. Nourse, age 49, $702,355 pay
EVP Operations; President, The Bombay Company Division: Michael L. Glazer, age 44, $632,618 pay
EVP, Treasurer, and CFO: James E. Herlihy, age 49, $469,413 pay
Secretary and General Counsel: Michael J. Veitenheimer, age 36, $291,408 pay
VP Human Resources: Robert S. Wyatt, age 45
Auditors: Price Waterhouse

WHERE

HQ: 550 Bailey Ave., Ste. 700, Fort Worth, TX 76107
Phone: 817-347-8200   **Fax:** 817-332-7066

1992 Stores

	No. of stores	% of total
Northeast	83	24
South	82	24
Midwest	77	23
West	53	15
Canada	47	14
Total	**342**	**100**

WHAT

1992 Sales

	% of total
Wood furniture & accessories	60
Prints, mirrors & sconces	23
Tabletop accessories, lamps & other	17
Total	**100**

KEY COMPETITORS

Armstrong World	Masco
Berkshire Hathaway	May
Carrefour	Mercantile Stores
Carter Hawley Hale	J.C. Penney
Dayton Hudson	Sears
Dillard	Service Merchandise
INTERCO	Tuesday Morning
Macy	

HOW MUCH

NYSE symbol: BBA FY ends: last Sunday in June	5-Year Growth	1987	1988	1989	1990	1991	1992
Sales ($ mil.)	21.2%	67.4	78.5	109.2	111.7	139.3	176.0
Net income ($ mil.)	—	(5.7)	2.4	5.4	5.9	5.9	9.6
Income as % of sales	—	(8.5%)	3.1%	5.0%	5.3%	4.2%	5.5%
Earnings per share ($)	—	(0.67)	0.25	0.47	0.43	0.41	0.65
Stock price – high ($)	—	6.22	4.89	12.28	12.39	11.89	36.50
Stock price – low ($)	—	2.22	3.17	4.89	4.28	4.33	10.00
Stock price – close ($)	59.3%	3.56	4.89	8.78	5.11	11.06	36.50
P/E – high	—	—	20	26	29	29	56
P/E – low	—	—	13	10	10	10	15
Dividends per share ($)	0.0%	0.00	0.00	0.00	0.00	0.00	0.00
Book value per share ($)	28.6%	1.17	1.66	3.15	3.86	3.38	4.13
Employees	18.5%	900	1,100	1,300	1,500	1,900	2,100

1992 Year-end:
Debt ratio: 0.0%
Return on equity: 17.4%
Cash (mil.): $10.1
Current ratio: 2.59
Long-term debt (mil.): $0.0
No. of shares (mil.): 14.3
Dividends:
    1992 average yield: 0.0%
    1992 payout: 0.0%
Market value (mil.): $522.3
R&D as % of sales: —
Advertising as % of sales: 6.8%

THE TEXAS 500

BRINKER INTERNATIONAL, INC.

RANK: 89

OVERVIEW

Brinker International, whose cornerstone restaurant, Chili's Grill & Bar, has grown into the 3rd largest casual dining chain in the US (after General Mills's Red Lobster and Olive Garden restaurants), also operates Romano's Macaroni Grill and Grady's American Grill. CEO Norman Brinker, who developed Steak and Ale and Bennigan's while with Pillsbury's restaurant group, owns 4% of the company.

Founded in Dallas in 1975 by Larry Lavine, Chili's had become by the early 1980s one of the Southwest's most popular "gourmet hamburger" chains. Brinker left Pillsbury and bought control of Chili's in 1983, and in 1984 the company made its first public offering. Chili's grew from 23 restaurants in 1983 to 275 in 1992, as Brinker and his management team aggressively recruited joint venture and franchise partners and expanded Chili's menu to include items such as fajitas, staking the company's growth on aging baby boomers, who were looking for something a step up from fast food. In 1989 Chili's Inc. bought Romano's Macaroni Grill and the Regas Grill (renamed Grady's), and the company changed its name to Brinker International in 1991.

The company plans to continue adding to the numbers of its existing restaurants and is also developing new restaurants, including Spaggedies (an Italian restaurant), a Mexican restaurant, and a steakhouse. The company is also expanding internationally, opening Chili's in Canada and Mexico in 1992 and signing an agreement with Hong Kong's Pac-Am Food Concepts to develop Chili's in Asia.

Norman Brinker suffered serious head injuries in a polo accident in January 1993 and was unconscious for several weeks. However, by May 1993 he had recovered enough to return to the company. Brinker continued its strong growth in the first half of fiscal 1993, with sales up by 23% and net income up 35% compared to the first half of fiscal 1993.

WHO

Chairman and CEO: Norman E. Brinker, age 62, $959,264 pay
President, and COO: Ronald A. McDougall, age 50, $764,288 pay
EVP and CFO: Debra L. Smithart-Weitzman, age 38
SVP Operations, Chili's Grill & Bar: Douglas H. Brooks, $297,460 pay
SVP Operations, Grady's American Grill: Douglas S. Lanham
SVP Operations, Romano's Macaroni Grill: Richard L. Federico
VP, General Counsel, and Secretary: Robert L. Callaway
VP Human Resources: Janet A. Coen
Auditors: KPMG Peat Marwick

WHERE

HQ: 6820 LBJ Freeway, Dallas, TX 75240
Phone: 214-980-9917 **Fax**: 214-770-9593

WHAT

	1992 Restaurants	
	No.	% of total
Chili's — owned	217	71
Chili's — franchised	58	19
Grady's	17	6
Macaroni Grill	13	4
Total	**305**	**100**

Chili's Grill & Bar
Hamburgers, fajitas, chicken, seafood, sandwiches, salads

Grady's American Grill
Seafood, prime rib, steaks, pasta, salads, sandwiches

Romano's Macaroni Grill
Family-style Italian seafood, steak, chicken, pasta, salads, antipasto

KEY COMPETITORS

Bertucci's
Carlson
Cracker Barrel Old Country Store
General Mills
Grand Metropolitan
Metromedia
PepsiCo
Outback Steakhouse
Uno Restaurant

HOW MUCH

NYSE symbol: EAT FY ends: June 30	5-Year Growth	1987	1988	1989	1990	1991	1992
Sales ($ mil.)	24.0%	177.2	218.3	284.7	347.1	426.8	519.3
Net income ($ mil.)	40.7%	6.5	8.1	14.0	18.1	26.1	35.7
Income as % of sales	—	3.7%	3.7%	4.9%	5.2%	6.1%	6.9%
Earnings per share ($)	28.4%	0.33	0.40	0.59	0.73	0.91	1.15
Stock price – high ($)	—	10.78	9.44	15.33	17.72	38.00	42.75
Stock price – low ($)	—	5.33	5.48	9.15	11.33	13.61	29.88
Stock price – close ($)	47.0%	6.00	9.33	14.61	15.39	37.50	41.13
P/E – high	—	33	24	26	24	42	37
P/E – low	—	16	14	16	15	15	26
Dividends per share ($)	0.0%	0.00	0.00	0.00	0.00	0.00	0.00
Book value per share ($)	28.5%	2.51	3.02	3.54	5.17	7.30	8.70
Employees	31.0%	7,365	10,480	14,000	15,000	20,000	28,000

1992 Year-end:
Debt ratio: 1.7%
Return on equity: 14.3%
Cash (mil.): $10.1
Current ratio: 0.50
Long-term debt (mil.): $4.2
No. of shares (mil.): 28.9
Dividends:
  1992 average yield: 0.0%
  1992 payout: 0.0%
Market value (mil.): $1,188.0
R&D as % of sales: —
Advertising as % of sales: 3.3%

THE TEXAS 500

CASH AMERICA INTERNATIONAL, INC.

RANK: 272

OVERVIEW

Cash America, "the blue-collar man's bank," operates over 200 pawnshops in the US and UK. With its 1992 purchase of the pawn business of the UK's Harvey & Thompson, Cash America became the world's largest pawn company and the only international one.

When Jack Daugherty was a student in Texas, he used to hock his guitar to finance dates. He quit school and in 1970 opened his own successful pawnshop. He used the proceeds to invest in oil, but when oil crashed he returned to the pawn business. Incorporated in 1984, the company went public in 1987. Cash America expanded through acquisitions initially. Since 1992 it has concentrated on new openings, which are cheaper, but the company still buys promising stores.

The company's average "borrower" earns $15,000–$30,000 per year and has several outstanding pawns of less than $100 at any time. Cash America has brought economies of scale and efficiency to the pawn business and has tried to address pawnshops' traditional image problem by maintaining a mainline discount store ambience and catering to bargain shoppers. It tries to maintain a collateral redemption rate of about 70% because pawn charge payments are preferable to carrying a large inventory of unredeemed goods.

Cash America has installed a computer system that, in addition to maintaining sales and loan information, also keeps records on individual customers' borrowing habits.

In 1992 the company began incorporating the UK acquisitions into its operations (UK pawn laws allow loans only on precious metals and jewelry and require that, for unredeemed items worth more than £25, any sale amount in excess of the pawn and service charges be returned to the original owner). In the first quarter of 1993, the company's earnings were flat, despite a 27% increase in sales over the first quarter in 1992.

WHO

Chairman and CEO: Jack R. Daugherty, age 45, $303,461 pay
President and COO: Daniel R. Feehan, age 42, $242,769 pay
EVP Operations: Terry R. Kuntz, age 46, $182,700 pay
VP, CFO, and Treasurer: Dale R. Westerfeld, age 39, $105,375 pay
VP, Secretary and General Counsel: Hugh A. Simpson, age 33
VP Human Resources: David F. Johns, age 53, $129,823 pay
Auditors: Coopers & Lybrand

WHERE

HQ: 1600 W. 7th St., Ste. 900, Fort Worth, TX 76102
Phone: 817-335-1100   **Fax:** 817-335-1119

	1992 Stores	
	No. of stores	% of total
Texas	131	52
Florida	22	9
Tennessee	19	8
Louisiana	17	7
Georgia	17	7
Oklahoma	15	6
Other states	4	2
UK	26	9
Total	**251**	**100**

WHAT

	1992 Sales	
	$ mil.	% of total
Sales	115.0	62
Pawn service charges	70.4	38
Total	**185.4**	**100**

KEY COMPETITORS

EZCORP

HOW MUCH

NYSE symbol: PWN FY ends: December 31	5-Year Growth	1987	1988	1989	1990	1991	1992
Sales ($ mil.)	36.4%	39.2	66.9	87.0	115.6	137.7	185.4
Net income ($ mil.)	36.5%	2.7	5.1	7.0	8.7	10.5	13.0
Income as % of sales	—	7.0%	7.6%	8.0%	7.5%	7.6%	7.0%
Earnings per share ($)	23.5%	0.16	0.22	0.29	0.36	0.43	0.45
Stock price – high ($)	—	5.50	6.00	7.54	10.25	9.81	12.88
Stock price – low ($)	—	3.50	3.25	3.21	5.75	6.00	7.25
Stock price – close ($)	18.0%	4.75	3.63	7.54	7.56	9.63	10.88
P/E – high	—	35	27	26	28	23	29
P/E – low	—	22	15	11	16	14	16
Dividends per share ($)	23.6%	0.02	0.02	0.02	0.03	0.04	0.05
Book value per share ($)	16.0%	2.60	3.24	3.46	3.79	4.21	5.46
Employees	28.9%	477	617	805	1,000	1,300	1,700

1992 Year-end:
Debt ratio: 24.5%
Return on equity: 9.3%
Cash (mil.): $4.2
Current ratio: 9.79
Long-term debt (mil.): $50.0
No. of shares (mil.): 28.2
Dividends:
    1992 average yield: 0.4%
    1992 payout: 10.7%
Market value (mil.): $306.6
R&D as % of sales: —
Advertising as % of sales: 1.9%

COMPUCOM SYSTEMS, INC.

RANK: 81

OVERVIEW

With a 45% compounded annual growth rate in both sales and earnings since 1988, CompuCom is one of the fastest-growing companies in the US, making *Fortune*'s list of top US growth companies in 1991 and 1992. The company operates 35 microcomputer sales and service centers across the US. Safeguard Scientifics, a venture capital firm that helped finance Novell, holds a 70.4% interest in the company.

Incorporated in Michigan under the name CytoSystems in 1981, the company changed its name in 1983 to Machine Vision International to reflect its focus on designing artificial vision systems for computers. In 1987 the company acquired TriStar Data Systems, adopted its present name, and shifted the thrust of its business to selling and supporting microcomputer systems. The next year CompuCom acquired CompuShop, Bell Atlantic's large computer chain. With the acquisition of The Computer Factory in 1991, the company became an authorized Apple dealer and gained a foothold in the northeastern US. To reduce debt, the retail outlets of The Computer Factory were grouped into superstores and sold. The acquisition of Photo & Sound's microcomputer business later that same year extended CompuCom's presence to the West Coast.

CompuCom has concentrated on selling to large corporate accounts. CEO Avery More, an immigrant from Israel, has melded the company's acquisitions by selling off retail operations but integrating the direct sales forces, streamlining the distribution process, shipping straight to the customer from the distribution center, and constructing an efficient information system. To counter the increasingly competitive computer resale market, the company is concentrating on providing consulting services with its products.

Sales and net income for the first quarter of 1993 were up 26% and 72%, respectively, over the same period for the prior year.

WHO

Chairman: James W. Dixon, age 46, $532,141 pay
President and CEO: Avery More, age 38, $532,141 pay
EVP Sales: Daniel F. Brown, age 47, $348,765 pay
SVP and CFO: Robert J. Boutin, age 35
SVP Direct Sales: Gary M. Sorkin, age 45
Manager of Social Services: Gayle Riley
Auditors: KPMG Peat Marwick

WHERE

HQ: 10100 N. Central Expwy., Dallas, TX 75231
Phone: 214-265-3600   **Fax:** 214-265-5220

WHAT

Microcomputer Brands
3Com
Apple
AST
Compaq
Epson
Hewlett-Packard
IBM
NEC
Toshiba

Software Brands
Lotus
Microsoft
Novell
WordPerfect

Services
CompuCom Technology Services (configuration evaluation, network integration support and installation, training, authorized warranty and repair service)

KEY COMPETITORS

Arthur Andersen
Babbage's
Best Buy
BLOC Development
Circuit City
CompuAdd
CompUSA
Damark International
DEC
Dell
Egghead
Gateway 2000
Kmart
Montgomery Ward
Random Access
Sears
Software Etc.
Software Spectrum
Tandy
Wal-Mart

HOW MUCH

NASDAQ symbol: CMPC FY ends: December 31	5-Year Growth	1987	1988	1989	1990	1991	1992
Sales ($ mil.)	75.7%	42.5	159.2	270.7	343.5	528.6	713.0
Net income ($ mil.)	48.7%	1.0	1.6	1.6	3.6	5.0	7.3
Income as % of sales	—	2.3%	1.0%	0.6%	1.1%	1.0%	1.0%
Earnings per share ($)	29.7%	0.06	0.06	0.06	0.13	0.16	0.22
Stock price – high ($)	—	3.38	2.63	2.31	2.13	3.56	2.88
Stock price – low ($)	—	0.38	1.13	1.00	0.75	1.31	1.44
Stock price – close ($)	0.6%	2.13	1.50	1.13	1.31	2.25	2.19
P/E – high	—	56	44	39	16	22	13
P/E – low	—	6	19	17	6	8	7
Dividends per share ($)	0.0%	0.00	0.00	0.00	0.00	0.00	0.00
Book value per share ($)	27.2%	0.42	0.72	0.81	0.93	1.14	1.39
Employees	35.5%	253	540	590	683	1,061	1,156

1992 Year-end:
Debt ratio: 68.0%
Return on equity: 17.4%
Cash (mil.): $3.3
Current ratio: 1.90
Long-term debt (mil.): $88.5
No. of shares (mil.): 29.9
Dividends:
   1992 average yield: 0.0%
   1992 payout: 0.0%
Market value (mil.): $65.5
R&D as % of sales: —
Advertising as % of sales: —

COMPUSA INC.

RANK: 51

OVERVIEW

By selling more merchandise per square foot than any other major US retailer, CompUSA has become the leading superstore computer retailer in the US, with about 1% of the PC market. As of December 1992 the company operated 38 outlets in 26 major cities throughout the US. Each store averages 24,000 square feet in size and is divided into 4 departments: hardware, software, accessories, and Apple products. The company sells its own line of products (Compudyne, about 8% of total company sales) and has a mail order subsidiary, Compudyne Direct.

CompUSA began operations in 1984 as Soft Warehouse, selling directly to business customers. The first retail operation was opened in April 1985 in Dallas. In April 1988 the company opened its first superstore. Decisions by Dell in 1990 and Apple in 1991 to sell their products through CompUSA contributed to the company's credibility within the market. In April 1991 the company adopted its present name and in December of that same year launched its initial public offering.

Based on his experience in Home Depot management, CEO Nathan Morton is advertising heavily and expanding rapidly to dominate the superstore market before competitors can respond. Rapid inventory turnover and a low cost structure allow CompUSA to offer low prices and broad product selection. Service is supplied by full-time, salaried employees and a well staffed technical department in each store. Training classes are offered for a separate fee. CompUSA's regional diversification allows it to match prices offered by local competitors.

As comparable store sales for the first quarter of fiscal 1993 increased 21%, CompUSA made plans to open 10 more outlets before the end of that year. Sales and net income for the first half of fiscal 1993 were up 60% and 75%, respectively, over the same period for the prior year.

WHO

Chairman and CEO: Nathan P. Morton, age 44, $481,167 pay (prior to promotion)
President and COO: James Halpin, age 42
EVP and CFO: Mervyn Benjet, age 53, $270,319 pay
President and CEO, CompUSA International: Keith R. Costine, age 51, $229,065 pay (prior to promotion)
President, CompUSA East: Lawrence N. Mondry, age 32, $242,672 pay (prior to promotion)
President, CompUSA West: Peter J. Buscetto, age 45, $242,672 pay (prior to promotion)
President, CompUSA Central (Personnel): Jack A. Phelps, age 43
VP; President, Compudyne Direct, Inc. and Compudyne Products, Inc.: Stephen A. Dukker, age 40, $280,776 pay
Auditors: Ernst & Young

WHERE

HQ: 14951 N. Dallas Pkwy., Dallas, TX 75240
Phone: 214-383-4000   **Fax:** 214-383-4520

WHAT

	1992 Sales % of total
Central processing units	30
Peripherals & accessories	20
Software	30
Services & training	20
Total	**100**

Major Brands Carried

Apple	Hewlett-Packard	Seagate Technology
Borland	Lotus	Software Publishing
Compaq	Microsoft	Sony
Compudyne	NEC	Texas Instruments
Dell	Packard Bell	Toshiba
Epson	Panasonic	WordPerfect

KEY COMPETITORS

Babbage's	Egghead	Service
BLOC Development	Gateway 2000	Merchandise
Circuit City	Kmart	Software
CompuAdd	Montgomery	Spectrum
CompuCom Systems	Ward	Staples
Costco Wholesale	Price Co.	Tandy
DEC	Sears	Wal-Mart
Dell		

HOW MUCH

NYSE symbol: CPU FY ends: June 30	Annual Growth	1987	1988	1989	1990	1991	1992
Sales ($ mil.)	91.5%	32.1	66.6	137.5	300.4	543.9	827.1
Net income ($ mil.)	102.8%	0.3	1.9	1.2	1.5	(9.7)	10.3
Income as % of sales	—	0.1%	2.9%	0.9%	0.5%	(1.8%)	1.2%
Earnings per share ($)	—	—	—	—	—	(1.58)	0.71
Stock price – high ($)	—	—	—	—	—	23.75	40.50
Stock price – low ($)	—	—	—	—	—	15.00	19.25
Stock price – close ($)	30.2%	—	—	—	—	21.50	28.00
P/E – high	—	—	—	—	—	—	57
P/E – low	—	—	—	—	—	—	27
Dividends per share ($)	0.0%	—	—	—	—	0.00	0.00
Book value per share ($)	—	—	—	—	—	(2.56)	5.59
Employees	72.1%	—	—	543	1,208	1,782	2,767

1992 Year-end:
Debt ratio: 5.3%
Return on equity: 46.9%
Cash (mil.): $12.8
Current ratio: 1.47
Long-term debt (mil.): $3.4
No. of shares (mil.): 14.9
Dividends:
    1992 average yield: 0.0%
    1992 payout: 0.0%
Market value (mil.): $418.2
R&D as % of sales: —
Advertising as % of sales: 1.5%

THE TEXAS 500

CYRIX CORPORATION

RANK: 483

OVERVIEW

Cyrix keeps putting chips on its shoulder and daring Intel to knock them off. That stance has resulted in large legal fees but has also allowed the small upstart to carve a 5% market share away from the computer chip Goliath. Cyrix designs and markets high-performance math coprocessors and microprocessors for PCs.

CEO Jerry Rogers founded Cyrix in 1988 with a former Texas Instruments buddy, Tom Brightman. The company's first product was a coprocessor designed to relieve a PC's main processor of performing large math equations and thereby boost overall computer performance. From conception to initial shipments, the entire design process took 14 months. With the revenues generated by the math coprocessor, Cyrix turned to the $10 billion main microprocessor market. Within 18 months a 6-engineer design team had developed a 486-compatible chip, duplicating a feat to which rival Intel had devoted hundreds of engineers for more than 4 years. Intel responded by filing suit, which Cyrix has successfully fended off so far.

In order to gain market share from its larger competitors, Cyrix competes on the basis of price and performance while emphasizing a fast design cycle with extensive simulations and compatibility verifications from early on in the process. Cyrix is targeting its chips for portable computers, desktop computers, and upgrade products. By "going fabless" (not making its own chips) the company can concentrate its resources on design and marketing rather than fabrication facilities. By entering joint ventures with licensees of Intel such as Texas Instruments and SGS Thompson, Cyrix has also obtained protection from lawsuits by Intel for patent infringement. Although Cyrix has an agreement with Texas Instruments to manufacture chips, the companies are currently renegotiating terms.

Sales doubled for the first quarter of 1993 as net income grew almost 4-fold. Until late in 1992 most of Cyrix's revenues were derived from math coprocessor sales, but microprocessor sales accounted for 68% of 1993 first-quarter revenues. Cyrix filed an IPO document in May 1993 and is working on a chip to compete with Intel's Pentium.

WHO

Chairman: Harvey Berry Cash, age 54
President and CEO: Gerald D. "Jerry" Rogers, age 49, $158,782 pay
VP Business and Technology Development: Thomas B. Brightman, age 38, $163,413 pay
VP Marketing: James N. Chapman, age 43, $287,179 pay
VP Sales: Robert T. Derby, age 53, $156,284 pay
VP Engineering: Kevin C. McDonough, age 43, $130,391 pay
VP; Managing Director, Cyrix International, Ltd.: Geoff Eccleston, age 46, $169,476 pay
VP; President, Cyrix K.K.: Stephen L. Domenik, age 41, $267,883 pay
VP Finance, Secretary, Treasurer, and CFO: Ronald P. Edgerton, age 41
Director Human Resources: Margaret Quinn
Auditors: Ernst & Young

WHERE

HQ: 2703 N. Central Expressway, Richardson, TX 75080
Phone: 214-994-8387   **Fax:** 214-699-9857

	1992 Sales $ mil.	% of total	1992 Operating Income $ mil.	% of total
US	60.2	83	13.6	—
Europe	12.7	17	(1.1)	—
Far East	—	—	0.1	—
Adjustments	—	—	0.6	—
Total	**72.9**	**100**	**13.2**	**100**

WHAT

Products
Microprocessors
  Cx486DLC
  Cx486DRu^2 microprocessor upgrade
  Cx486SLC
  Cx486S2/50 FasCache
Math coprocessors
  Cyrix 87SLC/DLC floating point units
  FasMath 82S87
  FasMath 83D87
  FasMath 83S87

KEY COMPETITORS

AMD
Chips and Technologies
Intel
IBM
Motorola
Sun Microsystems
Texas Instruments

HOW MUCH

NASDAQ symbol: CYRX FY ends: December 31	Annual Growth	1987	1988	1989	1990	1991	1992
Sales ($ mil.)	70.1%	—	—	—	25.2	55.3	72.9
Net Income ($ mil.)	—	—	(1.2)	(2.9)	9.8	12.7	8.4
Income as % of sales	—	—	—	—	38.9%	23.0%	11.5%
Employees	41.4%	—	—	—	70	125	140

1992 Year-end:
Debt ratio: 12.5%
Cash (mil.): $22.6
Long-term debt (mil.): $4.6
R&D as % of sales: 11.4%
Advertising as % of sales: 3.2%

136   THE TEXAS 500

DESTEC ENERGY, INC.

RANK: 119

OVERVIEW

The largest independent power producer and marketer in the US, Destec Energy produces energy in 2 ways — cogeneration and coal gasification. Cogeneration provides 2 or more forms of energy from a single source (in Destec's case, electricity and steam from natural gas), and coal gasification produces syngas, a replacement for natural gas. Destec is vertically integrated, involved in everything from the design of energy facilities to their construction and operation, and also owns coal, oil, and gas deposits in the southern and southwestern US. Dow Chemical owns 72.6% of Destec, and an agreement between the 2 companies to provide services to Houston Lighting and Power and Texas Utilities accounted for 21% of Destec's sales in 1992.

Destec was formed as a subsidiary of Dow in 1989 to take over Dow's cogeneration and syngas technologies, developed to take advantage of the Public Utilities Regulatory Policies Act of 1978, which encouraged independent producers to enter the electric power business. Destec acquired power developer PSE, Inc., in late 1989, and in 1991 Dow spun off Destec in a public offering. The financial and technical resources that Dow provides have been a major factor in Destec's rapid growth. However, Destec's reliance on the contracts with HL&P and Texas Utilities could pose a problem for the company if the contracts are not renewed in 1994 and 1995, respectively.

To reduce its exposure to the risk of losing such big contracts, Destec continues to seek new projects. The company has 9 cogeneration plants under development and is building a new coal gasification plant in Indiana.

In late 1992 Destec announced an agreement with utility company Ontario Hydro to build a cogeneration plant near Kingston, Ontario. Destec's sales were up 36% but net income dropped 14% in the first quarter of 1993 compared to the same period in 1992.

WHO

Chairman: Robert McFedries, age 62, $370,721 pay
President and CEO: Charles F. Goff, age 52, $269,582 pay
EVP and COO: Keys A. Curry, Jr., age 57, $316,343 pay
CFO: Enrique M. Larroucau
VP, Secretary, and General Counsel: Stephen R. Wright
VP Human Resources: Gerald Crone
Auditors: Deloitte & Touche

WHERE

HQ: 2500 City West Blvd., Ste. 150, Houston, TX 77042
Phone: 713-735-4000   **Fax:** 713-735-4201

WHAT

	1992 Sales	
	$ mil.	% of total
Power, steam & syngas	300.1	59
Development & engineering	151.5	30
Operations	42.0	8
Energy resources	14.0	3
Total	**507.6**	**100**

Projects in Operation
Badger Creek CoGen (Bakersfield, CA)
Chalk Cliff CoGen (Kern County, CA)
CoGen Lyondell (Channelview, TX)
CoGen Power (Port Arthur, TX)
Commonwealth Atlantic (Chesapeake, VA)
Corona CoGen (Corona, CA)
Double "C" CoGen (Kern County, CA)
High Sierra CoGen (Kern County, CA)
Kern Front CoGen (Kern County, CA)
Live Oak CoGen (Bakersfield, CA)
McKittrick CoGen (Bakersfield, CA)
San Joaquin CoGen (Stockton, CA)

Projects Under Construction
Hartwell Energy (Hart County, GA)
Oyster Creek CoGen (Freeport, TX)

KEY COMPETITORS

AES
California Energy
Magma Power

HOW MUCH

NYSE symbol: ENG FY ends: December 31	Annual Growth	1987	1988	1989	1990	1991	1992
Sales ($ mil.)	72.0%	33.7	77.2	152.7	412.3	437.0	507.6
Net income ($ mil.)	—	(16.9)	2.9	35.9	70.3	81.5	87.5
Income as % of sales	—	(50.1%)	3.8%	23.5%	17.1%	18.6%	17.2%
Earnings per share ($)	1.4%	—	—	—	—	1.39	1.41
Stock price – high ($)	—	—	—	—	—	28.63	22.75
Stock price – low ($)	—	—	—	—	—	15.00	13.00
Stock price – close ($)	(18.3%)	—	—	—	—	19.75	16.13
P/E – high	—	—	—	—	—	21	16
P/E – low	—	—	—	—	—	11	9
Dividends per share ($)	0.0%	—	—	—	0.00	0.00	0.00
Book value per share ($)	93.8%	—	—	—	2.45	7.62	9.20
Employees	18.1%	—	—	—	436	568	606

1992 Year-end:
Debt ratio: 0.0%
Return on equity: 16.8%
Cash (mil.): $314.2
Current ratio: 3.09
Long-term debt (mil.): $0.0
No. of shares (mil.): 62.2
Dividends:
    1992 average yield: 0.0%
    1992 payout: 0.0%
Market value (mil.): $1,003.4
R&D as % of sales: 0.2%
Advertising as % of sales: —

THE TEXAS 500

EZCORP, INC.

RANK: 418

OVERVIEW

EZCORP is the 2nd largest pawnshop chain in the US (after Cash America). Since going public in 1991 the company has grown from 45 to 133 stores, with sales more than doubling. MS Pawn, a limited partnership owned by Morgan Schiff & Co.'s owner, Phillip Cohen of New York, owns 81% of the voting stock (acquired in 1989); the remainder is held by founder and president Courtland Logue, Jr.

Logue opened the first EZ Pawn in Austin, Texas, in 1974. By 1989 the chain had grown to 16 stores and had incorporated. With a cash infusion from private investors, Logue, an admirer of Wal-Mart's Sam Walton, planned for future nationwide expansion by setting up the computer systems and management expertise that would allow EZCORP to expand most efficiently. The August 1991 IPO (and an offering in 1992) allowed the company to continue its program of acquisitions and openings.

The pawnshop business is fragmented, with chains operating fewer than 400 of about 10,000 stores in the US. It also suffers from an image problem, which EZCORP is addressing through more upscale siting and decoration, a professional management staff, and marketing that describes its business as a convenient source of consumer credit and as a specialty retailer of pre-owned jewelry, tools, electronics, and firearms (although the company buys new merchandise to maintain a balanced inventory). This has succeeded in Texas and other states where the failure of the thrift system left a void in the consumer credit market.

EZCORP has a computerized inventory system that generates a daily system-wide sales report. This allows the company to manage loans to maintain a collateral redemption rate (the percentage of items redeemed) of 75%.

In the first 6 months of fiscal 1993, the company's sales were up 153% and net income rose 201% over the same period in 1992.

WHO

Chairman: Sterling B. Brinkley, age 40, $100,000 pay
President and CEO: Courtland L. "Corky" Logue, Jr., age 45, $322,917 pay
EVP and CFO: Gary S. Kofnovec, age 39, $109,000 pay
VP: Ann Bradstreet
Secretary and Controller: Pamela C. Berger, age 34, $70,500 pay
Director of Human Resources: Jim Penny
Auditor: Ernst & Young

WHERE

HQ: 1901 Capital Parkway, Austin, TX, 78746
Phone: 512-314-3400   **Fax:** 512-314-3404

	1992 Stores	
	No. of stores	% of total
Texas	105	78
Mississippi	12	9
Oklahoma	7	5
Colorado	4	3
Tennessee	2	2
Alabama	2	2
Arkansas	1	1
Total	**133**	**100**

WHAT

	1992 Sales	
	$ mil.	% of total
Pawn service charges	27.6	54
Other	23.6	46
Total	**51.2**	**100**

KEY COMPETITORS

Cash America

HOW MUCH

NASDAQ symbol: EZPW FY ends: September 30	Annual Growth	1987	1988	1989	1990[1]	1991	1992
Sales ($ mil.)	50.6%	6.6	7.6	11.1	11.7	23.8	51.2
Net income ($ mil.)	70.7%	0.2	0.4	0.2	0.0	1.1	2.9
Income as % of sales	—	3.0%	5.3%	1.8%	—	4.5%	5.7%
Earnings per share ($)	—	—	—	—	(0.06)	0.20	0.33
Stock price – high ($)	—	—	—	—	—	16.00	25.50
Stock price – low ($)	—	—	—	—	—	9.00	9.75
Stock price – close ($)	75.4%	—	—	—	—	14.25	25.00
P/E – high	—	—	—	—	—	80	77
P/E – low	—	—	—	—	—	45	30
Dividends per share ($)	—	—	—	—	0.00	0.00	0.00
Book value per share ($)	—	—	—	—	2.49	5.03	7.16
Employees	118.3%	—	—	—	—	421	919

1992 Year-end:
Debt ratio: 3.3%
Return on equity: 5.4%
Cash (mil.): $5.0
Current ratio: 8.92
Long-term debt (mil.): $2.1
No. of shares (mil.): 9.7
Dividends:
  1992 average yield: 0.0%
  1992 payout: 0.0%
Market value (mil.): $241.9
R&D as % of sales: —
Advertising as % of sales: —

[1] 9-month year

HERITAGE MEDIA CORPORATION

RANK: 217

OVERVIEW

It isn't the end of the world when a Heritage Media FM radio station ranks #6 in Seattle or its Hanover, New Hampshire, TV station is #4, because Heritage's Actmedia subsidiary — its breadwinner — is #1 in the world. Actmedia provides in-store marketing — advertisements on carts, shelves, and freezers in over 36,000 supermarkets, drugstores, and other chains; product samples and coupons; POP (Point of Purchase) Radio, airing music and commercials under a joint operating agreement with Muzak (which gets 5% of POP revenues); and the Instant Coupon Machine, a shelf device that dispenses coupons next to the product. Hallmark Cards owns 15.5% of Heritage stock.

Heritage Media was formed in 1987, when Tele-Communications, Inc., bought Heritage Communications, Inc., for its cable systems. Investors led by HCI managers including Jim Hoak and David Walthall created Heritage Media as a spinoff for the 13 HCI TV and radio stations; in 1988 the company went public. In January 1989 Heritage bought 78% of Actmedia, and 6 months later it merged with Actmedia and made Actmedia its subsidiary. Heritage moved into Canada in 1990 with the purchase of Something Else Marketing (now Actmedia Canada). In 1992 Actmedia Europe bought Holland's MediaMeervoud.

Actmedia's strength is its presence — more than 14,000 people who service the stores of over 250 retailers. Heritage intends to improve Actmedia by developing new products for in-store marketing, expanding outside the US, increasing POP's presence, and going into other stores. In broadcasting, Heritage aims to focus on TV news and to grow in radio by buying and improving underperforming stations.

While Heritage has lost money every year, Actmedia is expected to make the company profitable. Heritage's 4th quarter of 1992 was its first profitable — $6.4 million net income, $87.8 million sales — since its founding.

WHO

Chairman: James M. Hoak, age 49, $334,557 pay
President and CEO: David N. Walthall, age 47, $440,748 pay
EVP and President, Actmedia, Inc.: Wayne W. LoCurto, age 49, $311,232 pay
EVP and President, Television Group: James J. Robinette, age 59, $289,314 pay
EVP and President, Radio Group: Paul W. Fiddick, age 43, $270,079 pay
EVP and CFO: Joseph D. Mahaffey, age 47
SVP and Secretary: Wayne Kern, age 60
Auditors: KPMG Peat Marwick

WHERE

HQ: 13355 Noel Rd., Ste. 1500, Dallas, TX 75240
Phone: 214-702-7380 **Fax:** 214-702-7382

WHAT

	1992 Sales	
	$ mil.	% of total
In-store marketing	186.5	74
Television	39.7	16
Radio	24.7	10
Total	**250.9**	**100**

In-Store Marketing
Actmedia
Actmedia Canada
Actmedia Europe (65%, joint venture with H.L. van Loon)
MediaMeervoud (Netherlands)
Actmedia, Inc.
BLS Retail Resource Group (Canada)

Television
KDLT-TV, Sioux Falls, SD
KEVN-TV, Rapid City, SD
KOKH-TV, Oklahoma City
WCHS-TV, Charleston, WV
WEAR-TV, Pensacola, FL
WNNE-TV, Hanover, NH
WPTZ-TV, Plattsburgh, NY

Radio
KCFX (FM), Kansas City, KS
KKSN (AM/FM), Portland, OR
KRPM (FM), Seattle
KULL (AM), Seattle
WBBF (AM), Rochester, NY
WBEE (AM), Rochester, NY
WEMP (AM), Milwaukee
WIL (FM), St. Louis
WMYX (FM), Milwaukee
WOFX (FM), Cincinnati
WRTH (AM), St. Louis

KEY COMPETITORS

Catalina Marketing
CBS
Citicorp
Dun & Bradstreet
Hearst
In-Store Advertising
Information Resources
E.W. Scripps
Viacom

HOW MUCH

AMEX symbol: HTG FY ends: December 31	Annual Growth	1987	1988	1989	1990	1991	1992
Sales ($ mil.)	70.9%	17.2	46.5	165.0	203.9	222.4	250.9
Net income ($ mil.)	—	(6.1)	(15.3)	(30.0)	(28.8)	(19.7)	(15.0)
Income as % of sales	—	(35.5%)	(32.8%)	(18.2%)	(14.1%)	(8.9%)	(6.0%)
Earnings per share ($)	—	—	(5.40)	(4.00)	(3.08)	(2.44)	(1.51)
Stock price – high ($)	—	—	18.50	23.00	22.50	20.00	15.50
Stock price – low ($)	—	—	15.50	10.00	10.50	9.50	5.63
Stock price – close ($)	(16.8%)	—	18.00	12.50	13.50	14.00	8.63
P/E – high	—	—	—	—	—	—	—
P/E – low	—	—	—	—	—	—	—
Dividends per share ($)	0.0%	0.00	0.00	0.00	0.00	0.00	0.00
Book value per share ($)	140.5%	0.05	2.85	8.25	5.84	4.02	4.40
Employees	98.2%	500	600	14,100	14,200	14,200	15,300

1992 Year-end:
Debt ratio: 77.8%
Return on equity: —
Cash (mil.): $1.2
Current ratio: 1.00
Long-term debt (mil.): $318.4
No. of shares (mil.): 17.1
Dividends:
  1992 average yield: 0.0%
  1992 payout: 0.0%
Market value (mil.): $147.1
R&D as % of sales: 0.3%
Advertising as % of sales: 1.9%

KANEB SERVICES, INC.

RANK: 284

OVERVIEW

Poised on the brink of bankruptcy a few years ago, Kaneb Services has metamorphosed into a growing energy services company through a series of sales and acquisitions. The most important acquisition Kaneb has made is Furmanite PLC. Based in the UK (where it has a 90% market share), Furmanite provides maintenance, testing, and emergency repair work to industrial process companies, principally those in the energy and chemical businesses. Kaneb also owns 62% of Kaneb Pipe Line Partners, which operates a 2,075-mile petroleum pipeline that runs from Kansas to North Dakota, and 100% of VIATA, which provides services including check verification, collateral insurance monitoring, and marketing information.

In 1953 Kaneb Pipe Line built its first pipeline between Kansas and Nebraska. As the pipeline grew through the Midwest so did Kaneb's interests in other operations, which included at various times offshore drilling, coal production, and savings and loans. When CEO John Barnes joined the company in 1986, it was $574 million in debt. Barnes sold all of Kaneb's energy-related business except the pipeline company, restructured Kaneb's debt, and in 1989 sold 1/3 of the pipeline company to the public for $100 million. Kaneb acquired Furmanite in 1991.

Furmanite, with its proprietary technology that can seal leaks without a costly plant shutdown, has proven to be the key to Kaneb's recent success. In early 1993 Kaneb acquired specialized liquid storage company Support Terminal Services and Germany's Kraftwerksund Anlagenbau, an engineering company. Kaneb is looking for additional opportunities in eastern Germany and plans to continue to expand its pipeline and terminaling business.

Kaneb's sales were up 33.7% in the first quarter of fiscal 1993, but the company posted a loss of more than $2 million.

WHO

Chairman, President, and CEO: John R. Barnes, age 48, $313,296 pay
SVP: Edward D. Doherty II, age 56, $251,580 pay
SVP: Jere M. Denton, age 46, $180,000 pay
VP Administration and Treasurer: Howard C. Wadsworth, age 48, $161,250 pay
VP, General Counsel, and Secretary: Stephen M. Hoffner, age 45
Director Human Resources: William Kettler
Auditors: Price Waterhouse

WHERE

HQ: 2400 Lakeside Blvd., Richardson, TX 75082
Phone: 214-699-4000   **Fax:** 214-699-4025

	1992 Sales	
	$ mil.	% of total
US	89.3	51
UK	37.7	21
Other countries	49.7	28
Total	**176.7**	**100**

WHAT

	1992 Sales	
	$ mil.	% of total
Industrial services	125.7	71
Pipeline services	42.2	24
VIATA	8.8	5
Total	**176.7**	**100**

Industrial Services
Emergency shutdown valve testing
Fugitive emissions inspection program tests
Maintenance outsourcing
On-line leak sealing
On-site machining
Passive fire protection
Valve testing and repair

Pipeline Services
Products transported
 Diesel fuel
 Gasoline
 Heating oil
 Propane

VIATA
Information services
Payment verification systems

KEY COMPETITORS

Amoco	Enron	Nabors Industries
Bechtel	Halliburton	Occidental
Chevron	Matrix Service	Serv-Tech
Coastal	McDermott	

HOW MUCH

NYSE symbol: KAB FY ends: December 31	5-Year Growth	1987	1988	1989	1990	1991	1992
Sales ($ mil.)	11.3%	103.6	72.0	37.5	40.9	135.0	176.7
Net income ($ mil.)	—	(38.3)	(77.8)	57.5	(3.4)	(8.1)	(5.5)
Income as % of sales	—	(37.0%)	(108.1%)	153.5%	(8.4%)	(6.0%)	(3.1%)
Earnings per share ($)	—	(1.36)	(2.66)	1.80	(0.16)	(0.30)	(0.22)
Stock price – high ($)	—	4.88	2.63	6.50	6.25	7.25	5.00
Stock price – low ($)	—	1.25	1.63	2.13	3.13	3.63	2.75
Stock price – close ($)	14.9%	1.63	2.13	5.00	3.63	4.25	3.25
P/E – high	—	—	—	4	—	—	—
P/E – low	—	—	—	1	—	—	—
Dividends per share ($)	0.0%	0.00	0.00	0.00	0.00	0.00	0.00
Book value per share ($)	—	—	3.11	0.49	0.46	0.36	(0.28)	(0.49)
Employees	17.7%	896	652	252	423	1,722	2,026

1992 Year-end:
Debt ratio: 101.0%
Return on equity: 56.9%
Cash (mil.): $10.6
Current ratio: 1.36
Long-term debt (mil.): $141.4
No. of shares (mil.): 31.8
Dividends:
 1992 average yield: 0.0%
 1992 payout: 0.0%
Market value (mil.): $103.3
R&D as % of sales: —
Advertising as % of sales: —

140   THE TEXAS 500

THE MEN'S WEARHOUSE, INC.

RANK: 295

OVERVIEW

George Zimmer, as anyone who watches any amount of television can tell you, wants you to shop at his stores. The ubiquitous TV adman runs Men's Wearhouse, which sells tailored business clothing and clothing accessories for men at prices about 20–30% below those found at typical department stores. The company operates 151 stores, which offer tailoring and alteration services (and free pressing for life), in 19 states, with an especially large presence in Texas and California. The Zimmer family controls about 52% of company shares; EVP Richard Goldman owns another 14%.

In 1973 the first Men's Wearhouse store opened in Houston, Texas. By 1986 the business had grown into a 25-store network. A new store push between 1989 and 1991 increased the number of stores further, to 113 by 1992. That year the company put up about 21% of its stock for public sale.

Two factors have aided Zimmer in building his large, successful empire. Knowing that men hate to shop, Zimmer has tried to create an easy, friendly shopping atmosphere. Each store, EVP Goldman relates, is more a "white collar army & navy store" than a fashionable clothing store, which Zimmer feels scares off men, and most are found in easily accessible shopping centers. Department store downsizing of tailored clothing departments is a 2nd factor; this trend has thrown market share the company's way. Comparable store sales for 1992 were up 6.2% over the previous year; Men's Wearhouse plans to open 40 stores (and enter 13 new markets) in 1993.

In 1992, in Houston, the company opened its first outlet store. It also introduced an in-store catalog program, which will allow shoppers to order sportswear by mail at Men's Wearhouse stores. Toward the end of 1992 the company entered the Phoenix market.

First-quarter fiscal 1993 sales rose by 34% over the fiscal 1992 period; profits rose 39%.

WHO

Chairman, President, and CEO: George Zimmer, age 44, $360,000 pay
EVP: Richard E. Goldman, age 42, $300,000 pay
SVP, Treasurer, CFO, and COO: David H. Edwab, age 38, $1,081,255 pay
SVP Merchandising: James E. Zimmer, age 41, $264,000 pay
SVP Real Estate: Robert E. Zimmer, age 69, $168,000 pay
SVP Planning and Systems and Chief Information Officer: Harry M. Levy, age 44
VP Administration (Personnel): Julia Maciag
Auditors: Deloitte & Touche

WHERE

HQ: 5803 Glenmont Dr., Houston, TX 77081
Phone: 713-664-3692   **Fax:** 713-664-1957

	1992 Stores No. of stores
California	43
Texas	37
Michigan	13
Washington	11
Georgia	10
Colorado	6
Minnesota	6
Other states	25
Total	**151**

WHAT

	1992 Sales % of total
Tailored clothing	78
Accessories & other	22
Total	**100**

KEY COMPETITORS

CML Group	May
Dayton Hudson	Melville
Dillard	Merry-Go-Round
Edison Brothers	Montgomery Ward
Harcourt General	Nordstrom
Lands' End	J.C. Penney
Macy	Woolworth
Marks and Spencer	

HOW MUCH

NASDAQ symbol: SUIT FY ends: January 31	Annual Growth	1987	1988	1989	1990	1991	1992
Sales ($ mil.)	36.9%	35.3	56.8	80.2	105.4	133.4	170.0
Net income ($ mil.)	29.8%	1.6	2.8	2.9	3.4	4.2	5.9
Income as % of sales	—	4.5%	4.9%	3.6%	3.2%	3.1%	3.5%
Earnings per share ($)	23.1%	—	—	—	—	0.65	0.80
Stock price – high ($)	—	—	—	—	—	—	17.75
Stock price – low ($)	—	—	—	—	—	—	8.50
Stock price – close ($)	—	—	—	—	—	—	17.00
P/E – high	—	—	—	—	—	—	22
P/E – low	—	—	—	—	—	—	11
Dividends per share ($)	0.0%	—	—	—	—	0.00	0.00
Book value per share ($)	63.0%	—	—	—	—	3.19	5.20
Employees	38.3%	—	—	—	—	1,277	2,125

1992 Year-end:
Debt ratio: 20.4%
Return on equity: 19.1%
Cash (mil.): $2.4
Current ratio: 1.99
Long-term debt (mil.): $8.9
No. of shares (mil.): 7.4
Dividends:
  1992 average yield: 0.0%
  1992 payout: 0.0%
Market value (mil.): $125.7
R&D as % of sales: —
Advertising as % of sales: 8.0%

SERV-TECH, INC.

RANK: 329

OVERVIEW

Serv-Tech has prospered by doing other companies' dirty work. With customers that include 9 of the top 10 oil companies in the US, Serv-Tech has grown as more and more big businesses farm out tasks to save money. In Serv-Tech's case that includes the periodic maintenance that oil refineries must undergo. Serv-Tech provides turnaround maintenance services, including heat exchanger cleaning and maintenance, tower and vessel maintenance, and specialty pipe welding and fabrication. A turnaround involves shutting down an operating unit, or sometimes an entire facility, to complete the maintenance work. Serv-Tech also provides environmental services, electrical and instrumentation contracting services, and engineering and design services. CEO Richard Krajicek owns 14% of the company.

Serv-Tech was founded in 1978 to provide hydroblasting and chemical cleaning services. In 1985 the company developed a new cleaning system, called Fast Clean, for heat exchangers used in petroleum refining and petrochemical processing. The process proved to be much faster and required less manpower than previous conventional hydroblasting methods. Serv-Tech sold its conventional cleaning business and added other turnaround services. The company went public in 1989. As part of its continued expansion, Serv-Tech acquired electrical and instrumentation contracting company SECO Industries in 1991.

With its growth spurred by the Fast Clean system, Serv-Tech continues to concentrate on expanding its services, and in 1992 it acquired engineering firm Talbert & Associates. The company is also looking to expand internationally. In 1992 the company formed Serv-Tech Europe in a joint venture with Thyssen.

Serv-Tech's sales rose by 12% but net income, hurt by the cost of expansion and new technology, dropped 28% in the first quarter of 1993 compared with the same period in 1992.

WHO

Chairman and CEO: Richard W. Krajicek, age 63, $273,000 pay
President and COO: James E. Dixon, age 44, $135,000 pay
President, SECO Industries: Frank L. Calandro, age 52, $234,160 pay
VP Finance, Secretary, and CFO: John M. Slack, $137,000 pay
Director Human Resources: Cheryl Cummings
Auditors: Coopers & Lybrand

WHERE

HQ: 5200 Cedar Crest Blvd., Houston, TX 77087
Phone: 713-644-9974   **Fax:** 713-644-0731

WHAT

	1992 Sales $ mil.	% of total
Turnaround services	88.9	60
Electrical & instrumentation contracting services	48.9	33
Environmental services	6.8	5
Engineering & design services	3.4	2
Total	**148.0**	**100**

Turnaround Services
Heat exchanger services
Planning and management services
Specialty pipe welding
Tower and vessel maintenance

Electrical and Instrumentation Contracting Services
System installation for:
Offshore production platforms
Petrochemical processing plants
Petroleum refineries

Environmental Services
Sludge control
Storage tank cleaning

Engineering and Design Services
Construction management
Drafting
Estimating services
Procurement

KEY COMPETITORS

Fluor
Halliburton
Kaneb Services
Matrix Service
Nabors Industries

HOW MUCH

NASDAQ symbol: STEC FY ends: December 31	Annual Growth	1987	1988	1989	1990	1991	1992
Sales ($ mil.)	74.7%	9.1	19.9	31.6	42.4	88.3	148.0
Net income ($ mil.)	126.0%	0.1	1.2	2.2	3.3	3.1	5.9
Income as % of sales	—	1.0%	5.9%	7.0%	7.8%	3.5%	4.0%
Earnings per share ($)	13.3%	—	0.62	0.60	0.75	0.59	1.02
Stock price – high ($)	—	—	—	20.00	18.00	21.75	15.75
Stock price – low ($)	—	—	—	10.50	11.75	9.25	6.00
Stock price – close ($)	9.7%	—	—	14.25	12.75	11.25	10.50
P/E – high	—	—	—	33	24	37	15
P/E – low	—	—	—	18	16	16	6
Dividends per share ($)	0.0%	—	0.00	0.00	0.00	0.00	0.00
Book value per share ($)	65.2%	—	1.21	4.53	5.32	8.00	9.02
Employees	101.4%	—	—	100	147	1,041	817

1992 Year-end:
Debt ratio: 13.5%
Return on equity: 12.0%
Cash (mil.): $3.9
Current ratio: 1.74
Long-term debt (mil.): $8.2
No. of shares (mil.): 5.8
Dividends:
  1992 average yield: 0.0%
  1992 payout: 0.0%
Market value (mil.): $61.0
R&D as % of sales: —
Advertising as % of sales: —

SNYDER OIL CORPORATION

RANK: 372

OVERVIEW

Snyder Oil is a developer and acquirer of oil and gas properties, with over 5,100 wells and properties in 19 states and the Gulf of Mexico. The company also gathers, processes, transports, and markets natural gas. After years of expanding almost wholly through acquisitions, Snyder Oil is now concentrating on developing properties it already owns, including those in the Wattenberg Field (Colorado), which account for over half of the company's reserves. In 1991 drilling costs exceeded acquisition costs for the first time in 10 years. This focus on production has sparked increases in net income (a 92% rise in 1992). Amoco accounted for 27% of sales in 1992 (virtually all resources pumped from Wattenberg are sold to Amoco per a lease agreement). Insiders own 19% of the company's stock.

Snyder Oil was founded in 1978 by independent oil operator John Snyder and banking executive Tom Edelman to explore for oil in the Rocky Mountains. In one of the first master limited partnerships, the company became the managing partner of Snyder Oil Properties (SOP) in 1982 and embarked upon an 8-year buying spree, finding bargains within a troubled industry while ignoring exploration and most drilling activities. Since 1983 the company has spent more than $600 million on over 100 acquisitions. Snyder Oil credits its success to low debt, heavy reinvestment, and an ability to adapt to market changes.

In 1990 the company merged with SOP, began selling off nonstrategic assets, and went public. It also began to emphasize production over acquisition. That same year Snyder Oil set up SOCO International to deal with opportunities in Russia and Tunisia.

In 1993 Barrett Resources sold its Wattenberg properties to Snyder for $18 million.

Sales and profits rose 88% and 105%, respectively, in the first half of 1993 over the same period in 1992.

WHO

Chairman and CEO: John C. Snyder, age 51, $595,912 pay
President: Thomas J. Edelman, age 42, $565,912 pay
EVP: John A. Fanning, age 53, $435,912 pay
SVP Gas Management: Robert J. Clark, age 48, $235,912 pay
SVP Legal Counsel and Secretary: Peter E. Lorenzen, age 43, $225,912 pay
SVP Production: William C. Melnar, age 57
SVP Special Projects: Rodney L. Waller, age 43
Controller: James H. Shonsey
President, SOCO International, Inc.: Edward T. Story
Auditors: Arthur Andersen & Co.

WHERE

HQ: 777 Main St., Ste. 2500, Fort Worth, TX 76102-5329
Phone: 817-338-4043 **Fax:** 817-882-5992

WHAT

	1992 Wells	
	No.	% of total
Wyoming	1,404	28
Texas	1,386	27
Wattenberg Field (Colorado)	838	16
Appalachian Basin	597	12
Thomasville Field (Alabama)	5	—
Other	873	17
Total	**5,103**	**100**

Subsidiaries
Snyder Acquisitions Corp.
Snyder Gas Marketing Inc.
SOCO 3300 L.P.
SOCO California Properties Inc.
SOCO International, Inc. (90%)
SOCO Wattenberg Corp.
Wyoming Gathering & Production Co.

KEY COMPETITORS

Ashland	Imperial Oil	Repsol
Associated Natural Gas	Mobil	Royal Dutch/
British Petroleum	Occidental	Shell
Chevron	Oryx	Sun
Coastal	Pennzoil	Texaco
Elf Aquitaine	Petrofina	
Exxon	Phillips Petroleum	

HOW MUCH

NYSE symbol: SNY FY ends: December 31	Annual Growth	1987	1988	1989	1990	1991	1992
Sales ($ mil.)	59.6%	11.6	14.7	26.5	82.2	92.5	120.2
Net income ($ mil.)	46.6%	2.5	3.4	4.8	7.5	8.8	16.9
Income as % of sales	—	—	—	23.3%	18.2%	9.1%	9.5%	14.0%
Earnings per share ($)	19.2%	.22	.31	.43	.36	.37	.53
Stock price – high ($)	—	—	—	—	9.50	8.50	10.50
Stock price – low ($)	—	—	—	—	4.75	4.75	5.88
Stock price – close ($)	33.3%	—	—	—	5.63	6.75	10.00
P/E – high	—	—	—	—	26	23	20
P/E – low	—	—	—	—	13	13	11
Dividends per share ($)	44.3%	.04	.08	.11	.16	.20	.25
Book value per share ($)	34.4%	1.85	2.25	2.80	5.59	7.66	8.12
Employees	34.4%	—	—	—	160	265	289

1992 Year-end:
Debt ratio: 34.4%
Return on equity: 9.4%
Cash (mil.): $20.5
Current ratio: 1.55
Long-term debt (mil.): $96.6
No. of shares (mil.): 22.7
Dividends:
 1992 average yield: 2.5%
 1992 payout: 47.2%
Market value (mil.): $227.0
R&D as % of sales: —
Advertising as % of sales: —

STERLING SOFTWARE, INC.

RANK: 212

OVERVIEW

EDI (Electronic Data Interchange) is the growing field of computer-to-computer transmission of documents between businesses using universal standards. Sterling became the leading EDI provider by working closely with the associations that set the standards. The company is organized into 3 groups: Systems Software supplies information management, storage management, and data communications products; EDI supplies software in several industries — health care (88% market share), hardware (70%), grocery (46%), transportation, retail, and banking; and Federal Systems works under long-term contracts mainly with the US Department of Defense and NASA in highly specialized areas, including supercomputing, virtual reality, automated messages, secure data links, and networking. The Wyly family controls the company.

Sam Wyly, Charles Wyly, Jr., Phillip Moore, and Sterling Williams, all former executives with University Computing, founded Sterling in 1981 with the goal of growing quickly by acquisition and internal development. Sterling went public and acquired 4 private software firms in 1983. In 1985 the company acquired Informatics General, a software firm 10 times the size of Sterling.

Most of Sterling's business is repeat business under long-term contracts: recurring revenue constituted 69% of 1992 revenues. The company is expanding the Systems Software group and transferring its EDI software to PCs and local area networks. With most of the debt from the Informatics acquisition paid off, Sterling has begun buying other firms.

In 1992 Sterling acquired Knowledge Systems Concepts, which supplies professional engineering services to the US military, and National Systems, which specializes in banking EDI products. Sales and net income for the first quarter of fiscal 1993 were up 17% and 41%, respectively, over the 1992 first quarter.

WHO

Chairman: Sam Wyly, age 58, $1,048,672 pay
VC: Charles J. Wyly, Jr., age 59, $511,176 pay
President and CEO: Sterling L. Williams, age 49, $870,249 pay
EVP; President, Systems Software Group: Werner L. Frank, age 63, $661,084 pay
EVP; President, EDI Group: Warner C. Blow, age 55, $544,550 pay
EVP; President, Federal Systems Group: Geno P. Tolari, age 49
SVP and CFO: George H. Ellis, age 43
SVP, General Counsel, and Secretary: Jeannette P. Meier, age 45
Auditors: Ernst & Young

WHERE

HQ: 8080 N. Central Expy., Ste. 1100, Dallas, TX 75206
Phone: 214-891-8600 **Fax:** 214-739-0535

	1992 Sales $ mil.	% of total	1992 Operating Profit $ mil.	% of total
North America	224.9	87	25.0	89
Other countries	34.4	13	3.0	11
Total	**259.3**	**100**	**28.0**	**100**

WHAT

	1992 Sales $ mil.	% of total	1992 Operating Profit $ mil.	% of total
Systems Software	100.0	40	24.1	57
EDI	56.5	22	12.2	29
Federal Systems	95.1	38	5.9	14
Adjustments	7.7	—	(14.2)	—
Total	**259.3**	**100**	**28.0**	**100**

Systems Software Group
Applications development and information management, data communications, storage management
EDI Group
Federal Systems Group

KEY COMPETITORS

BMC Software   General Electric
BT   IBM
Computer Associates   System Software Associates

HOW MUCH

NYSE symbol: SSW FY ends: September 30	5-Year Growth	1987	1988	1989	1990	1991	1992
Sales ($ mil.)	6.4%	190.1	169.8	180.2	200.2	224.4	259.3
Net income ($ mil.)	18.7%	5.8	4.6	8.6	10.5	12.7	13.8
Income as % of sales	—	3.1%	2.7%	4.8%	5.3%	5.7%	5.3%
Earnings per share ($)	16.7%	0.55	0.23	0.73	0.90	1.05	1.19
Stock price – high ($)	—	14.25	9.38	9.38	11.00	24.88	25.25
Stock price – low ($)	—	6.25	5.00	5.00	5.50	7.38	13.75
Stock price – close ($)	26.4%	6.50	5.75	9.13	8.50	24.63	21.00
P/E – high	—	26	41	13	12	24	21
P/E – low	—	11	22	7	6	7	12
Dividends per share ($)	0.0%	0.00	0.00	0.00	0.00	0.00	0.00
Book value per share ($)	(1.2%)	10.75	10.65	11.83	13.31	14.49	10.14
Employees	(2.6%)	2,450	1,840	1,800	1,900	2,000	2,150

1992 Year-end:
Debt ratio: 34.9%
Return on equity: 9.7%
Cash (mil.): $35.7
Current ratio: 1.58
Long-term debt (mil.): 52.8
No. of shares (mil.): 10
Dividends:
  1992 average yield: 0.0%
  1992 payout: 0.0%
Market value (mil.): $209.3
R&D as % of sales: —
Advertising as % of sales: —

TUESDAY MORNING CORPORATION

RANK: 309

OVERVIEW

Tuesday Morning is the largest national retailer of high-end, close-out gift merchandise, operating 190 stores that sell first class, quality merchandise. The company, whose motto is "Gifts. 50% to 80% Off Everything," buys the merchandise, which includes dinnerware, gourmet housewares, linens, luggage, and toys, at close-out discounts from manufacturers, marketing mostly unopened, but always new, merchandise. The most distinctive aspect of the company's marketing strategy, however, is its store schedule. All Tuesday Morning stores are open only 4 times a year, during what the company calls "sales events," which last 4–8 weeks. Chairman and founder Lloyd Ross owns 37% of company stock.

Tuesday Morning began retail operations in 1974 in Texas. Ross had always thought Tuesday the "most positive day of the week," and he named the company accordingly. From the beginning the company has relied on sales events to generate excitement in customers, who know that when the sales event is over, most of the merchandise will be gone for good. In 1991 the company began soliciting sales through catalogs (this operation was discontinued in 1993). Same-store sales increased by 8.2% in 1992 over 1991.

Tuesday Morning is practically the only store of its kind, with little direct competition. Its sales events strategy keeps overhead low, as does the company's no-frills — even spartan — approach to displaying merchandise. Its devotion to selling only top-quality, top-name goods at deep discount prices is unique as well. The company also owns its own fleet of trucks and runs a large distribution center in Dallas, where nationwide prices are set.

Tuesday Morning is testing a new store format, "Sofas by Design...Fast," a furniture store, in Virginia. First quarter 1993 sales increased by 11% over the same 1992 period; however, same-store sales fell by 5.4%.

WHO

Chairman and CEO: Lloyd L. Ross, age 57, $325,000 pay
President and COO: Stephen L. Higgins, age 43, $200,000 pay (prior to promotion)
SVP Advertising/Public Relations and Store Operations: Jerry M. Smith, age 56, $175,000 pay
SVP and CFO: Mark E. Jarvis
VP Sales and Marketing: Gary C. Grahnquist
VP Finance: Duane A. Huesers
VP Store Operations: William D. Flandermeyer
Director Human Resources: Debbie Steenrod
Auditors: KPMG Peat Marwick

WHERE

HQ: 14621 Inwood Rd., Dallas, TX 75244
Phone: 214-387-3562   **Fax:** 214-387-2344

Tuesday Morning Corporation operates 190 stores in Alabama, Arizona, Arkansas, California, Colorado, Florida, Georgia, Illinois, Indiana, Kansas, Kentucky, Louisiana, Maryland, Missouri, Mississippi, Nevada, New Mexico, North Carolina, Ohio, Oklahoma, South Carolina, Tennessee, Texas, Virginia, and Wisconsin.

WHAT

	1992 Sales % of total
Domestics	27
Tableware & china	11
Miscellaneous/seasonal products	34
Generic items	4
Other	24
Total	**100**

KEY COMPETITORS

50-Off Stores	Lechter's
Ames	May
Bombay Company	Montgomery Ward
Carter Hawley Hale	Nordstrom
Damark International	J.C. Penney
Dayton Hudson	Sears
Dillard	Service Merchandise
Kmart	Wal-Mart
Lands' End	Woolworth

HOW MUCH

NASDAQ symbol: TUES FY ends: December 31	5-Year Growth	1987	1988	1989	1990	1991	1992
Sales ($ mil.)	17.0%	72.9	81.6	96.8	107.4	123.4	160.1
Net income ($ mil.)	10.3%	4.0	3.5	4.3	4.7	5.0	6.6
Income as % of sales	—	5.5%	4.3%	4.5%	4.4%	4.1%	4.1%
Earnings per share ($)	7.4%	0.51	0.45	0.55	0.60	0.67	0.72
Stock price – high ($)	—	8.50	5.63	7.75	7.00	15.50	18.75
Stock price – low ($)	—	3.38	2.88	3.38	3.06	4.25	9.25
Stock price – close ($)	18.5%	4.44	3.75	6.81	5.13	15.00	10.38
P/E – high	—	17	13	14	12	23	26
P/E – low	—	7	6	6	5	6	13
Dividends per share ($)	0.0%	0.00	0.00	0.00	0.00	0.00	0.00
Book value per share ($)	17.7%	3.31	3.74	4.23	4.83	6.46	7.47
Employees	7.5%	2,000	1,200	1,410	1,535	1,725	2,877

1992 Year-end:
Debt ratio: 17.5%
Return on equity: 10.3%
Cash (mil.): $1.5
Current ratio: 3.24
Long-term debt (mil.): $8.9
No. of shares (mil.): 8.6
Dividends:
  1992 average yield: 0.0%
  1992 payout: 0.0%
Market value (mil.): $89.7
R&D as % of sales: —
Advertising as % of sales: 6.7%

THE TEXAS 500   145

U.S. LONG DISTANCE CORP.

RANK: 444

OVERVIEW

With Nolan Ryan delivering the pitch as corporate spokesperson, U.S. Long Distance is swinging for the fences. The company operates in 36 states through 2 subsidiaries: U.S. Long Distance, Inc., which provides operator-assisted and direct-dial long-distance services, and Zero Plus Dialing, Inc., the leading 3rd-party billing and information services provider for the long-distance telecommunications market, with more than a 40% market share.

In 1985 U.S. Long Distance entered the telecommunications business under the name International Telepool by acquiring a small pay-phone company. The following year Butch Holmes became CEO, and the company changed its name to US Pay-Tel of Texas. Learning that hotels needed operator services, the company sold the pay-phone operation and adopted its present name as a US corporation in 1987. In 1990 the company's stock began trading through the NASDAQ network. The following year the company acquired National Telephone Exchange, Valu-Line of Wichita Falls, and Central Texas Long Distance, collectively known as the NTX companies.

In the direct-dial long-distance market, U.S. Long Distance competes by pricing its services 25% lower than AT&T rates. The company's efforts to expand its operator services are focused on pay-telephone customers in Texas, California, Florida, and Michigan. Through its extensive agreements with local telephone concerns, the company is able to provide billing and information management services at a lower cost to telecommunications companies than they can do it for themselves, especially for smaller accounts. The company targets small- and medium-sized residential and commercial clients and cross-sells services to them from its 3 interrelated businesses.

On a 63% increase in first-half fiscal 1993 revenues as compared to the first half of fiscal 1992, net income almost tripled.

WHO

Chairman and CEO: Parris H. "Butch" Holmes, Jr., age 49, $247,500 pay
President: Larry M. James, age 45, $143,000 pay (prior to promotion)
EVP and COO: Charles P. Johnson
VP Finance & Treasurer: Kelly Simmons
General Counsel and SVP Legal and Regulatory Affairs: W. Audie Long, age 48, $150,000 pay
SVP Operations, Billing and Information Systems: Alan W. Saltzman, age 45, $110,000 pay
VP Human Resources: David S. Horne
Auditors: Arthur Andersen & Co.

WHERE

HQ: 9311 San Pedro, Ste. 300, San Antonio, TX 78216-4476
Phone: 210-525-9009   **Fax:** 210-525-0389

WHAT

	1992 Sales $ mil.	% of total
Billing services	31.1	36
Operator services	34.8	41
Direct-dial long-distance services	19.2	23
Total	**85.1**	**100**

Subsidiaries
Zero Plus Dialing, Inc. (3rd-party billing services)
U.S. Long Distance, Inc. (operator-assisted and direct-dial long-distance services)

KEY COMPETITORS

Ameritech	MCI
AT&T	NYNEX
Bell Atlantic	Pacific Telesis
BellSouth	Resurgens
Cable & Wireless	Southwestern Bell
General Motors	Sprint
GTE	U S WEST
IDB Communications	
LDDS Communications	

HOW MUCH

NASDAQ symbol: USLD FY ends: September 30	Annual Growth	1987	1988	1989	1990	1991	1992
Sales ($ mil.)	390.4%	0.03	1.8	8.7	19.3	36.7	85.1
Net income ($ mil.)	—	(2.3)	(3.0)	(1.5)	(0.5)	0.7	2.4
Income as % of sales	—	—	—	(17.1%)	(2.8%)	1.9%	2.9%
Earnings per share ($)	—	—	—	(0.36)	(0.09)	0.06	0.21
Stock price – high ($)	—	—	—	—	3.94	9.75	19.75
Stock price – low ($)	—	—	—	—	1.59	1.69	7.00
Stock price – close ($)	166.9%	—	—	—	2.44	7.25	17.38
P/E – high	—	—	—	—	—	163	94
P/E – low	—	—	—	—	—	28	33
Dividends per share ($)	0.0%	—	—	0.00	0.00	0.00	0.00
Book value per share ($)	—	—	—	(0.05)	0.40	0.61	1.13
Employees	84.6%	—	—	91	153	368	572

1992 Year-end:
Debt ratio: 82.2%
Return on equity: 24.1%
Cash (mil.): $13.9
Current ratio: 1.02
Long-term debt (mil.): $14.5
No. of shares (mil.): 9.3
Dividends:
  1992 average yield: 0.0%
  1992 payout: 0.0%
Market value (mil.): $161.1
R&D as % of sales: —
Advertising as % of sales: —

WHOLE FOODS MARKET, INC.

RANK: 365

OVERVIEW

Benefiting from the trend toward greater health awareness and environmental responsibility is Whole Foods Market, America's #1 natural foods supermarket chain. The company operates 22 stores, some of which are equipped with restaurants, and also does some wholesaling. The corporate culture of Whole Foods is unusual: employees are organized into teams with the power to set store policy. One page in the annual report is devoted to addressing employee complaints. Whole Foods donates at least 5% of profits to community and environmental causes. The Mackey family owns 9.4% of company stock.

Whole Foods began operation in 1978 in Austin, Texas, as Saferway Natural Foods. Two years later Saferway merged with Clarksville Natural Grocery, and Whole Foods was born, led by college dropout John Mackey. A full-sized, one-stop store soon opened in Texas's capital. Mackey developed a plan to add one new region and one new store in each existing region yearly, but in 1992, the year the company went public, Whole Foods bought Bread & Circus (Boston; the #3 natural foods store chain) and Wellspring Grocery (North Carolina), increasing the number of its stores to 19. It is now the only natural food chain with a presence in several regions of the US.

Making the stores large enough to fulfill customers' shopping needs in one stop was visionary; this strategy kept the customers coming back. The company is now in a good position to grow, through new store construction and acquisition, in a still highly fragmented market. In 1993 Whole Foods agreed to buy Los Angeles's Mrs. Gooch's Natural Foods, a 7-store chain, for $56 million. Same-store sales rose 7% in 1992 over 1991, far above the national grocery store average.

First quarter fiscal 1993 yielded ballooning increases in sales (85%) and net income (110%) over 1992's figures.

WHO

Chairman, President, and CEO: John Mackey, $175,000 pay
President, Northeast Region: Chris Hitt, $154,000 pay
VP and CFO: Glenda Flanagan, $129,000 pay
President, California Region: Peter Roy, $154,000 pay
General Manager, Texas Health Distributors: Craig Weller, $92,000 pay
VP and Chief Communications Officer: Jack Reed
Communications Coordinator (Personnel): Rema Cunningham
Auditors: KPMG Peat Marwick

WHERE

HQ: 2525 Wallingwood Dr., Ste. 1400, Austin, TX 78746
Phone: 512-328-7541   **Fax:** 512-328-5482

	1992 Stores No. of stores
Texas	8
Massachusetts	5
California	3
North Carolina	3
Louisiana	1
Illinois	1
Rhode Island	1
Total	**22**

WHAT

	1992 Sales % of total
Retail sales	96
Wholesale operations	4
Total	**100**

KEY COMPETITORS

Albertson's
American Stores
Food Lion
Fred Meyer
Great A&P
Kroger

Safeway
Stop & Shop
Supermarkets General
Vons
Winn-Dixie

HOW MUCH

NASDAQ symbol: WFMI FY ends: Last Fri. in Sept.	Annual Growth	1987	1988	1989	1990	1991	1992
Sales ($ mil.)	25.2%	39.0	44.7	62.6	74.7	92.5	119.9
Net income ($ mil.)	50.6%	0.4	0.7	(0.3)	0.7	1.6	3.1
Income as % of sales	—	1.0%	1.6%	(0.5%)	0.9%	1.7%	2.6%
Earnings per share ($)	45.7%	—	—	—	—	0.75	0.87
Stock price – high ($)	—	—	—	—	—	—	34.00
Stock price – low ($)	—	—	—	—	—	—	14.50
Stock price – close ($)	—	—	—	—	—	—	29.25
P/E – high	—	—	—	—	—	—	39
P/E – low	—	—	—	—	—	—	17
Dividends per share ($)	0.0%	—	—	—	—	0.00	0.00
Book value per share ($)	134.6%	—	—	—	—	4.25	9.97
Employees	23.3%	826	946	1,420	1,615	1,300	2,350

1992 Year-end:
Debt ratio: 1.5%
Return on equity: 12.2%
Cash (mil.): $16.0
Current ratio: 2.97
Long-term debt (mil.): $0.3
No. of shares (mil.): 3.6
Dividends:
   1992 average yield: 0.0%
   1992 payout: 0.0%
Market value (mil.): $106.5
R&D as % of sales: —
Advertising as % of sales: 0.0%

THE TEXAS 500

TEXAS 500

50-OFF STORES, INC. — RANK: 276

8750 Tesoro Dr.
San Antonio, TX 78217
Phone: 210-805-9300
Fax: 210-805-0067

CEO: Charles M. Siegel
CFO: Pat L. Ross
HR: Roy Springer
Employees: 2,849

1992 Sales: $181 million
Symbol: FOFF
Exchange: NASDAQ

Industry: Retail - discount-priced apparel, housewares, giftwares, and domestics

▶ See page 128 for a full profile of this company.

A. H. BELO CORP. — RANK: 115

400 S. Record St.
Dallas, TX 75202
Phone: 214-977-6606
Fax: 214-977-6603

CEO: Robert W. Decherd
CFO: Michael D. Perry
HR: Vicky Teherani
Employees: 2,788

1992 Sales: $516 million
Symbol: BLC
Exchange: NYSE

Industry: Broadcasting - TV (WFAA-TV [Dallas], KHOU-TV [Houston]); newspapers - The Dallas Morning News

ACADEMY CORP. — RANK: 320

1800 N. Mason Rd.
Katy, TX 77449
Phone: 713-579-1555
Fax: 713-492-5204

CEO: Arthur Gochman
CFO: James Pierce
HR: Sylvia Berrera
Employees: 1,700

1992 Sales: $154 million
Ownership: Private

Industry: Retail - sporting goods and apparel

ADAMS RESOURCES & ENERGY, INC. — RANK: 105

6910 Fannin St.
Houston, TX 77030
Phone: 713-797-9966
Fax: 713-795-4495

CEO: K. S. Adams, Jr.
CFO: Richard B. Abshire
HR: Jay Grimes
Employees: 309

1992 Sales: $550 million
Symbol: AE
Exchange: AMEX

Industry: Oil and gas - production and pipeline

ADMINISTAFF INC. — RANK: 149

19001 Crescent Springs Dr.
Kingwood, TX 77339
Phone: 713-358-8986
Fax: 713-358-3354

CEO: Paul Sarvadi
CFO: Richard Rawson
HR: Jim Wilkes
Employees: 12,800

1992 Sales: $410 million
Ownership: Private

Industry: Business services - employee leasing

TEXAS 500

AFFILIATED FOODS INCORPORATED — RANK: 104

6700 S. Washington
Amarillo, TX 79118
Phone: 806-372-3851
Fax: 806-372-1404

CEO: Benny R. Cooper
CFO: James Y'Barbo
HR: Don Barclay
Employees: 900

1992 Sales: $550 million
Ownership: Private

Industry: Food - wholesale groceries, drugs, toiletries, and sundries

AFG INDUSTRIES INC. — RANK: 111

301 Commerce St., Ste. 3300
Ft. Worth, TX 76102
Phone: 817-332-5006
Fax: 817-870-2685

CEO: R. D. Hubbard
CFO: Gary G. Miller
HR: Eugene Harris
Employees: 3,500

1992 Sales: $525 million
Ownership: Private

Industry: Glass products - flat glass manufacturing

AKIN, GUMP, STRAUSS, HAUER & FELD — RANK: 346

1700 Pacific Ave., Ste. 4100
Dallas, TX 75201
Phone: 214-969-2800
Fax: 214-969-4343

CEO: Alan D. Feld
CFO: Tom Atlas
HR: Laurel Digweed
Employees: 1,000

1992 Sales: $132 million
Ownership: Private

Industry: Business services - legal

ALLIANCE EMPLOYEE LEASING CORP. I — RANK: 307

2351 W. Northwest Hwy., Ste. 3100
Dallas, TX 75220
Phone: 214-902-9100
Fax: 214-353-0470

CEO: Tynes Hilderdrand
CFO: Valerie Duncan
HR: Valerie Duncan
Employees: 8,000

1991 Sales: $161 million
Ownership: Private

Industry: Business services - employee leasing

ALLRIGHT CORP. — RANK: 304

1111 Fannin St.
Houston, TX 77002
Phone: 713-222-2505
Fax: 713-222-6833

CEO: Bernard M. Meyer
CFO: Terry Chen
HR: A. J. Layden
Employees: 3,000

1992 Sales: $163 million
Ownership: Private

Industry: Business services - parking lot management

TEXAS 500

ALLWASTE, INC. RANK: 229

3040 Post Oak Blvd., Ste. 1300
Houston, TX 77056
Phone: 713-623-8777
Fax: 713-625-7087

CEO: Raymond L. Nelson, Jr.
CFO: I. T. Corley
HR: Julie Caturani
Employees: 3,263

1992 Sales: $234 million
Symbol: ALW
Exchange: NYSE

Industry: Pollution control equipment and services

AMERICAN ECOLOGY CORP. RANK: 487

5333 Westheimer
Houston, TX 77056
Phone: 713-624-1900
Fax: 713-624-1999

CEO: Harry J. Phillips, Jr.
CFO: C. Clifford Wright, Jr.
HR: Mike Walker
Employees: 249

1992 Sales: $71 million
Symbol: ECOL
Exchange: NASDAQ

Industry: Pollution control equipment and services - transportation and disposal of hazardous waste; operation of hazardous waste landfill; remediation services

AMERICAN GENERAL CORPORATION RANK: 23

2929 Allen Pkwy.
Houston, TX 77019
Phone: 713-522-1111
Fax: 713-831-3028

CEO: Harold S. Hook
CFO: Austin P. Young
HR: Tom Pulliam
Employees: 11,600

1992 Sales: $4,602 million
Symbol: AGC
Exchange: NYSE

Industry: Financial - investments and life insurance

See pages 54 – 55 for a full profile of this company.

AMERICAN INCOME HOLDING, INC. RANK: 288

1200 Wooded Acres Dr.
Waco, TX 76797
Phone: 817-772-3050
Fax: 817-751-8639

CEO: Bernard Rapoport
CFO: Mark E. Pape
HR: Curtis C. Moore
Employees: 235

1992 Sales: $175 million
Symbol: AIH
Exchange: NYSE

Industry: Insurance - multiline

AMERICAN INDEMNITY FINANCIAL CORP. RANK: 497

One American Indemnity Plaza
Galveston, TX 77550
Phone: 409-766-4600
Fax: 409-766-5531

CEO: J. F. Seinsheimer III
CFO: Synott L. McNeel
HR: William H. Felts, Jr.
Employees: 248

1992 Sales: $68 million
Symbol: AIFC
Exchange: NASDAQ

Industry: Insurance - property and casualty

AMERICAN MEDICAL HOLDINGS, INC. RANK: 44

8201 Preston Rd., Ste. 300
Dallas, TX 75225
Phone: 214-360-6300
Fax: 214-360-6363

CEO: Harry J. Gray
CFO: Wendy L. Simpson
HR: Charles N. Sabitino
Employees: 27,500

1992 Sales: $2,238 million
Symbol: AMI
Exchange: AMEX

Industry: Hospitals

AMERICAN NATIONAL INSURANCE CO. RANK: 52

One Moody Plaza
Galveston, TX 77550
Phone: 409-763-4661
Fax: 409-766-6589

CEO: Orson C. Clay
CFO: C. D. Thompson
HR: Bill McCollom
Employees: 1,266

1992 Sales: $1,318 million
Symbol: ANAT
Exchange: NASDAQ

Industry: Insurance - life

AMERICAN OIL AND GAS CORP. RANK: 142

333 Clay St., Ste. 2000
Houston, TX 77002
Phone: 713-739-2900
Fax: 713-739-2963

CEO: David M. Carmichael
CFO: Thomas H. Fanning
HR: William H. Spahr
Employees: 416

1992 Sales: $431 million
Symbol: AOG
Exchange: NYSE

Industry: Oil and gas - gathering, transporting, storing, processing, and marketing natural gas

AMERICAN PRODUCE AND VEGETABLE CO. RANK: 430

4721 Simonton Rd.
Dallas, TX 75244
Phone: 214-233-5750
Fax: 214-233-6909

CEO: Lucian La Barba
CFO: Mack Standlee
HR: Orville Poppe
Employees: 580

1992 Sales: $92 million
Ownership: Private

Industry: Food - wholesale groceries, fresh fruits and vegetables

AMERICAN RICE, INC. RANK: 285

16825 Northchase Dr., Ste. 1500
Houston, TX 77060
Phone: 713-873-8800
Fax: 713-873-2823

CEO: Douglas Murphy
CFO: Larry Dylla
HR: Marsha Donaghe
Employees: 230

1992 Sales: $176 million
Symbol: RICE
Exchange: OTC

Industry: Agricultural operations - rice milling (one of the largest rice millers in the U.S.)

TEXAS 500

AMERISERV FOOD CO. RANK: 71

13355 Noel Rd., Ste. 2225
Dallas, TX 75240
Phone: 214-385-8595
Fax: 214-702-7391

CEO: William R. Burgess
CFO: A. Scott Letier
HR: William Burgess
Employees: 1,200

1992 Sales: $806 million
Ownership: Private

Industry: Food - food service distribution

AMR CORPORATION RANK: 4

4333 Amon Carter Blvd.
Ft. Worth, TX 76155
Phone: 817-963-1234
Fax: 817-967-9641

CEO: Robert L. Crandall
CFO: Donald J. Carty
HR: Thomas J. Kiernan
Employees: 119,300

1992 Sales: $14,396 million
Symbol: AMR
Exchange: NYSE

Industry: Transportation - American Airlines (world's largest airline) and several regional airlines, including American Eagle; SABRE computer reservation system

🟊 See pages 56 – 57 for a full profile of this company.

AMRE, INC. RANK: 206

8585 N. Stemmons Fwy., Ste. 102
Irving, TX 75247
Phone: 214-819-7000
Fax: 214-819-4702

CEO: Ronald I. Wagner
CFO: John S. Vanecko
HR: Walker Williams
Employees: 3,250

1992 Sales: $274 million
Symbol: AMM
Exchange: NYSE

Industry: Building products - doors and trim

ANADARKO PETROLEUM CORP. RANK: 158

16855 Northchase Dr.
Houston, TX 77060
Phone: 713-875-1101
Fax: 713-874-3385

CEO: Robert J. Allison, Jr.
CFO: M. E. Rose
HR: Charles G. Manley
Employees: 970

1992 Sales: $375 million
Symbol: APC
Exchange: NYSE

Industry: Oil and gas - US exploration and production

ANCIRA ENTERPRISES INC. RANK: 299

6111 Bandera Rd.
San Antonio, TX 78238
Phone: 210-681-4900
Fax: 210-681-9413

CEO: Ernesto Ancira, Jr.
CFO: Gregory M. Spence
HR: Valerie Bibb
Employees: 300

1992 Sales: $169 million
Ownership: Private

Industry: Retail - automobiles

TEXAS 500

ANDERSON GRAIN CORP. — RANK: 390

PO Box 1117
Levelland, TX 79336
Phone: 806-894-4982
Fax: 806-894-1962

CEO: Buck Anderson
CFO: Dick Holland
HR: Bill Fitzherbert
Employees: 150

1993 Sales: $110 million
Ownership: Private

Industry: Wholesale distribution - grain, fertilizer, and farming supplies

ANDREWS AND KURTH — RANK: 429

4200 Texas Commerce
Houston, TX 77002
Phone: 713-220-4200
Fax: 713-220-4285

CEO: Rush Moody
CFO: Kevin Miller
HR: Dora Hightower
Employees: 515

1992 Sales: $93 million
Ownership: Private

Industry: Business services - legal

APACHE CORPORATION — RANK: 133

2000 Post Oak Blvd., Ste. 100
Houston, TX 77056
Phone: 713-296-6000
Fax: 713-296-6472

CEO: Raymond Plank
CFO: Mark Jackson
HR: Roger B. Rice
Employees: 844

1992 Sales: $454 million
Symbol: APA
Exchange: NYSE

Industry: Oil and gas - international integrated

APPLETREE MARKETS INC. — RANK: 99

7676 Hillmont, Ste. 300
Houston, TX 77040
Phone: 713-460-5000
Fax: 713-460-8262

CEO: R. Howard Stanworth
CFO: R. T. Kubicek
HR: Lynne Simons
Employees: 4,000

1992 Sales: $597 million
Ownership: Private

Industry: Retail - supermarkets

APS HOLDING CORPORATION — RANK: 150

3000 Pawnee St.
Houston, TX 77054
Phone: 713-741-2470
Fax: 713-749-8123

CEO: Richard Spelleri
CFO: Dave Barbeau
HR: Ray Rarey
Employees: 2,225

1992 Sales: $404 million
Ownership: Private

Industry: Auto parts - wholesale

TEXAS 500

ASSOCIATED MATERIALS INCORPORATED — RANK: 203
2200 Ross Ave., Ste. 4100
Dallas, TX 75201-6711
Phone: 214-220-4600
Fax: 214-220-4607

CEO: William W. Winspear
CFO: Robert L. Winspear
HR: Robert L. Winspear
Employees: 2,400

1992 Sales: $277 million
Ownership: Private

Industry: Building products - home improvement products including vinyl and aluminum siding, metal doors and windows, and kitchen cabinets

ASSOCIATED MILK PRODUCERS, INC. — RANK: 34
6609 Blanco Rd.
San Antonio, TX 78213
Phone: 210-340-9100
Fax: 210-340-9158

CEO: Noble Anderson
CFO: Telly Krueger
HR: Charles Warren
Employees: 4,364

1992 Sales: $2,835 million
Ownership: Private

Industry: Food - dairy products including milk, cheese, sour cream, frozen yogurt, nonfat dry milk, and canned sauces

ASSOCIATED PIPELINE CONTRACTORS INC. — RANK: 494
3535 Briarpark Dr.
Houston, TX 77042
Phone: 713-789-4311
Fax: 713-789-5232

CEO: Paul Somerville
CFO: C. Fowler
HR: Marcia Sinq-Mars
Employees: 600

1991 Sales: $69 million
Ownership: Private

Industry: Construction - water and sewer mains and pipeline

ATMOS ENERGY CORP. — RANK: 172
5430 LBJ Fwy.
Dallas, TX 75240
Phone: 214-934-9227
Fax: 214-991-5235

CEO: Charles K. Vaughan
CFO: James F. Purser
HR: H.F. Harber
Employees: 1,383

1992 Sales: $340 million
Symbol: ATO
Exchange: NYSE

Industry: Utility - gas distribution

AUSTIN INDUSTRIES INC. — RANK: 116
3535 Travis St.
Dallas, TX 75204
Phone: 214-443-5500
Fax: 214-443-5581

CEO: William T. Solomon
CFO: John P. Olsson
HR: Rob Brewer
Employees: 5,500

1992 Sales: $510 million
Ownership: Private

Industry: Construction - heavy, commercial, and industrial

TEXAS 500

AZTX CATTLE CO.   RANK: 413

PO Box 390
Hereford, TX 79045
Phone: 806-364-8871
Fax: 806-364-3842

CEO: Bob Josserand
CFO: Odess Lovin, Jr.
HR: Odess Lovin, Jr.
Employees: 140

1992 Sales: $100 million
Ownership: Private

Industry: Agricultural operations - cattle feedlots

BABBAGE'S, INC.   RANK: 248

10741 King William Dr.
Dallas, TX 75220
Phone: 214-401-9000
Fax: 214-401-9002

CEO: James B. McCurry
CFO: Opal P. Ferraro
HR: Michael A. Ivanich
Employees: 2,200

1992 Sales: $209 million
Symbol: BBGS
Exchange: NASDAQ

Industry: Retail - discount personal computer software, including games and entertainment systems and education and productivity software

➥ See page 129 for a full profile of this company.

BAKER AND BOTTS, L.L.P.   RANK: 322

3000 One Shell Plaza, 910 Louisiana
Houston, TX 77002
Phone: 713-229-1234
Fax: 713-229-1522

CEO: E. William Barnett
CFO: Jim Willis
HR: Sue Robinson
Employees: 1,307

1992 Sales: $154 million
Ownership: Private

Industry: Business services - legal

BAKER HUGHES INCORPORATED   RANK: 39

3900 Essex Ln.
Houston, TX 77027
Phone: 713-439-8600
Fax: 713-439-8699

CEO: James D. Woods
CFO: Eric L. Mattson
HR: Philip A. Rice
Employees: 19,600

1992 Sales: $2,539 million
Symbol: BHI
Exchange: NYSE

Industry: Oil field machinery and equipment

➥ See pages 106 – 107 for a full profile of this company.

BANCTEC, INC.   RANK: 231

4435 Spring Valley Rd.
Dallas, TX 75244
Phone: 214-450-7700
Fax: 214-450-7867

CEO: Grahame N. Clark, Jr.
CFO: Gary T. Robinson
HR: James R. Wimberley
Employees: 1,940

1993 Sales: $234 million
Symbol: BTEC
Exchange: NASDAQ

Industry: Computers - peripheral equipment; document image processing

TEXAS 500

BANK UNITED OF TEXAS FSB — RANK: 204

3200 Southwest Fwy.
Houston, TX 77027
Phone: 713-963-6500
Fax: 713-965-6883
Industry: Bank

CEO: Barry Burkholder
CFO: Tony Nocella
HR: Karen Hartnett
Employees: 2,200

1992 Sales: $276 million
Symbol: BKUA
Exchange: NYSE

BARNETT BROTHERS BROKERAGE COMPANY INC. — RANK: 424

2509 74th St.
Lubbock, TX 79423
Phone: 806-745-7575
Fax: 806-745-5709
Industry: Food - wholesale groceries

CEO: Clark Barnett
CFO: Tom Barnett
HR: Neil Burrus
Employees: 55

1992 Sales: $95 million
Ownership: Private

BAROID CORP. — RANK: 94

3000 N. Sam Houston Pkwy. East
Houston, TX 77032
Phone: 713-987-4000
Fax: 713-987-5742
Industry: Oil field machinery and equipment; being purchased by Dresser

CEO: J. Landis Martin
CFO: Joseph S. Campofelice
HR: Peggy D'Hemecourt
Employees: 5,450

1992 Sales: $628 million
Symbol: BRC
Exchange: NYSE

BARRETT & CROFOOT, LLP — RANK: 417

PO Box 670, 4 Rd. and J Rd.
Hereford, TX 79045
Phone: 806-364-6081
Fax: 806-357-2384
Industry: Agricultural operations - cattle feedlot

CEO: E.C. Barrett
CFO: James P. McDowell
HR: Anissa Stone
Employees: 100

1992 Sales: $98 million
Ownership: Private

BASS ENTERPRISES PRODUCTION CO. — RANK: 291

201 Main St., Ste. 300
Ft. Worth, TX 76102-3107
Phone: 817-390-8400
Fax: 817-390-8751
Industry: Oil and gas - exploration and production

CEO: Sid R. Bass
CFO: Robert Cotham
HR: Keith Bullard
Employees: 700

1992 Est. Sales: $174 mil.
Ownership: Private

BATTLE MOUNTAIN GOLD CO.   RANK: 275

333 Clay St., 42nd Fl.
Houston, TX 77002
Phone: 713-650-6400
Fax: 713-650-3636

CEO: Karl E. Elers
CFO: R. Dennis O'Connell
HR: Ken Row
Employees: 1,482

1992 Sales: $182 million
Symbol: BMG
Exchange: NYSE

Industry: Gold mining and processing

BAY HOUSTON TOWING CO.   RANK: 440

2243 Milford
Houston, TX 77098
Phone: 713-529-3755
Fax: 713-529-2591

CEO: Mark E. Kuebler
CFO: Milow Klein
HR: Bill McDonald
Employees: 318

1992 Sales: $86 million
Ownership: Private

Industry: Diversified operations - fertilizer manufacturing; tugboat services

BEHRENS INC.   RANK: 256

7500 Mars Dr.
Waco, TX 76712
Phone: 817-776-7583
Fax: 817-751-0857

CEO: William L. Clifton, Jr.
CFO: David Nemec
HR: David Nemec
Employees: 170

1992 Sales: $200 million
Ownership: Private

Industry: Drugs, proprietaries, and sundries - wholesale and distribution to independent pharmacies

BEN E. KEITH   RANK: 108

600 E. Ninth St.
Ft. Worth, TX 76102
Phone: 817-332-9171
Fax: 817-332-3471

CEO: Robert Hallam
CFO: Mel Cockrell
HR: Carolyn Marshall
Employees: 1,500

1992 Sales: $540 million
Ownership: Private

Industry: Wholesale distribution - beer and ale, food

BERRY-BARNETT GROCERY CO.   RANK: 445

900 N. Denton
Mexia, TX 76667
Phone: 817-562-9333
Fax: 817-562-7881

CEO: Dean Guerin
CFO: Dale Hamblett
HR: Phyllis Connell
Employees: 150

1992 Sales: $85 million
Ownership: Private

Industry: Food - wholesale groceries

TEXAS 500

BJ SERVICES CO.   RANK: 174
5500 NW Central Dr.
Houston, TX 77092
Phone: 713-462-4239
Fax: 713-895-5851

CEO: J. W. Stewart
CFO: Michael McShane
HR: Stephen A. Wright
Employees: 2,579

1992 Sales: $330 million
Symbol: BJS
Exchange: NYSE

Industry: Oil and gas - field services

BLOCK DISTRIBUTING COMPANY INC.   RANK: 408
827 Coliseum Rd.
San Antonio, TX 78219
Phone: 210-224-7531
Fax: 210-227-7810

CEO: E.L. Block
CFO: Raleigh Lair
HR: Raleigh Lair
Employees: 340

1992 Sales: $100 million
Ownership: Private

Industry: Wholesale distribution - wine, beer, and ale

BLUE BELL CREAMERIES   RANK: 279
Loop 577
Brenham, TX 77833
Phone: 409-836-7977
Fax: 409-830-2198

CEO: Howard Kruse
CFO: William J. Rankin
HR: Darrell Winklemann
Employees: 1,500

1992 Sales: $180 million
Ownership: Private

Industry: Food - dairy products, ice cream production (Blue Bell - Texas's favorite ice cream)

BLUE CROSS AND BLUE SHIELD OF TEXAS INC.   RANK: 54
901 S. Central Expwy.
Richardson, TX 75080
Phone: 214-669-6900
Fax: 214-669-5298

CEO: Rogers K. Coleman
CFO: Vernon Walker
HR: Mike Jarvis
Employees: 3,900

1992 Sales: $1,251 million
Ownership: Private

Industry: Insurance - health, hospital, and medical service plans

BMC SOFTWARE, INC.   RANK: 226
2101 CityWest Blvd.
Houston, TX 77042-2827
Phone: 713-918-8800
Fax: 713-918-8000

CEO: Max P. Watson, Jr.
CFO: David A. Farley
HR: Johnnie Horn
Employees: 921

1993 Sales: $239 million
Symbol: BMCS
Exchange: NASDAQ

Industry: Computers - mainframe database software

See page 130 for a full profile of this company.

BOMBAY COMPANY, INC., THE — RANK: 234

550 Bailey Ave., Ste. 700
Ft. Worth, TX 76107
Phone: 817-347-8200
Fax: 817-332-7066

CEO: Robert E. M. Nourse
CFO: James E. Herlihy
HR: William S. Goodlatte
Employees: 2,900

1993 Sales: $232 million
Symbol: BBA
Exchange: NYSE

Industry: Retail - home furnishings including accent furniture and decorative accessories

See page 131 for a full profile of this company.

BORDER STEEL MILLS INC. — RANK: 471

PO Box 12843, IH–10
El Paso, TX 79912
Phone: 915-886-2000
Fax: 915-886-2218

CEO: A. W. Lupia
CFO: F. P. Boyd
HR: Jill Rocha
Employees: 500

1992 Sales: $75 million
Ownership: Private

Industry: Steel - production of steel bars

BRACEWELL AND PATTERSON — RANK: 367

2900 S. Tower
Houston, TX 77002
Phone: 713-223-2900
Fax: 703-221-1212

CEO: Richard A. Royds
CFO: Mary Ann Jay
HR: Helen Lilienstren
Employees: 500

1992 Sales: $120 million
Ownership: Private

Industry: Business services - legal

BRAZOS ELECTRIC POWER COOPERATIVE INC. — RANK: 259

PO Box 2585
Waco, TX 76702-2585
Phone: 817-750-6500
Fax: 817-750-6290

CEO: Richard E. McCaskill
CFO: Clarence Carpenter
HR: J. T. Yows, Jr.
Employees: 290

1992 Sales: $199 million
Ownership: Private

Industry: Utility - electric power

BRENHAM WHOLESALE GROCERY CO. — RANK: 352

602 W. 1st St.
Brenham, TX 77833
Phone: 409-836-7925
Fax: 409-830-0346

CEO: Luther Utesch
CFO: Don Huebner
HR: Russell Engeling
Employees: 217

1992 Sales: $130 million
Ownership: Private

Industry: Food - wholesale groceries

TEXAS 500

BRINKER INTERNATIONAL, INC. RANK: 89

6820 LBJ Fwy.
Dallas, TX 75240
Phone: 214-980-9917
Fax: 214-770-9593

CEO: Norman E. Brinker
CFO: Debra Smithart-Weitzman
HR: Janet A. Coen
Employees: 28,000

1993 Sales: $653 million
Symbol: EAT
Exchange: NYSE

Industry: Retail - food and restaurants including Chili's Grill & Bar, Grady's American Grill, and Romano's Macaroni Grill

See page 132 for a full profile of this company.

BROOKSHIRE BROTHERS INCORPORATED RANK: 107

1201 Ellen Trout Dr.
Lufkin, TX 75901
Phone: 409-634-8155
Fax: 409-634-8646

CEO: Eugene Brookshire
CFO: Gene Nerren
HR: Tim Hale
Employees: 5,000

1992 Sales: $542 million
Ownership: Private

Industry: Retail - supermarkets under the names Budget Chopper and Brookshire Brothers Inc. in Texas and Louisiana

BROOKSHIRE GROCERY CO. RANK: 92

1600 SW Loop 323
Tyler, TX 75701
Phone: 903-534-3000
Fax: 903-534-3272

CEO: Bruce G. Brookshire
CFO: Harvey B. King
HR: Tim Brookshire
Employees: 7,300

1992 Sales: $640 million
Ownership: Private

Industry: Retail - supermarkets under the names Brookshire Grocery Co. and Super 1 Food Stores in Texas, Louisiana, and Arkansas

BROWNING-FERRIS INDUSTRIES, INC. RANK: 31

757 N. Eldridge
Houston, TX 77079
Phone: 713-870-8100
Fax: 713-870-7844

CEO: William D. Ruckelshaus
CFO: Jeffrey E. Curtiss
HR: Susan J. Piller
Employees: 29,400

1992 Sales: $3,288 million
Symbol: BFI
Exchange: NYSE

Industry: Pollution control equipment and services - collection and disposal of trash and medical waste, waste-to-energy conversion plants, sanitary landfills, recycling

See pages 108 – 109 for a full profile of this company.

BURLINGTON NORTHERN INC. RANK: 22

3800 Continental Plaza, 777 Main St.
Ft. Worth, TX 76102-5384
Phone: 817-878-2000
Fax: 817-878-2377

CEO: Gerald Grinstein
CFO: David C. Anderson
HR: James B. Dagnon
Employees: 31,204

1992 Sales: $4,630 million
Symbol: BNI
Exchange: NYSE

Industry: Transportation - Burlington Northern Railroad (longest rail system in the US)

See pages 58 – 59 for a full profile of this company.

BUSINESS RECORDS CORPORATION HOLDING CO.   RANK: 443

1111 W. Mockingbird, Ste. 1400
Dallas, TX 75247
Phone: 214-688-1800
Fax: 214-905-2303

CEO: Perry E. Esping
CFO: Thomas E. Kiraly
HR: Linda Hansen
Employees: 782

1992 Sales: $85 million
Symbol: BRCP
Exchange: NASDAQ

Industry: Business services - information management and data processing products and services to county and municipal governments

CABOT OIL & GAS CORP.   RANK: 330

15375 Memorial Dr.
Houston, TX 77079
Phone: 713-589-4600
Fax: 713-589-4653

CEO: John H. Lollar
CFO: John U. Clarke
HR: Gillian Payne
Employees: 410

1992 Sales: $148 million
Symbol: COG
Exchange: NYSE

Industry: Oil and gas - US exploration and production

CACTUS FEEDERS INCORPORATED   RANK: 177

2209 W. 7th St.
Amarillo, TX 79106
Phone: 806-373-2333
Fax: 806-371-4774

CEO: Paul F. Engler
CFO: Terry Manz
HR: Paul F. Engler
Employees: 375

1993 Sales: $325 million
Ownership: Private

Industry: Agricultural operations - cattle feedlots

CANTEY & HANGER LLP   RANK: 468

2100 Burnett Plaza
Ft. Worth, TX 76102
Phone: 817-877-2800
Fax: 817-877-2807

CEO: Allan Howeth
CFO: L. Joe Offutt
HR: L. Joe Offutt
Employees: 200

1992 Sales: $76 million
Ownership: Private

Industry: Business services - legal

CAP ROCK ELECTRIC COOPERATIVE   RANK: 415

Hwy. 80 West
Stanton, TX 79782
Phone: 915-756-3381
Fax: 915-756-3381 ext. 14

CEO: David W. Pruitt
CFO: John Parker
HR: Nancy Broadway
Employees: 100

1992 Sales: $100 million
Ownership: Private

Industry: Utility - electric power

TEXAS 500

CAPSTEAD MORTGAGE CORP.   RANK: 122

2001 Bryan Tower, Ste. 3300
Dallas, TX 75201
Phone: 214-999-2323
Fax: 214-999-2398
Industry: Real estate investment trust

CEO: Ronn K. Lytle
CFO: Andrew F. Jacobs
HR: Donna Howard
Employees: 6

1992 Sales: $504 million
Symbol: CMO
Exchange: NYSE

CASH AMERICA INTERNATIONAL, INC.   RANK: 272

1600 W. 7th St., Ste. 900
Ft. Worth, TX 76102
Phone: 817-335-1100
Fax: 817-335-1119

CEO: Jack R. Daugherty
CFO: Dale R. Westerfeld
HR: David F. Johns
Employees: 1,700

1992 Sales: $185 million
Symbol: PWN
Exchange: NYSE

Industry: Retail - world's largest (and only international) pawn company

▶ See page 133 for a full profile of this company.

CCC GROUP INC.   RANK: 470

5797 Dietrich
San Antonio, TX 78219
Phone: 210-661-4251
Fax: 210-661-6060

CEO: A. L. Greaves
CFO: A. D. Huebner
HR: Rita Jordan
Employees: 850

1992 Sales: $75 million
Ownership: Private

Industry: Machinery - industrial equipment and mining machinery installation and repair

CENTEX CORP.   RANK: 40

3333 Lee Pkwy.
Dallas, TX 75219
Phone: 214-559-6500
Fax: 214-559-6750

CEO: Laurence E. Hirsch
CFO: David W. Quinn
HR: Michael Albright
Employees: 6,500

1993 Sales: $2,503 million
Symbol: CTX
Exchange: NYSE

Industry: Building - residential and commercial, mortgage banking, and construction products (largest US builder of single-family homes)

CENTRAL AND SOUTH WEST CORP.   RANK: 30

1616 Woodall Rodgers Fwy.
Dallas, TX 75266
Phone: 214-754-1000
Fax: 214-754-1033

CEO: E. R. Brooks
CFO: Glenn D. Rosilier
HR: Dwight Corley
Employees: 8,595

1992 Sales: $3,289 million
Symbol: CSR
Exchange: NYSE

Industry: Utility - electric power; operates utilities in Texas, Oklahoma, Louisiana, and Arkansas

CHAPARRAL STEEL CO.   RANK: 146

300 Ward Rd.
Midlothian, TX 76065
Phone: 214-775-8241
Fax: 214-775-3627

CEO: Gordon E. Forward
CFO: Richard M. Fowler
HR: Jeffrey Roesler
Employees: 985

1993 Sales: $420 million
Symbol: CSM
Exchange: NYSE

Industry: Steel - production

CHEMICAL LIME CO.   RANK: 326

PO Box 121874
Ft. Worth, TX 76121
Phone: 817-732-8164
Fax: 817-732-3048

CEO: Tom Chambers
CFO: Joe Payne
HR: Tom Stokes
Employees: 800

1992 Sales: $150 million
Ownership: Private

Industry: Chemicals - lime

CHIEF AUTO PARTS INCORPORATED   RANK: 128

15303 Dallas Pkwy.
Dallas, TX 75248
Phone: 214-404-1114
Fax: 214-991-9259

CEO: David H. Eisenberg
CFO: Tom Hough
HR: Lynn Ashley
Employees: 5,800

1992 Sales: $473 million
Ownership: Private

Industry: Retail - automotive parts

CJC HOLDINGS INC.   RANK: 382

PO Box 149056
Austin, TX 78714
Phone: 512-444-0571
Fax: 512-441-0085

CEO: J.T. Waugh
CFO: Sharice Price
HR: Suzie Adams
Employees: 1,061

1992 Sales: $110 million
Ownership: Private

Industry: Precious metals and jewelry - manufacturing

CLEAR CHANNEL COMMUNICATIONS, INC.   RANK: 421

200 Concord Plaza #600
San Antonio, TX 78216
Phone: 210-822-2828
Fax: 210-822-2299

CEO: L. Lowry Mays
CFO: Mark P. Mays
HR: Herbert W. Hill, Jr.
Employees: 1,061

1992 Sales: $95 million
Symbol: CCU
Exchange: AMEX

Industry: Broadcasting - radio and TV stations

TEXAS 500

CLIFFS DRILLING CO. RANK: 466
1200 Smith St.	CEO: Douglas E. Swanson	1992 Sales: $77 million
Houston, TX 77002	CFO: James E. Mitchell, Jr.	Symbol: CLDR
Phone: 713-651-9426	HR: Douglas E. Swanson	Exchange: NASDAQ
Fax: 713-651-9466	Employees: 352	

Industry: Oil and gas - offshore drilling

CLUBCORP INTERNATIONAL RANK: 68
3030 LBJ Fwy.	CEO: Robert H. Dedman	1992 Sales: $870 million
Dallas, TX 75234	CFO: James P. McCoy	Ownership: Private
Phone: 214-243-6191	HR: Albert Chew	
Fax: 214-888-7721	Employees: 15,869	

Industry: Leisure and recreational services - owns or operates over 200 country clubs, athletic clubs, golf courses, and resorts in the US, Europe, and Asia; also owns Franklin Federal Bancorp

COASTAL CORPORATION, THE RANK: 7
Coastal Tower, Nine Greenway Plaza	CEO: Oscar S. Wyatt, Jr.	1992 Sales: $10,063 million
Houston, TX 77046-0995	CFO: David A. Arledge	Symbol: CGP
Phone: 713-877-1400	HR: E. C. Simpson	Exchange: NYSE
Fax: 713-877-6754	Employees: 16,570	

Industry: Oil and gas - exploration, production, marketing, and transmission; coal mining; chemicals; power production; trucking

See pages 60 – 61 for a full profile of this company.

COBURN SUPPLY COMPANY INC. RANK: 467
PO Box 2177	CEO: Don Maloney	1992 Sales: $77 million
Beaumont, TX 77704	CFO: Jay Shah	Ownership: Private
Phone: 409-838-6363	HR: Diane Blazek	
Fax: 409-838-4159	Employees: 330	

Industry: Wholesale distribution - hardware; plumbing, heating, and air conditioning equipment

COCA-COLA BOTTLING GROUP-SOUTHWEST RANK: 166
1999 Bryan, St. 300	CEO: Robert Hoffman	1992 Sales: $356 million
Dallas, TX 75201	CFO: Chuck Stephenson	Ownership: Private
Phone: 214-969-1910	HR: Barbara McMinn	
Fax: 214-969-5947	Employees: 1,000	

Industry: Beverages - soft drink bottler

TEXAS 500

COLOR TILE INC.   RANK: 100

515 Houston St.
Ft. Worth, TX 76102
Phone: 817-870-9400
Fax: 817-870-9589

CEO: Eddie Lesok
CFO: Dan Gilmartin
HR: Dick Andrews
Employees: 4,081

1992 Sales: $586 million
Ownership: Private

Industry: Retail - tile and floor covering products

COMMERCIAL METALS CO.   RANK: 57

7800 N. Stemmons Fwy.
Dallas, TX 75247
Phone: 214-689-4300
Fax: 214-689-4320

CEO: Stanley A. Rabin
CFO: Lawrence A. Engels
HR: Jesse Barnes
Employees: 3,793

1993 Sales: $1,166 million
Symbol: CMC
Exchange: NYSE

Industry: Metal processing and fabrication

COMPAQ COMPUTER CORPORATION   RANK: 25

20555 SH 249
Houston, TX 77070
Phone: 713-370-0670
Fax: 713-374-1740

CEO: Eckhard Pfeiffer
CFO: Daryl J. White
HR: Jerry G. Welch
Employees: 9,500

1992 Sales: $4,100 million
Symbol: CPQ
Exchange: NYSE

Industry: Computers - microcomputers, peripherals, and services

➤ **See pages 62 – 63 for a full profile of this company.**

COMPUADD, INC.   RANK: 112

12303 Technology Blvd.
Austin, TX 78727
Phone: 512-250-2000
Fax: 512-331-2794

CEO: Bill H. Hayden
CFO: Donald Amicucci
HR: Toni McIntosh
Employees: 1,300

1992 Sales: $525 million
Ownership: Private

Industry: Computers - mail-order microcomputers

COMPUCOM SYSTEMS, INC.   RANK: 81

10100 N. Central Expwy.
Dallas, TX 75231
Phone: 214-265-3600
Fax: 214-265-5220

CEO: Avery More
CFO: Robert J. Boutin
HR: Mark Esselman
Employees: 1,600

1992 Sales: $713 million
Symbol: CMPC
Exchange: NASDAQ

Industry: Computers - software and microcomputer sales and services

➤ **See page 134 for a full profile of this company.**

TEXAS 500

COMPUSA, INC. — RANK: 51

14951 N. Dallas Pkwy.
Dallas, TX 75240
Phone: 214-383-4000
Fax: 214-383-4276

CEO: Nathan P. Morton
CFO: Mervyn Benjet
HR: Paul Poyfair
Employees: 5,679

1993 Sales: $1,342 million
Symbol: CPU
Exchange: NYSE

Industry: Retail - computer hardware and software superstores, services and training

See page 135 for a full profile of this company.

COMPUTER LANGUAGE RESEARCH, INC. — RANK: 379

2395 Midway Rd.
Carrollton, TX 75006
Phone: 214-250-7000
Fax: 214-250-8181

CEO: Stephen T. Winn
CFO: M. Brian Healy
HR: Ron Castleman
Employees: 1,031

1992 Sales: $111 million
Symbol: CLRI
Exchange: NASDAQ

Industry: Computers - tax processing services

CONTINENTAL AIRLINES HOLDINGS, INC. — RANK: 17

2929 Allen Pkwy., Ste. 2010
Houston, TX 77019
Phone: 713-834-5000
Fax: 713-834-2087

CEO: Robert R. Ferguson III
CFO: Daniel P. Garton
HR: Robert F. Allen
Employees: 44,430

1992 Sales: $5,575 million
Symbol: CAIA; CAIB
Exchange: NYSE

Industry: Transportation - Continental Airlines, commuter airlines, airline catering

See pages 64 – 65 for a full profile of this company.

CONTINUUM COMPANY, INC., THE — RANK: 360

9500 Arboretum Blvd.
Austin, TX 78759-6399
Phone: 512-345-5700
Fax: 512-338-7041

CEO: W. Michael Long
CFO: John L. Westermann III
HR: Deborah Stafford
Employees: 1,080

1993 Sales: $124 million
Symbol: CNU
Exchange: NYSE

Industry: Computers - insurance industry software and services

CONTRAN CORP. — RANK: 58

5430 LBJ Freeway, #1700
Dallas, TX 75240
Phone: 214-233-1700
Fax: 214-239-0142

CEO: Harold C. Simmons
CFO: William C. Timm
HR: —
Employees: 19,950

1992 Sales: $1,128 million
Ownership: Private

Industry: Diversified operations - fast food, timber, sugar, steel. Mr. Simmons holds controlling interests in Valhi, Inc., NL Industries, and Tremont Corporation, as well as Contran.

CONVEX COMPUTER CORP.   RANK: 235

3000 Waterview Pkwy.　　　　CEO: Robert J. Paluck　　　　1992 Sales: $232 million
Richardson, TX 75080　　　　CFO: J. Cameron McMartin　　Symbol: CNX
Phone: 214-497-4000　　　　　HR: John P. O'Loughlin　　　Exchange: NYSE
Fax: 214-497-4441　　　　　　Employees: 1,164

Industry: Computers - mainframe: massively parallel processing supercomputers

COOPER INDUSTRIES, INC.   RANK: 16

1001 Fannin St., Ste. 4000　　CEO: Robert Cizik　　　　　1992 Sales: $6,119 million
Houston, TX 77002　　　　　　CFO: Dewain K. Cross　　　Symbol: CBE
Phone: 713-739-5400　　　　　HR: Carl J. Plesnicher, Jr.　Exchange: NYSE
Fax: 713-739-5555　　　　　　Employees: 52,900

Industry: Diversified operations - electrical equipment, automotive parts, hand tools, hardware, turbines, and petroleum industrial equipment

See pages 66 – 67 for a full profile of this company.

CRSS, INC.   RANK: 106

1177 West Loop South, Ste. 800　CEO: Bruce W. Wilkinson　1993 Sales: $546 million
Houston, TX 77027　　　　　　　CFO: William J. Gardiner　Symbol: CRX
Phone: 713-552-2000　　　　　　HR: Karen Holleyhead　　　Exchange: NYSE
Fax: 713-552-2538　　　　　　　Employees: 2,276

Industry: Construction - heavy

CULLEN/FROST BANKERS, INC.   RANK: 216

100 W. Houston St.　　　　　　CEO: T. C. Frost　　　　　1992 Sales: $252 million
San Antonio, TX 78205　　　　CFO: Phillip D. Green　　　Symbol: CFBI
Phone: 210-220-4011　　　　　HR: Jim L. Parker　　　　　Exchange: NASDAQ
Fax: 210-220-5557　　　　　　Employees: 1,754

Industry: Bank

CURTIS C. GUNN INC.   RANK: 233

7744 Broadway, Ste. 100　　　CEO: Robert Bomer　　　　　1992 Sales: $233 million
San Antonio, TX 78209　　　　CFO: Kelly Collins　　　　　Ownership: Private
Phone: 210-824-3208　　　　　HR: Cindy Rowley
Fax: 210-829-8226　　　　　　Employees: 700

Industry: Retail - automobiles

TEXAS 500

CYRIX CORPORATION   RANK: 483

2703 N. Central Expwy.   CEO: Gerald D. Rogers   1992 Sales: $73 million
Richardson, TX 75080   CFO: Ronald P. Edgerton   Symbol: CYRX
Phone: 214-994-8387   HR: Margaret Quinn   Exchange: NASDAQ
Fax: 214-699-9857   Employees: 140

Industry: Electrical components - semiconductors; coprocessors and microprocessors

🌵 See page 136 for a full profile of this company.

D. R. HORTON, INC.   RANK: 274

2221 E. Lamar Blvd., Ste. 950   CEO: Donald R. Horton   1992 Sales: $183 million
Arlington, TX 76006   CFO: David J. Keller   Symbol: DRHI
Phone: 817-640-8200   HR: Aricia Blasko   Exchange: NASDAQ
Fax: 817-856-8249   Employees: 268

Industry: Building - residential and commercial

DAL-TILE GROUP INC.   RANK: 238

PO Box 17130   CEO: Bill Cox   1992 Sales: $220 million
Dallas, TX 75217   CFO: Charles Nies   Ownership: Private
Phone: 214-398-1411   HR: Steve Smith
Fax: 214-944-4390   Employees: 2,500

Industry: Building products - ceramic wall and floor tile

DALFORT CORP.   RANK: 393

7701 Lemmon Ave.   CEO: Peter Chapman   1992 Sales: $107 million
Dallas, TX 75209   CFO: Stephen Lynn   Ownership: Private
Phone: 214-358-6019   HR: Dan Malin
Fax: 214-902-0938   Employees: 1,250

Industry: Transportation - aircraft maintenance

DALLAS AUTO AUCTION INC.   RANK: 255

5333 W. Keist Blvd.   CEO: Barry Roop   1992 Sales: $200 million
Dallas, TX 75236   CFO: Wayne Stroud   Ownership: Private
Phone: 214-330-1800   HR: Jan Mars
Fax: 214-339-3845   Employees: 380

Industry: Business services - auctioning of cars, trucks, and trailers

TEXAS 500

DALLAS SEMICONDUCTOR CORP. — RANK: 366

4401 S. Beltwood Pkwy.
Dallas, TX 75244
Phone: 214-450-0400
Fax: 214-450-0470

CEO: Charles V. Prothro
CFO: Alan Hale
HR: Gay Vencill
Employees: 696

1992 Sales: $120 million
Symbol: DS
Exchange: NYSE

Industry: Electrical components - semiconductors

DANIEL INDUSTRIES, INC. — RANK: 246

9753 Pine Lake Dr.
Houston, TX 77055
Phone: 713-467-6000
Fax: 713-827-3889

CEO: W. A. Griffin
CFO: Henry G. Schopfer III
HR: Jim McCoy
Employees: 1,700

1992 Sales: $210 million
Symbol: DAN
Exchange: NYSE

Industry: Oil field machinery and equipment

DARLING-DELAWARE COMPANY INC. — RANK: 123

251 O'Connor Ridge, Ste. 300
Irving, TX 75235
Phone: 214-717-0300
Fax: 214-717-1588

CEO: Frank W. Miller
CFO: Kenneth A. Ghazey
HR: Gil Gutierrez
Employees: 1,550

1992 Sales: $500 million
Ownership: Private

Industry: Agricultural operations - animal byproducts (animal and marine fats and oils)

DARR EQUIPMENT COMPANY — RANK: 183

2000 East Airport Freeway
Irving, TX 75062
Phone: 214-721-2000
Fax: 214-438-2481

CEO: Randall R. Engstrom
CFO: George Spencer
HR: Michael Shropshire
Employees: 1,000

1992 Sales: $310 million
Ownership: Private

Industry: Machinery - construction

DATAPOINT CORP. — RANK: 249

8400 Datapoint Dr.
San Antonio, TX 78229
Phone: 210-593-7000
Fax: 210-593-7921

CEO: Asher B. Edelman
CFO: Kenneth R. Kamp
HR: Angela Cooper
Employees: 1,777

1993 Sales: $208 million
Symbol: DPT
Exchange: NYSE

Industry: Computers - minicomputers and microcomputers

TEXAS 500

DAVID'S SUPERMARKETS INC.   RANK: 455

103-5 E. Criner
Grandview, TX 76050
Phone: 817-866-2651
Fax: 817-866-2659
Industry: Retail - supermarkets

CEO: Donald R. Moten
CFO: Reginald H. Denny
HR: Mary H. Basham
Employees: 700

1992 Sales: $80 million
Ownership: Private

DAVIS FOOD CITY INC.   RANK: 404

PO Box 262278
Houston, TX 77207
Phone: 713-644-2476
Fax: 713-644-0577
Industry: Retail - supermarkets

CEO: Al Davis
CFO: Ross Lewis
HR: Pat Dietz
Employees: 650

1992 Sales: $100 million
Ownership: Private

DELL COMPUTER CORPORATION   RANK: 47

9505 Arboretum Blvd.
Austin, TX 78759
Phone: 512-338-4400
Fax: 512-728-8700

CEO: Michael S. Dell
CFO: Thomas J. Meredith
HR: Savino R. Ferrales
Employees: 4,650

1992 Sales: $2,014 million
Symbol: DELL
Exchange: NASDAQ

Industry: Computers - microcomputers and software available primarily by mail order and through selected discount retailers

See pages 110 – 111 for a full profile of this company.

DELTA INDUSTRIAL OFFICES INC.   RANK: 458

PO Box 20115, Garth Rd.
Beaumont, TX 77720
Phone: 409-842-3326
Fax: 409-842-4049

CEO: D. W. Hearn, Jr.
CFO: G. Mabry
HR: D. W. Hearn, Jr.
Employees: 400

1992 Sales: $80 million
Ownership: Private

Industry: Building - industrial construction general contractors

DENTON COUNTY ELECTRIC COOPERATIVE   RANK: 480

PO Box 2147
Denton, TX 76202
Phone: 817-383-1671
Fax: 817-497-6525
Industry: Utility - electric power

CEO: Bill McGinnis
CFO: Donald R. Clary
HR: Jim Chism
Employees: 102

1992 Sales: $74 million
Ownership: Private

TEXAS 500

DESTEC ENERGY, INC.   RANK: 119

2500 City West Blvd., Ste. 150
Houston, TX 77042
Phone: 713-735-4000
Fax: 713-735-4201

CEO: Charles F. Goff
CFO: Enrique M. Larroucau
HR: Gerald Crone
Employees: 606

1992 Sales: $508 million
Symbol: ENG
Exchange: NYSE

Industry: Energy - cogeneration and coal gasification

🌟 **See page 137 for a full profile of this company.**

DIAMOND SHAMROCK, INC.   RANK: 38

9830 Colonnade Blvd.
San Antonio, TX 78230
Phone: 210-641-6800
Fax: 512-641-8687

CEO: Roger R. Hemminghaus
CFO: Robert C. Becker
HR: Patrick McConahy
Employees: 6,000

1992 Sales: $2,612 million
Symbol: DRM
Exchange: NYSE

Industry: Oil refining and marketing

DIGICON, INC.   RANK: 378

3701 Kirby Dr., Ste. 112
Houston, TX 77098
Phone: 713-526-5611
Fax: 713-630-4456

CEO: Edward R. Prince, Jr.
CFO: Allan C. Pogach
HR: Lisa Seeker
Employees: 1,140

1992 Sales: $111 million
Symbol: DGC
Exchange: AMEX

Industry: Oil and gas - field services

DR PEPPER BOTTLING COMPANY OF TEXAS   RANK: 296

8144 Walnut Hill
Dallas, TX 75231
Phone: 214-579-1024
Fax: 214-721-8147

CEO: Jim Turner
CFO: Marvin Montgomery
HR: Kelly DeFratus
Employees: 1,200

1992 Sales: $170 million
Ownership: Private

Industry: Beverages - soft drink bottler

DR PEPPER/SEVEN-UP COMPANIES, INC.   RANK: 88

8144 Walnut Hill Ln.
Dallas, TX 75231
Phone: 214-360-7000
Fax: 214-360-7981

CEO: John R. Albers
CFO: Ira M. Rosenstein
HR: John L. Quigley, Jr.
Employees: 930

1992 Sales: $659 million
Symbol: DPS
Exchange: NYSE

Industry: Beverages - soft drinks, including Dr Pepper, 7-Up, Welch's, and IBC (3rd largest soft drink manufacturer in the US)

🌟 **See pages 112 – 113 for a full profile of this company.**

TEXAS 500

DRESSER INDUSTRIES, INC.   RANK: 27

1600 Pacific
Dallas, TX 75201
Phone: 214-740-6000
Fax: 214-740-6584

CEO: John J. Murphy
CFO: Bill D. St. John
HR: Paul M. Bryant
Employees: 27,400

1992 Sales: $3,797 million
Symbol: DI
Exchange: NYSE

Industry: Oil field machinery and equipment - drill bits, drilling fluids, compressors, pumps, turbines, and pneumatic tools

🔶 See pages 114 – 115 for a full profile of this company.

DSC COMMUNICATIONS CORP.   RANK: 109

1000 Coit Rd.
Plano, TX 75075
Phone: 214-519-3000
Fax: 214-519-2322

CEO: James L. Donald
CFO: Gerald F. Montry
HR: Gerald Carlton
Employees: 3,301

1992 Sales: $536 million
Symbol: DIGI
Exchange: NASDAQ

Industry: Telecommunications equipment - including local area network equipment

DUNLAP CO.   RANK: 218

200 Greenleaf St.
Ft. Worth, TX 76107
Phone: 817-336-4985
Fax: 817-877-1302

CEO: Tom Hoskins
CFO: Gerald Stallard
HR: Ret Martin
Employees: 3,000

1992 Sales: $250 million
Ownership: Private

Industry: Retail - 50 department stores in Texas, Arkansas, Maine, Michigan, New Hampshire, and Vermont, including M.M. Cohn, Mark's, Marcom's, and Porteous

DUPEY MANAGEMENT CORP.   RANK: 420

9015 Sterling St.
Irving, TX 75063
Phone: 214-929-1719
Fax: 214-929-8283

CEO: Michael Dupey
CFO: Andy Jones
HR: Belinda Neal
Employees: 1,900

1992 Est. Sales: $95 mil.
Ownership: Private

Industry: Retail - 30 art supply stores in Texas and on the East Coast under the MJ Design name

E.R. FANT, INC.   RANK: 289

5800 Westview Dr.
Houston, TX 77055
Phone: 713-686-9631
Fax: 713-686-5358

CEO: Eugene R. Fant
CFO: Phil O. Kelley
HR: Jim Kollaja
Employees: 230

1992 Est. Sales: $175 mil.
Ownership: Private

Industry: Metal products - service centers

E Z MART STORES INCORPORATED RANK: 196

602 Falvey Ave.
Texarkana, TX 75501
Phone: 903-832-6502
Fax: 903-832-7903

CEO: Jim Yates
CFO: Sonya Hubbard
HR: Tom Coleman
Employees: 3,000

1992 Sales: $290 million
Ownership: Private

Industry: Retail - convenience stores and gas stations

E-SYSTEMS, INC. RANK: 46

6250 LBJ Fwy.
Dallas, TX 75266
Phone: 214-661-1000
Fax: 214-661-8508

CEO: E. Gene Keiffer
CFO: James W. Pope
HR: Gerald Shaver
Employees: 18,600

1992 Sales: $2,099 million
Symbol: ESY
Exchange: NYSE

Industry: Electronics - military

E-Z SERVE CORP. RANK: 140

2550 N. Loop West, Ste. 600
Houston, TX 77092
Phone: 713-684-4300
Fax: 713-684-4367

CEO: Neil H. McLaurin
CFO: John T. Miller
HR: Karl Miller
Employees: 3,016

1992 Sales: $434 million
Symbol: EZS
Exchange: AMEX

Industry: Retail - convenience stores and service stations, including Stop and Shop and Majic Market

EAST TEXAS DISTRIBUTING INC. RANK: 137

7171 Grand Blvd.
Houston, TX 77054
Phone: 713-748-2520
Fax: 713-748-2504

CEO: Ron Eisenberg
CFO: David Streusand
HR: Carol Nebrig
Employees: 800

1992 Est. Sales: $445 mil.
Ownership: Private

Industry: Wholesale distribution - magazines and books; videos

EASTEX ENERGY INC. RANK: 290

1000 Louisiana St., Ste. 1100
Houston, TX 77002
Phone: 713-650-6255
Fax: 713-650-6703

CEO: Robert G. Phillips
CFO: Jerry Pendleton
HR: Lisa Kell
Employees: 34

1992 Sales: $175 million
Symbol: ETEX
Exchange: NASDAQ

Industry: Oil and gas - marketing, storage, and pipeline

TEXAS 500

ECONOMY CASH AND CARRY INC.   RANK: 477

1000 E. Overland Ave.   CEO: Sam R. Sayklay   1992 Sales: $75 million
El Paso, TX 79901   CFO: Mike Dipp   Ownership: Private
Phone: 915-532-2660   HR: Paul Dipp
Fax: 915-534-7673   Employees: 69

Industry: Food - wholesale groceries

EDISTO RESOURCES CORP.   RANK: 155

2121 San Jacinto St., Ste. 2600   CEO: Michael Y. McGovern   1992 Sales: $386 million
Dallas, TX 75201   CFO: Jerry L. McNeill   Symbol: EDS
Phone: 214-880-0243   HR: Denise Harvey   Exchange: AMEX
Fax: 214-220-1054   Employees: 45

Industry: Oil and gas - offshore drilling

EL PASO ELECTRIC CO.   RANK: 113

303 N. Oregon St.   CEO: David H. Wiggs, Jr.   1992 Sales: $525 million
El Paso, TX 79901   CFO: William J. Johnson   Symbol: ELPAQ
Phone: 915-543-5711   HR: Susan Sickles   Exchange: NASDAQ
Fax: 915-542-3905   Employees: 1,100

Industry: Utility - electric power

EL PASO NATURAL GAS CO.   RANK: 72

One Paul Kayser Ctr., 304 Texas Ave.   CEO: William A. Wise   1992 Sales: $803 million
El Paso, TX 79901   CFO: Francis J. Boyle   Symbol: EPG
Phone: 915-541-2600   HR: Joel Richards III   Exchange: NYSE
Fax: 915-541-2600, ext. 215   Employees: 2,499

Industry: Utility - gas distribution

ELCOR CORP.   RANK: 292

14643 Dallas Pkwy., Ste. 1000   CEO: Roy E. Campbell   1993 Sales: $173 million
Dallas, TX 75240   CFO: Richard J. Rosebery   Symbol: ELK
Phone: 214-851-0500   HR: James J. Waibel   Exchange: NYSE
Fax: 214-851-0543   Employees: 796

Industry: Building products - roofing and other industrial products

ELECTROCOM AUTOMATION, INC. RANK: 129

2910 Ave. F East
Arlington, TX 76011
Phone: 817-640-5690
Fax: 817-695-5599

CEO: G. D. Thompson
CFO: T. G. Burmeister
HR: William C. Edwards, Jr.
Employees: 1,650

1992 Sales: $470 million
Symbol: ECA
Exchange: NYSE

Industry: Machinery - document processing automation

ELECTRONIC DATA SYSTEMS CORPORATION RANK: 10

5400 Legacy Dr.
Plano, TX 75024-3199
Phone: 214-604-6000
Fax: 214-605-8793

CEO: Lester M. Alberthal
CFO: Joseph M. Grant
HR: Joseph M. Grant
Employees: 70,500

1992 Sales: $8,155 million
Symbol: GME
Exchange: NYSE

Industry: Computers - the largest data processing corporation in the US; computer network systems integration (subsidiary of General Motors)

See pages 68 – 69 for a full profile of this company.

ELJER INDUSTRIES, INC. RANK: 154

17120 Dallas Pkwy., Ste. 205
Dallas, TX 75248
Phone: 214-407-7216
Fax: 214-407-2789

CEO: Scott G. Arbuckle
CFO: Henry Lehnerer
HR: Charles R. Wackenhuth
Employees: 3,750

1992 Sales: $397 million
Symbol: ELJ
Exchange: NYSE

Industry: Building products - plumbing and venting

EMERGENCY NETWORK INC. RANK: 490

545 E. John Carpenter Hwy., Ste. 1800
Irving, TX 75062
Phone: 214-401-4700
Fax: 214-401-4711

CEO: David Stull
CFO: Shannon Barry
HR: Sherry Denning
Employees: 2,800

1992 Est. Sales: $70 mil.
Ownership: Private

Industry: Building - residential security systems

ENDEVCO, INC. RANK: 225

8080 N. Central Expressway, Ste. 1200
Dallas, TX 75206
Phone: 214-691-5536
Fax: 214-691-5682

CEO: James W. Bryant
CFO: Jack W. Young
HR: Becky Erickson
Employees: 175

1992 Sales: $245 million
Symbol: EI
Exchange: AMEX

Industry: Oil and gas - production and pipeline

TEXAS 500

ENERGY SERVICE CO., INC. — RANK: 306

1445 Ross Ave.
Dallas, TX 75202
Phone: 214-922-1500
Fax: 214-855-0080

CEO: Carl F. Thorne
CFO: C. C. Gaut
HR: William S. Chadwick, Jr.
Employees: 890

1992 Sales: $162 million
Symbol: ESV
Exchange: AMEX

Industry: Oil and gas - offshore drilling and marine transportation

ENERGY VENTURES, INC. — RANK: 265

5 Post Oak Park, Ste. 1760
Houston, TX 77027
Phone: 713-297-8400
Fax: 713-297-8488

CEO: Bernard J. Duroc-Danner
CFO: Frances Powell
HR: Diana Lambert
Employees: 2,000

1992 Sales: $192 million
Symbol: ENGY
Exchange: NASDAQ

Industry: Oil field machinery and equipment

ENNIS BUSINESS FORMS, INC. — RANK: 355

107 N. Sherman St.
Ennis, TX 75119
Phone: 214-875-6581
Fax: 214-875-4915

CEO: Kenneth A. McCrady
CFO: Harve Cathey
HR: Richard Marsh
Employees: 1,354

1993 Sales: $129 million
Symbol: EBF
Exchange: NYSE

Industry: Paper - business forms

ENRON CORP. — RANK: 15

1400 Smith St.
Houston, TX 77002-7369
Phone: 713-853-6161
Fax: 713-853-3129

CEO: Kenneth L. Lay
CFO: Jack I. Tompkins
HR: James E. Street
Employees: 7,780

1992 Sales: $6,325 million
Symbol: ENE
Exchange: NYSE

Industry: Oil and gas - production, pipeline, and marketing; construction and management of power plants

See pages 70 – 71 for a full profile of this company.

ENSERCH CORP. — RANK: 35

300 South St. Paul St.
Dallas, TX 75201
Phone: 214-651-8700
Fax: 214-670-2520

CEO: David Biegler
CFO: Sanford R. Singer
HR: James Beard
Employees: 10,400

1992 Sales: $2,826 million
Symbol: ENS
Exchange: NYSE

Industry: Oil and gas - production and pipeline

ENTERPRISE PRODUCTS COMPANY — RANK: 126

2727 North Loop W., Ste. 700
Houston, TX 77008
Phone: 713-880-6500
Fax: 713-880-6573

CEO: Dan L. Duncan
CFO: Gary Miller
HR: John Tomerlin
Employees: 900

1992 Sales: $491 million
Ownership: Private

Industry: Oil and gas - processing and manufacturing natural gas liquids

ENTERRA CORP. — RANK: 324

13100 Northwest Fwy., Ste. 600
Houston, TX 77040
Phone: 713-462-7300
Fax: 713-462-7816

CEO: D. Dale Wood
CFO: Steven W. Krablin
HR: Don Guedry
Employees: 1,250

1992 Sales: $150 million
Symbol: EN
Exchange: NYSE

Industry: Oil and gas - field services

EPIC HOLDINGS, INC. — RANK: 64

3333 Lee Pkwy.
Dallas, TX 75219
Phone: 214-443-3333
Fax: 214-443-3599

CEO: Kenn S. George
CFO: Thomas T. Schleck
HR: Gary Griffith
Employees: 10,420

1992 Sales: $941 million
Ownership: Private

Industry: Hospitals

EXXON CORPORATION — RANK: 1

225 E. John W. Carpenter Fwy.
Irving, TX 75062-2298
Phone: 214-444-1000
Fax: 214-444-1505

CEO: Lee R. Raymond
CFO: E. A. Robinson
HR: M. E. Gillis
Employees: 95,000

1992 Sales: $103,160 million
Symbol: XON
Exchange: NYSE

Industry: Oil and gas - international integrated, including exploration, production, refining, and marketing (largest US oil company); petrochemical production; coal mining

See pages 72 - 73 for a full profile of this company.

EZCORP, INC. — RANK: 418

1901 Capital Pkwy.
Austin, TX 78746
Phone: 512-314-3400
Fax: 512-314-3404

CEO: Courtland L. Logue, Jr.
CFO: Gary S. Kofnovec
HR: Jim Penny
Employees: 919

1993 Est. Sales: $96 mil.
Symbol: EZPW
Exchange: NASDAQ

Industry: Retail - pawn shops

See page 138 for a full profile of this company.

TEXAS 500

FARAH INC. — RANK: 323

8889 Gateway West
El Paso, TX 79925
Phone: 915-593-4444
Fax: 915-593-4203

CEO: Richard C. Allender
CFO: James C. Swaim
HR: Mark Rose
Employees: 4,100

1992 Sales: $152 million
Symbol: FRA
Exchange: NYSE

Industry: Apparel - men's and boys' clothes

FARB COMPANIES LTD. — RANK: 388

PO Box 22770
Houston, TX 77227
Phone: 713-954-2100
Fax: 713-954-2114

CEO: Harold Farb
CFO: Mary Horton
HR: Gene Selph
Employees: 300

1992 Sales: $110 million
Ownership: Private

Industry: Real estate development

FFP PARTNERS, L.P. — RANK: 201

2801 Glenda Ave.
Ft. Worth, TX 76117
Phone: 817-838-4700
Fax: 817-838-4799

CEO: John Harvison
CFO: Steven B. Hawkins
HR: Steve Hawkins
Employees: 1,400

1992 Sales: $279 million
Symbol: FFP
Exchange: AMEX

Industry: Retail - convenience stores, including Direct Fuel, Kwik Pantry, and Hi-Lo

FIESTA MART INC. — RANK: 97

5235 Katy Fwy.
Houston, TX 77007
Phone: 713-869-5060
Fax: 713-869-6197

CEO: Donald L. Bonham
CFO: Robert Walker
HR: Gary Finney
Employees: 5,500

1992 Sales: $600 million
Ownership: Private

Industry: Retail - supermarkets

FINA, INC. — RANK: 29

FINA Plaza, 8350 N. Central Expwy.
Dallas, TX 75206
Phone: 214-750-2400
Fax: 214-750-2508

CEO: Ron W. Haddock
CFO: Christian Buggenhout
HR: Glenn Selvidge
Employees: 3,369

1992 Sales: $3,398 million
Symbol: FI
Exchange: AMEX

Industry: Oil and gas - international integrated; chemicals and paints (86% owned by Belgium oil giant Petrofina)

TEXAS 500

FIRST USA, INC.   RANK: 127

2001 Bryan Tower, 38th Fl.
Dallas, TX 75201
Phone: 214-746-8700
Fax: 214-746-8556

CEO: John C. Tolleson
CFO: Pamela H. Patsley
HR: Jan M. McKenney
Employees: 1,400

1993 Sales: $480 million
Symbol: FUS
Exchange: NYSE

Industry: Financial - business services, VISA and MasterCard issuer and credit card transaction processor

FISH ENGINEERING & CONSTRUCTION PARTNERS LTD.   RANK: 349

1990 Post Oak Blvd.
Houston, TX 77056
Phone: 713-621-8300
Fax: 713-850-7682

CEO: James A. Boyd
CFO: G. L. Turner
HR: G. L. Turner
Employees: 2,200

1992 Sales: $130 million
Ownership: Private

Industry: Building - petrochemical plant construction

FOJTASEK COMPANIES INC.   RANK: 403

PO Box 226957
Dallas, TX 75222
Phone: 214-438-4787
Fax: 214-438-8117

CEO: Joe Fojtasek
CFO: Shirley Crutcher
HR: Steven Rosenthal
Employees: 900

1992 Sales: $100 million
Ownership: Private

Industry: Building products - aluminum and wooden windows and patio doors

FOSSIL INC.   RANK: 479

11052 Grader St.
Dallas, TX 75238
Phone: 214-348-7400
Fax: 214-348-1366

CEO: Tom Kartsotis
CFO: Alan D. Moore
HR: Glenn Carlin
Employees: 164

1992 Sales: $74 million
Symbol: FOSL
Exchange: NASDAQ

Industry: Precious metals and jewelry - manufacture of fashion watches, parts, and accessories

FOXWORTH-GALBRAITH LUMBER COMPANY   RANK: 280

17111 Waterview Pkwy.
Dallas, TX 75252
Phone: 214-437-6100
Fax: 214-437-4236

CEO: Walter Foxworth
CFO: Jack Foxworth
HR: Jose Montalvo
Employees: 1,100

1992 Sales: $180 million
Ownership: Private

Industry: Retail - building products, lumber, and other building materials

TEXAS 500

FRANK PARRA CHEVROLET INC. RANK: 331

1000 E. Airport Fwy.
Irving, TX 75062
Phone: 214-721-4300
Fax: 214-579-0712

CEO: Tim Parra
CFO: Tim Parra
HR: Tim Parra
Employees: 284

1992 Sales: $147 million
Ownership: Private

Industry: Retail - automobiles

FREEMAN COMPANIES, THE RANK: 224

8801 Ambassador Row
Dallas, TX 75247-4622
Phone: 214-638-6450
Fax: 214-905-0957

CEO: Donald Freeman, Jr.
CFO: George Reinschmidt
HR: Dan Camp
Employees: 1,325

1991 Est. Sales: $245 mil.
Ownership: Private

Industry: Business services - trade show and convention arrangements, exhibit construction, equipment rental and leasing

FRIENDLY CHEVROLET RANK: 358

5601 Lemmon Ave.
Dallas, TX 75209
Phone: 214-526-8811
Fax: 214-523-1095

CEO: Mark A. Eddins
CFO: Mitch Vuckovich
HR: Sandy Anthony
Employees: 76

1992 Sales: $125 million
Ownership: Private

Industry: Retail - automobiles; nonresidential building operation

FRIONA INDUSTRIES LP RANK: 356

400 S. Taylor
Amarillo, TX 79101
Phone: 806-374-1811
Fax: 806-374-1324

CEO: James Herring
CFO: Dal Reid
HR: Jim Small
Employees: 230

1992 Sales: $129 million
Ownership: Private

Industry: Agricultural operations - cattle and cattle feedlots

FROZEN FOOD EXPRESS INDUSTRIES, INC. RANK: 261

318 Cadiz St.
Dallas, TX 75207
Phone: 214-630-8090
Fax: 214-819-5625

CEO: Stoney M. Stubbs, Jr.
CFO: Burl G. Cott
HR: Florence Ward
Employees: 1,822

1992 Sales: $195 million
Symbol: FFEX
Exchange: NASDAQ

Industry: Transportation - trucking

FULBRIGHT AND JAWORSKI — RANK: 242

1301 McKinney St.
Houston, TX 77010
Phone: 713-651-5151
Fax: 713-651-5246

CEO: Gibson Gale, Jr.
CFO: Scott Farrell
HR: Jane Williams
Employees: 1,590

1992 Sales: $214 million
Ownership: Private

Industry: Business services - legal

FURR'S/BISHOP'S, INCORPORATED — RANK: 209

6901 Quaker Ave.
Lubbock, TX 79413
Phone: 806-792-7151
Fax: 806-792-8277

CEO: Kevin E. Lewis
CFO: Joe W. Conner
HR: Carlene Stewart
Employees: 8,600

1992 Sales: $268 million
Symbol: CHI
Exchange: NYSE

Industry: Retail - cafeterias

GAINSCO, INC. — RANK: 441

500 Commerce St.
Ft. Worth, TX 76102
Phone: 817-336-2500
Fax: 817-335-1230

CEO: Joseph D. Macchia
CFO: Daniel J. Coots
HR: Brigitte Doyle
Employees: 149

1992 Sales: $86 million
Symbol: GNA
Exchange: AMEX

Industry: Insurance - property and casualty

GAL-TEX HOTEL CORP. — RANK: 380

Moody National Bank Bldg.
Galveston, TX 77550
Phone: 409-763-8536
Fax: 409-763-5304

CEO: Eugene Lucas
CFO: Dan Dick
HR: Mike Riley
Employees: 2,500

1992 Sales: $110 million
Ownership: Private

Industry: Hotels and motels - owns and operates hotels, including Holiday Inn North and Holiday Inn Southwest in Houston

GALVESTON-HOUSTON CO. — RANK: 399

4900 Woodway, Ste. 1200
Houston, TX 77056
Phone: 713-966-2500
Fax: 713-966-2575

CEO: Nathan M. Avery
CFO: Larry Medford
HR: Dennis G. Berryhill
Employees: 1,013

1992 Sales: $101 million
Symbol: GHX
Exchange: NYSE

Industry: Oil field machinery and equipment

TEXAS 500

GAMBRINUS COMPANY, THE   RANK: 484

14800 San Pedro
San Antonio, TX 78232
Phone: 210-490-9128
Fax: 210-490-9984

CEO: Carlos Alvarez
CFO: Jim Bolz
HR: Jim Bolz
Employees: 100

1992 Sales: $72 million
Ownership: Private

Industry: Beverages - brews Shiner Bock and Shiner Premium beers and imports Corona beer; wholesales beverages

GEORGE GRUBBS ENTERPRISES INC.   RANK: 263

310 Airport Fwy.
Bedford, TX 76021
Phone: 817-268-3121
Fax: 817-268-3628

CEO: George Grubbs, Jr.
CFO: Bobby D. Johnson
HR: Jenra Grubbs
Employees: 425

1992 Sales: $195 million
Ownership: Private

Industry: Retail - automobiles

GERLAND'S FOOD FAIR INC.   RANK: 247

3131 Pawnee
Houston, TX 77054
Phone: 713-746-3600
Fax: 713-746-3621

CEO: J. W. Morris
CFO: Jeff Reeder
HR: Dennis Chaivre
Employees: 1,500

1992 Sales: $210 million
Ownership: Private

Industry: Retail - supermarkets

GILLMAN COMPANIES, INC.   RANK: 232

7611 Bellaire Blvd.
Houston, TX 77036
Phone: 713-776-7000
Fax: 713-776-7057

CEO: Ramsay H. Gillman
CFO: Robert Kennedy
HR: Nancy Pavlik
Employees: 800

1992 Sales: $234 million
Ownership: Private

Industry: Retail - automobiles

GLAZER'S WHOLESALE DRUG COMPANY INC.   RANK: 156

14860 Landmark Blvd.
Dallas, TX 75240
Phone: 214-702-0900
Fax: 214-702-8508

CEO: Robert S. Glazer
CFO: Cary Rossel
HR: —
Employees: 1,050

1992 Sales: $385 million
Ownership: Private

Industry: Wholesale distribution - wine, beer, liquor, and bottled water

GLOBAL MARINE, INC.   RANK: 211

777 N. Eldridge Rd.   CEO: C. Russell Luigs   1992 Sales: $260 million
Houston, TX 77079   CFO: Jerry C. Martin   Symbol: GLM
Phone: 713-596-5100   HR: Dan Hansen   Exchange: NYSE
Fax: 713-531-1260   Employees: 1,500

Industry: Oil and gas - offshore drilling

GOODMAN MANUFACTURING CORPORATION   RANK: 153

1501 Seamist Dr.   CEO: Harold V. Goodman   1992 Sales: $400 million
Houston, TX 77008   CFO: Thomas O. Burkett   Ownership: Private
Phone: 713-861-2000   HR: Cliff Riley
Fax: 713-861-5428   Employees: 1,500

Industry: Building products - refrigeration and heating equipment

GRANT GEOPHYSICAL, INC.   RANK: 395

10550 Richmond Ave.   CEO: George W. Tilley   1992 Sales: $105 million
Houston, TX 77042   CFO: Michael P. Keirnan   Symbol: GRNT
Phone: 713-781-4000   HR: Sue Woelfel   Exchange: NASDAQ
Fax: 713-781-6934   Employees: 2,178

Industry: Oil and gas - field services

GREINER ENGINEERING, INC.   RANK: 345

909 E. Las Colinas Blvd., Ste 1900 CEO: Frank T. Callahan   1992 Sales: $132 million
Irving, TX 75039-3907   CFO: Robert L. Costello   Symbol: GII
Phone: 214-869-1001   HR: Carole Chaney   Exchange: NYSE
Fax: 214-869-3111   Employees: 1,425

Industry: Engineering - R&D services

GREYHOUND LINES, INC.   RANK: 84

15110 N. Dallas Pkwy.   CEO: Frank J. Schmieder   1992 Sales: $682 million
Dallas, TX 75248   CFO: Phillip Taft   Symbol: BUS
Phone: 214-715-7000   HR: Frank J. Schmieder   Exchange: AMEX
Fax: 214-419-3994   Employees: 9,700

Industry: Transportation - bus (only nationwide provider of intercity bus transportation in the US)

TEXAS 500

GROCERS SUPPLY CO. RANK: 53

3131 E. Holcombe Blvd.
Houston, TX 77021
Phone: 713-747-5000
Fax: 713-749-9320

CEO: Milton Levit
CFO: Max Levit
HR: Greg Belsheim
Employees: 1,900

1992 Sales: $1,300 million
Ownership: Private

Industry: Food - wholesale groceries

GSC ENTERPRISES, INC. RANK: 83

130 Hillcrest St.
Sulphur Springs, TX 75482
Phone: 903-885-7621
Fax: 903-439-3249

CEO: Michael K. McKenzie
CFO: Mike Mize
HR: Janet Mize
Employees: 1,250

1992 Sales: $699 million
Ownership: Private

Industry: Food - wholesale

GULF COAST SPORTSWEAR INC. RANK: 354

215 Flag Lake Dr.
Lake Jackson, TX 77566
Phone: 409-297-7552
Fax: 409-297-7355

CEO: Tom McKnight
CFO: Bill Boschma
HR: Buffie Robertson
Employees: 200

1992 Sales: $130 million
Ownership: Private

Industry: Apparel - wholesale sportswear

GULF MET HOLDINGS CORP. RANK: 452

PO Box 611
Houston, TX 77211
Phone: 713-926-1705
Fax: 713-923-1783

CEO: Jerome Robinson
CFO: Jamie Maddox
HR: —
Employees: 400

1992 Sales: $81 million
Ownership: Private

Industry: Metal processing and fabrication - copper and zinc recycling

GULF STATES INC. RANK: 454

6711 Hwy. 332
Freeport, TX 77541
Phone: 409-233-7821
Fax: 409-233-5556

CEO: Jim Linford
CFO: Gary Gibson
HR: Chuck Mitchell
Employees: 1,600

1992 Sales: $80 million
Ownership: Private

Industry: Building - electrical and mechanical contractor

TEXAS 500

GULF STATES TOYOTA — RANK: 98

7701 Wilshire Place Dr.
Houston, TX 77240
Phone: 713-744-3300
Fax: 713-744-3332

CEO: Jerry Pyle
CFO: F. R. Mason
HR: J. Brooks O'Hara
Employees: 1,100

1992 Sales: $600 million
Ownership: Private

Industry: Retail - automobiles

GUNDLE ENVIRONMENTAL SYSTEMS, INC. — RANK: 375

19103 Gundle Rd.
Houston, TX 77073
Phone: 713-443-8564
Fax: 713-875-6010

CEO: Thomas L. Caltrider
CFO: Daniel L. Shook
HR: Daniel L. Shook
Employees: 830

1993 Sales: $115 million
Symbol: GUN
Exchange: AMEX

Industry: Pollution control equipment and services - barrier systems, products, and services

H AND C COMMUNICATIONS INC. — RANK: 335

3050 Post Oak Blvd.
Houston, TX 77056
Phone: 713-993-2500
Fax: 713-993-2570

CEO: James E. Crowther
CFO: Cathy Leeson
HR: Jean Parsons
Employees: 900

1992 Sales: $140 million
Ownership: Private

Industry: Broadcasting - TV stations

H AND H MEAT PRODUCTS COMPANY INC. — RANK: 500

PO Box 358
Mercedes, TX 78570
Phone: 210-565-6363
Fax: 210-565-4108

CEO: Liborio Hinojosa
CFO: Ruben E. Hinojosa
HR: Erlinda Cavazos
Employees: 300

1992 Est. Sales: $67 mil.
Ownership: Private

Industry: Food - wholesale prepared Mexican foods for retail stores, hot deli, and food services

H.T. ARDINGER AND SON CO. — RANK: 493

9040 Governors Row
Dallas, TX 75247
Phone: 214-631-9830
Fax: 214-634-1270

CEO: H. T. Ardinger
CFO: Paula Acezedo
HR: H. T. Ardinger
Employees: 94

1992 Est. Sales: $70 mil.
Ownership: Private

Industry: Wholesale distribution - silk flowers and baskets

HAGGAR APPAREL
RANK: 184

6113 Lemmon Ave.
Dallas, TX 75209
Phone: 214-352-8481
Fax: 214-956-0367

CEO: J.M. Haggar, Jr.
CFO: Ralph Beattie
HR: George Greer
Employees: 6,500

1992 Sales: $300 million
Ownership: Private

Industry: Apparel - men's trousers, suits, and separates

HALLIBURTON COMPANY
RANK: 13

3600 Lincoln Plaza
Dallas, TX 75201
Phone: 214-978-2600
Fax: 214-978-2611

CEO: Thomas H. Cruikshank
CFO: Jerry H. Blurton
HR: Karen S. Stuart
Employees: 69,200

1992 Sales: $6,525 million
Symbol: HAL
Exchange: NYSE

Industry: Oil and gas - field services, including offshore drilling platform construction, underwater pipelines, well-logging and testing, environmental remediation, and casualty and marine insurance

See pages 74 – 75 for a full profile of this company.

HALLWOOD GROUP INC.
RANK: 374

3710 Rawlins St., Ste. 1500
Dallas, TX 75219
Phone: 214-528-5588
Fax: 214-528-8855

CEO: Anthony J. Gumbiner
CFO: Melvin J. Melle
HR: Holly McNeely
Employees: 697

1993 Sales: $116 million
Symbol: HWG
Exchange: NYSE

Industry: Diversified operations - investor in Show Biz Pizza, Monterey's Tex Mex Cafes, oil and gas, and hotels

HANDY ANDY SUPERMARKETS
RANK: 328

2001 S. Laredo St.
San Antonio, TX 78207
Phone: 210-227-8755
Fax: 210-225-0992

CEO: Jimmy Jimenez
CFO: Don Simmons
HR: Jeannie Wood
Employees: 1,705

1992 Sales: $148 million
Ownership: Private

Industry: Retail - supermarkets

HANDY HARDWARE WHOLESALE INC.
RANK: 453

8300 Tewantin
Houston, TX 77061
Phone: 713-644-1495
Fax: 713-644-3167

CEO: James D. Tipton
CFO: Tina Kirbie
HR: Mary Jane Anderson
Employees: 140

1992 Est. Sales: $81 mil.
Ownership: Private

Industry: Wholesale - hardware

HARBORAGE INC.
RANK: 310
11520 N. Central Expwy.
Dallas, TX 75243
Phone: 214-994-2000
Fax: 214-994-0111

CEO: Leon Carroll
CFO: Richard Mary
HR: Leon Carroll
Employees: 1,600

1992 Sales: $160 million
Ownership: Private

Industry: Real estate operations - commercial property management

HART GRAPHICS INC.
RANK: 438
8000 Shoal Creek Blvd.
Austin, TX 78758
Phone: 512-454-4761
Fax: 512-467-4583

CEO: William L. Hart
CFO: Britt Kaufman
HR: Brian Oetzel
Employees: 750

1992 Sales: $88 million
Ownership: Private

Industry: Printing - electronic typesetting and bookbinding

HARTE-HANKS COMMUNICATIONS HOLDINGS INCORPORATED
RANK: 144
200 Concord Plaza Dr., Ste. 800
San Antonio, TX 78216
Phone: 210-829-9000
Fax: 210-829-9403

CEO: Robert G. Marbut
CFO: Richard L. Ritchie
HR: Carolyn Oatman
Employees: 5,825

1992 Sales: $427 million
Symbol: HHS
Exchange: NYSE

Industry: Publishing - 58 newspapers, of which 8 are in Texas (including the Abilene Reporter-News, the Corpus Christi Caller-Times, and the Wichita Falls Times Record News)

HARTNETT, C.D. COMPANY, THE
RANK: 411
300 N. Main St.
Weatherford, TX 76086
Phone: 817-594-3813
Fax: 817-594-9714

CEO: Charles C. Milliken
CFO: Charles B. Milliken
HR: Diane DeSteiguer
Employees: 220

1992 Sales: $100 million
Ownership: Private

Industry: Food - wholesale groceries

HB ZACHRY CO.
RANK: 76
527 Logwood Ave.
San Antonio, TX 78221
Phone: 210-922-1213
Fax: 210-927-8060

CEO: H. B. Zachry, Jr.
CFO: Charles Ebrom
HR: Steve Hoech
Employees: 9,500

1992 Sales: $750 million
Ownership: Private

Industry: Construction - general contracting

HCB CONTRACTORS   RANK: 222

1400 Elm St., Ste. 4600
Dallas, TX 75202
Phone: 214-747-8541
Fax: 214-748-5063

CEO: Lawrence A. Wilson
CFO: James F. Russell
HR: Jerry D. Cooper
Employees: 210

1992 Sales: $250 million
Ownership: Private

Industry: Construction - general contracting and management

HEB GROCERY   RANK: 26

646 S. Main Ave.
San Antonio, TX 78204
Phone: 210-246-8060
Fax: 210-246-8169

CEO: Charles C. Butt
CFO: John C. Brouillard
HR: Louis LaGuardia
Employees: 42,000

1992 Sales: $3,800 million
Ownership: Private

Industry: Retail - supermarkets (largest independently held supermarket chain in Texas)

HELEN OF TROY CORP.   RANK: 343

6827 Market Ave.
El Paso, TX 79915
Phone: 915-779-6363
Fax: 915-774-4795

CEO: Gerald J. Rubin
CFO: Sam L. Henry
HR: Jeff Hubley
Employees: 348

1993 Sales: $137 million
Symbol: HELE
Exchange: NASDAQ

Industry: Cosmetics and toiletries

HELENA LABORATORIES   RANK: 447

1530 Lindbergh Dr.
Beaumont, TX 77707
Phone: 409-842-3714
Fax: 409-842-6241

CEO: Tipton Golias
CFO: Noel Bartlett
HR: Frankie Jordan
Employees: 650

1992 Sales: $84 million
Ownership: Private

Industry: Instruments - laboratory equipment and supplies

HERITAGE MEDIA CORPORATION   RANK: 217

13355 Noel Rd., Ste. 1500
Dallas, TX 75240
Phone: 214-702-7380
Fax: 214-702-7382

CEO: David N. Walthall
CFO: Joseph D. Mahaffey
HR: Kristen Springfield
Employees: 15,300

1992 Sales: $251 million
Symbol: HTG
Exchange: AMEX

Industry: Broadcasting - radio and TV stations in 12 states; in-store marketing

See page 139 for a full profile of this company.

HI-LO AUTO SUPPLY, INC.
RANK: 271

8601 Tavenor Ln.
Houston, TX 77075
Phone: 713-991-6052
Fax: 713-663-9296

CEO: T. Michael Young
CFO: Gary D. Walther
HR: Ed Fabritiis
Employees: 2,383

1992 Sales: $187 million
Symbol: HLO
Exchange: NYSE

Industry: Auto parts - wholesale and retail

HOLLY CORP.
RANK: 120

100 Crescent Court, Ste. 1600
Dallas, TX 75201
Phone: 214-871-3555
Fax: 214-871-3566

CEO: Lamar Norsworthy
CFO: Henry A. Teichholz
HR: Lamar Norsworthy
Employees: 438

1992 Sales: $507 million
Symbol: HOC
Exchange: AMEX

Industry: Oil refining and marketing

HOLLYWOOD CASINO CORP.
RANK: 205

13455 Noel Rd., Ste. 2200
Dallas, TX 75240
Phone: 214-386-9777
Fax: 214-386-7411

CEO: Jack E. Pratt
CFO: Albert J. Cohen
HR: Francis McCarthy
Employees: 3,200

1992 Sales: $275 million
Symbol: HWCC
Exchange: NASDAQ

Industry: Hotels and motels - owns Pratt Hotel Corp.; operates and manages casino and noncasino hotels

HOLLYWOOD MARINE INC.
RANK: 387

55 Waugh Dr., Ste. 1000
Houston, TX 77007
Phone: 713-868-1661
Fax: 713-868-6429

CEO: Charles B. Lawrence
CFO: Jill Cloud
HR: Ken Shaver
Employees: 550

1992 Est. Sales: $110 mil.
Ownership: Private

Industry: Transportation - canal barge shipping

HOME INTERIORS & GIFTS, INC.
RANK: 145

4550 Spring Valley Rd.
Dallas, TX 75244
Phone: 214-386-1000
Fax: 214-233-8825

CEO: Donald J. Carter
CFO: William Hendrix
HR: George Burton
Employees: 1,250

1992 Est. Sales: $425 mil.
Ownership: Private

Industry: Diversified operations - decorative home furnishings, picture frames, professional basketball team (the Dallas Mavericks), real estate management, construction and mining machinery, oil and gas

TEXAS 500

HOUSTON INDUSTRIES INCORPORATED   RANK: 24

4400 Post Oak Pkwy., Ste. 2700
Houston, TX 77027
Phone: 713-629-3000
Fax: 713-629-3129

CEO: Don D. Jordan
CFO: William Cropper
HR: Susan D. Fabre
Employees: 11,576

1992 Sales: $4,596 million
Symbol: HOU
Exchange: NYSE

Industry: Utility - electric power and cable TV

▶ See pages 76 – 77 for a full profile of this company.

HOUSTON MCLANE COMPANY, INC.   RANK: 427

Loop 610 and Kirby
Houston, TX 77021
Phone: 713-799-9629
Fax: 713-799-9718

CEO: Drayton McLane, Jr.
CFO: Gary Brooks
HR: Monica Rush
Employees: 1,200

1992 Sales: $93 million
Ownership: Private

Industry: Leisure and recreational services - operates the Houston Astrodome and owns professional baseball team the Houston Astros

HOUSTON PETERBILT INC.   RANK: 316

5219 I-45 N.
Houston, TX 77022
Phone: 713-691-4511
Fax: 713-695-9620

CEO: David Orf
CFO: David Orf
HR: David Orf
Employees: 300

1992 Sales: $160 million
Ownership: Private

Industry: Automotive and trucking - wholesale distribution of industrial trucks

HOWELL CORP.   RANK: 132

1010 Lamar, Ste. 1800
Houston, TX 77002
Phone: 713-658-4000
Fax: 713-658-4007

CEO: Paul W. Funkhouser
CFO: Allyn R. Skelton II
HR: Rick Robinson
Employees: 246

1992 Sales: $461 million
Symbol: HWL
Exchange: NYSE

Industry: Oil and gas - US integrated

HUNT BUILDING CORPORATION   RANK: 364

4401 N. Mesa, #201
El Paso, TX 79902
Phone: 915-533-1122
Fax: 915-545-2631

CEO: W. L. Hunt
CFO: William Sanders
HR: Patricia Minor
Employees: 200

1992 Sales: $122 million
Ownership: Private

Industry: Building - multi-family residential and commercial buildings

HUNT OIL COMPANY INC.   RANK: 79

Fountain Place, 1445 Ross at Field CEO: Ray L. Hunt   1992 Est. Sales: $720 mil.
Dallas, TX 75202   CFO: Don Robillard   Ownership: Private
Phone: 214-978-8000   HR: Chuck Mills
Fax: 214-978-8888   Employees: 2,000 (est.)

Industry: Oil and gas - petroleum and natural gas extraction; cattle ranching; inherited by Ruth Ray Hunt from her late husband, H. L. Hunt

HUNT PETROLEUM CORP.   RANK: 315

1601 Elm St.   CEO: Tom Hunt   1992 Sales: $160 million
Dallas, TX 75201   CFO: Terry Morris   Ownership: Private
Phone: 214-880-8800   HR: Joe Howard
Fax: 214-922-1060   Employees: 380

Industry: Oil and gas - exploration and production

HYDRIL CO.   RANK: 401

3300 N. Belt East   CEO: Richard Seaver   1992 Sales: $100 million
Houston, TX 77032   CFO: Larry Wilber   Ownership: Private
Phone: 713-449-2000   HR: Wayne Williams
Fax: 713-985-3457   Employees: 1,750

Industry: Oil field machinery and equipment

IGLOO HOLDINGS INC.   RANK: 351

1001 W. Sam Houston Pkwy. North   CEO: Jonathan H. Godshall   1992 Sales: $130 million
Houston, TX 77043   CFO: Sam E. Davis, Jr.   Ownership: Private
Phone: 713-465-2571   HR: Mary Alice Enreste
Fax: 713-935-7701   Employees: 1,250

Industry: Leisure and recreational products - ice chests and water coolers

IMPERIAL HOLLY CORP.   RANK: 90

8016 Hwy. 90-A   CEO: James C. Kempner   1993 Sales: $648 million
Sugar Land, TX 77478 CFO: James C. Kempner   Symbol: IHK
Phone: 713-491-9181   HR: William R. Krocak   Exchange: AMEX
Fax: 713-491-9198   Employees: 1,940

Industry: Food - sugar and refining

TEXAS 500

INDEPENDENT GROCERS INC. RANK: 396
4109 Vine St.
Abilene, TX 79602
Phone: 915-692-1440
Fax: 915-692-0848
Industry: Food - wholesale groceries

CEO: Jim Mullins
CFO: Roger Gibbs
HR: Shirley Moore
Employees: 140

1992 Est. Sales: $105 mil.
Ownership: Private

INTELLICALL, INC. RANK: 319
2155 Chenault, Ste. 410
Carrollton, TX 75006
Phone: 214-416-0022
Fax: 214-416-7213
Industry: Telecommunications equipment - private pay phones

CEO: William O. Hunt
CFO: Mike Barnes
HR: Lynn Zera
Employees: 325

1992 Sales: $155 million
Symbol: ICL
Exchange: NYSE

INTELOGIC TRACE, INC. RANK: 397
Turtle Creek Tower I, 8415 Datapoint Dr.
1992 Sales: $104 million
San Antonio, TX 78229
Phone: 210-593-5700
Fax: 210-593-2229
Industry: Computers - maintenance services to end users

CEO: Asher B. Edelman
CFO: Richard E. Wilson
HR: Sharon Johnson
Employees: 1,216

Symbol: IT
Exchange: NYSE

INTERNATIONAL BANCSHARES RANK: 308
1200 San Bernardo Ave.
Laredo, TX 78040-6301
Phone: 210-722-7611
Fax: 210-726-6647
Industry: Bank

CEO: Dennis Nixon
CFO: —
HR: Rosie Ramirez
Employees: 295

1992 Sales: $161 million
Ownership: Private

INTERTRANS CORP. RANK: 163
125 E. Carpenter Fwy., Ste. 900
Irving, TX 75062
Phone: 214-830-8888
Fax: 214-830-7488
Industry: Transportation - air and ocean transport; freight forwarding

CEO: Sam Wilson
CFO: John Witt
HR: Linda Crain
Employees: 1,108

1992 Sales: $367 million
Symbol: ITRN
Exchange: NASDAQ

TEXAS 500

J. C. PENNEY COMPANY, INC. RANK: 3

6501 Legacy Dr.
Plano, TX 75024-3698
Phone: 214-431-1000
Fax: 214-431-2212

CEO: William R. Howell
CFO: Robert E. Northam
HR: Richard T. Erickson
Employees: 192,000

1992 Sales: $19,085 million
Symbol: JCP
Exchange: NYSE

Industry: Retail - major department and catalog stores, selling apparel, shoes, jewelry, and home furnishings (4th largest retailer in the US)

➡ See pages 84 – 85 for a full profile of this company.

JACKSON AND WALKER LP RANK: 405

901 Main St.
Dallas, TX 75202
Phone: 214-953-6000
Fax: 214-953-5822

CEO: Mike Wilson
CFO: Rick Herlan
HR: Gail Richerson
Employees: 400

1992 Sales: $100 million
Ownership: Private

Industry: Business services - legal

JAGEE CORP RANK: 422

3228 Camp Bowie Rd.
Ft. Worth, TX 76107
Phone: 817-335-5881
Fax: 817-335-1905

CEO: Richard F. Garvey
CFO: Deborah Quillin
HR: Richard F. Garvey
Employees: 255

1992 Sales: $95 million
Ownership: Private

Industry: Agricultural operations - grains wholesaler

JONES BLAIR CO. RANK: 461

2728 Empire Central
Dallas, TX 75235
Phone: 214-353-1600
Fax: 214-350-7624

CEO: P.D. Dague
CFO: Michael Flanigan
HR: Betty Dunn
Employees: 480

1992 Sales: $78 million
Ownership: Private

Industry: Building products - plastic materials and resins

JULIUS SCHEPPS CO. RANK: 439

2535 Manana
Dallas, TX 75220
Phone: 214-357-8300
Fax: 214-351-2950

CEO: Lee M. Schepps
CFO: Fern Gleichenhous
HR: Karen McCain
Employees: 275

1992 Sales: $88 million
Ownership: Private

Industry: Wholesale distribution - wine, beer, and liquor

TEXAS 500

JUSTIN INDUSTRIES, INC.   RANK: 134

2821 W. 7th St.
Ft. Worth, TX 76107
Phone: 817-336-5125
Fax: 817-390-2477

CEO: John Justin
CFO: Richard J. Savitz
HR: John Bennett
Employees: 5,102

1992 Sales: $453 million
Symbol: JSTN
Exchange: NASDAQ

Industry: Shoes and related apparel

K.S.A. INDUSTRIES INC.   RANK: 332

6910 Fannin St.
Houston, TX 77030
Phone: 713-797-1500
Fax: 713-797-6631

CEO: Kenneth S. Adams, Jr.
CFO: A. O. Schulze
HR: Norma Russell
Employees: 587

1992 Sales: $141 million
Ownership: Private

Industry: Diversified operations - owns the professional football team, the Houston Oilers; oil and gas; California rice and melon farms; Texas ranches; automobile dealerships

KANEB SERVICES, INC.   RANK: 284

2400 Lakeside Blvd., Ste. 600
Richardson, TX 75082
Phone: 214-699-4000
Fax: 214-699-4025

CEO: John R. Barnes
CFO: Howard C. Wadsworth
HR: William Kettler
Employees: 2,026

1992 Sales: $177 million
Symbol: KAB
Exchange: NYSE

Industry: Diversified operations - specialized industrial services to the oil and gas industry, pipeline transportation and terminalling services

See page 140 for a full profile of this company.

KENT ELECTRONICS CORP.   RANK: 318

5600 Bonhomme Rd.
Houston, TX 77036
Phone: 713-780-7770
Fax: 713-978-5890

CEO: Morrie K. Abramson
CFO: Clarence J. Metzger
HR: Jim Corporron
Employees: 612

1993 Sales: $155 million
Symbol: KNT
Exchange: NYSE

Industry: Electrical components - wire, cable, and electronic connectors and components

KEYSTONE CONSOLIDATED INDUSTRIES, INC.   RANK: 180

5430 LBJ Fwy., Ste. 1440
Dallas, TX 75240
Phone: 214-458-0028
Fax: 214-458-8108

CEO: Glenn R. Simmons
CFO: Harold M. Curdy
HR: Lyle E. Pfeffinger
Employees: 2,000

1992 Sales: $316 million
Symbol: KES
Exchange: NYSE

Industry: Wire and cable products

KEYSTONE INTERNATIONAL, INC.   RANK: 110

9600 W. Gulf Bank Dr.
Houston, TX 77040
Phone: 713-466-1176
Fax: 713-937-5406

CEO: Raymond A. LeBlanc
CFO: Mark E. Baldwin
HR: Katherine Ruf
Employees: 4,100

1992 Sales: $528 million
Symbol: KII
Exchange: NYSE

Industry: Instruments - valves and systems that control the flow of gases and liquids

KIMBERLY-CLARK CORPORATION   RANK: 12

PO Box 619100, DFW Airport Station
Dallas, TX 75261-9100
Phone: 214-830-1200
Fax: 214-830-1289

CEO: Wayne R. Sanders
CFO: John W. Donehower
HR: Barbara Kimps
Employees: 42,902

1992 Sales: $7,091 million
Symbol: KMB
Exchange: NYSE

Industry: Paper and paper products - tissue, diapers, towels, napkins, surgical gowns, newsprint, and writing and technical papers; Midwest Commercial Airlines (Milwaukee)

    See pages 78 – 79 for a full profile of this company.

KINETIC CONCEPTS, INC.   RANK: 202

8023 Vantage Dr.
San Antonio, TX 78230
Phone: 210-524-9000
Fax: 210-308-3998

CEO: James R. Leininger
CFO: Bianca Rhodes
HR: Larry Baker
Employees: 2,460

1992 Sales: $278 million
Symbol: KNCI
Exchange: NASDAQ

Industry: Medical products - therapeutic beds

KING RANCH, INC.   RANK: 175

16825 Northchase, Ste. 1450
Houston, TX 77060
Phone: 713-872-5566
Fax: 713-872-7209

CEO: Roger L. Jarvis
CFO: Mark Kent
HR: Rickey Blackman
Employees: 700

1992 Sales: $330 million
Ownership: Private

Industry: Diversified operations - cattle and horse ranching, cotton, sugar cane, corn, wheat, sorghum, sod, wildflowers, real estate, oil and gas

    See pages 116 – 117 for a full profile of this company.

KINSEL MOTORS INC.   RANK: 432

PO Box 2470
Beaumont, TX 77704
Phone: 409-838-6611
Fax: 409-838-0663

CEO: Joe B. Kinsel, Jr.
CFO: Steven Odle
HR: Steven Odle
Employees: 299

1992 Sales: $92 million
Ownership: Private

Industry: Retail - automobiles

TEXAS 500

KIRBY CORP.   RANK: 208

1775 St. James Place, Ste. 300
Houston, TX 77056
Phone: 713-629-9370
Fax: 713-964-2200

CEO: George A. Peterkin, Jr.
CFO: Brian K. Harrington
HR: Jack Sims
Employees: 1,875

1992 Sales: $269 million
Symbol: KEX
Exchange: AMEX

Industry: Diversified operations - petrochemical transport, diesel repair, insurance

L&H PACKING COMPANY INC.   RANK: 313

647 Steves
San Antonio, TX 78210
Phone: 210-532-3241
Fax: 210-532-3399

CEO: Kenneth Leonard
CFO: Terry Black
HR: Mary Cheddie
Employees: 600

1992 Sales: $160 million
Ownership: Private

Industry: Food - wholesale meats and meat products

LA QUINTA MOTOR INNS, INC.   RANK: 214

10010 San Pedro Ave.
San Antonio, TX 78216
Phone: 210-366-6000
Fax: 210-302-6109

CEO: Sam Barshop
CFO: Walter J. Biegler
HR: Michael A. Nosil
Employees: 6,000

1992 Sales: $256 million
Symbol: LQM
Exchange: NYSE

Industry: Hotels and motels

LANDMARK GRAPHICS CORP.   RANK: 450

15150 Memorial Dr.
Houston, TX 77079
Phone: 713-560-1000
Fax: 713-560-1410

CEO: Robert P. Peebler
CFO: William H. Seippel
HR: Daniel L. Casaccia
Employees: 534

1992 Sales: $82 million
Symbol: LMRK
Exchange: NASDAQ

Industry: Computers - geoscientific exploration software

LAWRENCE MARSHALL CHEVROLET-OLDS, INC.   RANK: 353

905 Austin
Hempstead, TX 77445
Phone: 409-826-2411
Fax: 409-826-2411

CEO: Lawrence Marshall
CFO: Kenneth Siber
HR: Kenneth Siber
Employees: 215

1992 Sales: $130 million
Ownership: Private

Industry: Retail - automobiles

LEE LEWIS CONSTRUCTION, INC. — RANK: 362

7810 Orlando Ave.
Lubbock, TX 79423
Phone: 806-797-8400
Fax: 806-797-8492

CEO: Lee Lewis
CFO: M. R. Lawson
HR: Jim Hester
Employees: 300

1992 Sales: $123 million
Ownership: Private

Industry: Construction - commercial and industrial buildings

LEIF JOHNSON FORD INC. — RANK: 489

501 E. Koenig Ln.
Austin, TX 78765
Phone: 512-454-3711
Fax: 512-323-9200

CEO: Robert Johnson
CFO: Claude Baumbach
HR: Claude Baumbach
Employees: 200

1992 Sales: $71 million
Ownership: Private

Industry: Retail - automobiles

LENNOX INTERNATIONAL INC. — RANK: 59

2100 Lake Park Blvd.
Richardson, TX 75080
Phone: 214-497-5000
Fax: 214-497-5299

CEO: John W. Norris, Jr.
CFO: Clyde Wyant
HR: Harry Ashenhurst
Employees: 8,000

1992 Sales: $1,050 million
Ownership: Private

Industry: Building products - air conditioning and heating

LIFE INSURANCE COMPANY OF THE SOUTHWEST — RANK: 260

1300 W. Mockingbird
Dallas, TX 75247
Phone: 214-638-7100
Fax: 214-638-9120

CEO: Wade Mayo
CFO: Michael Goni
HR: Susan Jennings
Employees: 115

1992 Sales: $199 million
Ownership: Private

Industry: Insurance - life

LINBECK CONSTRUCTION CORP. — RANK: 391

3810 W. Alabama
Houston, TX 77027
Phone: 713-621-2350
Fax: 713-840-7525

CEO: Leo Linbeck
CFO: Glen Graff
HR: John Sylvester
Employees: 145

1992 Sales: $110 million
Ownership: Private

Industry: Building - contractors of commercial and healthcare facilities

TEXAS 500

LINCOLN PROPERTY CO. RANK: 56

500 N. Akard, Ste. 3300
Dallas, TX 75201
Phone: 214-740-3300
Fax: 214-740-3313

CEO: A. Mack Pogue
CFO: Mark Wallis
HR: Mark Wallis
Employees: 4,059

1992 Sales: $1,173 million
Ownership: Private

Industry: Real estate development and property management

LIVING CENTERS OF AMERICA, INC. RANK: 167

15415 Katy Fwy., Ste. 800
Houston, TX 77094
Phone: 713-578-4600
Fax: 713-578-4735

CEO: Edward L. Kuntz
CFO: Leroy D. Williams
HR: Teresa Tucker
Employees: 17,000

1992 Sales: $351 million
Symbol: LCA
Exchange: NYSE

Industry: Healthcare - long-term care (nursing homes)

LOCKE PURNELL RAIN HARRELL RANK: 371

2200 Ross Ave.
Dallas, TX 75201
Phone: 214-740-8000
Fax: 214-740-8800

CEO: Robert F. See, Jr.
CFO: Richard R. Woodmansee
HR: Mark E. Florence
Employees: 387

1992 Sales: $120 million
Ownership: Private

Industry: Business services - legal

LOMAS FINANCIAL CORP. RANK: 199

2001 Bryan Tower, 36th Fl.
Dallas, TX 75201
Phone: 214-746-7111
Fax: 214-879-5567

CEO: Jess Hay
CFO: Gene H. Bishop
HR: Kim Poole
Employees: 2,163

1992 Sales: $282 million
Symbol: LFC
Exchange: NYSE

Industry: Financial - investment management

LONE STAR PLYWOOD AND DOOR CORP. RANK: 462

600 N. Wildwood Dr.
Irving, TX 75061
Phone: 214-438-6611
Fax: 214-579-1720

CEO: B. W. Dean
CFO: Leroy Brodowski
HR: Sharon Inman
Employees: 350

1992 Sales: $78 million
Ownership: Private

Industry: Building products

LONE STAR TECHNOLOGIES, INC. — RANK: 148

2200 W. Mockingbird Ln.
Dallas, TX 75235
Phone: 214-386-3981
Fax: 214-353-6471

CEO: John P. Harbin
CFO: Judith Murrell
HR: John P. Harbin
Employees: 2,070

1992 Sales: $411 million
Symbol: LSST
Exchange: NASDAQ

Industry: Steel - production of tubular goods for the oil industry

LOTT GROUP INC., THE — RANK: 389

3500 S. Gessner
Houston, TX 77063
Phone: 713-266-5688
Fax: 713-266-6082

CEO: Alvin L. Jensen
CFO: Byron Wake
HR: Jose Puga
Employees: 300

1992 Sales: $110 million
Ownership: Private

Industry: Building - general contractor of office buildings, hotels, hospitals, stadiums, and other specialty commercial projects

LUBY'S CAFETERIAS, INC. — RANK: 171

2211 Northeast Loop 410
San Antonio, TX 78265
Phone: 210-654-9000
Fax: 210-654-3211

CEO: Ralph Erben
CFO: John E. Curtis, Jr.
HR: —
Employees: 9,200

1992 Sales: $346 million
Symbol: LUB
Exchange: NYSE

Industry: Retail - cafeterias

LUFKIN INDUSTRIES, INC. — RANK: 357

407 Kilen St.
Lufkin, TX 75901
Phone: 409-634-2211
Fax: 409-637-5474

CEO: F. B. Stevenson
CFO: C. J. Haley, Jr.
HR: Jim Riggs
Employees: 2,098

1992 Sales: $127 million
Symbol: LUFK
Exchange: NASDAQ

Industry: Oil field machinery and equipment

LYONDELL PETROCHEMICAL COMPANY — RANK: 20

1221 McKinney St., Ste. 1600
Houston, TX 77010
Phone: 713-652-7200
Fax: 713-652-7430

CEO: Bob G. Gower
CFO: Russell S. Young
HR: Richard W. Park
Employees: 2,312

1992 Sales: $4,805 million
Symbol: LYO
Exchange: NYSE

Industry: Chemicals - petrochemicals; gasoline, heating oil, lubricants, jet and diesel fuel

See pages 80 – 81 for a full profile of this company.

TEXAS 500

M/A/R/C GROUP, THE RANK: 499
7850 N. Belt Line Rd.
Irving, TX 75063
Phone: 214-506-3400
Fax: 214-506-3505
CEO: Sharon M. Munger
CFO: Harold R. Curtis
HR: Jim Farrell
Employees: 497
1992 Sales: $67 million
Symbol: MARC
Exchange: NASDAQ

Industry: Business services - market research

MACGREGOR MEDICAL ASSOCIATION RANK: 267
2550 Holly Hall
Houston, TX 77054
Phone: 713-741-8910
Fax: 713-880-9153
CEO: James Birte
CFO: Tim Hebert
HR: Donald Hand
Employees: 1,000
1992 Sales: $190 million
Ownership: Private

Industry: Medical services

MARATHON GROUP RANK: 6
5555 San Felipe Rd.
Houston, TX 77002
Phone: 713-629-6600
Fax: 713-871-0728
CEO: Victor G. Beghini
CFO: Jimmy D. Low
HR: Kenneth L. Matheny
Employees: 22,810
1992 Sales: $12,782 million
Symbol: MRO
Exchange: NYSE

Industry: Oil and gas - exploration and production (one of the three companies making up USX Corporation)

See pages 82 – 83 for a full profile of this company.

MARTIN GAS CORP. RANK: 270
101 E. Sabine
Kilgore, TX 75662
Phone: 903-983-1551
Fax: 903-983-6211
CEO: R. S. Martin, Jr.
CFO: Robert D. Bondurant
HR: R. S. Martin, Jr.
Employees: 590
1992 Sales: $189 million
Ownership: Private

Industry: Utility - liquefied petroleum gas distribution

MARY KAY COSMETICS INC. RANK: 96
8787 Stemmons Fwy.
Dallas, TX 75247
Phone: 214-630-8787
Fax: 214-905-5699
CEO: Richard R. Rogers
CFO: John P. Rochon
HR: —
Employees: 2,000
1992 Sales: $613 million
Ownership: Private

Industry: Cosmetics and toiletries, including fragrances and bath and body products

See pages 118 – 119 for a full profile of this company.

TEXAS 500

MAVERICK MARKETS INC.   RANK: 386

5440 Old Brownsville
Corpus Christi, TX 78469
Phone: 512-289-1585
Fax: 512-289-7824

CEO: Erich Wendl
CFO: Ricardo Elizondo
HR: Porfilio Silva
Employees: 580

1993 Sales: $110 million
Ownership: Private

Industry: Retail - convenience stores

MAXUS ENERGY CORP.   RANK: 69

717 N. Harwood St.
Dallas, TX 75201
Phone: 214-953-2000
Fax: 214-953-2901

CEO: Charles L. Blackburn
CFO: Michael J. Barron
HR: Mark J. Gentry
Employees: 2,190

1992 Sales: $851 million
Symbol: MXS
Exchange: NYSE

Industry: Oil and gas - international specialty

MAXXAM INC.   RANK: 45

5847 San Felipe, Ste. 2600
Houston, TX 77057
Phone: 713-975-7600
Fax: 713-267-3701

CEO: Charles E. Hurwitz
CFO: John T. La Duc
HR: Sharon Romere
Employees: 12,379

1992 Sales: $2,203 million
Symbol: MXM
Exchange: AMEX

Industry: Diversified operations - aluminum, forest products, and real estate development

MAXXIM MEDICAL, INC.   RANK: 469

104 Industrial Blvd.
Sugar Land, TX 77478
Phone: 713-240-2442
Fax: 713-240-9123

CEO: Kenneth W. Davidson
CFO: Peter M. Graham
HR: Donna Huestis
Employees: 1,800

1992 Sales: $75 million
Symbol: MAM
Exchange: AMEX

Industry: Medical products - disposable hospital products, surgical and medical instruments, physiotherapy equipment, electromedical equipment

MCCOY CORPORATION   RANK: 162

1200 IH-35 North, PO Box 1028
San Marcos, TX 78667
Phone: 512-353-5400
Fax: 512-396-5925

CEO: Emmett F. McCoy
CFO: Chuck Churchwell
HR: Rick Bell
Employees: 1,300

1992 Sales: $370 million
Ownership: Private

Industry: Building products - lumber and other building materials; hardware stores; paint, glass, and wallpaper stores

TEXAS 500

MEDIANEWS GROUP — RANK: 135

4888 Loop Central Dr., Ste. 525
Houston, TX 77081
Phone: 713-295-3800
Fax: 713-295-3893

CEO: W. Dean Singleton
CFO: E. Michael Fluker
HR: N. Lebra, Jr.
Employees: 8,000

1992 Sales: $450 million
Ownership: Private

Industry: Publishing - newspapers, including The Houston Post

MEDICAL CARE AMERICA INC. — RANK: 91

13455 Noel Rd., 20th Floor
Dallas, TX 75240
Phone: 214-701-2200
Fax: 214-385-3276

CEO: Donald E. Steen
CFO: Larry M. Mullen
HR: Jonathan Bond
Employees: 4,300

1992 Sales: $641 million
Symbol: MRX
Exchange: NYSE

Industry: Healthcare - outpatient surgical centers and home health care services (operates under names of Medical Care International and Critical Care America)

MEN'S WEARHOUSE, INC., THE — RANK: 295

5803 Glenmont Dr.
Houston, TX 77081
Phone: 713-664-3692
Fax: 713-664-1957

CEO: George Zimmer
CFO: David H. Edwab
HR: Julie Maciag
Employees: 2,125

1993 Sales: $170 million
Symbol: SUIT
Exchange: NASDAQ

Industry: Retail - discounted men's business apparel and accessories

See page 141 for a full profile of this company.

MERICHEM CO. — RANK: 409

4800 Texas Commerce
Houston, TX 77002
Phone: 713-224-3030
Fax: 713-224-4403

CEO: John T. Files
CFO: O. R. Cable
HR: Stephen L. Trncak
Employees: 300

1992 Sales: $100 million
Ownership: Private

Industry: Chemicals - cresylic acids, soda chemicals

MESA INC. — RANK: 228

2001 Ross Ave.
Dallas, TX 75201
Phone: 214-969-2200
Fax: 214-969-2228

CEO: T. Boone Pickens
CFO: W. Mark Womble
HR: Jeff Lamb
Employees: 382

1992 Sales: $237 million
Symbol: MXP
Exchange: NYSE

Industry: Oil and gas - US exploration and production

MICHAELS STORES, INC. — RANK: 125

5931 Campus Circle Dr.
Irving, TX 75063
Phone: 214-714-7700
Fax: 214-714-7155

CEO: Sam Wyly
CFO: R. Don Morris
HR: Donald C. Toby
Employees: 10,147

1993 Sales: $493 million
Symbol: MIKE
Exchange: NASDAQ

Industry: Retail - framing materials and arts and crafts

MIDDLEBERG, RIDDLE AND GIANNA — RANK: 486

2323 Bryan St., Ste. 1600
Dallas, TX 75201
Phone: 214-220-6300
Fax: 214-220-2785

CEO: Michael Riddle
CFO: Carol Riddle
HR: Marilyn Butler
Employees: 280

1992 Sales: $71 million
Ownership: Private

Industry: Business services - legal

MILLER AND MILLER AUCTIONEERS INC. — RANK: 359

2525 Ridgmar
Ft. Worth, TX 76116
Phone: 817-732-4888
Fax: 817-732-5552

CEO: William M. Miller
CFO: Terry Breedlove
HR: Terry Breedlove
Employees: 41

1992 Sales: $125 million
Ownership: Private

Industry: Business Services - auctioneering

MINYARD FOOD STORES INC. — RANK: 102

777 Freeport Pkwy.
Coppell, TX 75019
Phone: 214-393-8700
Fax: 214-462-9407

CEO: Liz Minyard
CFO: John Bennett
HR: Alan Zaughan
Employees: 6,100

1992 Sales: $550 million
Ownership: Private

Industry: Retail - supermarkets under Sack 'n Save, Carnival Food Store, and Minyard names

MITCHELL ENERGY & DEVELOPMENT CORP. — RANK: 66

2001 Timberloch Place
The Woodlands, TX 77380
Phone: 713-377-5500
Fax: 713-377-6910

CEO: George P. Mitchell
CFO: Philip S. Smith
HR: Clyde Black
Employees: 2,800

1992 Sales: $903 million
Symbol: MNDA
Exchange: NYSE

Industry: Oil and gas - US exploration and production; real estate development (The Woodlands)

TEXAS 500

MMI PRODUCTS INC.   RANK: 325

515 W. Greens Rd.
Houston, TX 77067
Phone: 713-876-0080
Fax: 713-876-1648

CEO: Julius Burns
CFO: Bob Tewczar
HR: Donna Pitre
Employees: 1,000

1992 Sales: $150 million
Ownership: Private

Industry: Wire and cable products - welded wire

MOORCO INTERNATIONAL, INC.   RANK: 262

2700 Post Oak Blvd., Ste. 5701
Houston, TX 77056
Phone: 713-993-0999
Fax: 713-993-7488

CEO: George A. Ciotti
CFO: David W. Pfleghar
HR: David Borth
Employees: 1,472

1993 Sales: $195 million
Symbol: MRC
Exchange: NYSE

Industry: Instruments - control

MORNINGSTAR GROUP, INC.   RANK: 168

5956 Sherry Ln., Ste. 1100
Dallas, TX 75225
Phone: 214-360-4700
Fax: 214-360-9100

CEO: James A. Bach
CFO: Tracy L. Noll
HR: Craig Forshag
Employees: 1,280

1992 Sales: $351 million
Symbol: MSTR
Exchange: NASDAQ

Industry: Food - dairy products

MRS. BAIRD'S BAKERIES INC.   RANK: 301

7301 South Fwy.
Ft. Worth, TX 76134
Phone: 817-293-6230
Fax: 817-568-3691

CEO: Allen Baird
CFO: Bradley Lummis
HR: —
Employees: 3,000

1992 Est. Sales: $165 mil.
Ownership: Private

Industry: Food - bread and other baked goods

MUNDY COS.   RANK: 252

11150 S. Wilcrest Dr.
Houston, TX 77099
Phone: 713-530-8711
Fax: 713-530-8561

CEO: Joe S. Mundy
CFO: David Hartsell
HR: William Nixon
Employees: 4,500

1992 Sales: $200 million
Ownership: Private

Industry: Building - petrochemical plant and petroleum refinery repairs

MUSTANG TRACTOR AND EQUIPMENT CO.   RANK: 314

12800 Northwest Fwy.   CEO: F. Louis Tucker, Jr.   1992 Sales: $160 million
Houston, TX 77040   CFO: Bradford Tucker   Ownership: Private
Phone: 713-460-2000   HR: Anna Keyes
Fax: 713-462-4032   Employees: 600

Industry: Machinery - wholesaler of Caterpillar construction equipment

NABORS INDUSTRIES, INC.   RANK: 198

515 W. Greens Rd., Ste. 1200   CEO: Eugene M. Isenberg   1992 Sales: $286 million
Houston, TX 77067   CFO: Harris Kaplan   Symbol: NBR
Phone: 713-874-0035   HR: Daniel McLachlin   Exchange: AMEX
Fax: 713-872-5205   Employees: 3,168

Industry: Oil and gas - field services, including engineering studies, environmental services, construction, and drilling

NATIONAL CONVENIENCE STORES   RANK: 62

100 Waugh Drive   CEO: V. H. Van Horn   1992 Sales: $959 million
Houston, TX 77007   CFO: Brian Fontan   Symbol: NCSI
Phone: 713-863-2200   HR: Dennis Edmunson   Exchange: NASDAQ
Fax: 713-863-2376   Employees: 4,500

Industry: Retail - convenience stores and gas stations under the Stop N Go name

NATIONAL INTERGROUP, INC.   RANK: 28

1220 Senlac Dr.   CEO: Abben J. Butler   1992 Sales: $3,411 million
Carrollton, TX 75006   CFO: Abben J. Butler   Symbol: NII
Phone: 214-446-4800   HR: Lawrence J. Pilon   Exchange: NYSE
Fax: 214-446-4499   Employees: 3,138

Industry: Drugs and sundries - pharmaceuticals, health and beauty aids, crafts merchandise distribution; owns 80.5% of FoxMeyer Corporation

NATIONAL WESTERN LIFE INSURANCE CO.   RANK: 151

850 E. Anderson Ln.   CEO: Robert L. Moody   1992 Sales: $401 million
Austin, TX 78752   CFO: Robert L. Busby III   Symbol: NWLIA
Phone: 512-836-1010   HR: Carol Jackson   Exchange: NASDAQ
Fax: 512-835-2729   Employees: 225

Industry: Insurance - life

TEXAS 500

NATIONAL-OILWELL RANK: 165
5555 San Felipe
Houston, TX 77056
Phone: 713-960-5100
Fax: 713-960-5428

CEO: Joel Staff
CFO: Diane Molinaro
HR: Tom Duessel
Employees: 3,400

1992 Sales: $360 million
Ownership: Private

Industry: Oil field machinery and equipment

NCH CORP. RANK: 85
2727 Chemsearch Blvd.
Irving, TX 75062
Phone: 214-438-0211
Fax: 214-438-0186

CEO: Irvin L. Levy
CFO: Tom Hetzer
HR: Neil Thomas
Employees: 10,477

1993 Sales: $680 million
Symbol: NCH
Exchange: NYSE

Industry: Soap and cleaning preparations

NEW PROCESS STEEL CORP. RANK: 433
5800 Westview Dr.
Houston, TX 77055
Phone: 713-686-9631
Fax: 713-686-5358

CEO: E.R. Fant
CFO: Jim Kollaja
HR: Jim Kollaja
Employees: 250

1992 Sales: $92 million
Ownership: Private

Industry: Metal products - service centers

NEWELL RECYCLING COMPANY INC. RANK: 268
726 Probandt
San Antonio, TX 78204
Phone: 210-227-3141
Fax: 210-227-8948

CEO: Alton S. Newell
CFO: Shirley Canady
HR: Alton S. Newell
Employees: 330

1992 Sales: $190 million
Ownership: Private

Industry: Metal products - wholesaler of processed scrap metals

NL INDUSTRIES, INC. RANK: 65
3000 N. Sam Houston Pkwy. East
Houston, TX 77032
Phone: 713-987-5000
Fax: 713-987-5742

CEO: J. Landis Martin
CFO: Susan E. Alderton
HR: Peggy D'Hemecourt
Employees: 3,600

1992 Sales: $914 million
Symbol: NL
Exchange: NYSE

Industry: Chemicals - titanium dioxide pigments and additives for paints, sealants, inks, cosmetics, and adhesives

TEXAS 500

NOBLE DRILLING CORP. RANK: 334

10370 Richmond Ave., Ste. 400
Houston, TX 77042
Phone: 713-974-3131
Fax: 713-974-3181

CEO: James C. Day
CFO: Byron L. Welliver
HR: Julie Robertson
Employees: 1,580

1992 Sales: $140 million
Symbol: NDCO
Exchange: NASDAQ

Industry: Oil and gas - field services, drilling contractor

OCEANEERING INTERNATIONAL, INC. RANK: 241

16001 Park Ten Place, Ste. 600
Houston, TX 77084
Phone: 713-578-8868
Fax: 713-578-5243

CEO: John R. Huff
CFO: T. Jay Collins
HR: Juanita Verdin
Employees: 1,800

1993 Sales: $216 million
Symbol: OII
Exchange: NYSE

Industry: Oil and gas - field services

OFFSHORE PIPELINES, INC. RANK: 161

5718 Westheimer
Houston, TX 77057
Phone: 713-952-1000
Fax: 713-268-6891

CEO: Franklin C. Wade
CFO: Howard D. Loyd III
HR: Don J. Hayden
Employees: 1,762

1992 Sales: $370 million
Symbol: OFP
Exchange: NYSE

Industry: Oil and gas - field services

OHMSTEDE INC. RANK: 457

895 N. Main
Beaumont, TX 77701
Phone: 409-833-6375
Fax: 409-833-4102

CEO: Will Ohmstede
CFO: Stephen Bender
HR: George Garrett
Employees: 463

1992 Sales: $80 million
Ownership: Private

Industry: Metal processing and fabrication - shell and tube heat exchangers

OLD AMERICA STORES INC. RANK: 446

811 North Collins Fwy.
Howe, TX 75459
Phone: 903-532-5547
Fax: 903-532-6708

CEO: C. W. Brush
CFO: Robert R. Mickey
HR: Cindy Young
Employees: 1,275

1992 Sales: $84 million
Ownership: Private

Industry: Retail - framing materials and arts and crafts

TEXAS 500

ORYX ENERGY CO. RANK: 50

13155 Noel Rd.
Dallas, TX 75240-5067
Phone: 214-715-4000
Fax: 214-715-3311

CEO: Robert P. Hauptfuhrer
CFO: Edward W. Moneypenny
HR: William P. Stokes
Employees: 1,600

1992 Sales: $1,392 million
Symbol: ORX
Exchange: NYSE

Industry: Oil and gas - international integrated; exploration, development, production, and marketing

OSHMAN'S SPORTING GOODS, INC. RANK: 182

2302 Maxwell Ln.
Houston, TX 77023
Phone: 713-928-3171
Fax: 713-967-8254

CEO: Alvin N. Lubetkin
CFO: Edward R. Carlin
HR: Will A. Clark
Employees: 3,700

1993 Sales: $313 million
Symbol: OSHM
Exchange: NASDAQ

Industry: Retail - sporting goods

OVERHEAD DOOR CORP. RANK: 187

6750 LBJ Fwy., Ste. 1200
Dallas, TX 75240
Phone: 214-233-6611
Fax: 214-233-0367

CEO: Brian J. Bolton
CFO: George E. Mangarelli
HR: Cal Brunson
Employees: 2,500

1992 Sales: $300 million
Ownership: Private

Industry: Building products - overhead doors, automatic entrances, and truck doors

OWEN HEALTHCARE INC. RANK: 200

9800 Centre Pkwy., Ste. 1100
Houston, TX 77036
Phone: 713-777-8173
Fax: 713-777-5417

CEO: Carl Isgren
CFO: Stan Florance
HR: Jean Grove
Employees: 1,600

1992 Sales: $280 million
Ownership: Private

Industry: Medical services - hospital pharmacy and materials services

PACE ENTERTAINMENT CORPORATION RANK: 373

515 Post Oak Blvd., Ste. 300
Houston, TX 77027-9407
Phone: 713-621-8600
Fax: 713-622-8461

CEO: Allen J. Becker
CFO: Robert Zlotnik
HR: —
Employees: 83

1992 Est. Sales: $120 mil.
Ownership: Private

Industry: Leisure and recreational services - theatrical production and operations; concert promotion; and management consultanting operations

TEXAS 500

PAGING NETWORK, INC.   RANK: 213

4965 Preston Park Blvd.
Plano, TX 75093
Phone: 214-985-4100
Fax: 214-985-6711

CEO: George M. Perrin
CFO: Terry L. Scott
HR: Paul M. Myers
Employees: 2,670

1992 Sales: $258 million
Symbol: PAGE
Exchange: NASDAQ

Industry: Telecommunications services

PALM HARBOR HOMES INC.   RANK: 286

15301 Dallas Pkwy.
Dallas, TX 75248
Phone: 214-991-2422
Fax: 214-991-5949

CEO: Lee Posey
CFO: Kelly Moore
HR: Tom Buncic
Employees: 1,700

1992 Sales: $175 million
Ownership: Private

Industry: Building - manufactured homes

PANCHO'S MEXICAN BUFFET, INC.   RANK: 481

3500 Noble Ave.
Ft. Worth, TX 76111
Phone: 817-831-0081
Fax: 817-838-1480

CEO: Hollis Taylor
CFO: David Oden
HR: David Dixon
Employees: 3,109

1992 Sales: $73 million
Symbol: PAMX
Exchange: NASDAQ

Industry: Retail - restaurants in 6 southern and southwestern states under the names Pancho's Mexican Buffet and Emiliano's Buffet Mexicano

PANHANDLE EASTERN CORP.   RANK: 41

5400 Westheimer Ct.
Houston, TX 77056
Phone: 713-627-5400
Fax: 713-627-4145

CEO: Dennis R. Hendrix
CFO: James B. Hipple
HR: Daniel Hennig
Employees: 5,000

1992 Sales: $2,434 million
Symbol: PEL
Exchange: NYSE

Industry: Oil and gas - production and pipeline

PANNELL KERR FORSTER   RANK: 428

5847 San Felipe, Ste. 2300
Houston, TX 77057
Phone: 713-780-8007
Fax: 713-784-3360

CEO: Arthur L. Brien
CFO: Randall C. Houston
HR: Sandy Griffith
Employees: 1,000

1992 Sales: $93 million
Ownership: Private

Industry: Business services - accounting

TEXAS 500

PARAGON GROUP — RANK: 103

7557 Rambler Rd., Ste. 1200
Dallas, TX 75231
Phone: 214-891-2000
Fax: 214-891-2019

CEO: W. R. Cooper
CFO: Jerry Bonner
HR: Jerry Meritt
Employees: 1,646

1992 Sales: $550 million
Ownership: Private

Industry: Real estate development - including management

PARK PLACE MOTOR CARS — RANK: 376

4023 Oak Lawn Ave.
Dallas, TX 75219
Phone: 214-526-8701
Fax: 214-443-8205

CEO: Kenneth Schnitzer, Jr.
CFO: Bryon K. Dobbs
HR: Janet Delapp
Employees: 192

1992 Sales: $115 million
Ownership: Private

Industry: Retail - automobiles

PARKER & PARSLEY PETROLEUM CO. — RANK: 250

600 W. Illinois, Ste. 103
Midland, TX 79701
Phone: 915-683-4768
Fax: 915-571-5696

CEO: Scott D. Sheffield
CFO: A. Frank Kubica
HR: Larry Paulsen
Employees: 674

1992 Sales: $208 million
Symbol: PDP
Exchange: AMEX

Industry: Oil and gas - US exploration and production

PAY 'N SAVE INC. — RANK: 400

1804 Hall Ave.
Littlefield, TX 79339
Phone: 806-385-3366
Fax: 806-385-5438

CEO: R.C. Lowe
CFO: D. Arthro
HR: Angela Evans
Employees: 900

1992 Sales: $101 million
Ownership: Private

Industry: Retail - supermarkets

PEARCE INDUSTRIES INC. — RANK: 303

12312 Main St.
Houston, TX 77035
Phone: 713-723-1050
Fax: 713-551-0427

CEO: Gary M. Pearce
CFO: Richard E. Bean
HR: —
Employees: 750

1992 Sales: $164 million
Ownership: Private

Industry: Machinery - wholesale industrial machinery and equipment, oil and gas field machinery, and general construction machinery and equipment

TEXAS 500

PEDERNALES ELECTRIC COOPERATIVE INC. — RANK: 407

200 Ave. F
Johnson City, TX 78636
Phone: 210-868-7155
Fax: 210-868-4999

CEO: Bennie Fuelberg
CFO: Ron Borchers
HR: Nickie Cox
Employees: 370

1992 Sales: $100 million
Ownership: Private

Industry: Utility - electric power

PENNZOIL COMPANY — RANK: 43

PO Box 2967, Pennzoil Place
Houston, TX 77252-2967
Phone: 713-546-4000
Fax: 713-546-6639

CEO: James L. Pate
CFO: David P. Alderson II
HR: Harold C. Mitchell
Employees: 9,125

1992 Sales: $2,357 million
Symbol: PZL
Exchange: NYSE

Industry: Oil and gas - US integrated, including exploration, production, and marketing; sulphur mining and production; real estate management; Jiffy Lube centers

🌵 See pages 120 – 121 for a full profile of this company.

PERIODICAL MANAGEMENT GROUP INC. — RANK: 312

1011 N. Frio St.
San Antonio, TX 78207
Phone: 210-226-6820
Fax: 210-226-5716

CEO: Brian Weiner
CFO: Walter Biegler
HR: Steve Parma
Employees: 650

1992 Sales: $160 million
Ownership: Private

Industry: Wholesale distribution - periodicals

PEROT SYSTEMS CORP. — RANK: 223

12377 Merit Dr., Ste. 1100
Dallas, TX 75251
Phone: 214-383-5600
Fax: 214-383-5827

CEO: Morton H. Meyerson
CFO: John Vonesh
HR: Jack Woodmansee
Employees: 1,500

1992 Sales: $247 million
Ownership: Private

Industry: Computers - services and custom software design

PETRO INC. — RANK: 152

6080 Surety Dr.
El Paso, TX 79905
Phone: 915-779-4711
Fax: 915-778-2991

CEO: James A. Cardwell
CFO: Evonne Cardwell
HR: Jinny Louis
Employees: 2,572

1992 Sales: $400 million
Ownership: Private

Industry: Oil and gas - truck gas service stations under Petro Stopping Centers name at 53 locations throughout the US

TEXAS 500

PHILP CO. — RANK: 33

4809 Cole Ave., Ste. 350
Dallas, TX 75205
Phone: 214-528-6200
Fax: 214-528-4340

CEO: John P. Thompson, Sr.
CFO: Dean Renkes
HR: Dean Renkes
Employees: 4,820

1992 Sales: $2,910 million
Ownership: Private

Industry: Diversified operations - petroleum refining, fuel additives, boat building, inboard and outboard motorboats, food additives, drugs and sundries, toys

PIER 1 IMPORTS, INC. — RANK: 93

301 Commerce St., Ste. 600
Ft. Worth, TX 76102
Phone: 817-878-8000
Fax: 817-878-7883

CEO: Clark A. Johnson
CFO: Robert G. Herndon
HR: E. Mitchell Weatherly
Employees: 7,600

1993 Sales: $629 million
Symbol: PIR
Exchange: NYSE

Industry: Retail - imported home furnishings and apparel

PILGRIM'S PRIDE CORPORATION — RANK: 67

110 S. Texas St.
Pittsburg, TX 75686
Phone: 903-856-7901
Fax: 903-856-7505

CEO: Lonnie A. Pilgrim
CFO: Clifford E. Butler
HR: Ray Gameson
Employees: 10,500

1993 Sales: $887 million
Symbol: CHX
Exchange: NYSE

Industry: Food - world's largest chicken preparing and processing plant

PILLOWTEX CORP. — RANK: 207

4111 Mint Way
Dallas, TX 75237
Phone: 214-333-3225
Fax: 214-330-6016

CEO: Charles Hansen
CFO: Steve Richman
HR: Rudy Sanchez
Employees: 1,700

1992 Sales: $273 million
Symbol: PTX
Exchange: NYSE

Industry: Textiles - home furnishings

PIONEER CHLOR ALKALI INVESTMENTS INC. — RANK: 281

700 Louisiana St.
Houston, TX 77002
Phone: 713-225-5383
Fax: 713-225-4426

CEO: Richard C. Kellogg
CFO: George T. Henning
HR: Raymond A. Bart
Employees: 600

1992 Sales: $180 million
Ownership: Private

Industry: Chemicals - industrial

TEXAS 500

PIONEER CONCRETE OF AMERICA
RANK: 220

800 S. Gessner, #1100
Houston, TX 77024
Phone: 713-468-6868
Fax: 713-468-8742

CEO: Gary Bullock
CFO: Ron Mattingly
HR: Donna Ashabranner
Employees: 1,625

1992 Sales: $250 million
Ownership: Private

Industry: Building products - concrete

PLACID OIL CO.
RANK: 131

3800 Thanksgiving Tower
Dallas, TX 75201
Phone: 214-880-1000
Fax: 214-880-1185

CEO: Jerry R. Wright
CFO: Jack Tate
HR: Robert M. Adkins
Employees: 611

1992 Sales: $464 million
Ownership: Private

Industry: Oil and gas - US exploration and production

PLAINS COOPERATIVE OIL MILL INC.
RANK: 460

2901 Ave. A
Lubbock, TX 79404
Phone: 806-747-3434
Fax: 806-744-3221

CEO: Wayne Martin
CFO: J. Sebastian
HR: Diana Blount
Employees: 250

1992 Sales: $80 million
Ownership: Private

Industry: Food - cottonseed oil

PLAINS COTTON COOPERATIVE ASSOCIATION
RANK: 124

3301-11 E. 50th St.
Lubbock, TX 79404
Phone: 806-763-8011
Fax: 806-762-7333

CEO: Van May
CFO: Bill Morton
HR: Lee Phenix
Employees: 800

1992 Sales: $500 million
Ownership: Private

Industry: Textiles - cotton marketing

PLAINS RESOURCES INC.
RANK: 344

1600 Smith St., Ste. 1500
Houston, TX 77002
Phone: 713-654-1414
Fax: 713-759-1416

CEO: Greg L. Armstrong
CFO: Phillip D. Kramer
HR: Mary O. Peters
Employees: 214

1992 Sales: $133 million
Symbol: PLX
Exchange: AMEX

Industry: Oil and gas - international integrated; exploration and production, including marketing, transportation, storage, and terminalling

TEXAS 500

PLANTATION FOODS INC.
RANK: 350

2510 E. Lake Shore
Waco, TX 76705
Phone: 817-799-6211
Fax: 817-799-6499

CEO: Joel D. Taylor
CFO: Pete Palasota
HR: Don Hay
Employees: 1,500

1992 Sales: $130 million
Ownership: Private

Industry: Food - poultry processing

POGO PRODUCING COMPANY
RANK: 333

5 Greenway Plaza, Ste. 2700
Houston, TX 77046
Phone: 713-297-5000
Fax: 713-297-5100

CEO: Paul G. Van Wagenen
CFO: D. Stephen Slack
HR: John O. McCoy, Jr.
Employees: 100

1992 Sales: $141 million
Symbol: PPP
Exchange: NYSE

Industry: Oil and gas - US exploration and production

POOL ENERGY SERVICES CO.
RANK: 243

10375 Richmond Ave.
Houston, TX 77042
Phone: 713-954-3000
Fax: 713-954-3319

CEO: James T. Jongebloed
CFO: Ernest J. Spillard
HR: Richard K. Sanders
Employees: 4,519

1992 Sales: $213 million
Symbol: PESC
Exchange: NASDAQ

Industry: Oil and gas - field services

PORT CITY AUTOMOTIVE PARTNERS
RANK: 431

4601 S. Staples
Corpus Christi, TX 78411
Phone: 512-994-6200
Fax: 512-994-6287

CEO: J. Sulephen
CFO: Robert G. Westrup
HR: —
Employees: 325

1992 Sales: $92 million
Ownership: Private

Industry: Retail - automobiles

POWELL INDUSTRIES, INC.
RANK: 342

8550 Mosley Rd.
Houston, TX 77075
Phone: 713-944-6900
Fax: 713-947-4453

CEO: Thomas W. Powell
CFO: J. F. Ahart
HR: Robert Murphy
Employees: 783

1992 Sales: $137 million
Symbol: POWL
Exchange: NASDAQ

Industry: Machinery - electrical

PRIDE COMPANIES, LP — RANK: 87

500 Chestnut St.
Abilene, TX 79602
Phone: 915-674-8000
Fax: 915-676-8792

CEO: Brad Stephens
CFO: Brad Stephens
HR: Dave Caddell
Employees: 550

1992 Sales: $668 million
Symbol: PRF
Exchange: NYSE

Industry: Oil refining and marketing

PRIDE PETROLEUM SERVICES, INC. — RANK: 398

3040 Post Oak Blvd., Ste. 1500
Houston, TX 77056
Phone: 713-871-8567
Fax: 713-789-1430

CEO: Ray H. Tolson
CFO: Eugene C. Fowler
HR: Paul Drury
Employees: 1,875

1992 Sales: $101 million
Symbol: PRDE
Exchange: NASDAQ

Industry: Oil and gas - field services

PRODUCTION OPERATORS CORP — RANK: 473

11302 Tanner Rd.
Houston, TX 77041
Phone: 713-466-0980
Fax: 713-896-2528

CEO: Carl W. Knobloch, Jr.
CFO: William S. Robinson, Jr.
HR: Caleta Byrd
Employees: 383

1992 Sales: $75 million
Symbol: PROP
Exchange: NASDAQ

Industry: Oil and gas - field services

QUANEX CORP. — RANK: 101

1900 W. Loop South, Ste. 1500
Houston, TX 77027
Phone: 713-961-4600
Fax: 713-877-5333

CEO: Robert C. Snyder
CFO: Wayne M. Rose
HR: Joseph K. Peery
Employees: 2,697

1992 Sales: $572 million
Symbol: NX
Exchange: NYSE

Industry: Steel - pipes, tubes, and bars; aluminum building products

QUINTANA PETROLEUM CORP. — RANK: 178

601 Jefferson, Ste. 3800
Houston, TX 77002
Phone: 713-651-8600
Fax: 713-651-8663

CEO: H. Pat Riley
CFO: James W. Carroll
HR: Wilburn V. Lunn, Jr.
Employees: 325

1992 Sales: $325 million
Ownership: Private

Industry: Oil and gas - exploration and production

TEXAS 500

R CORP.   RANK: 298

1000 IH–10 North
Beaumont, TX 77702
Phone: 409-892-6696
Fax: 409-892-7690

CEO: Kenneth E. Ruddy
CFO: Charles R. King
HR: Jamie Ross
Employees: 508

1992 Sales: $170 million
Ownership: Private

Industry: Retail - automobiles

RANDALL'S FOOD MARKETS, INC.   RANK: 32

3663 Briarpark
Houston, TX 77042
Phone: 713-268-3500
Fax: 713-268-3601

CEO: Robert R. Onstead
CFO: Bob Gowens
HR: Ron Barclay
Employees: 20,000

1992 Sales: $3,200 million
Ownership: Private

Industry: Retail - supermarkets, including Randall's, Tom Thumb, and Simon David

RAYCO   RANK: 370

4800 Fredericksburg
San Antonio, TX 78229
Phone: 210-349-1111
Fax: 210-308-1307

CEO: John H. Willome
CFO: Jack Biagler
HR: Doris Gatton
Employees: 400

1992 Sales: $120 million
Ownership: Private

Industry: Building - residential

READING & BATES CORP.   RANK: 317

901 Threadneedle, Ste. 200
Houston, TX 77079
Phone: 713-496-5000
Fax: 713-496-2298

CEO: Paul B. Loyd, Jr.
CFO: Tim W. Nagle
HR: D.L. McIntire
Employees: 1,700

1992 Sales: $157 million
Symbol: RB
Exchange: NYSE

Industry: Oil and gas - offshore drilling and floating production

RECOGNITION EQUIPMENT INC.   RANK: 258

2701 E. Grauwyler Rd.
Irving, TX 75061
Phone: 214-579-6000
Fax: 214-579-6830

CEO: Robert A. Vanourek
CFO: Robert M. Swartz
HR: Robert M. Swartz
Employees: 1,695

1992 Sales: $199 million
Symbol: REC
Exchange: NYSE

Industry: Optical character recognition equipment

TEXAS 500

REDMAN INDUSTRIES INC.   RANK: 164

2550 Walnut Hill Ln., Ste. 200
Dallas, TX 75229
Phone: 214-353-3600
Fax: 214-351-2983

CEO: Tom Sturgess
CFO: Fergus Walker
HR: Rich Morris
Employees: 3,500

1993 Sales: $365 million
Symbol: RDMN
Exchange: NASDAQ

Industry: Building - manufactured housing

RELIABLE CHEVROLET INC.   RANK: 193

800 N. Central Expwy.
Richardson, TX 75080
Phone: 214-952-1500
Fax: 214-952-8171

CEO: Cecil Van Tuyl
CFO: Dave Anderson
HR: Dave Anderson
Employees: 265

1992 Sales: $300 million
Ownership: Private

Industry: Retail - automobiles

REMINGTON HOTEL CORPORATION   RANK: 293

14180 Dallas Pkwy.
Dallas, TX 75240
Phone: 214-980-2700
Fax: 214-980-2705

CEO: Archie Bennett, Jr.
CFO: Monty Bennett
HR: Mary Villarreal
Employees: 3,000

1992 Sales: $170 million
Ownership: Private

Industry: Hotels and motels - management

REXENE CORP.   RANK: 147

5005 LBJ Fwy.
Dallas, TX 75244
Phone: 915-333-7200
Fax: 915-333-8238

CEO: Andrew J. Smith
CFO: Kevin W. McAleer
HR: Joann Sibley
Employees: 1,300

1992 Sales: $415 million
Symbol: RXN
Exchange: NYSE

Industry: Chemicals - diversified and plastics

RICE FOOD MARKETS INC.   RANK: 189

5333 Gulfton St.
Houston, TX 77081
Phone: 713-662-7700
Fax: 713-662-7757

CEO: Alfred L. Friedlander
CFO: James Potter
HR: Kent Milton
Employees: 1,600

1992 Sales: $300 million
Ownership: Private

Industry: Retail - supermarkets

TEXAS 500

RICHARDS GROUP INC.   RANK: 283
10000 N. Central Expressway   CEO: Stan Richards   1992 Sales: $180 million
Dallas, TX 75231   CFO: Scott Dykema   Ownership: Private
Phone: 214-891-5700   HR: Stan Richards
Fax: 214-891-5844   Employees: 242
Industry: Business services - advertising

RIP GRIFFIN TRUCK/TRAVEL CENTERS INC.   RANK: 221
5202 4th St.   CEO: Rip Griffin   1992 Sales: $250 million
Lubbock, TX 79416   CFO: Ronnie Owens   Ownership: Private
Phone: 806-795-8785   HR: Risa Barron
Fax: 806-795-6574   Employees: 1,200
Industry: Diversified operations - gas stations; motels

RIVIANA FOODS INC.   RANK: 136
2777 Allen Pkwy.   CEO: Joseph A. Hafner, Jr. 1992 Sales: $450 million
Houston, TX 77019   CFO: Wayne Ray   Ownership: Private
Phone: 713-529-3251   HR: Jack Nolingberg
Fax: 713-529-1661   Employees: 2,400
Industry: Food - rice milling, canning, and baking

ROWAN COMPANIES, INC.   RANK: 219
2800 Post Oak Blvd., Ste. 5450   CEO: C. R. Palmer   1992 Sales: $250 million
Houston, TX 77056   CFO: E. E. Thiele   Symbol: RDC
Phone: 713-621-7800   HR: Bill S. Person   Exchange: NYSE
Fax: 713-960-7560   Employees: 2,333
Industry: Oil and gas - offshore drilling

ROYAL INTERNATIONAL OPTICAL CORP.   RANK: 341
2760 Irving Blvd.   CEO: William A. Schwartz   1992 Sales: $137 million
Dallas, TX 75207   CFO: George E. McHenry   Symbol: RIOC
Phone: 214-638-1397   HR: Susan Hahn   Exchange: NASDAQ
Fax: 214-634-7215   Employees: 3,200
Industry: Retail - optical goods

TEXAS 500

RSR CORP. — RANK: 311

1111 W. Mockingbird Ln.
Dallas, TX 75247
Phone: 214-631-6070
Fax: 214-631-6146

CEO: Albert P. Lospinoso
CFO: Sandra M. Anderson
HR: William White
Employees: 750

1992 Sales: $160 million
Ownership: Private

Industry: Metals - nonferrous, primarily lead

SAMMONS ENTERPRISES — RANK: 42

300 Crescent Court, Ste. 700
Dallas, TX 75201
Phone: 214-855-2800
Fax: 214-855-2899

CEO: Robert W. Korba
CFO: Joe Ethridge
HR: Larry Beach
Employees: 5,000

1992 Sales: $2,400 million
Ownership: Private

Industry: Diversified operations - insurance, cable TV, industrial equipment; company built by late billionaire Charles A. Sammons

SANIFILL, INC. — RANK: 449

1225 N. Loop West, Ste. 550
Houston, TX 77008
Phone: 713-865-9800
Fax: 713-865-9899

CEO: Lorne D. Bain
CFO: J. Chris Brewster
HR: Ken Rose
Employees: 650

1992 Sales: $82 million
Symbol: FIL
Exchange: NYSE

Industry: Pollution control equipment and services - solid waste disposal

SANTA FE ENERGY RESOURCES, INC. — RANK: 143

1616 S. Voss, Ste. 1000
Houston, TX 77057
Phone: 713-783-2401
Fax: 713-268-5341

CEO: James L. Payne
CFO: Michael J. Rosinski
HR: Charles Hain
Employees: 839

1992 Sales: $428 million
Symbol: SFR
Exchange: NYSE

Industry: Oil and gas - international integrated

SCHULTZ INDUSTRIES INC. — RANK: 419

131 Ava Dr.
Hewitt, TX 76643
Phone: 817-666-5155
Fax: 817-666-4472

CEO: Fred Schultz
CFO: Phillip Mitchell
HR: Ron Oden
Employees: 450

1992 Sales: $96 million
Ownership: Private

Industry: Leisure and recreational products

TEXAS 500

SEAGULL ENERGY CORP. — RANK: 227

1001 Fannin St., Ste. 1700
Houston, TX 77002
Phone: 713-951-4700
Fax: 713-951-4819

CEO: Barry J. Galt
CFO: Robert W. Shower
HR: Jack M. Robertson
Employees: 704

1992 Sales: $239 million
Symbol: SGO
Exchange: NYSE

Industry: Oil and gas - production and pipeline

SEMATECH, INC. — RANK: 244

2706 Montopolis Dr.
Austin, TX 78741
Phone: 512-356-3500
Fax: 512-356-3083

CEO: William Spencer
CFO: Dan Damon
HR: Vern Ogden
Employees: 700

1992 Sales: $213 million
Consortium

Industry: Engineering - R&D services, semiconductor technology

SERV-TECH, INC. — RANK: 329

5200 Cedar Crest Blvd.
Houston, TX 77087
Phone: 713-644-9974
Fax: 713-644-0731

CEO: Richard W. Krajicek
CFO: John M. Slack
HR: Cheryl Cummings
Employees: 817

1992 Sales: $148 million
Symbol: STEC
Exchange: NASDAQ

Industry: Oil and gas - field services, including cleaning and maintenance, welding, construction, environmental services, and engineering and design services

See page 142 for a full profile of this company.

SERVICE CORPORATION INTERNATIONAL — RANK: 75

1929 Allen Pkwy.
Houston, TX 77019
Phone: 713-522-5141
Fax: 713-525-5586

CEO: Robert L. Waltrip
CFO: Samuel W. Rizzo
HR: W. Blair Waltrip
Employees: 11,818

1992 Sales: $772 million
Symbol: SRV
Exchange: NYSE

Industry: Funeral services

SEWELL VILLAGE CADILLAC — RANK: 435

7310 Lemmon Ave.
Dallas, TX 75209
Phone: 214-350-2000
Fax: 214-956-2261

CEO: Carl Sewell, Jr.
CFO: Rich Clonts
HR: Lisa Brion
Employees: 300

1992 Sales: $90 million
Ownership: Private

Industry: Retail - automobiles

TEXAS 500

SHELL OIL COMPANY RANK: 2

One Shell Plaza
Houston, TX 77002
Phone: 713-241-6161
Fax: 713-241-6781

CEO: Philip J. Carroll
CFO: L. E. Sloan
HR: B. W. Levan
Employees: 25,308

1992 Sales: $21,702 million
Symbol: SC
Exchange: NYSE

Industry: Oil and gas - international integrated (owned by Royal Dutch/Shell Group, the largest oil company in the world)

🔶 See pages 86 – 87 for a full profile of this company.

SHOWBIZ PIZZA TIME, INC. RANK: 215

4441 W. Airport Fwy.
Irving, TX 75062
Phone: 214-258-8507
Fax: 214-258-8545

CEO: Richard M. Frank
CFO: Michael H. Magusiak
HR: Rob Harig
Employees: 12,000

1992 Sales: $253 million
Symbol: SHBZ
Exchange: NASDAQ

Industry: Retail - food and restaurants

SID RICHARDSON CARBON AND GASOLINE CO. RANK: 456

201 Main St.
Ft. Worth, TX 76102
Phone: 817-390-8600
Fax: 817-390-8663

CEO: John M. Hogg
CFO: Robert Cotham
HR: Keith Bullard
Employees: 500

1992 Sales: $80 million
Ownership: Private

Industry: Diversified operations - manufacturing of carbon black; natural gas liquids production

SIGEL LIQUOR STORES INC. RANK: 488

2960 Anode Ln.
Dallas, TX 75220
Phone: 214-350-1271
Fax: 214-357-3490

CEO: Louis Glazer
CFO: Al Miller
HR: Mike Ivie
Employees: 230

1992 Sales: $71 million
Ownership: Private

Industry: Wholesale distribution - wholesale and retail liquor

SKY CHEFS, INC. RANK: 130

524 E. Lamar Blvd.
Arlington, TX 76011
Phone: 817-792-2123
Fax: 817-792-2343

CEO: James J. O'Neill
CFO: Patrick Tolbert
HR: Joe Primavera
Employees: 7,300

1992 Sales: $467 million
Ownership: Private

Industry: Food - airline catering

TEXAS 500

SLM POWER GROUP INC.   RANK: 254

424 Southport Ave.
Corpus Christi, TX 78405
Phone: 512-883-4358
Fax: 512-887-6439

CEO: Lee Stockseth
CFO: Angie Estrada
HR: Terrie Steen
Employees: 400

1992 Sales: $200 million
Ownership: Private

Industry: Automotive and trucking - wholesale truck distribution

SMITH INTERNATIONAL, INC.   RANK: 245

16740 Hardy Rd.
Houston, TX 77032
Phone: 713-443-3370
Fax: 713-443-7102

CEO: Doug Rock
CFO: Dan Steigerwald
HR: Joe Sizemore
Employees: 1,800

1992 Sales: $211 million
Symbol: SII
Exchange: NYSE

Industry: Oil field machinery and equipment

SNYDER OIL CORPORATION   RANK: 372

777 Main St., Ste. 2500
Ft. Worth, TX 76102-5329
Phone: 817-338-4043
Fax: 817-882-5993

CEO: John C. Snyder
CFO: James H. Shonsey
HR: Susan Bodycomb
Employees: 289

1992 Sales: $120 million
Symbol: SNY
Exchange: NYSE

Industry: Oil and gas - US exploration and production

See page 143 for a full profile of this company.

SNYDERGENERAL CORP.   RANK: 73

3219 McKinney Ave.
Dallas, TX 75204
Phone: 214-754-0500
Fax: 214-754-0901

CEO: Richard W. Snyder
CFO: James F. Brum
HR: Bart L. Bailey
Employees: 6,300

1992 Sales: $800 million
Ownership: Private

Industry: Building products - heating, ventilating, air conditioning, and filtration products for commercial, industrial, and institutional applications

SOFTWARE SPECTRUM, INC.   RANK: 240

2140 Merritt Dr.
Garland, TX 75041
Phone: 214-840-6600
Fax: 214-864-7878

CEO: Judy O. Sims
CFO: Keith R. Coogan
HR: Judy Shoning
Employees: 303

1993 Sales: $220 million
Symbol: SSPE
Exchange: NASDAQ

Industry: Computers - microcomputer software and peripheral products; support services, training, and technical publications

TEXAS 500

SOLO SERV CORP.   RANK: 321

1610 Cornerway Blvd.	CEO: Robert J. Grimm	1993 Sales: $154 million
San Antonio, TX 78219	CFO: Timothy L. Grady	Symbol: SOLO
Phone: 210-225-7163	HR: Janet Pollock	Exchange: NASDAQ
Fax: 210-662-6461	Employees: 1,500	

Industry: Retail - discount fragrances, apparel, home furnishings

SOUND WAREHOUSE INCORPORATED   RANK: 139

10911 Petal St.	CEO: Mark Siegel	1992 Sales: $440 million
Dallas, TX 75238	CFO: John Vollmer	Ownership: Private
Phone: 214-343-4700	HR: —	
Fax: 214-503-5981	Employees: 2,800	

Industry: Retail - audio and video

SOUTHDOWN, INC.   RANK: 118

1200 Smith St., Ste. 2400	CEO: Clarence C. Comer	1992 Sales: $508 million
Houston, TX 77002	CFO: James L. Persky	Symbol: SDW
Phone: 713-650-6200	HR: Joseph W. Devine	Exchange: NYSE
Fax: 713-653-6815	Employees: 2,600	

Industry: Construction - cement and concrete

SOUTHERN FOODS GROUPS INCORPORATED   RANK: 169

3114 S. Haskell Ave.	CEO: Pete Schenkel	1992 Sales: $350 million
Dallas, TX 75223	CFO: Jerry Fry	Ownership: Private
Phone: 214-824-8163	HR: Stu Gibson	
Fax: 214-824-0967	Employees: 1,500	

Industry: Food - dairy products

SOUTHERN UNION CO.   RANK: 266

400 W. 15th St., Ste. 615	CEO: George L. Lindemann	1992 Sales: $192 million
Austin, TX 78701	CFO: Ronald J. Endres	Symbol: SUG
Phone: 512-477-5852	HR: Ronald J. Endres	Exchange: AMEX
Fax: 512-370-3599	Employees: 900	

Industry: Utility - gas distribution

TEXAS 500

SOUTHLAND CORPORATION, THE   RANK: 14

2711 N. Haskell Ave.
Dallas, TX 75204-2906
Phone: 214-828-7011
Fax: 214-828-7848

CEO: Clark. J. Matthews II
CFO: Jim Keyes
HR: David M. Finley
Employees: 35,646

1992 Sales: $6,439 million
Symbol: SLCMC
Exchange: NASDAQ

Industry: Retail - convenience stores and gas stations: 7-Eleven, selling Citgo gasoline

See pages 88 – 89 for a full profile of this company.

SOUTHWEST AIRLINES CO.   RANK: 48

2702 Love Field Dr.
Dallas, TX 75235
Phone: 214-904-4000
Fax: 214-904-4200

CEO: Herbert D. Kelleher
CFO: Gary C. Kelly
HR: Margaret Ann Rhoades
Employees: 11,397

1992 Sales: $1,685 million
Symbol: LUV
Exchange: NYSE

Industry: Transportation - Southwest Airlines

See pages 122 – 123 for a full profile of this company.

SOUTHWEST RESEARCH INSTITUTE INC.   RANK: 230

6220 Culebra Rd.
San Antonio, TX 78228
Phone: 210-522-2122
Fax: 210-522-3496

CEO: Martin Goland
CFO: Jesse D. Bates
HR: Bill Crumlett
Employees: 2,606

1992 Sales: $234 million
Ownership: Private

Industry: Engineering - R&D services, noncommercial

SOUTHWEST SECURITIES GROUP INC.   RANK: 498

1201 Elm St., Ste. 4300
Dallas, TX 75270
Phone: 214-651-1800
Fax: 214-749-0810

CEO: Don A. Buchholz
CFO: Robert A. Buchholz
HR: Pat Mincinski
Employees: 376

1992 Sales: $68 million
Symbol: SWST
Exchange: NASDAQ

Industry: Financial - securities brokers

SOUTHWEST TOYOTA, INC.   RANK: 348

9400 Southwest Fwy.
Houston, TX 77074
Phone: 713-270-3900
Fax: 713-270-3909

CEO: Sterling McCall
CFO: —
HR: Michelle Norris
Employees: 200

1992 Sales: $131 million
Ownership: Private

Industry: Retail - automobiles

TEXAS 500

SOUTHWESTERN BELL CORPORATION   RANK: 9

175 E. Houston
San Antonio, TX 78299-2933
Phone: 210-821-4105
Fax: 210-351-2071

CEO: Edward E. Whitacre, Jr.
CFO: Robert G. Pope
HR: Richard A. Harris
Employees: 59,500

1992 Sales: $10,015 million
Symbol: SBC
Exchange: NYSE

Industry: Utility - telephone, including local phone service, access to long distance carriers, PBX and data communications systems, and cellular and mobile communications; directory publishing

See pages 90 – 91 for a full profile of this company.

SOUTHWESTERN IRRIGATED COTTON GROWERS ASSOCIATION   RANK: 436

3500 Donithan Dr.
El Paso, TX 79922
Phone: 915-581-5441
Fax: 915-581-4138

CEO: David L. Hand
CFO: Philip Egger
HR: Philip Egger
Employees: 125

1992 Sales: $90 million
Ownership: Private

Industry: Agricultural operations - wholesale cotton and cottonseed

SOUTHWESTERN PUBLIC SERVICE CO.   RANK: 77

600 S. Tyler St.
Amarillo, TX 79101
Phone: 806-378-2121
Fax: 806-378-2995

CEO: Bill D. Helton
CFO: Bill D. Helton
HR: John L. Anderson
Employees: 2,030

1992 Sales: $749 million
Symbol: SPS
Exchange: NYSE

Industry: Utility - electric power

SPECIALTY RETAILERS INC.   RANK: 121

10201 S. Main St.
Houston, TX 77025
Phone: 713-667-5601
Fax: 713-669-2708

CEO: Bernard Fuchs
CFO: Jerry Ivie
HR: Jack Chipperfield
Employees: 7,500

1992 Sales: $505 million
Ownership: Private

Industry: Retail - apparel stores under Palais Royal, Beall's, and Fashion Bar names

SPECTRUM INFORMATION TECHNOLOGIES, INC.   RANK: 414

2710 Stemmons Fwy.
Dallas, TX 75207
Phone: 214-999-6000
Fax: 214-880-0006

CEO: Peter T. Caserta
CFO: Christopher McGowan
HR: Steve Allenda
Employees: 129

1993 Sales: $100 million
Symbol: SPCL
Exchange: NASDAQ

Industry: Telecommunications equipment - wireless data transmission

TEXAS 500

SPI HOLDING, INC. RANK: 297
1501 N. Plano Rd.
Richardson, TX 75081
Phone: 214-234-2721
Fax: 214-301-9234

CEO: Al Jerome
CFO: Dan Hair
HR: Scott Campbell
Employees: 747

1992 Est. Sales: $170 mil.
Symbol: SPH B
Exchange: AMEX

Industry: Cable TV - hospitality pay-per-view TV; owns Spectradyne

STANDARD FRUIT AND VEGETABLE COMPANY INC. RANK: 474
1400 Parker St.
Dallas, TX 75215
Phone: 214-428-3600
Fax: 214-428-8834

CEO: Martin H. Rutchik
CFO: Morris Rutlik
HR: Steve Gray
Employees: 250

1992 Sales: $75 million
Ownership: Private

Industry: Food - wholesale produce (fruits and vegetables)

STANLEY STORES INC. RANK: 239
1400 8th St.
Bay City, TX 77414
Phone: 409-245-6355
Fax: 409-245-1032

CEO: O. B. Stanley
CFO: John Hancock
HR: Ester Gomez
Employees: 1,425

1992 Sales: $220 million
Ownership: Private

Industry: Retail - supermarkets under Stanley Stores, Foods 4 Less, and Price-Low Foods names

STEAKLEY CHEVROLET INC. RANK: 492
6411 E. Northwest Hwy.
Dallas, TX 75231
Phone: 214-363-8341
Fax: 214-691-2918

CEO: John W. Steakley
CFO: Kelly McCrory
HR: John W. Steakley
Employees: 200

1992 Est. Sales: $70 mil.
Ownership: Private

Industry: Retail - automobiles

STERLING CHEMICALS, INC. RANK: 141
1200 Smith St., Ste. 1900
Houston, TX 77002
Phone: 713-650-3700
Fax: 713-654-9551

CEO: J. Virgil Waggoner
CFO: Douglas W. Metten
HR: Bob McAlister
Employees: 1,225

1992 Sales: $431 million
Symbol: STX
Exchange: NYSE

Industry: Chemicals - diversified

TEXAS 500

STERLING ELECTRONICS CORP. RANK: 327

4201 Southwest Fwy.
Houston, TX 77027
Phone: 713-627-9800
Fax: 713-629-3938

CEO: Michael S. Spolane
CFO: Leon Webb, Jr.
HR: Sheila Babin
Employees: 473

1993 Sales: $150 million
Symbol: SEC
Exchange: AMEX

Industry: Electrical components - raw materials and subassemblies

STERLING SOFTWARE, INC. RANK: 212

8080 N. Central Expwy., Ste. 1100
Dallas, TX 75206
Phone: 214-891-8600
Fax: 214-739-0535

CEO: Sterling L. Williams
CFO: George H. Ellis
HR: Rich Connelly
Employees: 2,150

1992 Sales: $259 million
Symbol: SSW
Exchange: NYSE

Industry: Computers - software and network services

See page 144 for a full profile of this company.

STEVENS GRAPHICS CORP. RANK: 448

5500 Airport Fwy.
Ft. Worth, TX 76117
Phone: 817-831-3911
Fax: 817-838-4344

CEO: Paul I. Stevens
CFO: James A. Cole
HR: Ken Green
Employees: 624

1992 Sales: $84 million
Symbol: SVGA
Exchange: AMEX

Industry: Machinery - printing

STEWART INFORMATION SERVICES CORP. RANK: 195

2200 W. Loop South
Houston, TX 77027
Phone: 713-871-1100
Fax: 713-552-9523

CEO: Carloss Morris
CFO: Max Crisp
HR: Nita Hanks
Employees: 3,471

1992 Sales: $290 million
Symbol: SISC
Exchange: NASDAQ

Industry: Business services - title insurance and real estate database

STEWART & STEVENSON SERVICES, INC. RANK: 70

2707 N. Loop West
Houston, TX 77008
Phone: 713-868-7700
Fax: 713-868-7692

CEO: Bob O'Neal
CFO: Robert L. Hargrave
HR: Bobby Brown
Employees: 2,850

1993 Sales: $813 million
Symbol: SSSS
Exchange: NASDAQ

Industry: Engines - internal combustion

TEXAS 500

STRAFCO INC. — RANK: 363

1964 S. Alamo
San Antonio, TX 78204
Phone: 210-226-0101
Fax: 210-271-7495

CEO: Jack D. Trawick
CFO: Huey Rhudy
HR: Murray Betts
Employees: 1,260

1992 Sales: $122 million
Ownership: Private

Industry: Auto parts - tire distribution

STRASBURGER AND PRICE — RANK: 406

901 Main St.
Dallas, TX 75202
Phone: 214-651-4300
Fax: 214-651-4330

CEO: David Meyercord
CFO: Bob Kratus
HR: Eunice Newton
Employees: 400

1992 Sales: $100 million
Ownership: Private

Industry: Business services - legal

SUN COAST RESOURCES INC. — RANK: 442

14825 Willis
Houston, TX 77039
Phone: 713-449-7274
Fax: 713-449-7288

CEO: Kathy Prasnicki
CFO: Kathy Prasnicki
HR: Lisa Smith
Employees: 17

1992 Sales: $86 million
Ownership: Private

Industry: Wholesale distribution - gasoline and diesel fuel

SUNBELT CORP. — RANK: 383

600 Travis
Houston, TX 77002
Phone: 713-225-2245
Fax: 713-225-2442

CEO: Jose Domene
CFO: Jeff Smith
HR: Larry Douthitt
Employees: 1,050

1992 Sales: $110 million
Ownership: Private

Industry: Construction - concrete

SUNBELT NURSERY GROUP, INC. — RANK: 338

6500 West Fwy., Ste. 600
Ft. Worth, TX 76116
Phone: 817-738-8111
Fax: 817-735-0948

CEO: Donald W. Davis
CFO: Donald W. Davis
HR: Tim Hinaman
Employees: 2,150

1993 Sales: $139 million
Symbol: SBN
Exchange: AMEX

Industry: Retail - garden centers

TEXAS 500

SUPER CLUB NORTH AMERICA CORPORATION — RANK: 117

4560 Belt Line Rd., Ste. 200
Dallas, TX 75244
Phone: 214-701-9929
Fax: 214-701-9920

CEO: Darrel Baldwin
CFO: Keith Horniman
HR: Al Hagman
Employees: 3,500

1992 Sales: $510 million
Ownership: Private

Industry: Retail - audio (Record Bar, Tracks, Turtles, Rhythm and Views) and video (Alfalfa Video, Movieland, Movietime, Movies at Home, Video Towne) tape sales and rentals

SUPERTRAVEL — RANK: 336

361 Greens Rd.
Houston, TX 77060
Phone: 713-876-2900
Fax: 713-920-7180

CEO: Stanley St. Pierre
CFO: Gene McDaniel
HR: Bob Gregg
Employees: 300

1992 Sales: $140 million
Ownership: Private

Industry: Leisure and recreational services - travel agency

SYSCO CORPORATION — RANK: 8

1390 Enclave Pkwy.
Houston, TX 77077-2099
Phone: 713-584-1390
Fax: 713-584-1188

CEO: John F. Woodhouse
CFO: E. James Lowrey
HR: Philip C. Thompson
Employees: 24,000

1993 Sales: $10,022 million
Symbol: SYY
Exchange: NYSE

Industry: Food - wholesale, including frozen, canned, and dry goods; fresh meat and produce; disposable and reusable utensils and dishes; kitchen equipment; cleaning supplies

See pages 92 – 93 for a full profile of this company.

TANDY CORPORATION — RANK: 21

1800 One Tandy Center
Ft. Worth, TX 76102
Phone: 817-390-3700
Fax: 817-390-2774

CEO: John V. Roach
CFO: Dwain H. Hughes
HR: George J. Berger
Employees: 39,000

1992 Sales: $4,743 million
Symbol: TAN
Exchange: NYSE

Industry: Retail - consumer electronics and appliances: Radio Shack, Computer City, The Edge in Electronics, Incredible Universe, Video Concepts, and McDuff

See pages 94 – 95 for a full profile of this company.

TANDYCRAFTS, INC. — RANK: 347

1400 Everman Pkwy.
Ft. Worth, TX 76140
Phone: 817-551-9600
Fax: 817-551-5763

CEO: Jerry L. Roy
CFO: Michael J. Walsh
HR: Jerry L. Roy
Employees: 2,000

1992 Sales: $131 million
Symbol: TAC
Exchange: NYSE

Industry: Diversified operations - retail outlets, leather products, frames, furniture

TEXAS 500

TARRANT DISTRIBUTORS INC. RANK: 282

9835 Genard Rd.
Houston, TX 77041
Phone: 713-690-8888
Fax: 713-690-1169

CEO: N. B. Strauss
CFO: David Ritch
HR: Rose Clark
Employees: 250

1992 Sales: $180 million
Ownership: Private

Industry: Wholesale distribution - alcoholic beverages

TAUBER OIL CO. RANK: 78

55 Waugh Dr., Ste. 700
Houston, TX 77007
Phone: 713-869-8700
Fax: 713-869-8069

CEO: O. J. Tauber, Jr.
CFO: Pat O'Neal
HR: Nancy Dillard
Employees: 52

1993 Sales: $747 million
Ownership: Private

Industry: Oil refining and marketing - petroleum and petrochemical marketing

TAYLOR MEDICAL RANK: 451

2155 I-10 East
Beaumont, TX 77701
Phone: 409-835-1847
Fax: 409-832-1879

CEO: Todd Christopher
CFO: Eugene Humphery
HR: Linda Carter
Employees: 550

1992 Sales: $81 million
Ownership: Private

Industry: Medical products - wholesale

TCA CABLE TV, INC. RANK: 339

3015 SSE Loop 323
Tyler, TX 75701
Phone: 903-595-3701
Fax: 903-595-1929

CEO: Robert M. Rogers
CFO: Jimmie F. Taylor
HR: Jerry Yawdall
Employees: 772

1992 Sales: $139 million
Symbol: TCAT
Exchange: NASDAQ

Industry: Cable TV

TDINDUSTRIES INC. RANK: 495

13850 Diplomat Dr.
Dallas, TX 75234
Phone: 214-888-9500
Fax: 214-888-9338

CEO: Jack Lowe, Jr.
CFO: Michael J. Fitzpatrick
HR: Jessie McCain
Employees: 579

1992 Sales: $69 million
Ownership: Private

Industry: Building - mechanical contracting

TEXAS 500

TEAM, INC. RANK: 464

1001 Fannin, Ste. 4656
Houston, TX 77602
Phone: 713-659-3600
Fax: 713-659-3420

CEO: H. Wesley Hall
CFO: Russell G. Donham
HR: Clark Ingram
Employees: 1,076

1993 Sales: $77 million
Symbol: TMI
Exchange: AMEX

Industry: Pollution control equipment and services - emissions monitoring and manufacture of equipment for repair of leaks from chemical, volatile gas, and hazardous waste sources

TECH-SYM CORP. RANK: 278

10500 Westoffice Dr., Ste. 200
Houston, TX 77042
Phone: 713-785-7790
Fax: 713-780-3524

CEO: Wendell W. Gamel
CFO: Ray F. Thompson
HR: —
Employees: 1,812

1992 Sales: $180 million
Symbol: TSY
Exchange: NYSE

Industry: Electronics - parts distribution

TECNOL INC. RANK: 485

7201 Industrial Park Blvd.
Ft. Worth, TX 76180
Phone: 817-581-6424
Fax: 817-581-9354

CEO: Vance M. Hubbard
CFO: Vance M. Hubbard
HR: John Meadows
Employees: 861

1992 Sales: $71 million
Symbol: TCNL
Exchange: NASDAQ

Industry: Medical products

TEJAS GAS CORP. RANK: 114

1301 McKinney St., Ste. 700
Houston, TX 77010
Phone: 713-658-0509
Fax: 713-658-9600

CEO: Jay A. Precourt
CFO: Maurice D. McNeil
HR: Diane LaCount
Employees: 273

1992 Sales: $524 million
Symbol: TEJ
Exchange: NYSE

Industry: Oil and gas - production and pipeline

TEJAS POWER CORP. RANK: 273

200 Westlake Park Blvd.
Houston, TX 77079
Phone: 713-597-6200
Fax: 713-597-6500

CEO: Larry W. Bickle
CFO: J. Chris Jones
HR: Marianne Finch
Employees: 90

1992 Sales: $184 million
Symbol: TPC
Exchange: AMEX

Industry: Oil and gas - production and pipeline

TEXAS 500

TELECHECK SERVICES, INC.   RANK: 340

5251 Westheimer
Houston, TX 77056
Phone: 713-599-7600
Fax: 713-599-7854

CEO: J.D. Chaney
CFO: Roby Ogan
HR: Dominic Gallo
Employees: 1,500

1993 Sales: $138 million
Ownership: Private

Industry: Business services - check guarantee and verification

TEMPLE-INLAND INC.   RANK: 37

303 S. Temple Dr.
Diboll, TX 75941
Phone: 409-829-5511
Fax: 409-829-1366

CEO: Clifford J. Grum
CFO: Kenneth M. Jastrow II
HR: Vernon Burkhalter
Employees: 15,000

1992 Sales: $2,713 million
Symbol: TIN
Exchange: NYSE

Industry: Paper and paper products

TENNECO INC.   RANK: 5

Tenneco Bldg., 1010 Milam St.
Houston, TX 77002
Phone: 713-757-2131
Fax: 713-757-1410

CEO: Michael H. Walsh
CFO: Robert T. Blakely
HR: Barry R. Schuman
Employees: 79,000

1992 Sales: $13,139 million
Symbol: TGT
Exchange: NYSE

Industry: Diversified operations - construction and farm equipment, natural gas pipelines, shipbuilding, automotive parts, paperboard, and chemicals

See pages 96 – 97 for a full profile of this company.

TEPPCO PARTNERS, L.P.   RANK: 300

2929 Allen Pkwy.
Houston, TX 77019
Phone: 713-759-3636
Fax: 713-759-4726

CEO: Clifford Rackley
CFO: Charles H. Leonard
HR: Sharon Stratton
Employees: 500

1992 Sales: $166 million
Symbol: TPP
Exchange: NYSE

Industry: Oil and gas - pipeline

TESORO PETROLEUM CORP.   RANK: 63

8700 Tesoro Dr.
San Antonio, TX 78217
Phone: 210-828-8484
Fax: 210-828-8600

CEO: Michael D. Burke
CFO: Bruce A. Smith
HR: Thomas E. Reardon
Employees: 900

1992 Sales: $954 million
Symbol: TSO
Exchange: NYSE

Industry: Oil refining and marketing

TETCO INC.   RANK: 425

1777 NE Loop 410 #1500   CEO: Tom E. Turner   1992 Sales: $94 million
San Antonio, TX 78217   CFO: Dayton Simms   Ownership: Private
Phone: 210-821-5900   HR: William Bach
Fax: 210-826-3003   Employees: 1,200

Industry: Transportation - nationwide trucking

TEXAS INDUSTRIES, INC.   RANK: 95

7610 N. Stemmons Fwy.   CEO: Robert D. Rogers   1993 Sales: $614 million
Dallas, TX 75247   CFO: Richard M. Fowler   Symbol: TXI
Phone: 214-647-6700   HR: Brooke E. Brewer   Exchange: NYSE
Fax: 214-647-3878   Employees: 2,700

Industry: Building products - steel; concrete readymix, block and brick, pipe, and precast concrete

TEXAS INSTRUMENTS INCORPORATED   RANK: 11

13500 N. Central Expwy.   CEO: Jerry R. Junkins   1992 Sales: $7,440 million
Dallas, TX 75265   CFO: William A. Aylesworth   Symbol: TXN
Phone: 214-995-2551   HR: Charles F. Nielson   Exchange: NYSE
Fax: 214-995-3340   Employees: 60,577

Industry: Electrical components - semiconductors and microprocessors; calculators, weapons systems, missile guidance and navigation systems; laptop computers, printers, and software

See pages 98 – 99 for a full profile of this company.

TEXAS KENWORTH CO.   RANK: 491

4040 Irving Blvd.   CEO: V. E. Salvino   1992 Est. Sales: $70 mil.
Dallas, TX 75247   CFO: Lonnie Whiddon   Ownership: Private
Phone: 214-920-7300   HR: Bill Keutzer
Fax: 214-920-7318   Employees: 250

Industry: Automotive and trucking - wholesale truck tractors and trailers

TEXAS MILL SUPPLY INC.   RANK: 463

2413 Ave. K   CEO: Monte K. Legro   1992 Sales: $78 million
Galena Park, TX 77547   CFO: Leonard Truett   Ownership: Private
Phone: 713-675-2421   HR: Stephanie Williams
Fax: 713-675-0068   Employees: 265

Industry: Wholesale distribution - industrial, janitorial, and safety supplies

TEXAS 500

TEXAS OLEFINS CO. RANK: 192

8707 Katy Fwy., Ste. 300
Houston, TX 77024
Phone: 713-461-2223
Fax: 713-461-1029

CEO: B.W. Waycaster
CFO: C.E. Manning
HR: Jimmy Rhodes
Employees: 280

1992 Sales: $300 million
Ownership: Private

Industry: Chemicals - hydrocarbon fluids and industrial organic chemicals

TEXAS PIPE AND SUPPLY COMPANY INC. RANK: 476

2330 Holmes Rd.
Houston, TX 77051
Phone: 713-799-9235
Fax: 713-799-8701

CEO: Jerry R. Rubenstein
CFO: James R. Dunn
HR: Ruth Villamar
Employees: 115

1992 Sales: $75 million
Ownership: Private

Industry: Metal products - service center

TEXAS STADIUM CORPORATION RANK: 377

2401 E. Airport Fwy.
Irving, TX 75062
Phone: 214-438-7676
Fax: 214-438-4171

CEO: Jerry Jones
CFO: Bruce Hardy
HR: —
Employees: 50

1992 Sales: $112 million
Ownership: Private

Industry: Leisure and recreational services - management of Texas Stadium; owns professional football team the Dallas Cowboys

TEXAS UNITED CORP RANK: 478

2000 W. Loop South
Houston, TX 77027
Phone: 713-877-1778
Fax: 713-877-2605

CEO: Raymond W. Verhoeve
CFO: Bob Duboise
HR: Joe Pribyl
Employees: 400

1992 Sales: $74 million
Ownership: Private

Industry: Chemicals - industrial inorganic chemicals

TEXAS UTILITIES COMPANY RANK: 19

2001 Bryan Tower
Dallas, TX 75201
Phone: 214-812-4600
Fax: 214-812-4079

CEO: Jerry S. Farrington
CFO: H. Jarrell Gibbs
HR: Pitt Pittman
Employees: 14,023

1992 Sales: $4,908 million
Symbol: TXU
Exchange: NYSE

Industry: Utility - electric power, natural gas pipeline, and coal production

See pages 100 – 101 for a full profile of this company.

TEXAS 500

THOMPSON AND KNIGHT PC   RANK: 368

3300 1st City Center
Dallas, TX 75201
Phone: 214-969-1700
Fax: 214-969-1751

CEO: B. Berry
CFO: Mitch Hopwood
HR: Sam Phillips
Employees: 500

1992 Sales: $120 million
Ownership: Private

Industry: Business services - legal

TIC UNITED CORP.   RANK: 188

4645 N. Central Expwy.
Dallas, TX 75205
Phone: 214-559-0580
Fax: 214-559-9510

CEO: Stratton J. Georgoulis
CFO: Dean Marcy
HR: Harold Hatley
Employees: 2,000

1992 Sales: $300 million
Ownership: Private

Industry: Machinery - farm

TNP ENTERPRISES, INC.   RANK: 138

4100 International Plaza, Tower 2
Ft. Worth, TX 76109
Phone: 817-731-0099
Fax: 817-737-1384

CEO: James M. Tarpley
CFO: D. R. Barnard
HR: Dennis Cash
Employees: 1,086

1992 Sales: $444 million
Symbol: TNP
Exchange: NYSE

Industry: Utility - electric power

TRACOR INC.   RANK: 210

6500 Tracor Ln.
Austin, TX 78725
Phone: 512-926-2800
Fax: 512-929-2241

CEO: James B. Skaggs
CFO: Robert K. Floyd
HR: Murray Shaw
Employees: 3,400

1992 Sales: $262 million
Symbol: TTRR
Exchange: NASDAQ

Industry: Electronics - military and engineering

TRAMMELL CROW COMPANY   RANK: 294

2001 Ross Ave.
Dallas, TX 75201
Phone: 214-979-5100
Fax: 214-979-6058

CEO: H. Don Williams
CFO: Mike Decker
HR: Steve Laver
Employees: 2,400

1992 Sales: $170 million
Ownership: Private

Industry: Real estate operations - property management, hospital facilities management

See pages 124 – 125 for a full profile of this company.

TEXAS 500

TRANSCO ENERGY CO. RANK: 36
2800 Post Oak Blvd.
Houston, TX 77056
Phone: 713-439-2000
Fax: 713-439-2440

CEO: John P. DesBarres
CFO: John U. Clarke
HR: Thomas W. Spencer
Employees: 4,708

1992 Sales: $2,724 million
Symbol: E
Exchange: NYSE

Industry: Oil and gas - production and pipeline

TRI-GAS INC. RANK: 472
4545 Fuller Dr., Ste. 200
Irving, TX 75038
Phone: 214-650-1700
Fax: 214-717-2996

CEO: Jeff Ellis
CFO: John Olsen
HR: Lee Elder
Employees: 390

1992 Sales: $75 million
Ownership: Private

Industry: Chemicals - industrial gases such as oxygen, nitrogen, and argon

TRI-STATE WHOLESALE ASSOCIATED GROCERS INC. RANK: 191
1000 Hawkins Blvd.
El Paso, TX 79915
Phone: 915-774-6400
Fax: 915-774-6443

CEO: Stanton L. Irvin
CFO: Maxine H. Hixon
HR: Christine Wade
Employees: 325

1992 Sales: $300 million
Ownership: Private

Industry: Food - wholesale groceries

TRIANGLE PACIFIC CORP. RANK: 194
16803 Dallas Pkwy.
Dallas, TX 75248
Phone: 214-931-3000
Fax: 214-931-3284

CEO: Floyd Sherman
CFO: M. Joseph McHugh
HR: Debbie Wetterlin
Employees: 3,400

1992 Sales: $293 million
Symbol: TRIP
Exchange: NASDAQ

Industry: Building products - hardwood floors and wood kitchen cabinets

TRINITY INDUSTRIES, INC. RANK: 49
2525 Stemmons Fwy.
Dallas, TX 75207
Phone: 214-631-4420
Fax: 214-689-0501

CEO: W. Ray Wallace
CFO: K. W. Lewis
HR: Jack Cunningham
Employees: 13,000

1993 Sales: $1,540 million
Symbol: TRN
Exchange: NYSE

Industry: Transportation - manufacture and leasing of transportation equipment; rail freight cars, containers for liquefied gases, boats and barges, structural products (guardrails, girders, and beams)

TRITON ENERGY CORP. RANK: 385

6688 N. Central Expwy.
Dallas, TX 75206
Phone: 214-691-5200
Fax: 214-987-0571

CEO: William I. Lee
CFO: Robert W. Puetz
HR: Linda V. Austin
Employees: 628

1993 Sales: $110 million
Symbol: OIL
Exchange: NYSE

Industry: Oil and gas - US exploration and production

TRUMAN ARNOLD COMPANIES RANK: 170

701 S. Robinson Rd.
Texarkana, TX 75501
Phone: 903-794-3835
Fax: 903-838-5803

CEO: Truman Arnold
CFO: Larry Fincher
HR: Johnnie Edwards
Employees: 180

1992 Sales: $348 million
Ownership: Private

Industry: Oil and gas - wholesale petroleum products including gas and diesel fuel; airports, flying fields, and services

TTI INC. RANK: 369

2441 Northeast Pkwy.
Ft. Worth, TX 76106
Phone: 817-740-9000
Fax: 817-740-9988

CEO: Jack Darcy
CFO: Nick Kypreos
HR: Sharon Carrell
Employees: 500

1992 Sales: $120 million
Ownership: Private

Industry: Electronics - parts distribution, resistors and capacitors

TUBOSCOPE VETCO INTERNATIONAL INC. RANK: 302

2835 Holmes Rd.
Houston, TX 77051
Phone: 713-799-5100
Fax: 713-799-1460

CEO: William V. Larkin, Jr.
CFO: Ronald L. Koons
HR: Kenneth L. Nibling
Employees: 1,918

1992 Sales: $165 million
Symbol: TUBO
Exchange: NASDAQ

Industry: Oil and gas - field services

TUESDAY MORNING CORPORATION RANK: 309

14621 Inwood Rd.
Dallas, TX 75244
Phone: 214-387-3562
Fax: 214-387-2344

CEO: Lloyd L. Ross
CFO: Mark E. Jarvis
HR: Deborah Steenrod
Employees: 2,877

1992 Sales: $160 million
Symbol: TUES
Exchange: NASDAQ

Industry: Retail - discount variety merchandise including giftware, housewares, linens, luggage, and toys

See page 145 for a full profile of this company.

TEXAS 500

TYLER CORP. — RANK: 197

2121 San Jacinto St., Ste. 3200
Dallas, TX 75201
Phone: 214-754-7800
Fax: 214-969-9352

CEO: Joseph F. McKinney
CFO: W. Michael Kipphut
HR: Sandie Shepherd
Employees: 3,470

1992 Sales: $286 million
Symbol: TYL
Exchange: NYSE

Industry: Diversified operations - cast iron pipe and fittings, retail auto parts

U.S. CONTRACTORS INC. — RANK: 381

622 Commerce
Clute, TX 77531
Phone: 409-265-7451
Fax: 409-265-9281

CEO: Harold E. Monical
CFO: Lynn D. Monical
HR: Floyd Scott
Employees: 2,500

1992 Sales: $110 million
Ownership: Private

Industry: Building - general contractor of industrial plants

U.S. HOME CORP. — RANK: 86

1800 W. Loop South, Ste. 1850
Houston, TX 77027
Phone: 713-877-2311
Fax: 713-877-2387

CEO: Robert J. Strudler
CFO: Thomas A. Napoli
HR: Frank Matthews
Employees: 970

1992 Sales: $679 million
Symbol: UH
Exchange: NYSE

Industry: Building - residential and commercial

U.S. INTEC, INC. — RANK: 482

1212 Brai Dr.
Port Arthur, TX 77640
Phone: 409-724-7024
Fax: 409-724-2348

CEO: Danny J. Adair
CFO: Roane Ruddy
HR: Jody Young
Employees: 320

1992 Sales: $73 million
Symbol: USI
Exchange: AMEX

Industry: Building products - roofing materials

U.S. LONG DISTANCE CORP. — RANK: 444

9311 San Pedro Ave., Ste. 300
San Antonio, TX 78216-4476
Phone: 210-525-9009
Fax: 210-525-0389

CEO: Parris H. Holmes, Jr.
CFO: Kelly Simmons
HR: David S. Horne
Employees: 572

1992 Sales: $85 million
Symbol: USLD
Exchange: NASDAQ

Industry: Telecommunications services - including operator assistance and direct-dial long-distance services, 3rd party billing and information services

▶ See page 146 for a full profile of this company.

TEXAS 500

UETA INC. RANK: 253

3407 NE Pkwy.
San Antonio, TX 78218
Phone: 210-828-8382
Fax: 210-826-7588

CEO: John Edmondson
CFO: Ramon Bosquez
HR: Mary Ince
Employees: 600

1992 Sales: $200 million
Ownership: Private

Industry: Diversified operations - transportation; alcohol storage; wholesale (distilled liquors)

UNION TEXAS PETROLEUM HOLDINGS, INC. RANK: 80

1330 Post Oak Blvd.
Houston, TX 77056
Phone: 713-623-6544
Fax: 713-968-2771

CEO: A. Clark Johnson
CFO: Larry Kalmbach
HR: Vicki Pollman
Employees: 1,000

1992 Sales: $714 million
Symbol: UTH
Exchange: NYSE

Industry: Oil and gas - US exploration and production

UNITED INSURANCE COMPANIES, INC. RANK: 160

4001 McEwen Dr., Ste. 200
Dallas, TX 75244
Phone: 214-960-8497
Fax: 214-851-9097

CEO: Ronald L. Jensen
CFO: Vernon R. Woelke
HR: Linda Flowers
Employees: 650

1992 Sales: $371 million
Symbol: UICI
Exchange: NASDAQ

Industry: Insurance - health and accident

UNITED SUPERMARKETS INCORPORATED RANK: 173

7830 Orlando Ave.
Lubbock, TX 79423
Phone: 806-791-0220
Fax: 806-791-7480

CEO: Robert Snell
CFO: Kent Moore
HR: Jim Tye
Employees: 2,600

1992 Sales: $330 million
Ownership: Private

Industry: Retail - supermarkets (42 stores in Texas under the United Supermarkets name)

USAA RANK: 18

9800 Fredericksburg Rd.
San Antonio, TX 78288-0001
Phone: 210-498-2211
Fax: 210-498-9940

CEO: Robert T. Herres
CFO: Staser Holcomb
HR: Bill Tracy
Employees: 14,667

1992 Sales: $5,434 million
Ownership: Private

Industry: Insurance - multiline: automobile, health, and life; travel, retirement, and brokerage services; mutual funds; banking; retirement plans and services

See pages 102 – 103 for a full profile of this company.

TEXAS 500

VALERO ENERGY CORP.   RANK: 55

530 McCullough Ave.
San Antonio, TX 78215
Phone: 210-246-2000
Fax: 210-246-2103

CEO: William E. Greehey
CFO: Don Heep
HR: Steven Fry
Employees: 1,735

1992 Sales: $1,235 million
Symbol: VLO
Exchange: NYSE

Industry: Oil refining and marketing - natural gas pipeline and natural gas liquids

VALLEN CORP.   RANK: 287

13333 Northwest Fwy.
Houston, TX 77040
Phone: 713-462-8700
Fax: 713-462-7634

CEO: J.M. Wayne Code
CFO: Don B. Hair
HR: Kent M. Edwards
Employees: 720

1993 Sales: $175 million
Symbol: VALN
Exchange: NASDAQ

Industry: Protection - safety equipment and services

VANGUARD ENERGY CORP.   RANK: 159

1111 N. Loop West
Houston, TX 77008
Phone: 713-880-8750
Fax: 713-880-9311

CEO: Phillip Trotter
CFO: Phillip Trotter
HR: Phillip Trotter
Employees: 19

1992 Sales: $375 million
Ownership: Private

Industry: Oil and gas - wholesale petroleum and liquid petroleum gases

VAUGHAN AND SONS INC.   RANK: 459

10800 Sentinel
San Antonio, TX 78217
Phone: 210-590-9300
Fax: 210-590-1438

CEO: Curtis Vaughan III
CFO: Robert Vaughan
HR: Curtis Vaughan III
Employees: 300

1992 Sales: $80 million
Ownership: Private

Industry: Building products - wholesale and retail

VERAGON CORP.   RANK: 337

1415 West Loop North
Houston, TX 77055
Phone: 713-682-6848
Fax: 713-682-3104

CEO: Terry Tognietti
CFO: Wally Klemp
HR: Joan Cunningham
Employees: 110

1992 Sales: $140 million
Ownership: Private

Industry: Paper and paper products - diapers sold under the Drypers brand name (number one on the 1993 Inc. list of the fastest growing private companies)

VICTORIA BANKSHARES, INC. RANK: 361

One O'Connor Plaza
Victoria, TX 77902
Phone: 512-573-9432
Fax: 512-574-5612

CEO: Charles R. Hrdlicka
CFO: Edwin W. Dentler
HR: Barry Lacey
Employees: 981

1992 Sales: $123 million
Symbol: VICT
Exchange: NASDAQ

Industry: Bank

VINMAR INC. RANK: 257

523 N. Sam Houston
Houston, TX 77060
Phone: 713-445-0800
Fax: 713-445-1724

CEO: Vijay P. Goradia
CFO: Robert Whatley
HR: Cindy Taylor
Employees: 30

1992 Sales: $200 million
Ownership: Private

Industry: Chemicals - wholesale distributors of plastic raw materials and chemicals

VINSON & ELKINS L.L.P. RANK: 264

1001 Fannin St.
Houston, TX 77002-6760
Phone: 713-758-2222
Fax: 713-758-2346

CEO: Harry M. Reasoner
CFO: John W. Spire
HR: Sandra K. Hickle
Employees: 1,500

1992 Sales: $194 million
Ownership: Private

Industry: Business services - legal

VISTA CHEMICAL INC. RANK: 82

900 Threadneedle St.
Houston, TX 77079
Phone: 713-588-3000
Fax: 713-588-3119

CEO: James R. Ball
CFO: Robert Whitlow
HR: James R. Ball
Employees: 1,750

1992 Sales: $700 million
Ownership: Private

Industry: Chemicals - polyvinyl chloride resins

VISTA OIL CO. RANK: 269

PO Box 5127, 6 1/2 mi. N. 10th St.
McAllen, TX 78502
Phone: 210-381-0976
Fax: 210-383-1744

CEO: Gus E. Clemons, Jr.
CFO: Gary Clemons
HR: Gus E. Clemons, Jr.
Employees: 20

1992 Sales: $190 million
Ownership: Private

Industry: Diversified operations - wholesaler of rubber tires and petroleum products

TEXAS 500

VOLUNTARY HOSPITALS OF AMERICA INC. RANK: 384

5215 N. O'Connor Rd.
Irving, TX 75039
Phone: 214-830-0000
Fax: 214-830-0141

CEO: C. Thomas Smith
CFO: Curt Nonomaque
HR: Ellie Johnson
Employees: 950

1992 Sales: $110 million
Ownership: Private

Industry: Medical products - medical supplies, pharmaceuticals, and information systems

W. O. BANKSTON ENTERPRISES INC. RANK: 277

4755 McEwen Rd.
Dallas, TX 75244
Phone: 214-788-5400
Fax: 214-490-6753

CEO: James G. Bankston
CFO: Chris Price
HR: James G. Bankston
Employees: 530

1992 Sales: $181 million
Ownership: Private

Industry: Retail - automobiles

W.S. BELLOWS CONSTRUCTION CORP. RANK: 423

1906 Afton
Houston, TX 77055
Phone: 713-680-2132
Fax: 713-680-0643

CEO: Thomas F. Bellows
CFO: John Vague
HR: Thomas F. Bellows
Employees: 100

1992 Sales: $95 million
Ownership: Private

Industry: Building - commercial and heavy plant construction

WAGNER AND BROWN, LTD. RANK: 434

PO Box 1714, Summit Bldg.
Midland, TX 79702
Phone: 915-682-7936
Fax: 915-686-5928

CEO: Joel L. Reed
CFO: A. J. Brune III
HR: Sherri Rotan
Employees: 280

1992 Sales: $91 million
Ownership: Private

Industry: Oil and gas - exploration and production

WAINOCO OIL CORP. RANK: 465

1200 Smith St., Ste. 1500
Houston, TX 77002
Phone: 713-658-9900
Fax: 713-658-8136

CEO: John B. Ashmun
CFO: James Gibbs
HR: Wayne Meyer
Employees: 434

1992 Sales: $77 million
Symbol: WOL
Exchange: NYSE

Industry: Oil and gas - US exploration and production

WALSH-LUMPKIN DRUG CO. — RANK: 416

5005 State Line Ave.
Texarkana, TX 75503
Phone: 903-794-5141
Fax: 903-794-3728

CEO: Ron Nelson
CFO: David Harrel
HR: Lou Lynch
Employees: 100

1992 Sales: $100 million
Ownership: Private

Industry: Drugs and sundries - wholesale

WARREN ELECTRIC CO. — RANK: 410

2929 McKinney
Houston, TX 77003
Phone: 713-236-0971
Fax: 713-236-0971

CEO: R.V. Bob Williams
CFO: Wil Parmley
HR: Anna Eldred
Employees: 250

1992 Sales: $100 million
Ownership: Private

Industry: Electronics - parts and equipment

WEATHERFORD INTERNATIONAL INC. — RANK: 251

1360 Post Oak Blvd., Ste. 1000
Houston, TX 77056
Phone: 713-439-9400
Fax: 713-621-0994

CEO: Philip Burguieres
CFO: Norman W. Nolen
HR: Jon Nicholson
Employees: 2,763

1992 Sales: $206 million
Symbol: WII
Exchange: AMEX

Industry: Oil and gas - field services

WEEKLEY HOMES INC. — RANK: 176

1300 Post Oak Blvd.
Houston, TX 77056
Phone: 713-963-0500
Fax: 713-621-8384

CEO: David Weekley
CFO: Barry Kulpa
HR: Steve Miller
Employees: 500

1992 Sales: $330 million
Ownership: Private

Industry: Building - residential single-unit homes

WEINERS ENTERPRISES — RANK: 179

6005 Westview
Houston, TX 77055
Phone: 713-688-1331
Fax: 713-688-6976

CEO: Leon Weiner
CFO: Robert Shapiro
HR: Larry Kleypas
Employees: 5,500

1992 Sales: $320 million
Ownership: Private

Industry: Retail - discount and variety apparel, housewares, domestics, and toys

TEXAS 500

WEINGARTEN REALTY INVESTORS — RANK: 437
2600 Citadel Plaza Dr.
Houston, TX 77292
Phone: 713-866-6000
Fax: 713-866-6049
CEO: Stanford Alexander
CFO: Joseph W. Robertson, Jr.
HR: Judy Barnes
Employees: 13
1992 Sales: $90 million
Symbol: WRI
Exchange: NYSE

Industry: Real estate investment trust

WELLTECH INC. — RANK: 426
3535 Briarpark, Ste. 200
Houston, TX 77042
Phone: 713-975-1600
Fax: 713-977-7331
CEO: Douglas B. Thompson
CFO: Ted Owen
HR: Leslye Carter
Employees: 1,200
1992 Sales: $94 million
Ownership: Private

Industry: Oil field machinery and equipment - drill equipment repairs

WEST TEXAS EQUIPMENT CO. — RANK: 475
2301 Production Ln.
Midland, TX 79761
Phone: 915-332-1681
Fax: 915-563-1871
CEO: Johnny Warren
CFO: Rick Bartholomee
HR: Sharon McCrary
Employees: 250
1992 Est. Sales: $75 mil.
Ownership: Private

Industry: Machinery - wholesale Caterpillar construction equipment

WESTERN CO. OF NORTH AMERICA — RANK: 181
515 Post Oak Blvd.
Houston, TX 77027
Phone: 713-629-2600
Fax: 713-629-2722
CEO: Sheldon R. Erikson
CFO: Thomas R. Hix
HR: Jane Crowder
Employees: 2,700
1992 Sales: $315 million
Symbol: WSN
Exchange: NYSE

Industry: Oil and gas - field services

WHATABURGER SYSTEMS — RANK: 236
4600 Parkdale Dr.
Corpus Christi, TX 78411
Phone: 512-855-3836
Fax: 512-878-0647
CEO: G. W. Dobson
CFO: Bruce Able
HR: Pete Opel
Employees: 8,500
1992 Sales: $230 million
Ownership: Private

Industry: Retail - restaurants

TEXAS 500

WHITE SWAN INC.   RANK: 74

400 Fuller-Wiser Rd., Ste. 300
Euless, TX 76039
Phone: 817-283-5444
Fax: 817-283-1391

CEO: Ronald E. Elmquist
CFO: Robert Smith
HR: Rudy Zinsmeister
Employees: 1,500

1992 Sales: $780 million
Ownership: Private

Industry: Food - institutional distribution

WHOLE FOODS MARKET, INC.   RANK: 365

2525 Wallingwood Dr., Ste. 1400
Austin, TX 78746
Phone: 512-328-7541
Fax: 512-328-5482

CEO: John Mackey
CFO: Glenda Flanagan
HR: Rema Cunningham
Employees: 2,350

1992 Sales: $120 million
Symbol: WFMI
Exchange: NASDAQ

Industry: Retail - natural foods supermarkets

See page 147 for a full profile of this company.

WHOLESALE ELECTRIC SUPPLY COMPANY OF HOUSTON, INC.   RANK: 412

4040 Gulf Fwy.
Houston, TX 77004
Phone: 713-748-6100
Fax: 713-749-8415

CEO: Clyde G. Rutland
CFO: Joe R. Jones, Sr.
HR: Joe R. Jones, Sr.
Employees: 215

1992 Est. Sales: $100 mil.
Ownership: Private

Industry: Electrical products - wholesaler of electric apparatus and equipment

WILLIAMSON-DICKIE MANUFACTURING CO.   RANK: 186

319 Lipscomb
Ft. Worth, TX 76104
Phone: 817-336-7201
Fax: 817-877-5027

CEO: Steven Lefler
CFO: Frank E. Brock
HR: Estelle Lewis
Employees: 4,000

1992 Sales: $300 million
Ownership: Private

Industry: Apparel - men's trousers and work clothing

WILSON INDUSTRIES INCORPORATED   RANK: 190

1301 Conti
Houston, TX 77002
Phone: 713-237-3700
Fax: 713-237-3300

CEO: Wallace S. Wilson
CFO: James K. Andrews
HR: Anne Gray
Employees: 736

1992 Sales: $300 million
Ownership: Private

Industry: Oil field machinery and equipment - wholesale

TEXAS 500

WING INDUSTRIES INC. RANK: 496
11999 Plano Rd., Ste. 110
Dallas, TX 75243
Phone: 214-699-9900
Fax: 214-470-9304
Industry: Textiles - millwork

CEO: Sam A. Wing, Jr.
CFO: Tom Cox
HR: Lonnie Duke
Employees: 400

1992 Est. Sales: $69 mil.
Ownership: Private

WINGATE PARTNERS LP RANK: 60
750 N. Saint Paul St.
Dallas, TX 75201
Phone: 214-720-1313
Fax: 214-871-8799

CEO: James Callier
CFO: James Callier
HR: Janet Holderness
Employees: 8,800

1992 Sales: $1,000 million
Ownership: Private

Industry: Financial - leveraged buyout firm; partners: James Callier, Frederick B. Hegi, James Johnson, Thomas Sturgess

WINN'S STORES INCORPORATED RANK: 237
4342 N. Panam Expwy.
San Antonio, TX 78218
Phone: 210-227-4747
Fax: 210-222-8527
Industry: Retail - variety stores

CEO: Doug Wise
CFO: Bill Hale
HR: Patsy Beck
Employees: 3,200

1992 Sales: $221 million
Ownership: Private

WRIGHT BRAND FOODS INC. RANK: 392
1306 Main St.
Vernon, TX 76384
Phone: 817-553-1811
Fax: 817-552-2912
Industry: Food - bacon and ham products

CEO: W. D. Wright
CFO: Bob Williamson
HR: Sarah Lowery
Employees: 510

1992 Sales: $108 million
Ownership: Private

WYATT CAFETERIAS INC. RANK: 185
10726 Plano Rd.
Dallas, TX 75238
Phone: 214-349-0060
Fax: 214-553-7798
Industry: Retail - restaurants and food (wholesale groceries)

CEO: Richard Gozia
CFO: Matt Peiffer
HR: Nancy Schuerr
Employees: 5,500

1992 Sales: $300 million
Ownership: Private

TEXAS 500

WYNDHAM HOTEL COMPANY LTD. — RANK: 157

2001 Bryan St., Ste. 2300
Dallas, TX 75201
Phone: 214-978-4500
Fax: 214-978-4695

CEO: Jim Carreker
CFO: John P. Klumph
HR: Brian Goodwin
Employees: 6,000

1992 Sales: $384 million
Ownership: Private

Industry: Hotels and motels - administrative hotel management

XERON INC. — RANK: 305

9301 S.W. Fwy.
Houston, TX 77074
Phone: 713-988-0051
Fax: 713-988-3476

CEO: Ernest Allen
CFO: Patrick E. Armand
HR: Patrick E. Armand
Employees: 8

1992 Sales: $163 million
Ownership: Private

Industry: Oil refining and marketing - petroleum bulk stations and terminals; wholesale liquefied petroleum gas from bulk

YORK GROUP INC., THE — RANK: 402

9430 Old Katy Rd.
Houston, TX 77055
Phone: 713-984-5500
Fax: 713-984-5569

CEO: Eldon Nuss
CFO: Dave Beck
HR: Tony Wheeler
Employees: 1,000

1992 Sales: $100 million
Ownership: Private

Industry: Wholesale distribution - funeral caskets

ZALE HOLDING CORPORATION — RANK: 61

901 W. Walnut Hill Ln.
Irving, TX 75038
Phone: 214-580-4000
Fax: 214-580-5523

CEO: Andreas Ludwig
CFO: Andreas Ludwig
HR: Wayne Majors
Employees: 9,000

1993 Sales: $981 million
Symbol: ZALE
Exchange: NASDAQ

Industry: Retail - jewelry stores

ZAPATA CORP. — RANK: 394

711 Louisiana St., Zapata Tower
Houston, TX 77002
Phone: 713-226-6000
Fax: 713-940-6111

CEO: Ronald C. Lassiter
CFO: Marvin J. Migura
HR: Kay Guhlin
Employees: 1,200

1992 Sales: $106 million
Symbol: ZOS
Exchange: NYSE

Industry: Oil and gas - offshore drilling

MORE TEXAS INFORMATION

TEXAS COMERS*

AMTECH CORPORATION

17304 Preston Rd., East 100
Dallas, TX 75252
Phone: 214-733-6600
Fax: 214-733-6699

CEO: G. Russell Mortenson
CFO: Steve M. York
HR: Joe Crumpton
Employees: 272

1992 Sales: $40 million
Symbol: AMTC
Exchange: NASDAQ

Industry: Computer software - radio frequency electronic identification (RFID) tagging used in transportation systems, including rail, intermodal freight, air freight, and electronic toll and traffic management.

BENCHMARK ELECTRONICS INC.

802 W. Brazos Park Dr.
Clute, TX 77531
Phone: 409-265-0991
Fax: 409-266-4271

CEO: Donald E. Nigbor
CFO: Cary T. Fu
HR: Gwen Holden
Employees: 307

1992 Sales: $51 million
Symbol: BHE
Exchange: AMEX

Industry: Electrical components - circuit boards and manufacturing services to makers of communications equipment, medical devices and instruments, business computers, and testing equipment.

DATA RACE INC.

11550 IH-10 West, Ste. 395
San Antonio, TX 78230
Phone: 210-558-1900
Fax: 210-558-1929

CEO: Herbert T. Hensley
CFO: Steven W. Riebel
HR: Herbert T. Hensley
Employees: 150

1992 Sales: $44 million
Symbol: RACE
Exchange: NASDAQ

Industry: Telecommunications equipment - design, manufacture, and marketing of data communications products for faxing from portable computers; also data/fax modems and multiplexers.

DF & R RESTAURANTS INC.

2350 Airport Fwy., Ste. 640
Bedford, TX 76022
Phone: 817-571-6682
Fax: 817-354-9640

CEO: David P. Frazier
CFO: Lawrence M. Folk
HR: Liz Starkey
Employees: 1,508

1992 Sales: $45 million
Symbol: DFNR
Exchange: NASDAQ

Retail - restaurants, under the names Harrigan's and Don Pablo's, operating in the Southwest as well as Ohio and Indiana.

INPUT-OUTPUT INC.

4235 Grenbriar Dr.
Staford, TX 77477
Phone: 713-240-2200
Fax: 713-240-2419

CEO: Charles E. Selecman
CFO: Robert P. Brindley
HR: Lacey Rice
Employees: 166

1992 Sales: $54 million
Symbol: IPOP
Exchange: NASDAQ

Industry: Oil field equipment - seismic data acquisition systems and peripheral seismic instruments for oil and gas exploration and production.

TEXAS COMERS*

INTERVOICE INC.

17811 Waterview Pwy.
Dallas, TX 75252
Phone: 214-669-3988
Fax: 214-907-1079

CEO: Daniel D. Hammon
CFO: Donald B. Crosbie
HR: Cathy Hackney
Employees: 262

1992 Sales: $45 million
Symbol: INTV
Exchange: NASDAQ

Industry: Telecommunications equipment - voice automation systems to access computer databases by telephone, credit card terminal, or voice.

STECK-VAUGHN CO.

3520 Executive Center Dr., Ste. 300
Austin, TX 78731-1671
Phone: 512-343-8227
Fax: 512-343-8293

CEO: Roy Mayers
CFO: Floyd Rogers
HR: Patricia Frisbie
Employees: 293

1992 Sales: $45 million
Symbol: STEK
Exchange: NASDAQ

Industry: Publishing - books, workbooks, and other materials used in elementary, secondary, and adult education.

TACO CABANA INC.

3309 San Pedro Ave.
San Antonio, TX 78212
Phone: 210-231-6090
Fax: 210-231-6099

CEO: Richard Cervera
CFO: Judith Reitzer
HR: Judith Reitzer
Employees: 2,040

1992 Sales: $59 million
Symbol: TACO
Exchange: NASDAQ

Industry: Retail - restaurants under the Taco Cabana name.

TANKOLOGY ENVIRONMENTAL, INC.

5225 Hollister St.
Houston, TX 77040-6294
Phone: 713-690-8265
Fax: 713-690-2255

CEO: Robert L. Waltrip
CFO: Rick Berry
HR: Beth Martin
Employees: 337

1992 Sales: $38 million
Symbol: TANK
Exchange: NASDAQ

Industry: Pollution control - detection of leaks in above-ground and underground storage tanks, vapor recovery systems, and tank supply lines.

USA WASTE SERVICES, INC.

5000 Quorum Dr., Ste. 445
Dallas, TX 75240
Phone: 214-233-4212
Fax: 214-385-1757

CEO: Donald F. Moorehead
CFO: Earl E. Defrates
HR: Diana Neal
Employees: 400

1992 Sales: $52 million
Symbol: USAS
Exchange: NASDAQ

Industry: Pollution control - solid waste management, including collection, transfer, and disposal; recycling; and landfill operation.

---

* These public companies were just a bit too small to make the Texas 500. However, based on their rapid rate of growth we think they merit your attention and will likely show up in the next edition of this book.

80 OF THE LARGEST TEXAS EMPLOYERS HEADQUARTERED OUT OF STATE

ABBOTT LABORATORIES
Diagnostic Division
1921 Hurd Dr.
Irving, Texas 75015
Phone: 214-518-6000
Number of Texas Employees: 11,866

ADVANCED MICRO DEVICES, INC.
5204 E. Ben White Blvd.
Austin, TX 78741
Phone: 512-385-8542
Number of Texas Employees: 2,200

ALBERTSON'S INC.
7580 Oak Grove Rd.
Fort Worth, Texas 76140
Phone: 817-568-2900
Number of Texas Employees: 11,306

ALCON LABORATORIES, INC.
Alcon Precision Device
6201 South Fwy.
Fort Worth, TX 76134
Phone: 817-293-0450
Number of Texas Employees: 4,600
Parent: Nestle SA

AMERICAN BUILDING MAINTENANCE INDUSTRIES, INC.
330 South R. L. Thornton Fwy.
Dallas, TX 75203
Phone: 214-941-0584
Number of Texas Employees: 4,960

AMERICAN TELEPHONE AND TELEGRAPH COMPANY
Business Network Services
5501 Lyndon Johnson Fwy.
Dallas, TX 75240-6202
Phone: 214-851-4556
Number of Texas Employees: 10,259

AMOCO OIL CO.
2401 5th Ave. South
Texas City, TX 77592
Phone: 409-945-1011
Fax: 409-942-4083
Number of Texas Employees: 15,951
Parent: Amoco Corporation

ANHEUSER-BUSCH COMPANIES, INC.
775 Gellhorn
Houston, TX 77229
Phone: 713-675-2311
Number of Texas Employees: 3,888

ARCO OIL AND GAS CO.
1601 Bryan St.
Dallas, TX 75201-3420
Phone: 214-880-2500
Fax: 214-880-5100
Number of Texas Employees: 7,172
Parent: Atlantic Richfield Company

ASSOCIATES CORPORATION OF NORTH AMERICA
250 E. John W. Carpenter Fwy.
Irving, TX 75062
Phone: 214-541-4000
Fax: 214-541-4001
Number of Texas Employees: 12,226
Parent: Ford Motor Company

Note: Not all Texas employees may be at the location indicated in the entry.

80 OF THE LARGEST TEXAS EMPLOYERS HEADQUARTERED OUT OF STATE

BANC ONE CORPORATION
1717 Main St.
Dallas, Texas 75201
Phone: 214-290-2000
Number of Texas Employees: 11,211

BELL HELICOPTER TEXTRON INC.
Hwy 10, PO Box 482
Fort Worth, Texas 76101-0482
Phone: 817-280-2011
Fax: 817-280-2321
Number of Texas Employees: 7,720
Parent: Textron Inc.

BEVERLY ENTERPRISES, INC.
Leisure Lodge
1205 Santa Fe Dr.
Weatherford, TX 76086-5819
Phone: 817-594-2786
Number of Texas Employees: 6,970

BOEING ELECTRONICS
3131 Story Rd. West
Irving, TX 75038-3514
Phone: 214-659-2600
Number of Texas Employees: 3,670
Parent: The Boeing Company

CALTEX PETROLEUM CORPORATION
125 E. John Carpenter Fwy.
Irving, TX 75062
Phone: 214-830-1000
Fax: 214-830-1081
Number of Texas Employees: 7,800
Joint Venture, Texaco Inc. and Chevron Corporation

CENTRAL FREIGHT LINES INC.
5601 W. Waco Dr.
Waco, TX 76710
Phone: 817-772-2120
Fax: 817-772-4944
Number of Texas Employees: 4,592
Parent: Roadway Services, Inc.

CHAMPION INTERNATIONAL CORPORATION
Champion Papers Division
11611 5th St.
Houston, TX 77044-8780
Phone: 713-456-8780
Number of Texas Employees: 4021

CHEVRON INDUSTRIES INC.
Chevron Exploration and Production
2811 Hayes Rd.
Houston, Texas 77082
Phone: 713-596-2000
Fax: 713-754-2016
Number of Texas Employees: 9,251
Parent: Chevron Corporation

CHRYSLER TECHNOLOGIES AIRBORNE SYSTEMS
7500 Maehr Rd.
Waco, TX 76705
Phone: 817-799-5533
Number of Texas Employees: 5,328
Parent: Chrysler Corporation

COCA-COLA BOTTLING COMPANY OF NORTH TEXAS
6011 Lemmon Ave.
Dallas, TX 75209-2005
Phone: 214-357-1781
Number of Texas Employees: 5,833
Parent: Coca-Cola Enterprises, Inc.

Note: Not all Texas employees may be at the location indicated in the entry.

80 OF THE LARGEST TEXAS EMPLOYERS HEADQUARTERED OUT OF STATE

COLLINS INTERNATIONAL SERVICE CO.
3200 E. Renner Rd.
Richardson, Texas 75082
Phone: 214-705-0000
Number of Texas Employees: 9,115
Parent: Rockwell International Corporation

DOW CHEMICAL USA TEXAS OPERATION
2301 Francis Brazos
Freeport, TX 77541
Phone: 409-238-2011
Fax: 409-238-2276
Number of Texas Employees: 18,223
Parent: The Dow Chemical Company

CROWN MEDIA, INC.
1 Galleria Tower 1650
Dallas, TX 75240
Phone: 214-702-7380
Number of Texas Employees: 2,000
Parent: Hallmark Cards Incorporated

E.I. DUPONT DE NEMOURS & CO.
Hwy. 347, Box 3269
Beaumont, TX 77704
Phone: 409-722-3451
Fax: 409-727-9673
Number of Texas Employees: 16,646

DAYTON HUDSON CORP.
777 Nicollet Mall
Minneapolis, MN 55402
Phone: 612-370-6948
Fax: 612-370-5502
Number of Texas Employees: 13,921

EASTMAN KODAK COMPANY
District Marketing Center
Greenspoint 4
6945 N. Chase Dr., Ste. 1800
Houston, TX 77060-2133
Phone: 713-874-6897
Fax: 713-874-6897
Number of Texas Employees: 3,067

DECKER FOOD CO.
3200 W. Kingsley
Garland, TX 75041
Phone: 214-278-6192
Fax: 214-278-1983
Number of Texas Employees: 6,430
Parent: ConAgra, Inc.

FLUOR TEXAS INC.
One Fluor Daniel Dr.
Sugarland, TX 77478
Phone: 713-263-1000
Number of Texas Employees: 3,338
Parent: Flour Corporation

DILLARD DEPARTMENT STORES, INC.
4501 North Beach St.
Fort Worth, Texas 76111
Phone: 817-568-3900
Number of Texas Employees: 11,437

FOLEY'S DEPARTMENT STORE
1110 Main St.
Houston, TX 77002
Phone: 713-651-7038
Fax: 713-651-6937
Number of Texas Employees: 11,957
Parent: The May Department Stores Co.

Note: Not all Texas employees may be at the location indicated in the entry.

80 OF THE LARGEST TEXAS EMPLOYERS HEADQUARTERED OUT OF STATE

FOODMAKER, INC.
1111 N. Loop West, Ste. 600
Houston, TX 77008-1778
Phone: 713-863-0300
Fax: 713-863-1219
Number of Employees in Texas: 3,762

FRITO-LAY INC.
7701 Legacy Dr.
Plano, TX 75024
Phone: 214-334-7000
Fax: 214-334-2019
Number of Texas Employees: 12,000
Parent: PepsiCo, Inc.

GENERAL ELECTRIC COMPANY
Distributing Equipment Division
3530 W. 12th St.
Houston, TX 77008
Phone: 713-864-4431
Fax: 713-880-7441
Number of Texas Employees: 8,721

GENERAL MOTORS CORPORATION
C-P-C Group
2525 E. Abram
Arlington, TX 76010-2071
Phone: 817-652-2580
Fax: 817-652-2190
Number of Texas Employees: 47,466

W.R. GRACE & CO. INC.
Composite Technology
1005 Blue Mound Rd.
Ft. Worth, TX 76131-1403
Phone: 817-232-1127
Number of Texas Employees: 3,537

GTE SOUTHWEST INC.
290 E. Carpenter Fwy.
Irving, Texas 75062
Phone: 214-717-7700
Fax: 214-859-9212
Number of Texas Employees: 14,950
Parent: GTE Corporation

GULF COAST MEDICAL CENTER
1400 Hwy. 59 Bypass
Wharton, TX 77488
Phone: 409-532-2500
Number of Texas Employees: 7,060
Parent: HealthTrust Inc., The Hospital Co.

HARCOURT GENERAL, INC.
27 Boylston St.
Boston, MA 02116
Phone: 617-232-8200
Number of Texas Employees: 6,351

HALL-MARK ELECTRONICS CORP.
11333 Pagemill Rd.
Dallas, TX 75243
Phone: 214-343-5000
Number of Texas Employees: 1,546
Parent: Avnet Inc.

HUMANA HEALTH PLAN OF TEXAS
8431 Fredericksburg Rd.
San Antonio, TX 78229
Phone: 210-617-1000
Number of Texas Employees: 7,517
Parent: Humana Inc.

Note: Not all Texas employees may be at the location indicated in the entry.

80 OF THE LARGEST TEXAS EMPLOYERS HEADQUARTERED OUT OF STATE

INTERCRAFT COMPANY, INC.
One Intercraft Plaza
Taylor, TX 76574
Phone: 512-352-8501
Number of Texas Employees: 1,800
Parent: The A. Newell Company

THE KROGER COMPANY
1014 Vine St.
Cincinnati, OH 45402
Phone: 513-762-4000
Fax: 513-762-4454
Number of Texas Employees: 24,692

INTERNATIONAL BUSINESS MACHINES
11400 Burnet Rd.
Austin, Texas 78758-3406
Phone: 512-823-0000
Fax: 512-823-8449
Number of Texas Employees: 8,664

LOCKHEED ENGINEERING AND SCIENCES COMPANY
2625 Bay Area Blvd.
Houston, TX 77058
Phone: 713-333-6200
Fax: 713-283-4660
Number of Texas Employees: 27,826
Parent: Lockheed Corporation

JOHNSON & JOHNSON MEDICAL INC.
2500 E. Arbrook Blvd.
Arlington, TX 76014-3631
Phone: 817-465-3141
Number of Texas Employees: 3,985
Parent: Johnson & Johnson

LORAL CORPORATION
1902 W. Freeway
Grand Prarie, TX 75051
Phone: 214-603-1000
Number of Texas Employees: 11,840

KELLY SPRINGFIELD TIRE CO.
SH 31 West
Tyler, Texas 75709
Phone: 903-535-1500
Fax: 903-535-1643
Number of Texas Employees: 4,934
Parent: The Goodyear Tire and Rubber Co.

MARRIOT CORPORATION
Regional Center
5151 Belt Line Rd.
Dallas, TX 75240-7545
Phone: 214-385-1600
Number of Texas Employees: 9,011

KMART CORPORATION
3100 W. Big Beaver Rd.
Troy, MI 48084
Phone: 313-643-1000
Fax: 313-643-5249
Number of Texas Employees: 23,278

MCI COMMUNICATIONS CORP.
2400 N. Glenville Dr.
Richardson TX, 75082
Phone: 214-918-3000
Number of Texas Employees: 3,452

Note: Not all Texas employees may be at the location indicated in the entry.

80 OF THE LARGEST TEXAS EMPLOYERS HEADQUARTERED OUT OF STATE

MILLER BREWING CO.

7001 South Fwy.
Fort Worth, TX 76314-4099
Phone: 817-551-3300
Number of Texas Employees: 5,115
Parent: Philip Morris Companies Inc.

MINNESOTA MINING AND MANUFACTURING CO.

Electronic Products Division
3M Austin Center, 6801 River Place Blvd.
Austin, Texas 78726
Phone: 512-984-1800
Number of Texas Employees: 5,706

MOBIL OIL CORP., BEAUMONT REFINERY

End of Burt St., PO Box 3311
Beaumont, TX 77701
Phone: 409-833-9411
Fax: 409-757-3798
Number of Texas Employees: 15,079
Parent: Mobil Corporation

MOTOROLA INC.

Microprocessor and Memory Technologies Group
6501 William Cannon Dr. W.
Austin, Texas 78735
Phone: 512-891-2553
Number of Texas Employees: 9,914

NATIONAL MEDICAL ENTERPRISES, INC.

Cedar Creek Hospital
7200 W. 9th Ave.
Amarillo, TX 79106-1703
Phone: 806-354-7500
Number of Texas Employees: 6,583

NATIONSBANK OF TEXAS

910 Main St.
Dallas, TX 75202
Phone: 214-508-6262
Fax: 214-508-1490
Number of Texas Employees: 14,645
Parent: NationsBank Corporation

OCCIDENTAL CHEMICAL CORP.

5005 Lyndon B. Johnson Fwy.
Dallas, TX 75244
Phone: 214-404-3800
Fax: 214-408-3669
Number of Texas Employees: 7,885
Parent: Occidental Petroleum Corporation

PHIBRO ENERGY INC.

One Allen Center, Ste. 3200
Houston, TX 77002
Phone: 713-646-5200
Fax: 713-646-5275
Number of Texas Employees: 1,650
Parent: Salomon Inc.

PHILLIPS PETROLEUM CO., BORGER REFINERY

300 W. 6th
Borger, Texas 79007
Phone: 806-273-2831
Fax: 806-275-1361
Number of Texas Employees: 11,912
Parent: Phillips Petroleum Company

PINKERTON'S SECURITY SERVICE

6024 Gateway Blvd. E 1c
El Paso, TX 79905-2003
Phone: 915-778-9261
Number of Texas Employees: 4,304
Parent: Pinkerton's Inc.

Note: Not all Texas employees may be at the location indicated in the entry.

80 OF THE LARGEST TEXAS EMPLOYERS HEADQUARTERED OUT OF STATE

PRIMERICA FINANCIAL SERVICES INC.
450 N. Sam Houston Pkwy. E.
Houston, TX 77060-3520
Phone: 713-448-4100
Number of Texas Employees: 3,536
Parent: Primerica Corp.

RYDER SYSTEM INC.
Airline Services Division
7515 Lemmon Ave, Bldg. J
Dallas, TX 75209
Phone: 214-956-5000
Number of Texas Employees: 8,339

RADIAN CORPORATION
8501 Mopac Expy.
Austin, TX 78759
Phone: 512-454-4797
Number of Texas Employees: 2,391
Parent: The Hartford Steam Boiler Inspection and Insurance Company

SCHLUMBERGER TECHNOLOGY CORP.
Well Service Division
5000 Gulf Fwy.
Houston, Texas 77023
Phone: 713-928-4000
Number of Texas Employees: 6,148
Parent: Schlumberger NV

RALPH WILSON PLASTICS CO., INC.
600 General Bruce Dr.
Temple, TX 76504
Phone: 817-778-2711
Number of Texas Employees: 2600
Parent: Premark International, Inc.

SEARS, ROEBUCK AND CO.
Sears Tower, 233 S. Wacker Dr.
Chicago, IL 60684
Phone: 312-875-2500
Fax: 312-875-8351
Number of Texas Employees: 20,354

RANK HOTELS, INC.
15303 Dallas Pkwy.
Dallas, TX 75248
Phone: 214-458-7265
Fax: 214-991-5647
Number of Texas Employees: 2,500
Parent: The Rank Organisation PLC

STAR ENTERPRISE
12700 Northborough Dr.
Houston, TX 77067
Phone: 713-874-7000
Fax: 713-874-3879
Number of Texas Employees: 4,000
Joint Venture, Texaco, Inc. and Aramco

RUST ENCLEAN, INC.
6750 West Loop South, Ste. 1000
Bellaire, TX 77401
Phone: 713-661-4777
Fax: 713-661-0742
Number of Texas Employees: 1,750
Parent: WMX Technologies, Inc.

TEXACO CHEMICAL COMPANY
3040 Post Oak Blvd.
Houston, Texas 77056
Phone: 713-961-3711
Fax: 713-235-6480
Number of Texas Employees: 9,277
Parent: Texaco Inc.

Note: Not all Texas employees may be at the location indicated in the entry.

80 OF THE LARGEST TEXAS EMPLOYERS HEADQUARTERED OUT OF STATE

TEXAS COMMERCE BANKSHARES

712 Main St.
Houston, Texas 77002
Phone: 713-236-4865
Fax: 713-216-6071
Number of Texas Employees: 13,839
Parent: Chemical Banking Corporation

TYSON FOODS, INC.

1019 Shelbyville St.
Center, TX 75935-3741
Phone: 409-598-2723
Number of Texas Employees: 3,655

UNION CARBIDE CORP.

10235 W. Little York, 3rd Fl.
Houston, TX 77040
Phone: 713-466-4433
Number of Texas Employees: 3,867

USPCI INC.

515 W. Greens Rd., Ste. 500
Houston, TX 77067
Phone: 713-775-7800
Number of Texas Employees: 3,982
Parent: Union Pacific Corporation

VOUGHT AIRCRAFT COMPANY

9314 W. Jefferson Blvd.
Dallas, TX 75211
Phone: 214-266-2011
Number of Texas Employees: 7,000
Joint Venture, The LTV Corporation and Lockheed Corporation

WALGREEN CO.

200 Wilmot Rd.
Deerfield, IL 60015
Phone: 708-940-2500
Fax: 708-940-2804
Number of Texas Employees: 3,752

WESTERN ATLAS INTERNATIONAL INC.

Western Geophysical
10205 Westheimer Rd.
Houston, Texas 77042
Phone: 713-963-2224
Fax: 713-952-9837
Number of Texas Employees: 14,784
Parent: Litton Industries, Inc.

WESTERN MERCHANDISERS AND WAL-MART STORES

421 E. 34th Ave., PO Box 32270
Amarillo, TX 79103-1702
Phone: 806-376-6251
Fax: 806-374-0095
Number of Texas Employees: 35,971
Parent: Wal-Mart Stores, Inc.

WINN-DIXIE STORES, INC.

5050 Edgewood Court
Jacksonville, FL 32205
Phone: 904-783-5000
Fax: 904-783-5294
Number of Texas Employees: 4,258

YOPLAIT U.S.A. INC.

15100 Midway Rd.
Dallas, TX 75244-2420
Phone: 214-991-1200
Fax: 214-991-0425
Number of Texas Employees: 5,312
Parent: General Mills, Inc.

Note: Not all Texas employees may be at the location indicated in the entry.

BIG 6 ACCOUNTING FIRMS — AUSTIN

ANDERSEN CONSULTING
701 Brazos, Ste. 1020
Austin, TX 78701
Phone: 512-472-2323
Fax: 512-320-5970
CEO: Warner Croft

COOPERS & LYBRAND
600 Congress Ave., Ste. 1800
Austin, TX 78701
Phone: 512-477-1300
Fax: 512-477-8681
CEO: Gary C. Prasher

DELOITTE & TOUCHE
700 Lavaca St.
Austin, TX 78701
Phone: 512-476-7661
Fax: 512-476-3415
CEO: Robert Campbell

ERNST & YOUNG
700 Lavaca St., Ste. 1400
Austin, TX 78701
Phone: 512-478-9881
Fax: 512-473-3499
CEO: Ronald G. Garrick

KPMG PEAT MARWICK
111 Congress Ave., Ste. 1100
Austin, TX 78701
Phone: 512-320-5200
Fax: 512-320-5100
CEO: William C. Love

PRICE WATERHOUSE
600 Congress Ave., Ste. 2000
Austin, TX 78701
Phone: 512-476-6700
Fax: 512-320-7291
CEO: Ryan D. Burdeno

BIG 6 ACCOUNTING FIRMS — DALLAS - FT. WORTH

ARTHUR ANDERSEN & CO.
901 Main St., Ste. 5600
Dallas, TX 75202
Phone: 214-741-8300
Fax: 214-741-8989
CEO: Dale V. Kesler

COOPERS & LYBRAND
1999 Bryan St., Ste. 3000
Dallas, TX 75201
Phone: 214-754-5000
Fax: 214-953-0669
CEO: Jerry W. Walker

DELOITTE & TOUCHE
Texas Commerce Bank Tower
2200 Ross Ave., Ste. 1600
Dallas, TX 75201
Phone: 214-777-7000
Fax: 214-777-7033
CEO: Gary F. McMahon

ERNST & YOUNG
2121 San Jacinto, Ste. 500
Dallas, TX 75201
Phone: 214-969-8000
Fax: 214-969-8115
CEO: Dennis J. Wander

KPMG PEAT MARWICK
1601 Elm St., Ste. 1400
Dallas, TX 75201
Phone: 214-754-2000
Fax: 214-754-2244
CEO: Cecil H. Moore

PRICE WATERHOUSE
1700 Pacific Ave., Ste. 1400
Dallas, TX 75201
Phone: 214-922-8040
Fax: 214-754-7991
CEO: Paul E. Weaver

BIG 6 ACCOUNTING FIRMS — HOUSTON

ARTHUR ANDERSEN & CO.
711 Louisiana
Houston, TX 77002
Phone: 713-237-2323
Fax: 713-237-2786
CEO: H. Devon Graham, Jr.

COOPERS & LYBRAND
1100 Louisiana St., Ste. 4100
Houston, TX 77002
Phone: 713-757-5200
Fax: 713-757-5249
CEO: Carroll W. Phillips

DELOITTE & TOUCHE
333 Clay St., Ste. 2300
Houston, TX 77002
Phone: 713-756-2000
Fax: 713-756-2001
CEO: R. Terry Seitz

ERNST & YOUNG
1221 McKinney St., Ste. 2400
Houston, TX 77010
Phone: 713-750-1500
Fax: 713-750-1501
CEO: Dennis R. Purdum

KPMG PEAT MARWICK
700 Louisiana
Houston, TX 77002
Phone: 713-224-4262
Fax: 713-224-4566
CEO: Frank W. Maresh

PRICE WATERHOUSE
1201 Louisiana, Ste. 2900
Houston, TX 77002
Phone: 713-654-4100
Fax: 713-750-4717
CEO: G. Edward Powell

BIG 6 ACCOUNTING FIRMS — SAN ANTONIO

ARTHUR ANDERSEN & CO.
70 N.E. Loop 410, Ste. 1100
San Antonio, TX 78216
Phone: 210-979-3700
Fax: 210-979-3795
CEO: James Thailing

DELOITTE & TOUCHE
711 Navarro St., Ste. 337
San Antonio, TX 78205
Phone: 210-224-1041
Fax: 210-224-9456
CEO: Richard Banta

ERNST & YOUNG
1900 East Bank Tower
San Antonio, TX 78205
Phone: 210-228-9696
Fax: 210-554-0253
CEO: Louis Brill

KPMG PEAT MARWICK
112 E. Pecan St., Ste. 2400
San Antonio, TX 78205
Phone: 210-227-9272
Fax: 210-224-0126
CEO: Paul Reddy

PRICE WATERHOUSE
One Riverwalk Place, Ste. 900
San Antonio, TX 78205
Phone: 210-226-7700
Fax: 210-226-7412
CEO: Beuford Shirley

MAJOR BANKS — AUSTIN

CATTLEMEN'S STATE BANK
912 Bastrop Hwy.
Austin, TX 78741
Phone: 512-389-1200
CEO: F. Gary Valdez

FIRST STATE BANK
400 W. 15th St.
Austin, TX 78701
Phone: 512-495-1000
CEO: Joe R. Long

FROST BANK — AUSTIN
816 Congress
Austin, Texas 78701
Phone: 512-473-4343
CEO: Bob Huthnance

HARTLAND BANK
10711 Burnet Rd.
Austin, TX 78758
Phone: 512-836-6622
CEO: David A. Hartman

HILL COUNTRY BANK
7709 N. RR 620
Austin, Texas 78720
Phone: 512-258-3333
CEO: Danny Clayton

LIBERTY NATIONAL BANK
900 Congress Ave.
Austin, TX 78701
Phone: 512-479-0011
CEO: Edward Z. Safady

NATIONSBANK OF TEXAS, N.A.
501 Congress Ave.
Austin, TX 78701
Phone: 512-397-2200
CEO: Andrew C. Elliott, Jr.

TEXAS COMMERCE BANK, N.A.
700 Lavaca St.
Austin, TX 78701
Phone: 512-479-2444
CEO: Merriman Morton

THE BANK OF THE WEST
609 Castle Ridge Rd.
Austin, TX 78746
Phone: 512-327-6516
CEO: Jack Collins

WORTHEN NATIONAL BANK OF TEXAS
919 Congress Ave.
Austin, TX 78701
Phone: 512-867-1000
CEO: William J. Renfro

MAJOR BANKS — DALLAS–FT. WORTH

BANK OF AMERICA — TEXAS
1925 W. Carpenter Fwy.
Irving, TX 75061
Phone: 214-444-5555
CEO: Larry McNabb

COMERICA BANK — TEXAS
801 Cherry St.
Fort Worth, TX 76102
Phone: 817-339-6100
CEO: Charles L. Gummer

BANK ONE, TEXAS N.A.
1717 Main Street
Dallas, TX 75201
Phone: 214-290-2000
CEO: Harvey R. Mitchell

CENTRAL BANK & TRUST
777 W. Rosedale
Fort Worth, TX 76104
Phone: 817-347-8800
CEO: J. Andy Thompson

BANK ONE, TEXAS N.A.
500 Throckmorton
Fort Worth, TX 76102
Phone: 817-884-4000
CEO: John T. Hickey, Jr.

GUARANTY FEDERAL BANK F.S.B.
8333 Douglas Ave.
Dallas, TX 75225
Phone: 214-360-3360
CEO: Robert Adelizzi

BLUEBONNET SAVINGS BANK F.S.B.
3100 Monticello
Dallas, TX 75205
Phone: 214-443-9000
CEO: R. Brad Oates

NATIONSBANK OF TEXAS, N.A.
901 Main St.
Dallas, TX 75202
Phone: 214-508-6262
CEO: Timothy P. Hartman

COMERICA BANK — TEXAS
1909 Woodall Rodgers Fwy.
Dallas, TX 75201
Phone: 214-841-1400
CEO: Charles L. Gummer

TEXAS COMMERCE BANK, N.A.
2200 Ross Ave.
Dallas, TX 75201
Phone: 214-922-2300
CEO: John L. Adams

MAJOR BANKS — HOUSTON

BANK ONE, TEXAS N.A.
2800 Post Oak Blvd.
Houston, TX 77056
Phone: 713-626-3420
CEO: David Smith

FROST BANK — CULLEN CENTER
600 Smith at Jefferson
Houston, TX 77002
Phone: 713-652-7600
CEO: David Beck

COMPASS BANK — RIVER OAKS
2001 Kirby Dr.
Houston, TX 77019
Phone: 713-526-2211
CEO: Charles E. McMahen

NATIONSBANK OF TEXAS, N.A.
700 Louisiana St.
Houston, TX 77002
Phone: 713-247-6000
CEO: Larry Mallard

CHANNELVIEW BANK
811 Sheldon Rd.
Channelview, TX 77530
Phone: 713-452-1551
CEO: Fredric M. Saunders

SOUTHWEST BANK OF TEXAS, N.A.
4295 San Felipe
Houston, TX 77027
Phone: 713-235-8800
CEO: Walter E. Johnson

CHARTER NATIONAL BANK — HOUSTON
2600 Citadel Plaza Dr., Ste. 100
Houston, TX 77008
Phone: 713-692-6121
CEO: Mark T. Giles

STERLING BANK
15000 Northwest Fwy.
Houston, TX 77040
Phone: 713-466-8300
CEO: George Martinez

FIRST INTERSTATE BANK OF TEXAS, N.A.
1000 Louisiana
Houston, TX 77002
Phone: 713-224-6611
CEO: Linnet Deily

TEXAS COMMERCE BANK, N.A.
712 Main St.
Houston, TX 77002
Phone: 713-216-4865
CEO: Marc J. Shapiro

MAJOR BANKS — SAN ANTONIO

BROADWAY NATIONAL BANK
1717 N.E. Loop 410
San Antonio, TX 78209
Phone: 210-283-6500
CEO: Greg Crane

KELLY FIELD NATIONAL BANK
6100 Bandera Rd.
San Antonio, TX 78238
Phone: 210-681-5100
CEO: Greg Oveland

EISENHOWER NATIONAL BANK
2302 Stanley Rd.
Ft. Sam Houston, TX 78234
Phone: 210-227-7131
CEO: Donald Gudinas

NATIONSBANK OF TEXAS, N.A.
300 Convent St.
San Antonio, TX 78205
Phone: 210-270-5555
CEO: Guy Bodine III

FROST NATIONAL BANK
100 W. Houston St.
San Antonio, TX 78205
Phone: 210-220-4011
CEO: Patrick Frost

SECURITY NATIONAL BANK
100 St. Cloud Rd.
San Antonio, TX 78228
Phone: 210-734-7361
CEO: James B. Cox

GROOS BANK, N.A.
40 N.E. Loop 410
San Antonio, TX 78216
Phone: 210-340-5000
CEO: R. Tom Roddy

TEXAS COMMERCE BANK, N.A.
1020 N.E. Loop 410
San Antonio, TX 78209
Phone: 210-829-6100
CEO: Joe C. McKinney

JEFFERSON STATE BANK
2900 Fredericksburg Rd.
San Antonio, TX 78201
Phone: 210-734-4311
CEO: Byron LeFlore

THE BANK OF THE WEST
109 N. San Saba
San Antonio, TX 78285
Phone: 210-224-2261
CEO: William Hudson

TOP 10 ADVERTISING AGENCIES — AUSTIN[1]

GSD&M
1250 Capital of Texas Hwy. South, Ste. 400
Austin, TX 78746
Phone: 512-327-8810
Fax: 512-327-1775
CEO: Roy Spence
Employees: 179
1992 Billings: $201.1 million

SICOLA MARTIN KOONS FRANK
6850 Austin Center Blvd. #270
Austin, TX 78731
Phone: 512-343-0264
Fax: 512-343-0659
CEO: Tom Sicola
Employees: 23
1991 Billings: $11.6 million

U.S. CREATIVE INC.
901 S. MoPac, Ste. 595
Austin, TX 78746
Phone: 512-328-2040
Fax: 512-328-0871
CEO: Candice Medlin
Employees: 20
1991 Billings: $11.2 million

LEE TILFORD AGENCY INC.
1201 Spyglass, Ste. 100
Austin, TX 78746
Phone: 512-329-9000
Fax: 512-329-8816
CEO: Anthony L. Tilford
Employees: 14
1991 Billings: $8.2 million

BONNER & TATE
316 Congress Ave.
Austin, TX 78701
Phone: 512-476-7696
Fax: 512-476-7722
CEO: Kerry Tate
Employees: 6
1991 Billings: $7.3 million

STAATS FALKENBERG & PARTNERS
919 Congress Ave., Ste. 800
Austin, TX 78701
Phone: 512-482-8897
Fax: 512-482-8950
CEO: Howard Falkenberg
Employees: 14
1991 Billings: $6.6 million

SHERRY MATTHEWS ADVERTISING & PUBLIC RELATIONS
101 San Jacinto Blvd.
Austin, TX 78701
Phone: 512-478-4397
Fax: 512-478-4978
CEO: Sherry Matthews
Employees: 16
1991 Billings: $5.0 million

FOX ADVERTISING INC.
110 Wild Basin Rd., Ste. 220
Austin, TX 78746
Phone: 512-328-6044
Fax: 512-327-4042
CEO: Jan Patschke
Employees: 9
1991 Billings: $5.0 million

WARREN MARTINO INC.
1512 W. 35th St. Cut-off, Ste. 200
Austin, TX 78703
Phone: 512-458-6302
Fax: 512-458-8331
CEO: Gay Warren Gaddis
Employees: 9
1991 Billings: $4.5 million

PRICE, HOOPER & ASSOCIATES
11940 Jollyville Rd., Ste. 200 S.
Austin, TX 78759
Phone: 512-258-3759
Fax: 512-335-5964
CEO: Wallace Price
Employees: 8
1992 Billings: $3.0 million

[1]Ranked by billings

TOP 10 ADVERTISING AGENCIES — DALLAS–FT. WORTH[1]

TEMERLIN McCLAIN INC.
201 E. Carpenter Fwy.
Irving, TX 75062
Phone: 214-556-1100
Fax: 214-830-2619
CEO: J. L. Temerlin
Employees: 476
1992 Billings: $440.0 million

TRACY-LOCKE INC.
200 Crescent Court
Dallas, TX 75201
Phone: 214-969-9000
Fax: 214-855-2087
CEO: Mike Rawlings
Employees: 454
1992 Billings: $320.4 million

RICHARDS GROUP
10000 N. Central Expy., Ste. 1200
Dallas, TX 75231
Phone: 214-891-5700
Fax: 214-891-5714
CEO: Stan Richards
Employees: 240
1992 Billings: $182.5 million

BLOOM FCA! INC.
3500 Maple Ave.
Dallas, TX 75219
Phone: 214-443-9900
Fax: 214-443-0002
CEO: Robert H. Bloom
Employees: 149
1992 Billings: $123.6 million

BRIERLEY & PARTNERS
1 Main Place
Dallas, TX 75202
Phone: 214-760-8700
Fax: 214-651-7718
CEO: Harold Brierley
Employees: 55
1992 Billings: $64.4 million

PUSKAR GIBBON CHAPIN INC.
3500 Maple Ave., Ste. 900
Dallas, TX 75219
Phone: 214-528-5400
Fax: 214-521-4538
CEO: Ross Puskar
Employees: 45
1992 Billings: $48.0 million

LARKIN, MEEDER & SCHWEIDEL INC.
7800 Stemmons Fwy., Ste. 770
Dallas, TX 75247
Phone: 214-688-7070
Fax: 214-979-5005
CEO: Carl Larkin
Employees: 70
1992 Billings: $48.0 million

LEVENSON, LEVENSON & HILL INC.
600 N. Pearl, Ste. 910
Dallas, TX 75201
Phone: 214-880-0200
Fax: 214-880-0602
CEO: Barbara Levenson
Employees: 75
1992 Billings: $46.1 million

MOROCH & ASSOCIATES INC.
3625 N. Hall St.
Dallas, TX 75219
Phone: 214-520-9700
Fax: 214-520-6464
CEO: Thomas F. Moroch
Employees: 78
1992 Billings: $33.3 million

ANDERSON FISCHEL THOMPSON
350 N. St. Paul St., Ste. 1500
Dallas, TX 75201
Phone: 214-855-5155
Fax: 214-871-7204
CEO: Joe Anderson
Employees: 40
1992 Billings: $29.0 million

[1]Ranked by billings

TOP 10 ADVERTISING AGENCIES — HOUSTON[1]

OGILVY & MATHER – HOUSTON
1415 Louisiana
Houston, TX 77002
Phone: 713-659-6688
Fax: 713-655-3721
CEO: James S. Hine
Employees: 97
1992 Billings: $98.0 million

FOGARTY & KLEIN/WINIUS BRANDON
7155 Old Katy Rd.
Houston, TX 77024
Phone: 713-862-5100
Fax: 713-869-6566
CEO: William H. Fogarty
Employees: 94
1992 Billings: $87.8 million

CME/GDL&W
5847 San Felipe, Ste. 400
Houston, TX 77057
Phone: 713-266-7676
Fax: 713-267-7222
CEO: Gerald R. Kerr
Employees: 117
1992 Billings: $71.7 million

McCANN–ERICKSON INC.
1360 Post Oak Blvd.
Houston, TX 77056
Phone: 713-965-0303
Fax: 713-439-9349
CEO: Jim G. Hetherly
Employees: 104
1992 Billings: $66.0 million

BLACK GILLOCK & LANGBERG
5851 San Felipe, Ste. 100
Houston, TX 77057
Phone: 713-781-6666
Fax: 713-783-1592
CEO: Wm. Scott Black
Employees: 63
1991 Billings: $41.2 million

EISAMAN, JOHNS & LAWS ADVERTISING INC.
2121 Sage Rd., Ste. 200
Houston, TX 77056
Phone: 713-961-4355
Fax: 713-961-9508
CEO: Dick Westman
Employees: 32
1991 Billings: $37.0 million

TAYLOR SMITH
2000 W. Loop South, 16th Floor
Houston, TX 77027
Phone: 713-877-1220
Fax: 713-877-1672
CEO: Larry Taylor
Employees: 55
1992 Billings: $34.6 million

RIVES CARLBERG
5599 San Felipe, Ste. 1111
Houston, TX 77056
Phone: 713-965-0764
Fax: 713-965-0135
CEO: W. Charles Carlberg
Employees: 45
1991 Billings: $30.1 million

THE QUEST BUSINESS AGENCY INC.
2900 N. Loop West, Ste. 1020
Houston, TX 77092
Phone: 713-956-6569
Fax: 713-956-2593
CEO: Alan D. Vera
Employees: 34
1992 Billings: $23.7 million

PENNY & SPEIER INC.
1800 W. Loop South, Ste. 400
Houston, TX 77027
Phone: 713-965-0331
Fax: 713-961-4128
CEO: C. R. Penny
Employees: 24
1992 Billings: $15.0 million

---

[1] Ranked by billings

TOP 10 ADVERTISING AGENCIES — SAN ANTONIO[1]

SOSA BROMLEY AGUILAR & ASSOCIATES
321 Alamo Plaza, Ste. 300
San Antonio, TX 78205
Phone: 210-227-2013
Fax: 210-227-2102
CEO: Lionel Sosa
Employees: 85
1991 Billings: $42.6 million

THE ATKINS AGENCY
1777 NE Loop 410, 11th Floor
San Antonio, TX 78217
Phone: 210-826-5500
Fax: 210-826-1247
CEO: Steve Atkins
Employees: 44
1991 Billings: $24.2 million

ANDERSON ADVERTISING INC.
1017 N. Main Ave., Ste. 300
San Antonio, TX 78212
Phone: 210-223-6233
Fax: 210-223-9692
CEO: Charles Anderson
Employees: 49
1991 Billings: $24.0 million

GROVES CHENEY & ASSOCIATES
7800 I-10 West, Ste. 500
San Antonio, TX 78230
Phone: 210-344-4332
Fax: 210-344-1567
CEO: Janie Groves
Employees: 14
1991 Billings: $11.7 million

MONTEMAYOR Y ASOCIADOS INC.
70 NE Loop 410, Ste. 870
San Antonio, TX 78216
Phone: 210-342-1990
Fax: 210-525-1052
CEO: Carlos Montemayor
Employees: 15
1991 Billings: $10.2 million

MARKETING MERCADEO INTERNATIONAL
6243 I-10 West, Ste. 315
San Antonio, TX 78201
Phone: 210-733-3588
Fax: 210-733-0402
CEO: Robert Whitt III
Employees: 16
1991 Billings: $7.1 million

HOWELL BOYD ADVERTISING INC.
14800 San Pedro Ave., Ste. 200
San Antonio, TX 78232
Phone: 210-491-9005
Fax: 210-491-9383
CEO: Hal Boyd
Employees: 12
1992 Billings: $5.0 million

ALAMO AD CENTER INC.
217 Arden Grove
San Antonio, TX 78215
Phone: 210-225-6294
Fax: 210-225-6327
CEO: Carlton Mertens
Employees: 10
1991 Billings: $4.8 million

KICH/COTTER
100 W. Olmos St., Ste. 102
San Antonio, TX 78212
Phone: 210-829-7891
Fax: 210-829-7895
CEO: Greg Cotter
Employees: 8
1991 Billings: $3.9 million

WOMACK/KLEYPAS ADVERTISING INC.
10205 Oasis St., Ste. 220
San Antonio, TX 78216
Phone: 210-349-3609
Fax: 210-349-3974
CEO: James Kleypas
Employees: 7
1991 Billings: $3.8 million

[1] Ranked by billings

TOP 10 LAW FIRMS — AUSTIN[1]

BROWN McCARROLL & OAKS HARTLINE
1400 Franklin Plaza, 111 Congress Ave.
Austin, TX 78701
Phone: 512-472-5456
Fax: 512-479-1101
CEO: R. Kinnan Golemon
Local lawyers: 84

CLARK, THOMAS, WINTERS & NEWTON
700 Lavaca St.
Austin, TX 78701
Phone: 512-472-8800
Fax: 512-474-1129
CEO: Larry McNeill
Local lawyers: 78

GRAVES, DOUGHERTY, HEARON & MOODY
515 Congress Ave., Ste. 2300
Austin, TX 78701
Phone: 512-480-5600
Fax: 512-478-1976
CEO: James A. Williams
Local lawyers: 70

McGINNIS, LOCHRIDGE & KILGORE
919 Congress Ave., Ste. 1300
Austin, TX 78701
Phone: 512-495-6000
Fax: 512-495-6093
CEO: Tom Barton
Local lawyers: 58

SMALL, CRAIG & WERKENTHIN
100 Congress Ave., Ste. 1100
Austin, TX 78701
Phone: 512-472-8355
Fax: 512-320-9734
CEO: Ed Coultas
Local lawyers: 58

WRIGHT & GREENHILL, P.C.
221 W. Sixth St., Ste. 1800
Austin, TX 78701
Phone: 512-476-4600
Fax: 512-476-5382
CEO: Mel Waxler
Local lawyers: 38

BICKERSTAFF, HEATH & SMILEY, L.L.P.
96 San Jacinto Blvd., Ste. 1800
Austin, TX 78701
Phone: 512-472-8021
Fax: 512-320-5638
CEO: Andrew Kever
Local lawyers: 37

FULBRIGHT & JAWORSKI
600 Congress Ave., Ste. 2400
Austin, TX 78701
Phone: 512-474-5201
Fax: 512-320-4598
CEO: Pike Powers
Local lawyers: 34

JENKENS & GILCHRIST
2200 One American Center
600 Congress Ave.
Austin, TX 78701
Phone: 512-499-3800
Fax: 512-404-3520
CEO: Rod Edens, Jr.
Local lawyers: 31

SCOTT, DOUGLASS & LUTON, L.L.P.
600 Congress Ave., 15th Floor
Austin, TX 78701
Phone: 512-495-6300
Fax: 512-474-0731
CEO: Tom W. Reavley
Local lawyers: 30

[1] Ranked by number of local lawyers

TOP 10 LAW FIRMS — DALLAS – FT. WORTH[1]

THOMPSON & KNIGHT P.C.
1700 Pacific Ave., Ste. 3300
Dallas, TX 75201
Phone: 214-969-1700
Fax: 214-969-1651
CEO: Buford P. Berry
Local lawyers: 194

GARDERE & WYNNE L.L.P.
1601 Elm St., Ste. 3000
Dallas, TX 75201
Phone: 214-999-3000
Fax: 214-999-4967
CEO: Donald C. McCleary
Local lawyers: 166

STRASBURGER & PRICE L.L.P.
901 Main St., Ste. 4300
Dallas, TX 75202
Phone: 214-651-4300
Fax: 214-651-4330
CEO: David K. Meyercord
Local lawyers: 166

LOCKE PURNELL RAIN HARRELL P.C.
2200 Ross Ave., Ste. 2200
Dallas, TX 75201
Phone: 214-740-8000
Fax: 214-740-8800
CEO: Rob See, Jr.
Local lawyers: 160

JOHNSON & GIBBS P.C.
900 Jackson St., Ste. 100
Dallas, TX 75202
Phone: 214-977-9000
Fax: 214-977-9004
CEO: Michael D. Wortley
Local lawyers: 152

HAYNES AND BOONE L.L.P.
901 Main St., Ste. 3100
Dallas, TX 75202
Phone: 214-651-5000
Fax: 214-651-5940
CEO: Michael M. Boone, George W. Bramblett, and Robert E. Wilson
Local lawyers: 140

JONES, DAY, REAVIS & POGUE
2001 Ross Ave., Ste. 2300
Dallas, TX 75201
Phone: 214-220-3939
Fax: 214-969-5100
CEO: Francis P. Hubach, Jr.
Local lawyers: 139

JENKENS & GILCHRIST P.C.
1445 Ross Ave., Ste. 3200
Dallas, TX 75202
Phone: 214-855-4500
Fax: 214-855-4300
CEO: David M. Laney
Local lawyers: 127

HUGHES & LUCE L.L.P.
1717 Main St., Ste. 2800
Dallas, TX 75201
Phone: 214-939-5500
Fax: 214-939-6100
CEO: Alan J. Bogdanow
Local lawyers: 121

JACKSON & WALKER L.L.P.
901 Main St., Ste. 6000
Dallas, TX 75202
Phone: 214-953-6000
Fax: 214-953-5822
CEO: Mike Wilson
Local lawyers: 116

[1]Ranked by number of local lawyers

TOP 10 LAW FIRMS — HOUSTON[1]

VINSON & ELKINS L.L.P.
1001 Fannin St.
Houston, TX 77002
Phone: 713-758-2222
Fax: 713-758-2346
CEO: Harry M. Reasoner
Local lawyers: 374

FULBRIGHT & JAWORSKI
1301 McKinney, Ste. 5100
Houston, TX 77010
Phone: 713-651-5151
Fax: 713-651-5246
CEO: A. T. Blackshear, Jr.
Local lawyers: 333

BAKER & BOTTS
910 Louisiana, Ste. 3000
Houston, TX 77002
Phone: 713-229-1234
Fax: 713-229-1522
CEO: E. W. Barnett
Local lawyers: 254

ANDREWS & KURTH L.L.P.
4200 Texas Commerce Tower
Houston, TX 77002
Phone: 713-220-4200
Fax: 713-220-4285
CEO: Rush Moody, Jr.
Local lawyers: 174

BRACEWELL & PATTERSON
711 Louisiana St., Ste. 2900
Houston, TX 77002
Phone: 713-223-2900
Fax: 713-221-1212
CEO: Richard A. Royds
Local lawyers: 150

LIDDELL, SAPP, ZIVLEY, HILL & LABOON L.L.P
3400 Texas Commerce Tower
Houston, TX 77002
Phone: 713-226-1200
Fax: 713-223-3717
CEO: R. Bruce LaBoon
Local lawyers: 112

BUTLER & BINION
1000 Louisiana, Ste. 1600
Houston, TX 77002
Phone: 713-237-3111
Fax: 713-237-3201
CEO: Louis Paine
Local lawyers: 103

WEIL, GOTSHAL & MANGES
700 Louisiana, Ste. 1600
Houston, TX 77002
Phone: 713-546-5000
Fax: 713-224-9511
CEO: D. J. Baker
Local lawyers: 67

ARNOLD, WHITE & DURKEE
P.O. Box 4433
Houston, TX 77210
Phone: 713-787-1400
Fax: 713-789-2679
CEO: John D. Norris
Local lawyers: 66

MAYOR, DAY, CALDWELL & KEETON L.L.P.
700 Louisiana, Ste. 1800
Houston, TX 77002
Phone: 713-225-7000
Fax: 713-225-7047
CEO: Jonathan Day
Local lawyers: 66

[1] Ranked by number of local lawyers

TOP 10 LAW FIRMS — SAN ANTONIO[1]

MATTHEWS & BRANSCOMB

One Alamo Center
106 S. St. Mary's St., Ste. 800
San Antonio, TX 78205
Phone: 210-226-4211
Fax: 210-226-0521
CEO: Tullos Wells
Local lawyers: 64

COX & SMITH INC.

112 E. Pecan St., Ste. 2000
San Antonio, TX 78205
Phone: 210-554-5500
Fax: 210-226-8395
CEO: Dan Webster III
Local lawyers: 58

PLUNKETT GIBSON & ALLEN INC.

6243 N. W. Expressway, Ste. 600
San Antonio, TX 78201
Phone: 210-734-7092
Fax: 210-734-0379
CEO: Mark Stein
Local lawyers: 42

FULBRIGHT & JAWORSKI

300 Convent St, Ste. 2200
San Antonio, TX 78205
Phone: 210-224-5575
Fax: 210-224-8336
CEO: Philip Pfeiffer
Local lawyers: 41

AKIN GUMP HAUER & FELD L.L.P.

300 Convent St., Ste. 1500
San Antonio, TX 78205
Phone: 210-270-0800
Fax: 210-224-2035
CEO: Cecil Schenker
Local lawyers: 40

GROCE LOCKE & HEBDON

1800 Frost Bank Tower
San Antonio, TX 78205
Phone: 210-246-5000
Fax: 210-246-5999
CEO: Norman Nevins
Local lawyers: 35

FOSTER LEWIS LANGLEY GARDNER & BANACK INC.

112 E. Pecan St., Ste. 1100
San Antonio, TX 78205-1533
Phone: 210-226-3116
Fax: 210-226-1065
CEO: Emerson Banack, Jr.
Local lawyers: 32

THORNTON SUMMERS BIECHLIN DUNHAM & BROWN INC.

100 N.E. Loop 410, Ste. 800
San Antonio, TX 78216
Phone: 210-342-5555
Fax: 210-525-0666
CEO: Robert Thornton
Local lawyers: 31

OPPENHEIMER ROSENBERG & KELLEHER INC.

711 Navarro St.
San Antonio, TX 78205
Phone: 210-224-2000
Fax: 210-224-7540
CEO: Stanley Blend
Local lawyers: 31

BALL & WEED, P.C.

745 E. Mulberry Ave., Ste. 500
San Antonio, TX 78212
Phone: 210-731-6300
Fax: 210-7316499
CEO: Ray Weed
Local lawyers: 28

Sources: *Austin Business Journal, 1992–1993 Book of Lists; Dallas Business Journal, 1993 Book of Lists; Houston Business Journal, The 1993 Book of Lists; San Antonio Business Journal, Top 25 Lists 1993; The American Lawyer, The AmLaw 100,* July/August 1993; *The National Law Journal, The NLJ 250,* September 28, 1992.

[1]Ranked by number of local lawyers

MAJOR TEXAS PUBLICATIONS

TEXAS HIGHWAYS
State Department of Highways and Public
 Transportation
Travel & Information Division
PO Box 141009
Austin, TX 78714-1009
Phone: 512-483-3675

TEXAS MONTHLY
PO Box 1569
Austin, TX 78767
Phone: 512-320-6900

TEXAS PARKS AND WILDLIFE
State Department of Parks and Wildlife
4200 Smith School Rd.
Austin, TX 78744
Phone: 512-707-1833

MAJOR MEDIA — AUSTIN

TELEVISION
KTBC-TV (CBS)
119 E. 10th St.
Austin, TX 78701
Phone: 512-476-7777

KVUE-TV (ABC)
3201 Steck
Austin, TX 78757
Phone: 512-459-6521

KXAN-TV (NBC)
908 W. Martin Luther King Jr. Blvd.
Austin, TX 78701
Phone: 512-476-3636

KBVO-TV (Fox)
10700 Metric
Austin, TX 78758
Phone: 512-835-0042

KLRU-TV (PBS)
Box 7158
Austin, TX 78713
Phone: 512-471-4811

RADIO
KUT-FM (Public)
26th and Guadalupe Streets
Austin, TX 78752
Phone: 512-471-1631

DAILY NEWSPAPER
Austin American-Statesman
305 S. Congress Ave.
Austin, TX 78704
Phone: 512-445-3500

OTHER
Austin Business Journal
1301 Capital of Texas Hwy.
Austin, TX 78746
Phone: 512-328-0180

Austin Chronicle
PO Box 49066
Austin, TX 78765
Phone: 512-473-8995

MAJOR MEDIA — DALLAS-FORT WORTH

TELEVISION

WFAA-TV (ABC)
Communications Center
606 Young St.
Dallas, TX 75202
Phone: 214-748-9631

KXAS-TV (NBC)
3900 Barnett St.
Fort Worth, TX 76103
Phone: 817-429-1550

KDFW-TV (CBS)
400 N. Griffin St.
Dallas, TX 76102
Phone: 214-720-4444

KDAF-TV (Fox)
8001 John Carpenter Fwy.
Dallas, TX 75247
Phone: 214-634-8833

KERA-TV (PBS)
3000 Harry Hines Blvd.
Dallas, TX 75201
Phone: 214-871-1390

RADIO

KERA-FM (Public)
3000 Harry Hines Blvd.
Dallas, TX 75201
Phone: 214-871-1390

DAILY NEWSPAPERS

The Dallas Morning News
PO Box 655237
Dallas, TX 75265
Phone: 214-977-8222

Fort Worth Star-Telegram
400 W. 7th St.
Fort Worth, TX 76101
Phone: 817-429-2655

OTHER

Dallas Business Journal
4131 N. Central Expressway, Ste. 310
Dallas, TX 75204
Phone: 214-263-0449

MAJOR MEDIA — HOUSTON

TELEVISION

KHOU-TV (CBS)
1945 Allen Pkwy.
Houston, TX 77019
Phone: 713-526-1111

KPRC-TV (NBC)
8181 Southwest Fwy.
Houston, TX 77051
Phone: 713-771-4631

KRIV-TV (Fox)
3935 Westheimer
Houston, TX 77027
Phone: 713-626-2610

KTRK-TV (ABC)
3310 Bissonnet
Houston, TX 77005
Phone: 713-666-0713

KUHT-TV (PBS)
4513 Cullen Blvd.
Houston, TX 77004
Phone: 713-748-8888

RADIO

KUHF-FM (Public)
4800 Calhoun Rd.
Houston, TX 77204-4061
Phone: 713-7497186

DAILY NEWSPAPERS

Houston Chronicle
PO Box 4260
Houston, TX 77210
Phone: 713-220-7171

The Houston Post
PO Box 4747
Houston, TX 77210
Phone: 713-840-5600

OTHER

Houston Business Journal
One West Loop South, Ste. 650
Houston, TX 77027-9875
Phone: 713-688-8811

MAJOR MEDIA — SAN ANTONIO

TELEVISION

KMOL (NBC)
PO Box 2641
San Antonio, TX 78299
Phone: 210-226-4444

KENS (CBS)
PO Box TV 5
San Antonio, TX 78229
Phone: 210-366-5000

KSAT (ABC)
PO Box 2478
San Antonio, TX 78298
Phone: 210-351-1200

KRRT (Fox)
6218 NW Loop 410
San Antonio, TX 78238
Phone: 210-684-0035

KLRN-TV (PBS)
801 S. Bowie
San Antonio, TX 78205
Phone: 210-270-9000

RADIO

KSTYX-FM (PBS)
8401 Data Pt. Drive
San Antonio, TX
Phone: 210-614-8977

DAILY NEWSPAPER

San Antonio *Express-News*
PO Box 2171
San Antonio, TX 78297
Phone: 210-225-7411

OTHER

The San Antonio Business Journal
8200 IH-10 West, Ste. 300
San Antonio, TX 78230
Phone: 210-341-3202

San Antonio Monthly Magazine
Business Times Publishing Co., Inc.
2700 NE Loop 410, #560
San Antonio, TX 78217-4835

LARGEST NOT-FOR-PROFIT HOSPITALS — AUSTIN

SETON MEDICAL CENTER INC.
Daughters of Charity Health Systems of Austin
1201 W. 38th St.
Austin, TX 78705
Phone: 512-323-1000
CEO: Thomas Gallagher
Employees: 1,900
1992 Est. Sales: $160 mil.

PCA HEALTH PLANS OF TEXAS, INC.
8303 N. Mo-Pac Expy.
Austin, TX 78759
Phone: 512-338-6100
CEO: Donald Gessler
Employees: 200
1992 Est. Sales: $150 mil.

ST. DAVID'S HEALTH CARE SYSTEM INC.
919 E. 32nd St.
Austin, TX 78705
Phone: 512-476-7111
CEO: Cynthia Brouillette
Employees: 1,900
1992 Est. Sales: $140 mil.

THE AUSTIN DIAGNOSTIC CLINIC ASSOCIATION
801 W. 34th St.
Austin, TX 78705
Phone: 512-459-1111
CEO: Jonathan F. Decherd
Employees: 650
1992 Est. Sales: $60 mil.

AUSTIN REGIONAL CLINIC
Occupational Health Centers of Austin
3410 Far West Blvd.
Austin, TX 78731
Phone: 512-346-6611
CEO: Norman Chenven
Employees: 650
1992 Est. Sales: $50 mil.

LARGEST NOT-FOR-PROFIT HOSPITALS — DALLAS–FT. WORTH

BAYLOR HEALTH CARE SYSTEM INC.
3409 Worth St., Bldg. 605
Dallas, TX 75246
Phone: 214-820-0111
CEO: Boone Powell
Employees: 7,500
1992 Est. Sales: $600 mil.

HARRIS METHODIST HEALTH SYSTEM INC.
510 S. Ballinger St.
Ft. Worth, TX 76104
Phone: 817-878-1100
CEO: Ronald L. Smith
Employees: 7,000
1992 Est. Sales: $520 mil.

PRESBYTERIAN HEALTHCARE SYSTEMS INC.
5750 Pineland Dr., Ste. 204
Dallas, TX 75231
Phone: 214-345-2638
CEO: Douglas Hawthorne
Employees: 4,500
1992 Est. Sales: $340 mil.

DALLAS COUNTY HOSPITAL DISTRICT
5201 Harry Hines Blvd.
Dallas, TX 75235
Phone: 214-590-8000
CEO: Ron Anderson
Employees: 5,700
1992 Est. Sales: $310 mil.

METHODIST HOSPITALS OF DALLAS INC.
1441 N. Beckley Ave.
Dallas, TX 75208
Phone: 214-944-8132
CEO: David H. Hitt
Employees: 2,400
1992 Est. Sales: $180 mil.

LARGEST NOT-FOR-PROFIT HOSPITALS — HOUSTON

SCH HEALTH CARE SYSTEM
2600 N. Loop West
Houston, TX 77092
Phone: 713-681-8877
CEO: Stanley Urban
Employees: 20,000
1992 Est. Sales: $1,250 mil.

THE METHODIST HOSPITAL
6565 Fannin St.
Houston, TX 77030
Phone: 713-790-3311
CEO: Larry Mathis
Employees: 6,450
1992 Est. Sales: $480 mil.

HARRIS COUNTY HOSPITAL DISTRICT
2525 Holly Hall St.
Houston, TX 77054
Phone: 713-746-5791
CEO: Lois J. Moore
Employees: 5,250
1992 Est. Sales: $420 mil.

BAYLOR COLLEGE OF MEDICINE INC.
1 Baylor Plaza
Houston, TX 77030
Phone: 713-798-4951
CEO: William T. Butler
Employees: 6,400
1992 Est. Sales: $410 mil.

MEMORIAL HEALTHCARE SYSTEM
Central Business Office
9494 SW F
Houston, TX 77074
Phone: 713-776-5000
CEO: Dan Wilford
Employees: 3,800
1992 Est. Sales: $350 mil.

LARGEST NOT-FOR-PROFIT HOSPITALS — SAN ANTONIO

INCARNATE WORD HEALTH SERVICES
9311 San Pedro Ave.
San Antonio, TX 78216
Phone: 210-524-4100
CEO: William McGuire
Employees: 7,350
1992 Est. Sales: $600 mil.

BEXAR COUNTY HOSPITAL DISTRICT
4502 Medical Dr.
San Antonio, TX 78229
Phone: 210-616-4000
CEO: John Guest
Employees: 3,000
1992 Est. Sales: $210 mil.

BAPTIST MEMORIAL HOSPITAL SYSTEM
111 Dallas St.
San Antonio, TX 78205
Phone: 210-222-8431
CEO: Callie Smith
Employees: 4,450
1992 Est. Sales: $200 mil.

SOUTHWEST TEXAS METHODIST HOSPITAL INC.
7700 Floyd Curl Dr.
San Antonio, TX 78229
Phone: 210-692-4000
CEO: John Hornbeak
Employees: 2,500
1992 Est. Sales: $190 mil.

ST. LUKE'S LUTHERAN HOSPITAL INC.
7930 Floyd Curl Dr., PO Box 29100
San Antonio, TX 78229
Phone: 210-617-7000
CEO: William Hyslop
Employees: 1,100
1992 Est. Sales: $70 mil.

LARGEST NOT-FOR-PROFIT HOSPITALS — OTHER TEXAS CITIES

SCOTT AND WHITE MEMORIAL HOSPITAL
2401 S. 31st St.
Temple, TX 76508
Phone: 817-774-2111
CEO: Robert E. Myers
Employees: 5,000
1992 Est. Sales: $230 mil.

ST. ELIZABETH HOSPITAL INC.
2830 Calder St.
Beaumont, TX 77702
Phone: 409-892-7171
CEO: Sister M. McCarthy
Employees: 2,350
1992 Est. Sales: $220 mil.

PROVIDENCE MEMORIAL HOSPTIAL INC.
2001 N. Oregon St.
El Paso, TX 79902
Phone: 915-542-6011
CEO: David P. Buchmueller
Employees: 1,850
1992 Est. Sales: $200 mil.

SISTERS OF ST. JOSEPH OF TEXAS INC.
4000 24th St.
Lubbock, TX 79410
Phone: 806-796-6840
CEO: Charley Trimble
Employees: 1,600
1992 Est. Sales: $190 mil.

METHODIST HOSPITAL OF LUBBOCK, TEXAS INC.
3615 19th St.
Lubbock, TX 79410
Phone: 806-792-1011
CEO: W. D. Poteet
Employees: 8,450
1992 Est. Sales: $190 mil.

PROFESSIONAL SPORTS TEAMS IN TEXAS

DALLAS COWBOYS (FOOTBALL)
1 Cowboys Pkwy.
Irving, TX 75063
Phone: 214-556-9900
Fax: 214-556-9970
Owner: Jerry Jones
Head Coach: Jimmy Johnson
1992-93 Season Record: 13-3 (Super Bowl champions)
1992 Sales: $55 million

DALLAS MAVERICKS (BASKETBALL)
Reunion Arena
777 Sports St.
Dallas, TX 75207
Phone: 214-988-0117
Fax: 214-748-0510
Owner: Donald Carter
Head Coach: Quinn Buckner
1992-93 Season Record: 11-71 (Did not make playoffs)
1992 Sales: $29 million

DALLAS STARS (HOCKEY)
901 Main St., Ste. 2301
Dallas, TX 75202
Phone: 214-712-2890
Fax: 214-712-2860
Owner: Norman Green
Head Coach: Bob Gainey
1992-93 Season Record: 36-38-10 (Did not make playoffs)
1992 Sales: $20 million

HOUSTON ASTROS (BASEBALL)
8400 Kirby Dr.
Houston, TX 77054
Phone: 713-799-9500
Fax: 713-799-9562
Owner: Drayton McLane, Jr.
Manager: Vacant
1993 Season Record: 85-77 (Did not make playoffs)
1992 Sales: $43 million

HOUSTON OILERS (FOOTBALL)
6910 Fannin St.
Houston, TX 77030
Phone: 713-797-9111
Fax: 713-797-6631
Owner: K. S. "Bud" Adams, Jr.
Head Coach: Jack Pardee
1992-93 Season Record: 10-6 (Lost to Buffalo in the 2nd round of the NFL Playoffs)
1992 Sales: $55 million

HOUSTON ROCKETS (BASKETBALL)
10 Greenway Plaza East
Houston, TX 77046
Phone: 713-627-0600
Fax: 713-627-8159
Owner: Leslie Alexander
Head Coach: Rudy Tomjanovich
1992-93 Season Record: 55-27 (Lost to Seattle in the 2nd round of the NBA Playoffs)
1992 Sales: $32 million

SAN ANTONIO SPURS (BASKETBALL)
100 Montana
San Antonio, TX 78023
Phone: 210-554-7787
Fax: 210-554-7701
Owner: Consortium of San Antonio investors
Head Coach: John Lucas
1992-93 Season Record: 49-33 (Lost to Phoenix in the 2nd Round of the NBA Playofffs)
1992 Sales: $31 million

TEXAS RANGERS (BASEBALL)
1250 E. Copeland Rd., Ste. 1100
Arlington, TX 76011
Phone: 817-273-5222
Fax: 817-273-5206
Owners: George W. Bush and Edward "Rusty" Rose (general managing partners)
Manager: Kevin Kennedy
1993 Season Record: 86-76 (did not make play-offs)
1992 Sales: $66 million

Source: *Financial World;* May 25, 1993

TEXAS ZIP CODE MAP

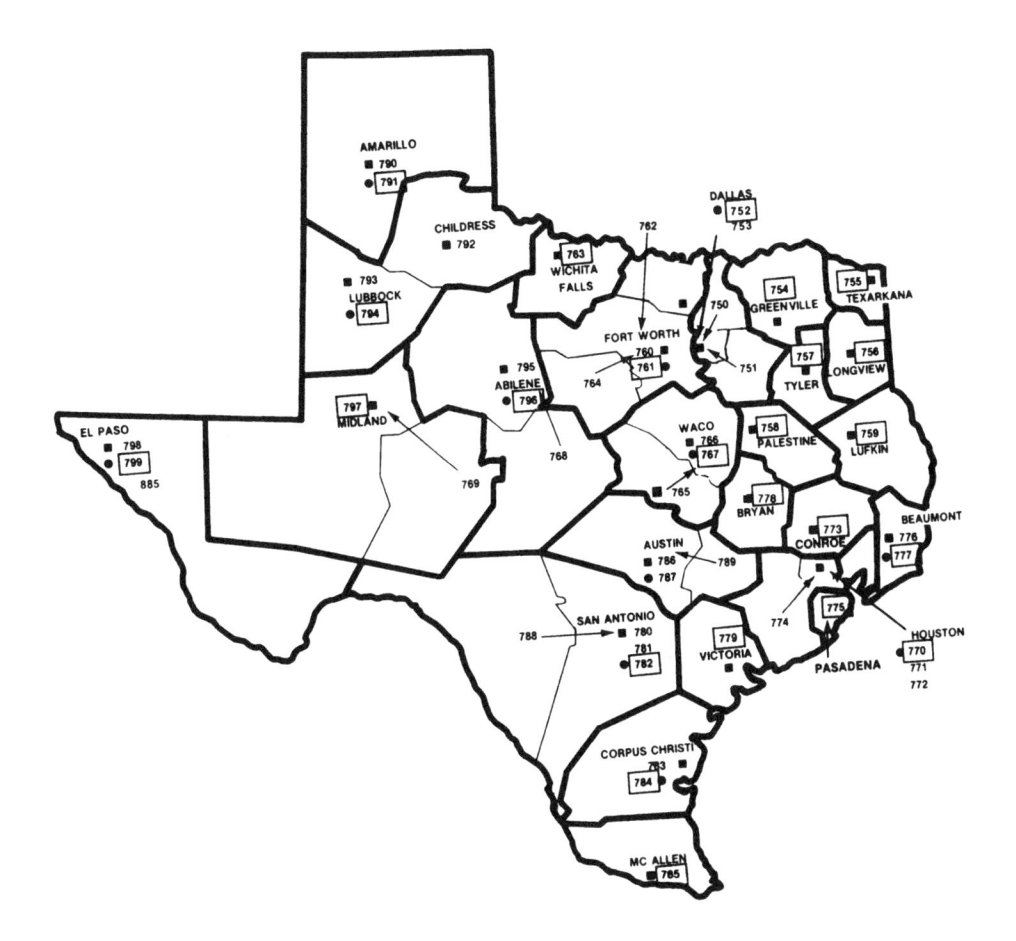

THE INDEXES

INDEX OF COMPANIES BY INDUSTRY

> Note: Bold numbers refer to in-depth company profiles; all others refer to capsule company profiles.

Agricultural operations
American Rice, Inc. 153
AZTX Cattle Co. 157
Barrett & Crofoot, LLP 158
Cactus Feeders Incorporated 163
Darling-Delaware Company Inc. 171
Friona Industries LP 182
JaGee Corp 195
Southwestern Irrigated Cotton Growers Association 227

Apparel
Farah Inc. 180
Gulf Coast Sportswear Inc. 186
Haggar Apparel 188
Williamson-Dickie Manufacturing Co. 247

Auto parts — retail & wholesale
APS Holding Corporation 155
Hi-Lo Auto Supply, Inc. 191
Strafco Inc. 230

Automotive & trucking — original equipment & wholesale
Houston Peterbilt Inc. 192
SLM Power Group Inc. 224
Texas Kenworth Co. 235

Banks
Bank United of Texas FSB 158
Cullen/Frost Bankers, Inc. 169
International Bancshares 194
Victoria Bankshares, Inc. 243

Beverages — alcoholic
Gambrinus Company, The 184

Beverages — soft drinks
Coca-Cola Bottling Group-Southwest 166

Dr Pepper Bottling Company of Texas 173
Dr Pepper/Seven-Up Companies, Inc. **112**, 173

Broadcasting — radio & TV
A. H. Belo Corp. 150
Clear Channel Communications, Inc. 165
H and C Communications Inc. 187
Heritage Media Corporation **139**, 190

Building — maintenance & services
Emergency Network Inc. 177
Gulf States Inc. 186
Mundy Cos. 206

Building — mobile homes & RV
Palm Harbor Homes Inc. 211
Redman Industries Inc. 219

Building — residential & commercial
Centex Corp. 164
D. R. Horton, Inc. 170
Delta Industrial Offices Inc. 172
Fish Engineering & Construction Partners Ltd. 181
Hunt Building Corporation 192
Linbeck Construction Corp. 199
Lott Group Inc., The 201
Rayco 218
TDIndustries Inc. 232
U.S. Contractors Inc. 240
U.S. Home Corp. 240
W.S. Bellows Construction Corp. 244
Weekley Homes Inc. 245

Building products — a/c & heating
Goodman Manufacturing Corporation 185
Lennox International Inc. 199
SnyderGeneral Corp. 224

Building products — doors and trim
AMRE, Inc. 154
Fojtasek Companies Inc. 181
Overhead Door Corp. 210

Building products — misc.
Associated Materials Incorporated 156
Dal-Tile Group Inc. 170
Elcor Corp. 176
Eljer Industries, Inc. 177
Jones Blair Co. 195
Lone Star Plywood and Door Corp. 200
Pioneer Concrete of America 215
Texas Industries, Inc. 235
Triangle Pacific Corp. 238
U.S. Intec, Inc. 240

Building products — retail & wholesale
McCoy Corporation 203
Vaughan and Sons Inc. 242

Business services
Administaff Inc. 150
Akin, Gump, Strauss, Hauer & Feld 151
Alliance Employee Leasing Corp. 151
Allright Corp. 151
Andrews and Kurth 155
Baker and Botts, L.L.P. 157
Bracewell and Patterson 161
Business Records Corporation Holding Co. 163
Cantey & Hanger LLP 163
Dallas Auto Auction Inc. 170
Freeman Companies, The 182
Fulbright and Jaworski 183
Jackson and Walker LP 195
Locke Purnell Rain Harrell 200
M/A/R/C Group, The 202
Middleberg, Riddle and Gianna 205
Miller and Miller Auctioneers Inc. 205
Pannell Kerr Forster 211
Richards Group Inc. 220

286   THE TEXAS 500

INDEX OF COMPANIES BY INDUSTRY

Stewart Information
  Services Corp. 229
Strasburger and Price 230
TeleCheck Services, Inc.
  234
Thompson and Knight PC
  237
Vinson & Elkins L.L.P. 243

Cable TV
SPI Holding, Inc. 228
TCA Cable TV, Inc. 232

Chemicals — diversified
Lyondell Petrochemical
  Company **80**, 201
Rexene Corp. 219
Sterling Chemicals, Inc.
  228

Chemicals — fibers
Texas Olefins Co. 236

Chemicals — plastics
Vinmar Inc. 243

Chemicals — specialty
Chemical Lime Co. 165
Merichem Co. 204
NL Industries, Inc. 208
Pioneer Chlor Alkali
  Investments Inc. 214
Texas United Corp 236
Tri-Gas Inc. 238
Vista Chemical Inc. 243

Computers — mainframe
CONVEX Computer Corp.
  169

Computers — mini & micro
Compaq Computer
  Corporation **62**, 167
CompuAdd, Inc. 167
Datapoint Corp. 171
Dell Computer Corporation
  110, 172

Computers — peripheral equipment
BancTec, Inc. 157

Computers — services
Computer Language
  Research, Inc. 168
Electronic Data Systems
  Corporation **68**, 177
Intelogic Trace, Inc. 194
Perot Systems Corp. 213

Computers — software
BMC Software, Inc. **130**,
  160
CompuCom Systems, Inc.
  134, 167
Continuum Company, Inc.,
  The 168
Landmark Graphics Corp.
  198
Software Spectrum, Inc.
  224
Sterling Software, Inc.
  144, 229

Construction — cement & concrete
Southdown, Inc. 225
Sunbelt Corp. 230

Construction — heavy
Associated Pipeline
  Contractors Inc. 156
Austin Industries Inc. 156
CRSS, Inc. 169
HB Zachry Co. 189
HCB Contractors 190
Lee Lewis Construction,
  Inc. 199

Cosmetics & toiletries
Helen of Troy Corp. 190
Mary Kay Cosmetics Inc.
  118, 202

Diversified operations
Bay Houston Towing Co.
  159
Contran Corp. 168
Cooper Industries, Inc. **66**,
  169
Hallwood Group Inc. 188
Home Interiors & Gifts, Inc.
  191
K.S.A. Industries Inc. 196
Kaneb Services, Inc. **140**,
  196
King Ranch, Inc. **116**, 197
Kirby Corp. 198
MAXXAM Inc. 203
Philp Co. 214
Rip Griffin Truck/Travel
  Centers Inc. 220
Sammons Enterprises 221
Sid Richardson Carbon and
  Gasoline Co. 223
Tandycrafts, Inc. 231
Tenneco Inc. **96**, 234
Tyler Corp. 240
UETA Inc. 241
Vista Oil Co. 243

Drugs & sundries — wholesale
Behrens Inc. 159
National Intergroup, Inc.
  207
Walsh-Lumpkin Drug Co.
  245

Electrical components — misc.
Kent Electronics Corp.
  196
Sterling Electronics Corp.
  229

Electrical components — semiconductors
Cyrix Corporation **136**,
  170
Dallas Semiconductor Corp.
  171
Texas Instruments
  Incorporated **98**, 235

Electrical products — wholesale
Wholesale Electric Supply
  Company of Houston, Inc.
  247

Electronics — military
E-Systems, Inc. 175
Tracor Inc. 237

Electronics — parts distribution
Tech-Sym Corp. 233
TTI Inc. 239
Warren Electric Co. 245

Energy — cogeneration
Destec Energy, Inc. **137**,
  173

Engineering — R & D services
Greiner Engineering, Inc.
  185
Sematech, Inc. 222
Southwest Research
  Institute Inc. 226

Engines — internal combustion
Stewart & Stevenson
  Services, Inc. 229

Financial — business services
First USA, Inc. 181

THE TEXAS 500

INDEX OF COMPANIES BY INDUSTRY

Southwest Securities Group Inc. 226
Wingate Partners LP 248

Financial — investment management
American General Corporation **54**, 152
Lomas Financial Corp. 200

Food — dairy products
Associated Milk Producers, Inc. 156
Blue Bell Creameries 160
MorningStar Group, Inc. 206
Southern Foods Groups Incorporated 225

Food — flour & grain
Mrs. Baird's Bakeries Inc. 206
Riviana Foods Inc. 220

Food — meat products
H and H Meat Products Company Inc. 187
L&H Packing Company Inc. 198
Pilgrim's Pride Corporation 214
Plantation Foods Inc. 216
Wright Brand Foods Inc. 248

Food — misc.
AmeriServ Food Co. 154
Sky Chefs, Inc. 223

Food — sugar & refining
Imperial Holly Corp. 193

Food — wholesale
Affiliated Foods Incorporated 151
American Produce and Vegetable Co. 153
Barnett Brothers Brokerage Company Inc. 158
Berry-Barnett Grocery Co. 159
Brenham Wholesale Grocery Co. 161
Economy Cash and Carry Inc. 176
Grocers Supply Co. 186
GSC Enterprises, Inc. 186
Hartnett, C.D. Company, The 189
Independent Grocers Inc. 194

Plains Cooperative Oil Mill Inc. 215
Standard Fruit and Vegetable Company Inc. 228
SYSCO Corporation **92**, 231
Tri-State Wholesale Associated Grocers Inc. 238
White Swan Inc. 247

Funeral services & related
Service Corporation International 222

Glass products
AFG Industries Inc. 151

Gold mining & processing
Battle Mountain Gold Co. 159

Healthcare — outpatient & home
Living Centers of America, Inc. 200
Medical Care America Inc. 204

Hospitals
American Medical Holdings, Inc. 153
Epic Holdings, Inc. 179

Hotels & motels
Gal-Tex Hotel Corp. 183
Hollywood Casino Corp. 191
La Quinta Motor Inns, Inc. 198
Remington Hotel Corporation 219
Wyndham Hotel Company Ltd. 249

Instruments — control
Keystone International, Inc. 197
Moorco International, Inc. 206

Instruments — scientific
Helena Laboratories 190

Insurance — accident & health
Blue Cross and Blue Shield of Texas Inc. 160
United Insurance Companies, Inc. 241

Insurance — life
American National Insurance Co. 153
Life Insurance Company of the Southwest 199
National Western Life Insurance Co. 207

Insurance — multi line & misc.
American Income Holding, Inc. 152
USAA **102**, 241

Insurance — property & casualty
American Indemnity Financial Corp. 152
GAINSCO, INC. 183

Leisure & recreational products
Igloo Holdings Inc. 193
Schultz Industries Inc. 221

Leisure & recreational services
ClubCorp International 166
Houston McLane Company, Inc. 192
Pace Entertainment Corporation 210
Supertravel 231
Texas Stadium Corporation 236

Machinery — construction & mining
Darr Equipment Company 171
Mustang Tractor and Equipment Co. 207
West Texas Equipment Co. 246

Machinery — electrical
Powell Industries, Inc. 216

Machinery — farm
TIC United Corp. 237

Machinery — general industrial
CCC Group Inc. 164
Pearce Industries Inc. 212

THE TEXAS 500

INDEX OF COMPANIES BY INDUSTRY

Machinery — printing
ElectroCom Automation, Inc. 177
Stevens Graphics Corp. 229

Medical products
Kinetic Concepts, Inc. 197
MAXXIM Medical, Inc. 203
Taylor Medical 232
Tecnol Inc. 233
Voluntary Hospitals of America Inc. 244

Medical services
MacGregor Medical Association 202
Owen Healthcare Inc. 210

Metal processing & fabrication
Commercial Metals Co. 167
Gulf Met Holdings Corp. 186
Ohmstede Inc. 209

Metal producers — distribution
E.R. Fant, Inc. 174
New Process Steel Corp. 208
Newell Recycling Company Inc. 208
Texas Pipe and Supply Company Inc. 236

Metals — non ferrous
RSR Corp. 221

Oil & gas — field services
BJ Services Co. 160
Digicon, Inc. 173
Enterra Corp. 179
Grant Geophysical, Inc. 185
Halliburton Company **74**, 188
Nabors Industries, Inc. 207
Noble Drilling Corp. 209
Oceaneering International, Inc. 209
Offshore Pipelines, Inc. 209
Pool Energy Services Co. 216
Pride Petroleum Services, Inc. 217
Production Operators Corp 217
Serv-Tech, Inc. **142**, 222

Tuboscope Vetco International Inc. 239
Weatherford International Inc. 245
Western Co. of North America 246

Oil & gas — international integrated
Apache Corporation 155
Exxon Corporation **72**, 179
FINA, Inc. 180
Oryx Energy Co. 210
Plains Resources Inc. 215
Santa Fe Energy Resources, Inc. 221
Shell Oil Company **86**, 223

Oil & gas — international specialty
Maxus Energy Corp. 203

Oil & gas — offshore drilling
Cliffs Drilling Co. 166
Edisto Resources Corp. 176
Energy Service Co., Inc. 178
Global Marine, Inc. 185
Reading & Bates Corp. 218
Rowan Companies, Inc. 220
Zapata Corp. 249

Oil & gas — production & pipeline
Adams Resources & Energy, Inc. 150
American Oil and Gas Corp. 153
Eastex Energy Inc. 175
Endevco, Inc. 177
Enron Corp. **70**, 178
ENSERCH Corp. 178
Enterprise Products Company 179
Panhandle Eastern Corp. 211
Seagull Energy Corp. 222
Tejas Gas Corp. 233
Tejas Power Corp. 233
Teppco Partners, L.P. 234
Transco Energy Co. 238

Oil & gas — US exploration & production
Anadarko Petroleum Corp. 154

Bass Enterprises Production Co. 158
Cabot Oil & Gas Corp. 163
Coastal Corporation, The **60**, 166
Hunt Oil Company Inc. 193
Hunt Petroleum Corp. 193
Marathon Group **82**, 202
Mesa Inc. 204
Mitchell Energy & Development Corp. 205
Parker & Parsley Petroleum Co. 212
Placid Oil Co. 215
Pogo Producing Company 216
Quintana Petroleum Corp. 217
Snyder Oil Corporation **143**, 224
Triton Energy Corp. 239
Union Texas Petroleum Holdings, Inc. 241
Wagner and Brown, Ltd. 244
Wainoco Oil Corp. 244

Oil & gas — US integrated
Howell Corp. 192
Pennzoil Company **120**, 213

Oil field machinery & equipment
Baker Hughes Incorporated **106**, 157
Baroid Corp. 158
Daniel Industries, Inc. 171
Dresser Industries, Inc. **114**, 174
Energy Ventures, Inc. 178
Galveston-Houston Co. 183
Hydril Co. 193
Lufkin Industries, Inc. 201
National-Oilwell 208
Smith International, Inc. 224
WellTech Inc. 246
Wilson Industries Incorporated 247

Oil refining & marketing
Diamond Shamrock, Inc. 173
Holly Corp. 191
Petro Inc. 213
Pride Companies, LP 217
Tauber Oil Co. 232

THE TEXAS 500   289

INDEX OF COMPANIES BY INDUSTRY

Tesoro Petroleum Corp. 234
Truman Arnold Companies 239
Valero Energy Corp. 242
Vanguard Energy Corp. 242
Xeron Inc. 249

Optical character recognition
Recognition Equipment Inc. 218

Paper — business forms
Ennis Business Forms, Inc. 178

Paper & paper products
Kimberly-Clark Corporation **78**, 197
Temple-Inland Inc. 234
Veragon Corp. 242

Pollution control equipment & services
Allwaste, Inc. 152
American Ecology Corp. 152
Browning-Ferris Industries, Inc. **108**, 162
Gundle Environmental Systems, Inc. 187
Sanifill, Inc. 221
Team, Inc. 233

Precious metals & jewelry
CJC Holdings Inc. 165
Fossil Inc. 181

Printing — commercial
Hart Graphics Inc. 189

Protection— safety equipment & services
Vallen Corp. 242

Publishing — newspapers
Harte-Hanks Communications Holdings Incorporated 189
MediaNews Group 204

Real estate development
Farb Companies Ltd. 180
Lincoln Property Co. 200
Paragon Group 212

Real estate investment trust
Capstead Mortgage Corp. 164
Weingarten Realty Investors 246

Real estate operations
Harborage Inc. 189
Trammell Crow Company **124**, 237

Retail — apparel & shoes
Men's Wearhouse, Inc., The **141**, 204
Specialty Retailers Inc. 227

Retail — consumer electronics
Babbage's, Inc. **129**, 157
Tandy Corporation **94**, 231

Retail — convenience stores
E Z Mart Stores Incorporated 175
E-Z Serve Corp. 175
FFP Partners, L.P. 180
Maverick Markets Inc. 203
National Convenience Stores 207
Southland Corporation, The **88**, 226

Retail — discount & variety
50-Off Stores, Inc. **128**, 150
Solo Serv Corp. 225
Tuesday Morning Corporation **145**, 239
Weiners Enterprises 245
Winn's Stores Incorporated 248

Retail — food & restaurants
Brinker International, Inc. **132**, 162
Furr's/Bishop's, Incorporated 183
Luby's Cafeterias, Inc. 201
Pancho's Mexican Buffet, Inc. 211
ShowBiz Pizza Time, Inc. 223
Whataburger Systems 246
Wyatt Cafeterias Inc. 248

Retail — home furnishings
Bombay Company, Inc., The **131**, 161
Pier 1 Imports, Inc. 214

Retail — jewelry stores
Zale Holding Corporation 249

Retail — major department stores
J. C. Penney Company, Inc. **84**, 195

Retail — misc.
Academy Corp. 150
Ancira Enterprises Inc. 154
Cash America International, Inc. **133**, 164
Chief Auto Parts Incorporated 165
Color Tile Inc. 167
CompUSA, Inc. **135**, 168
Curtis C. Gunn Inc. 169
Dupey Management Corp. 174
EZCORP, Inc. **138**, 179
Foxworth-Galbraith Lumber Company 181
Frank Parra Chevrolet Inc. 182
Friendly Chevrolet 182
George Grubbs Enterprises Inc. 184
Gillman Companies, Inc. 184
Gulf States Toyota 187
Kinsel Motors Inc. 197
Lawrence Marshall Chevrolet-Olds, Inc. 198
Leif Johnson Ford Inc. 199
Michaels Stores, Inc. 205
Old America Stores Inc. 209
Oshman's Sporting Goods, Inc. 210
Park Place Motor Cars 212
Port City Automotive Partners 216
R Corp. 218
Reliable Chevrolet Inc. 219
Royal International Optical Corp. 220
Sewell Village Cadillac 222
Sound Warehouse Incorporated 225
Southwest Toyota, Inc. 226

INDEX OF COMPANIES BY INDUSTRY

Steakley Chevrolet Inc. 228
Sunbelt Nursery Group, Inc. 230
Super Club North America Corporation 231
W. O. Bankston Enterprises Inc. 244

Retail — regional department stores
Dunlap Co. 174

Retail — supermarkets
AppleTree Markets Inc. 155
Brookshire Brothers Incorporated 162
Brookshire Grocery Co. 162
David's Supermarkets Inc. 172
Davis Food City Inc. 172
Fiesta Mart Inc. 180
Gerland's Food Fair Inc. 184
Handy Andy Supermarkets 188
HEB Grocery 190
Minyard Food Stores Inc. 205
Pay 'N Save Inc. 212
Randall's Food Markets, Inc. 218
Rice Food Markets Inc. 219
Stanley Stores Inc. 228
United Supermarkets Incorporated 241
Whole Foods Market, Inc. **147**, 247

Shoes & related apparel
Justin Industries, Inc. 196

Soap & cleaning preparations
NCH Corp. 208

Steel — pipes & tubes
Quanex Corp. 217

Steel — production
Border Steel Mills Inc. 161
Chaparral Steel Co. 165
Lone Star Technologies, Inc. 210

Telecommunications equipment
DSC Communications Corp. 174
Intellicall, Inc. 194
Spectrum Information Technologies, Inc. 227

Telecommunications services
Paging Network, Inc. 211
U.S. Long Distance Corp. **146**, 240

Textiles — home furnishings
Pillowtex Corp. 214

Textiles — mill products
Plains Cotton Cooperative Association 215
Wing Industries Inc. 248

Transportation — airline
AMR Corporation **56**, 154
Continental Airlines Holdings, Inc. **64**, 168
Southwest Airlines Co. **122**, 226

Transportation — bus
Greyhound Lines, Inc. 185

Transportation — equipment & leasing
Trinity Industries, Inc. 238

Transportation — rail
Burlington Northern Inc. **58**, 162

Transportation — services
Dalfort Corp. 170
Intertrans Corp. 194

Transportation — shipping
Hollywood Marine Inc. 191

Transportation — truck
Frozen Food Express Industries, Inc. 182
Tetco Inc. 235

Utility — electric power
Brazos Electric Power Cooperative Inc. 161
Cap Rock Electric Cooperative 163
Central and South West Corp. 164
Denton County Electric Cooperative 172
El Paso Electric Co. 176
Houston Industries Incorporated **76**, 192
Pedernales Electric Cooperative Inc. 213
Southwestern Public Service Co. 227
Texas Utilities Company **100**, 236
TNP Enterprises, Inc. 237

Utility — gas distribution
Atmos Energy Corp. 156
El Paso Natural Gas Co. 176
Martin Gas Corp. 202
Southern Union Co. 225

Utility — telephone
Southwestern Bell Corporation **90**, 227

Wholesale distribution — consumer products
Anderson Grain Corp. 155
Ben E. Keith 159
Block Distributing Company Inc. 160
Coburn Supply Company Inc. 166
East Texas Distributing Inc. 175
Glazer's Wholesale Drug Company Inc. 184
H.T. Ardinger and Son Co. 187
Handy Hardware Wholesale Inc. 188
Julius Schepps Co. 195
Periodical Management Group Inc. 213
Sigel Liquor Stores Inc. 223
Sun Coast Resources Inc. 230
Tarrant Distributors Inc. 232
Texas Mill Supply Inc. 235
York Group Inc., The 249

Wire & cable products
Keystone Consolidated Industries, Inc. 196
MMI Products Inc. 206

THE TEXAS 500   291

INDEX OF COMPANIES BY HEADQUARTERS LOCATION

> **Note:** Bold numbers refer to in-depth company profiles; all others refer to capsule company profiles.

Abilene
Independent Grocers Inc. 194
Pride Companies, LP 217

Amarillo
Affiliated Foods Incorporated 151
Cactus Feeders Incorporated 163
Friona Industries LP 182
Southwestern Public Service Co. 227

Arlington
D. R. Horton, Inc. 170
ElectroCom Automation, Inc. 177
Sky Chefs, Inc. 223

Austin
CJC Holdings Inc. 165
CompuAdd, Inc. 167
Continuum Company, Inc., The 168
Dell Computer Corporation **110**, 172
EZCORP, Inc. **138**, 179
Hart Graphics Inc. 189
Leif Johnson Ford Inc. 199
National Western Life Insurance Co. 207
Sematech, Inc. 222
Southern Union Co. 225
Tracor Inc. 237
Whole Foods Market, Inc. **147**, 247

Bay City
Stanley Stores Inc. 228

Beaumont
Coburn Supply Company Inc. 166
Delta Industrial Offices Inc. 172
Helena Laboratories 190
Kinsel Motors Inc. 197
Ohmstede Inc. 209
R Corp. 218
Taylor Medical 232

Bedford
George Grubbs Enterprises Inc. 184

Brenham
Blue Bell Creameries 160
Brenham Wholesale Grocery Co. 161

Carrollton
Computer Language Research, Inc. 168
Intellicall, Inc. 194
National Intergroup, Inc. 207

Clute
U.S. Contractors Inc. 240

Coppell
Minyard Food Stores Inc. 205

Corpus Christi
Maverick Markets Inc. 203
Port City Automotive Partners 216
SLM Power Group Inc. 224
Whataburger Systems 246

Dallas
A. H. Belo Corp. 150
Akin, Gump, Strauss, Hauer & Feld 151
Alliance Employee Leasing Corp. I 151
American Medical Holdings, Inc. 153
American Produce and Vegetable Co. 153
AmeriServ Food Co. 154
Associated Materials Incorporated 156
Atmos Energy Corp. 156
Austin Industries Inc. 156
Babbage's, Inc. **129**, 157
BancTec, Inc. 157
Brinker International, Inc. **132**, 162
Business Records Corporation Holding Co. 163
Capstead Mortgage Corp. 164
Centex Corp. 164
Central and South West Corp. 164
Chief Auto Parts Incorporated 165
ClubCorp International 166
Coca-Cola Bottling Group-Southwest 166
Commercial Metals Co. 167

CompuCom Systems, Inc. **134**, 167
CompUSA, Inc. **135**, 168
Contran Corp. 168
Dal-Tile Group Inc. 170
Dalfort Corp. 170
Dallas Auto Auction Inc. 170
Dallas Semiconductor Corp. 171
Dr Pepper Bottling Company of Texas 173
Dr Pepper/Seven-Up Companies, Inc. **112**, 173
Dresser Industries, Inc. **114**, 174
E-Systems, Inc. 175
Edisto Resources Corp. 176
Elcor Corp. 176
Eljer Industries, Inc. 177
Endevco, Inc. 177
Energy Service Co., Inc. 178
ENSERCH Corp. 178
Epic Holdings, Inc. 179
FINA, Inc. 180
First USA, Inc. 181
Fojtasek Companies Inc. 181
Fossil Inc. 181
Foxworth-Galbraith Lumber Company 181
Freeman Companies, The 182
Friendly Chevrolet 182
Frozen Food Express Industries, Inc. 182
Glazer's Wholesale Drug Company Inc. 184
Greyhound Lines, Inc. 185
H.T. Ardinger and Son Co. 187
Haggar Apparel 188
Halliburton Company **74**, 188
Hallwood Group Inc. 188
Harborage Inc. 189
HCB Contractors 190
Heritage Media Corporation **139**, 190
Holly Corp. 191
Hollywood Casino Corp. 191
Home Interiors & Gifts, Inc. 191
Hunt Oil Company Inc. 193
Hunt Petroleum Corp. 193

292   THE TEXAS 500

INDEX OF COMPANIES BY HEADQUARTERS LOCATION

Jackson and Walker LP 195
Jones Blair Co. 195
Julius Schepps Co. 195
Keystone Consolidated Industries, Inc. 196
Kimberly-Clark Corporation **78**, 197
Life Insurance Company of the Southwest 199
Lincoln Property Co. 200
Locke Purnell Rain Harrell 200
Lomas Financial Corp. 200
Lone Star Technologies, Inc. 201
Mary Kay Cosmetics Inc. **118**, 202
Maxus Energy Corp. 203
Medical Care America Inc. 204
Mesa Inc. 204
Middleberg, Riddle and Gianna 205
MorningStar Group, Inc. 206
Oryx Energy Co. 210
Overhead Door Corp. 210
Palm Harbor Homes Inc. 211
Paragon Group 212
Park Place Motor Cars 212
Perot Systems Corp. 213
Philp Co. 214
Pillowtex Corp. 214
Placid Oil Co. 215
Redman Industries Inc. 219
Remington Hotel Corporation 219
Rexene Corp. 219
Richards Group Inc. 220
Royal International Optical Corp. 220
RSR Corp. 221
Sammons Enterprises 221
Sewell Village Cadillac 222
Sigel Liquor Stores Inc. 223
SnyderGeneral Corp. 224
Sound Warehouse Incorporated 225
Southern Foods Groups Incorporated 225
Southland Corporation, The **88**, 226
Southwest Airlines Co. **122**, 226
Southwest Securities Group Inc. 226

Spectrum Information Technologies, Inc. 227
Standard Fruit and Vegetable Company Inc. 228
Steakley Chevrolet Inc. 228
Sterling Software, Inc. **144**, 229
Strasburger and Price 230
Super Club North America Corporation 231
TDIndustries Inc. 232
Texas Industries, Inc. 235
Texas Instruments Incorporated **98**, 235
Texas Kenworth Co. 235
Texas Utilities Company **100**, 236
Thompson and Knight PC 237
TIC United Corp. 237
Trammell Crow Company **124**, 237
Triangle Pacific Corp. 238
Trinity Industries, Inc. 238
Triton Energy Corp. 239
Tuesday Morning Corporation **145**, 239
Tyler Corp. 240
United Insurance Companies, Inc. 241
W. O. Bankston Enterprises Inc. 244
Wing Industries Inc. 248
Wingate Partners LP 248
Wyatt Cafeterias Inc. 248
Wyndham Hotel Company Ltd. 249

Denton
Denton County Electric Cooperative 172

Diboll
Temple-Inland Inc. 234

El Paso
Border Steel Mills Inc. 161
Economy Cash and Carry Inc. 176
El Paso Electric Co. 176
El Paso Natural Gas Co. 176
Farah Inc. 180
Helen of Troy Corp. 190
Hunt Building Corporation 192
Petro Inc. 213
Southwestern Irrigated Cotton Growers Association 227

Tri-State Wholesale Associated Grocers Inc. 238

Ennis
Ennis Business Forms, Inc. 178

Euless
White Swan Inc. 247

Freeport
Gulf States Inc. 186

Ft. Worth
AFG Industries Inc. 151
AMR Corporation **56**, 154
Bass Enterprises Production Co. 158
Ben E. Keith 159
Bombay Company, Inc., The **131**, 161
Burlington Northern Inc. **58**, 162
Cantey & Hanger LLP 163
Cash America International, Inc. **133**, 164
Chemical Lime Co. 165
Color Tile Inc. 167
Dunlap Co. 174
FFP Partners, L.P. 180
GAINSCO, INC. 183
JaGee Corp 195
Justin Industries, Inc. 196
Miller and Miller Auctioneers Inc. 205
Mrs. Baird's Bakeries Inc. 206
Pancho's Mexican Buffet, Inc. 211
Pier 1 Imports, Inc. 214
Sid Richardson Carbon and Gasoline Co. 223
Snyder Oil Corporation **143**, 224
Stevens Graphics Corp. 229
Sunbelt Nursery Group, Inc. 230
Tandy Corporation **94**, 231
Tandycrafts, Inc. 231
Tecnol Inc. 233
TNP Enterprises, Inc. 237
TTI Inc. 239
Williamson-Dickie Manufacturing Co. 247

Galena Park
Texas Mill Supply Inc. 235

THE TEXAS 500   293

INDEX OF COMPANIES BY HEADQUARTERS LOCATION

Galveston
American Indemnity Financial Corp. 152
American National Insurance Co. 153
Gal-Tex Hotel Corp. 183

Garland
Software Spectrum, Inc. 224

Grandview
David's Supermarkets Inc. 172

Hempstead
Lawrence Marshall Chevrolet-Olds, Inc. 198

Hereford
AZTX Cattle Co. 157
Barrett & Crofoot, LLP 158

Hewitt
Schultz Industries Inc. 221

Houston
Adams Resources & Energy, Inc. 150
Allright Corp. 151
Allwaste, Inc. 152
American Ecology Corp. 152
American General Corporation **54**, 152
American Oil and Gas Corp. 153
American Rice, Inc. 153
Anadarko Petroleum Corp. 154
Andrews and Kurth 155
Apache Corporation 155
AppleTree Markets Inc. 155
APS Holding Corporation 155
Associated Pipeline Contractors Inc. 156
Baker and Botts, L.L.P. 157
Baker Hughes Incorporated **106**, 157
Bank United of Texas FSB 158
Baroid Corp. 158
Battle Mountain Gold Co. 159
Bay Houston Towing Co. 159
BJ Services Co. 160

BMC Software, Inc. **130**, 160
Bracewell and Patterson 161
Browning-Ferris Industries, Inc. **108**, 162
Cabot Oil & Gas Corp. 163
Cliffs Drilling Co. 166
Coastal Corporation, The **60**, 166
Compaq Computer Corporation **62**, 167
Continental Airlines Holdings, Inc. **64**, 168
Cooper Industries, Inc. **66**, 169
CRSS, Inc. 169
Daniel Industries, Inc. 171
Davis Food City Inc. 172
Destec Energy, Inc. **137**, 173
Digicon, Inc. 173
E.R. Fant, Inc. 174
E-Z Serve Corp. 175
East Texas Distributing Inc. 175
Eastex Energy Inc. 175
Energy Ventures, Inc. 178
Enron Corp. **70**, 178
Enterprise Products Company 179
Enterra Corp. 179
Farb Companies Ltd. 180
Fiesta Mart Inc. 180
Fish Engineering & Construction Partners Ltd. 181
Fulbright and Jaworski 183
Galveston-Houston Co. 183
Gerland's Food Fair Inc. 184
Gillman Companies, Inc. 184
Global Marine, Inc. 185
Goodman Manufacturing Corporation 185
Grant Geophysical, Inc. 185
Grocers Supply Co. 186
Gulf Met Holdings Corp. 186
Gulf States Toyota 187
Gundle Environmental Systems, Inc. 187
H and C Communications Inc. 187
Handy Hardware Wholesale Inc. 188

Hi-Lo Auto Supply, Inc. 191
Hollywood Marine Inc. 191
Houston Industries Incorporated **76**, 192
Houston McLane Company, Inc. 192
Houston Peterbilt Inc. 192
Howell Corp. 192
Hydril Co. 193
Igloo Holdings Inc. 193
K.S.A. Industries Inc. 196
Kent Electronics Corp. 196
Keystone International, Inc. 197
King Ranch, Inc. **116**, 197
Kirby Corp. 198
Landmark Graphics Corp. 198
Linbeck Construction Corp. 199
Living Centers of America, Inc. 200
Lott Group Inc., The 201
Lyondell Petrochemical Company **80**, 201
MacGregor Medical Association 202
Marathon Group **82**, 202
MAXXAM Inc. 203
MediaNews Group 204
Men's Wearhouse, Inc., The **141**, 204
Merichem Co. 204
MMI Products Inc. 206
Moorco International, Inc. 206
Mundy Cos. 206
Mustang Tractor and Equipment Co. 207
Nabors Industries, Inc. 207
National Convenience Stores 207
National-Oilwell 208
New Process Steel Corp. 208
NL Industries, Inc. 208
Noble Drilling Corp. 209
Oceaneering International, Inc. 209
Offshore Pipelines, Inc. 209
Oshman's Sporting Goods, Inc. 210
Owen Healthcare Inc. 210
Pace Entertainment Corporation 210
Panhandle Eastern Corp. 211
Pannell Kerr Forster 211

294   THE TEXAS 500

INDEX OF COMPANIES BY HEADQUARTERS LOCATION

Pearce Industries Inc. 212
Pennzoil Company **120**, 213
Pioneer Chlor Alkali Investments Inc. 214
Pioneer Concrete of America 215
Plains Resources Inc. 215
Pogo Producing Company 216
Pool Energy Services Co. 216
Powell Industries, Inc. 216
Pride Petroleum Services, Inc. 217
Production Operators Corp 217
Quanex Corp. 217
Quintana Petroleum Corp. 217
Randall's Food Markets, Inc. 218
Reading & Bates Corp. 218
Rice Food Markets Inc. 219
Riviana Foods Inc. 220
Rowan Companies, Inc. 220
Sanifill, Inc. 221
Santa Fe Energy Resources, Inc. 221
Seagull Energy Corp. 222
Serv-Tech, Inc. **142**, 222
Service Corporation International 222
Shell Oil Company **86**, 223
Smith International, Inc. 224
Southdown, Inc. 225
Southwest Toyota, Inc. 226
Specialty Retailers Inc. 227
Sterling Chemicals, Inc. 228
Sterling Electronics Corp. 229
Stewart Information Services Corp. 229
Stewart & Stevenson Services, Inc. 229
Sun Coast Resources Inc. 230
Sunbelt Corp. 230
Supertravel 231
SYSCO Corporation **92**, 231
Tarrant Distributors Inc. 232
Tauber Oil Co. 232
Team, Inc. 233
Tech-Sym Corp. 233

Tejas Gas Corp. 233
Tejas Power Corp. 233
TeleCheck Services, Inc. 234
Tenneco Inc. **96**, 234
Teppco Partners, L.P. 234
Texas Olefins Co. 236
Texas Pipe and Supply Company Inc. 236
Texas United Corp 236
Transco Energy Co. 238
Tuboscope Vetco International Inc. 239
U.S. Home Corp. 240
Union Texas Petroleum Holdings, Inc. 241
Vallen Corp. 242
Vanguard Energy Corp. 242
Veragon Corp. 242
Vinmar Inc. 243
Vinson & Elkins L.L.P. 243
Vista Chemical Inc. 243
W.S. Bellows Construction Corp. 244
Wainoco Oil Corp. 244
Warren Electric Co. 245
Weatherford International Inc. 245
Weekley Homes Inc. 245
Weiners Enterprises 245
Weingarten Realty Investors 246
WellTech Inc. 246
Western Co. of North America 246
Wholesale Electric Supply Company of Houston, Inc. 247
Wilson Industries Incorporated 247
Xeron Inc. 249
York Group Inc., The 249
Zapata Corp. 249

Howe
Old America Stores Inc. 209

Irving
AMRE, Inc. 154
Darling-Delaware Company Inc. 171
Darr Equipment Company 171
Dupey Management Corp. 174
Emergency Network Inc. 177
Exxon Corporation **72**, 179

Frank Parra Chevrolet Inc. 182
Greiner Engineering, Inc. 185
Intertrans Corp. 194
Lone Star Plywood and Door Corp. 200
M/A/R/C Group, The 202
Michaels Stores, Inc. 205
NCH Corp. 208
Recognition Equipment Inc. 218
ShowBiz Pizza Time, Inc. 223
Texas Stadium Corporation 236
Tri-Gas Inc. 238
Voluntary Hospitals of America Inc. 244
Zale Holding Corporation 249

Johnson City
Pedernales Electric Cooperative Inc. 213

Katy
Academy Corp. 150

Kilgore
Martin Gas Corp. 202

Kingwood
Administaff Inc. 150

Lake Jackson
Gulf Coast Sportswear Inc. 186

Laredo
International Bancshares 194

Levelland
Anderson Grain Corp. 155

Littlefield
Pay 'N Save Inc. 212

Lubbock
Barnett Brothers Brokerage Company Inc. 158
Furr's/Bishop's, Incorporated 183
Lee Lewis Construction, Inc. 199
Plains Cooperative Oil Mill Inc. 215
Plains Cotton Cooperative Association 215
Rip Griffin Truck/Travel Centers Inc. 220

THE TEXAS 500

INDEX OF COMPANIES BY HEADQUARTERS LOCATION

United Supermarkets Incorporated 241

Lufkin
Brookshire Brothers Incorporated 162
Lufkin Industries, Inc. 201

McAllen
Vista Oil Co. 243

Mercedes
H and H Meat Products Company Inc. 187

Mexia
Berry-Barnett Grocery Co. 159

Midland
Parker & Parsley Petroleum Co. 212
Wagner and Brown, Ltd. 244
West Texas Equipment Co. 246

Midlothian
Chaparral Steel Co. 165

Pittsburg
Pilgrim's Pride Corporation 214

Plano
DSC Communications Corp. 174
Electronic Data Systems Corporation **68**, 177
J. C. Penney Company, Inc. **84**, 195
Paging Network, Inc. 211

Port Arthur
U.S. Intec, Inc. 240

Richardson
Blue Cross and Blue Shield of Texas Inc. 160
CONVEX Computer Corp. 169
Cyrix Corporation **136**, 170
Kaneb Services, Inc. **140**, 196
Lennox International Inc. 199

Reliable Chevrolet Inc. 219
SPI Holding, Inc. 228

San Antonio
50-Off Stores, Inc. **128**, 150
Ancira Enterprises Inc. 154
Associated Milk Producers, Inc. 156
Block Distributing Company Inc. 160
CCC Group Inc. 164
Clear Channel Communications, Inc. 165
Cullen/Frost Bankers, Inc. 169
Curtis C. Gunn Inc. 169
Datapoint Corp. 171
Diamond Shamrock, Inc. 173
Gambrinus Company, The 184
Handy Andy Supermarkets 188
Harte-Hanks Communications Holdings Incorporated 189
HB Zachry Co. 189
HEB Grocery 190
Intelogic Trace, Inc. 194
Kinetic Concepts, Inc. 197
L&H Packing Company Inc. 198
La Quinta Motor Inns, Inc. 198
Luby's Cafeterias, Inc. 201
Newell Recycling Company Inc. 208
Periodical Management Group Inc. 213
Rayco 218
Solo Serv Corp. 225
Southwest Research Institute Inc. 226
Southwestern Bell Corporation **90**, 227
Strafco Inc. 230
Tesoro Petroleum Corp. 234
Tetco Inc. 235
U.S. Long Distance Corp. **146**, 240

UETA Inc. 241
USAA **102**, 241
Valero Energy Corp. 242
Vaughan and Sons Inc. 242
Winn's Stores Incorporated 248

San Marcos
McCoy Corporation 203

Stanton
Cap Rock Electric Cooperative 163

Sugar Land
Imperial Holly Corp. 193
MAXXIM Medical, Inc. 203

Sulphur Springs
GSC Enterprises, Inc. 186

Texarkana
E Z Mart Stores Incorporated 175
Truman Arnold Companies 239
Walsh-Lumpkin Drug Co. 245

The Woodlands
Mitchell Energy & Development Corp. 205

Tyler
Brookshire Grocery Co. 162
TCA Cable TV, Inc. 232

Vernon
Wright Brand Foods Inc. 248

Victoria
Victoria Bankshares, Inc. 243

Waco
American Income Holding, Inc. 152
Behrens Inc. 159
Brazos Electric Power Cooperative Inc. 161
Plantation Foods Inc. 216

Weatherford
Hartnett, C.D. Company, The 189

296   THE TEXAS 500

For more information on other valuable business reference products, see pages 298–300.

To order, use the reply card in the back of the book, or call 800-486-8666 for credit card orders.

ATTENTION: Sales Executives, Career Changers, Investors, Information Professionals, and Fund Raisers

If you need to contact the companies in this book, and thousands of other public and major private companies, at a price you can afford — **less than 1 cent per name for unlimited personal use** — then you need the *Executive Desk Register*. Updated daily and published monthly by Demand Research Corporation, the *Executive Desk Register* provides hard-to-get information in computer-readable format at incredibly reasonable prices.

The *Executive Desk Register* contains information on approximately 5,300 public companies in IBM-compatible personal computer format. It includes all companies traded on the NYSE, AMEX, and NASDAQ National Market System.

Each entry contains the following information:
- Company name & address
- Telephone number
- Fax number (not all companies)
- Ticker symbol
- Exchange affiliation
- Full name of the CEO
- Full name of the CFO
- Industry description

Price:
$59.95 — one month's edition
$100.00 — 4 quarterly editions
$249.00 — 12 monthly editions

The *Executive Desk Register Plus* contains all the information from the *Executive Desk Register* plus information on approximately 1,000 major private companies, including nearly all the companies on the *Forbes* Private 400 and the *Inc.* 500 lists.

Each private company entry contains the following information:
- Company name & address
- Full name of the CEO
- Telephone number
- Number of employees
- Annual sales
- Industry description

Price:
$69.95 — one month's edition
$110.00 — 4 quarterly editions
$259.00 — 12 monthly editions

Other specialized databases of public company executives available in IBM-compatible PC format include:
MIS Executives — 500 names
Human Resource Executives — 900 names
Marketing & Sales Executives — 900 names
Corporate Treasurers — 1,000 names
Corporate Controllers — 1,400 names
Manufacturing Executives — 200 names
R&D Executives — 200 names

Each entry includes the following information:
- Full name
- Exact title
- Company name
- Address
- Telephone number
- Industry description

Any of these databases is available at no extra charge with an order for the *Executive Desk Register* or *Executive Desk Register Plus*.

All databases are available in 4 different formats:
- ASCII, text
- ASCII, comma-delimited
- Lotus 1-2-3™
- dBASE III PLUS™

When ordering, please be sure to specify 3 1/2" or 5 1/4" floppy disk format.

TO ORDER OR FOR MORE INFORMATION, CALL (312) 664-6500 OR FAX US AT (312) 266-2016.

DEMAND RESEARCH CORPORATION
625 NORTH MICHIGAN AVENUE CHICAGO, ILLINOIS 60611 (312) 664-6500

VALUABLE RESOURCES FOR BUSINESS EXECUTIVES, INVESTORS, SALESPERSONS, CAREER CHANGERS, AND STUDENTS

THE TEXAS 500: HOOVER'S GUIDE TO THE TOP TEXAS COMPANIES
$24.95 hardcover, ISBN 1-878753-46-0
The definitive guide to the top 500 public and private companies features in-depth profiles of 55 of Texas's largest and fastest-growin companies, capsule profiles of 445 major Texas companies, and information on major out-of-state employers, plus an overview of th Texas economy and major industries.

HOOVER'S HANDBOOK OF AMERICAN BUSINESS 1994
$34.95 hardcover, ISBN 1-878753-22-3
Profiles over 500 of the largest and most influential enterprises in America, including company histories and strategies, up to 10 yea of key financial and employment data, products, competitors, key officers, addresses, and phone and fax numbers. Fully indexed.

HOOVER'S HANDBOOK OF EMERGING COMPANIES 1993–1994
$32.95 hardcover, ISBN 1-878753-18-5
The only reasonably priced guide to 250 of America's most exciting growth enterprises. Company profiles include overviews and strategies, up to 6 years of key financial and stock data, lists of products and key competitors, names of key officers, addresses, and phone and fax numbers.

HOOVER'S HANDBOOK OF WORLD BUSINESS 1993
$32.95 hardcover, ISBN 1-878753-06-1
Profiles 191 non-U.S.-based companies that employ thousands of Americans in the U.S. and abroad. Includes a discussion of the wor economy and business/economic profiles of 66 countries and 5 regions, plus a combined index that covers this book and *Hoover's Handbook of American Business 1993*. **1994 Edition available August 1994.**

HOOVER'S MASTERLIST OF MAJOR U.S. COMPANIES 1993
$49.95 hardcover, ISBN 1-878753-14-2 • $129.95 computer disk • $149.95 book and disk combo • $99.95 CD-ROM
Names, addresses, phone and fax numbers, key officers, industry descriptions, sales and employment data, stock symbols, and stock exchanges for nearly 6,000 of the largest public and private companies in the U.S. Also available on IBM-compatible or Macintosh computer disk in ASCII, spreadsheet, or database format. The data must be imported into your own word processing, spreadsheet, o database software for use. Technical support is not available. CD-ROM version comes with its own application program. **1994 Editio available in May 1994.**

STATISTICAL ABSTRACT OF THE UNITED STATES 1993
$19.95 hardcover, ISBN 1-878753-31-2
The Bureau of the Census's annual compendium of who we are, where we live, what we do, and how we spend our national resource Available from The Reference Press at 48% off the government price.

THE NATIONAL BOOK OF BUSINESS LISTS 1994
$24.95 hardcover, ISBN 1-878753-29-0 • Available January 1994
The top 40 companies or organizations in more than 50 categories, such as biotechnology, exporters, government agencies, private companies, SBA lenders, semiconductor manufacturers, and venture capital firms. Includes company names, addresses, phone and fax numbers, names and titles of top management, ranking criteria, and more.

OTHER PRODUCTS AVAILABLE FROM THE REFERENCE PRESS
THE LEADER IN REASONABLY PRICED BUSINESS REFERENCE INFORMATION

The 1994 National Directory of Addresses and Telephone Numbers	$84.95
The Computer Industry Almanac 1993	$55.00
Microcomputer Market Place 1993	$29.95
National Trade and Professional Associations of the U.S. 1993 and State and Regional Associations of the U.S. 1993 (2-volume set)	$114.95
National Directory of Corporate Public Affairs 1993	$79.95
Washington Representatives 1993	$69.95
Washington '93	$74.95
1993 NASDAQ Fact Book & Company Directory	$19.95
The Business One Irwin Business and Investment Almanac 1993	$74.95
'994 Information Please Business Almanac & Desk Reference	$29.95
he 100 Best Companies to Work for in America	$27.95
he 100 Best Stocks to Own in America, 3rd Edition	$22.95
'ompanies With a Conscience	$19.95
he U.S.-Mexico Trade Pages	$59.95
lexico Company Handbook 1993	$29.95
razil Company Handbook 1993	$29.95
enezuela Company Handbook 1992–1993	$29.95
rgentina Company Handbook 1993	$29.95
Cracking Latin America	$44.95
Canada Company Handbook 1993	$39.95
Henry Holt International Desk Reference	$39.95
European Companies: A Guide to Sources of Information	$89.95
Company Handbook Spain	$84.95
Cracking Eastern Europe	$44.95
French Company Handbook 1993	$49.95
Access Nippon 1993	$34.95
Cracking the Pacific Rim	$44.95
Asia Pacific Securities Handbook 1993	$99.95
Company Handbook—Hong Kong	$44.95
The Wilson Directory of Emerging Market Funds 1992–1993	$99.95
The World's Emerging Stock Markets	$59.95
Russia '94	$64.95
Information China (3-volume set)	$124.95
Weissmann Travel Planner for Western and Eastern Europe 1993–1994	$49.95
Weissmann Travel Reports: International Profiles	$349.95
Weissmann Travel Reports: North America Profiles	$349.95
Weissmann Travel Reports on CD-ROM	$399.95

CALL 800-486-8666 FOR A FREE CATALOG

NEW MEDIA FROM THE REFERENCE PRESS

On the cutting edge of electronic publishing, The Reference Press offers business reference information in more electronic formats than any other publisher. Choose the formats that best meet your needs — CD-ROMs, floppy disks, electronic books, or on-line services.

THE TEXAS 500 MAILING LIST ON DISK $29.95
Names, addresses, phone and fax numbers, and key officers of the top 500 Texas companies, plus about 100 major out-of-state employers. **Available January 1994.**

HOOVER'S HANDBOOK OF AMERICAN BUSINESS 1994: MULTIMEDIA BUSINESS 500 $49.95
This CD-ROM contains the entire contents of *Hoover's Handbook of American Business 1994*. Search by company, key word, region, or industry. Access competitive information by using the hot spot to jump to numerous competitors. See and hear 30 minutes of multimedia video clips from over 20 top corporations. Cut and paste information into your own word processing documents and generate mailing lists. CD-ROM drive and DOS Windows required for use.

HOOVER'S MASTERLIST OF MAJOR U.S. COMPANIES ON DISK $129.95
The entire contents of *Hoover's MasterList of Major U.S. Companies 1993* is available on a PC or Macintosh disk in ASCII or database format. PC disk available in 3-1/2" or 5-1/4" size. Approximately 6,000 companies and 12,000 executives' names. Data **MUST** be imported into your own software for use. License permits use of disk for creating labels for personal use only, and technical support is not available.

MASTERLIST CD-ROM: BEST BUSINESSES $99.95
Contains the same information as *MasterList on Disk* above, in a CD-ROM format. Locate companies by company name or industry, or page through the database alphabetically. Select companies by state, zip code, or industry and then export company names and addresses to your word processor in ASCII format, or print them out. CD-ROM drive and DOS Windows required for use.

SONY DATA DISCMAN
The Sony Data Discman plays 3" electronic book CDs and comes with *Hoover's Handbook of American and World Business*. The player measures 4-1/4" x 7" x 1-1/2" and weighs 17 ounces.
Sony Data Discman with *Hoover's Handbook* $299.95
Hoover's Handbook disc only $39.95

SONY MMCD MULTIMEDIA CD-ROM PLAYER
The Sony MMCD player plays 5" electronic book CDs and comes with the *Hoover's Handbook Plus* disc. The *Hoover's Handbook Plus* disc contains the company profiles in *Hoover's Handbook of American Business 1993* and *Hoover's Handbook of World Business 1992*, plus a database of over 5,000 companies. The player measures approximately 7" x 6" x 2" and weighs 2 pounds.
Sony MMCD Player with *Hoover's Handbook* disc $999.95
Hoover's Handbook disc only $59.95

FRANKLIN DIGITAL BOOK SYSTEM
The Franklin Digital Book System provides instant access to a continuously expanding library of Digital Books, each containing up to 45 megabytes of information. It stores two Digital Books simultaneously and allows communication between the two books. The Digital Books are 2-1/4" cartridges that are inserted into the player. Our package includes the player and *Hoover's Handbook of American Business*. The player measures just 3" x 5" x 1/2" and weighs only 5 ounces. **Available January 1994.**

APPLE'S NEWTON MESSAGE PAD
The Newton Message Pad is a revolutionary new personal digital assistant that stores and retrieves information, takes notes, sends faxes, makes appointments, and much more. *The FORTUNE Guide to American Business*, one of the titles available for Newton, includes company profile information from *Hoover's Handbooks*. Look for Newton in your favorite electronics stores.

ON-LINE SERVICES
Company profiles from *Hoover's Handbooks* are available on the following on-line services:
- Mead's LEXIS/NEXIS — under "Hoover" in the "COMPNY" file
- America Online — in the "News and Finance" section under Company Profiles — Hoover's Handbooks
- Bloomberg Financial Network — type HHB [GO]

— SEE REVERSE FOR MORE PRODUCTS —

I want to order the indicated quantities of the following publications:

____ *The Texas 500: Hoover's Guide to the Top Texas Companies*	$24.95 hardcover	ISBN 1-878753-46-0
____ *The Texas 500 Mailing List on Disk*	$29.95 Specify disk: PC❑ Mac❑ Format: tab text❑ spreadsheet❑ database❑	
____ *Hoover's Handbook of American Business 1994*	$34.95 hardcover	ISBN 1-878753-22-3
____ *Hoover's Handbook of Emerging Companies 1993–1994*	$32.95 hardcover	ISBN 1-878753-18-5
____ *Hoover's Handbook of World Business 1993*	$32.95 hardcover	ISBN 1-878753-06-1
____ *Hoover's MasterList of Major U.S. Companies 1993*	$49.95 hardcover	ISBN 1-878753-14-2
____ *Hoover's MasterList of Major U.S. Companies 1993 on Disk*	$129.95 Specify disk: PC❑ Mac❑ Format: tab text❑ spreadsheet❑ database❑	ISBN 1-878753-32-0
____ *Hoover's MasterList of Major U.S. Companies 1993 book and disk combo*	$149.95 Specify disk: PC❑ Mac❑ Format: tab text❑ spreadsheet❑ database❑	ISBN 1-878753-33-9
____ *Statistical Abstract of the United States 1993*	$19.95 hardcover	ISBN 1-878753-31-2
____ *The National Book of Business Lists 1994*	$24.95 hardcover	ISBN 1-878753-29-0

List additional titles here: Price

____ _____   _____

____ _____   _____

Subtotal   _____

(Texas residents add 8% of subtotal or provide proof of exemption.) Texas sales tax   _____

Shipping and handling   _____

Total $ _____

SHIPPING & HANDLING
Unless otherwise indicated, shipping and handling to U.S. addresses is $3.50 per item ordered for the first 3 items and $1.50 for each additional item.

❑ Make mine a standing order.

❑ Send me information about your other business reference products.

❑ I have the following suggestions for reference books: _____

_____

❑ I bought this book from/at _____

Name _____ Telephone No. (_____) _____

Affiliation _____ Title _____

Street Address _____

City _____ State _____ Zip _____

Credit card or prepayment required, except for public libraries and academic institutions.

❑ MasterCard ❑ Visa ❑ American Express   Acct. No. _____

Signature _____ Expiration Date _____

❑ Check for $ _____ enclosed.   ❑ Library/school PO# _____

TO ORDER CALL 800-486-8666 OR FAX US AT 512-454-9401.

The Reference Press, Inc. • 6448 Highway 290 East, Ste. E-104, Austin, Texas 78723 • 512-454-7778

TX 93

Please tape along edge before mailing. Do NOT staple.

BUSINESS REPLY MAIL
FIRST-CLASS MAIL PERMIT NO. 7641 AUSTIN TX

POSTAGE WILL BE PAID BY ADDRESSEE

THE REFERENCE PRESS INC
6448 E HIGHWAY 290 STE E104
AUSTIN TX 78723-9965

NO POSTAGE
NECESSARY
IF MAILED
IN THE
UNITED STATES

OFFICIAL SWEEPSTAKES ENTRY

Register to Win a Free Copy of The TexasMonthly Guidebook TEXAS

Return this questionnaire to register to win one of 25 copies of **TEXAS**, the completely revised third edition of the definitive guidebook to the Lone Star State. This new edition is completely updated to feature many new attractions and describes in detail all major cities and towns. An $18.95 value, this book is a valuable resource for natives and tourists.

To help us better meet your needs for business reference information, please answer the following questions, then fill in your name and address on the reverse side. All entries received by April 1, 1994, will be eligible for the prize drawing. Winners will be notified by mail.

1. Did you buy this book primarily for
   - ❏ General reference
   - ❏ Selling to the companies in it
   - ❏ Academic use
   - ❏ Investment information
   - ❏ Job hunting
   - ❏ Other _____

2. Where did you first hear about/see *The Texas 500*?
   - ❏ Advertisement in _____
   - ❏ Book review in _____
   - ❏ Other media mention in _____
   - ❏ Received as gift
   - ❏ Direct mail
   - ❏ Library
   - ❏ Friend
   - ❏ Co-worker
   - ❏ Teacher
   - ❏ Bookstore: name _____ city _____ state _____
   - ❏ Other retail outlet: name _____ city _____ state _____

3. What is your primary job description (e.g., executive, salesperson, student, librarian, etc.)? _____

4. What features in *The Texas 500* did you find the most helpful? _____

5. What features did you find least helpful? _____

6. How could we improve this book? _____

7. Are there any companies that should be added to the book? _____

8. What other books would you like to see us publish? _____

Thank you! Please complete the reverse side and mail.

TXSW93

THE REFERENCE PRESS, INC.
6448 Highway 290 East, Suite E-104
Austin, Texas 78723-9828

PLACE STAMP HERE
The Post Office will not deliver without postage.

OFFICIAL SWEEPSTAKES ENTRY

Name _____

Organization _____

Title _____

Street address _____

City _____ State _____ Zip _____

Telephone number (_____) _____

Fax number (_____) _____

Please tape this edge before mailing. Do not staple.